"Stephen Um's dynamic ministry in downtown Boston is grounded in his faithful, weekly ministry of the Word of God. His experience there makes him an ideal expositor of 1 Corinthians, because today's secular city is an ideal context for understanding and applying the same gospel message that Paul first preached to the Christians in cosmopolitan Corinth."

Philip Graham Ryken, President, Wheaton College

"*1 Corinthians: The Word of the Cross* is not only a journeyman's exposition of 1 Corinthians; it's also a demonstration of a culturally astute pastor at work. Stephen Um combines his pastor's heart, his disciplined mind, and his communicator's gifts to bring us a commentary that will remind the Church of the gospel Paul preached to us."

George W. Robertson, Senior Minister, First Presbyterian Church, Augusta, Georgia; author, *Deuteronomy: More Grace, More Love*

"Stephen Um demonstrates the intellect of a scholar, the heart of a pastor, and the experience of the city to relate the truths of the gospel for city dwellers of the apostles' time that were no less cultured, urbane, or sophisticated than we imagine ourselves to be."

Bryan Chapell, President Emeritus, Covenant Theological Seminary; Senior Pastor, Grace Presbyterian Church, Peoria, Illinois

"Stephen Um's pastoral and preaching ministry has been a bright spot in the evangelical world. I have benefited from his wisdom and insights for a long time, so I am glad to see the arrival of this volume. Pastors will benefit from Um's ability to apply the Biblical text to the human heart and the idols of our culture. Stephen is a wise exegete and good pastor."

John Starke, Pastor of Preaching, Apostles Church, New York City, New York; coeditor, *One God in Three Persons*

1 CORINTHIANS

PREACHING THE WORD
Edited by R. Kent Hughes

(((PREACHING *the* WORD)))

1 CORINTHIANS

The WORD *of the* CROSS

STEPHEN T. UM

R. Kent Hughes
Series Editor

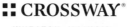
CROSSWAY®

WHEATON, ILLINOIS

1 Corinthians

Copyright © 2015 by Stephen T. Um

Published by Crossway
          1300 Crescent Street
          Wheaton, Illinois 60187

Cover design: Jon McGrath, Simplicated Studio

Cover image: Adam Greene, illustrator

First printing 2015

Printed in the United States of America

Hardcover ISBN: 978-1-4335-1200-1
ePub ISBN: 978-1-4335-2396-0
PDF ISBN: 978-1-4335-1201-8
Mobipocket ISBN: 978-1-4335-1202-5

Library of Congress Cataloging-in-Publication Data

Um, Stephen T.
   1 Corinthians : the word of the cross / Stephen Um.
     pages cm. – (Preaching the word)
   Includes bibliographical references and index.
ISBN 978–1–4335–1200–1 (hc) – ISBN 1–4335–1200–9 (hc) – ISBN 978–1–4335–1201–8 (PDF) – ISBN 978–1–4335–1202–5 (Mobipocket) – ISBN 978143523960 (ePub)
   1. Bible. Corinthians, 1st–Commentaries. I. Title. II. Title: One Corinthians.
BS2675.53.U4   2015
227'.207–dc23   2015007840

Crossway is a publishing ministry of Good News Publishers.

To my beautiful wife Kathleen,
who has shaped my preaching more than anyone

Contents

A Word to Those Who Preach the Word

There are times when I am preaching that I have especially sensed the pleasure of God. I usually become aware of it through the unnatural silence. The ever-present coughing ceases, and the pews stop creaking, bringing an almost physical quiet to the sanctuary—through which my words sail like arrows. I experience a heightened eloquence, so that the cadence and volume of my voice intensify the truth I am preaching.

There is nothing quite like it—the Holy Spirit filling one's sails, the sense of his pleasure, and the awareness that something is happening among one's hearers. This experience is, of course, not unique, for thousands of preachers have similar experiences, even greater ones.

What has happened when this takes place? How do we account for this sense of his smile? The answer for me has come from the ancient rhetorical categories of *logos*, *ethos*, and *pathos*.

The first reason for his smile is the *logos*—in terms of preaching, God's Word. This means that as we stand before God's people to proclaim his Word, we have done our homework. We have exegeted the passage, mined the significance of its words in their context, and applied sound hermeneutical principles in interpreting the text so that we understand what its words meant to its hearers. And it means that we have labored long until we can express in a sentence what the theme of the text is—so that our outline springs from the text. Then our preparation will be such that as we preach, we will not be preaching our own thoughts about God's Word, but God's actual Word, his *logos*. This is fundamental to pleasing him in preaching.

The second element in knowing God's smile in preaching is *ethos*—what you are as a person. There is a danger endemic to preaching, which is having your hands and heart cauterized by holy things. Phillips Brooks illustrated it by the analogy of a train conductor who comes to believe that he has been to the places he announces because of his long and loud heralding of them. And that is why Brooks insisted that preaching must be "the bringing of truth through personality." Though we can never perfectly embody the truth we preach, we must be subject to it, long for it, and make it as much a part of our ethos as possible. As the Puritan William Ames said, "Next to the Scriptures, nothing makes a sermon more to pierce, than when it comes out of the inward affection of the heart without any affectation." When a preacher's *ethos* backs up his *logos*, there will be the pleasure of God.

Last, there is *pathos*—personal passion and conviction. David Hume, the Scottish philosopher and skeptic, was once challenged as he was seen going to hear George Whitefield preach: "I thought you do not believe in the gospel." Hume replied, "I don't, but he does." Just so! When a preacher believes what he preaches, there will be passion. And this belief and requisite passion will know the smile of God.

The pleasure of God is a matter of *logos* (the Word), *ethos* (what you are), and *pathos* (your passion). As you preach the Word may you experience his smile—the Holy Spirit in your sails!

R. Kent Hughes
Wheaton, Illinois

Preface

Having been involved in full-time pastoral ministry for over twenty-five years, I've had the opportunity to preach the Word of God in many contexts. I've preached numerous sermons, but have heard my fair share of sermons as well. When it comes to delivering God's Word, every preacher wants to preach a good sermon for the glory of God and the benefit of his listeners. However, preachers are merely called to present good sermons through careful exegetical study. In terms of crafting a good sermon to potentially become a great one—that is the work of the Holy Spirit. Just as priests were called to set up the altar to make sacrifices to honor God, and only God could provide the fire; so it is with preaching. It is the preacher's responsibility to do all the preparatory work necessary to deliver a good sermon, but it will be the work of the Holy Spirit to take a hold of it and change the hearts of its listeners.

I believe a sermon needs to do three things to the glory of God: (1) contain a careful exposition; (2) create sensation for the listener; and (3) provide contextual application. In this sense, the sermon has to be tri-perspectival. It first needs to explain the text. Then it needs to understand the people's existential needs to help them gain a sense for what the Word of God is saying. And finally, it should apply gospel truths into every dimension of life and ministry.

Another tri-perspectival way of looking at a sermon is to understand it within the context of the three offices of the Messiah: prophet, priest, and king. The sermon has to be prophetic, in that it needs to explain the normative truth of God's Word. It has to be priestly by recognizing human need and addressing the hearts of its hearers. And lastly, it needs to be situational, recognizing the immediate context for which these truths will be applied and implemented in the life of the Christian.

When developing the material for this commentary, many of the thoughts and reflections were directly created from my weekly sermon preparation. In all, I preached nearly thirty sermons through the entire book of 1 Corinthians to my urban congregation in Boston. This particular setting often reminds me that there are always mildly curious skeptics who are present in the audience while I am preaching. With that in mind, I cannot assume that people have basic biblical categories for what the gospel is. I believe that the gospel is the power onto salvation; it is the power that not only gets people into the kingdom of God, but also the power that sustains them in the kingdom. And so, in the context of the city, I am always aware of the apologetic sidebars; or the so-called "Christian defeaters." Countless times throughout my preaching through 1 Corinthians, questions, doubts, and rebuttals are going through the mind of many of the listeners.

In addition, I was forced to be aware of the cultural and corporate idols that exist within my current setting and city (Boston, MA). In order to address them, the bulk of my preaching effort was directed to present the person of Jesus, who is the only satisfying answer to the longings of our culture. When I was expositing a given text, my approach was not only to merely explain the main idea of a given text—which is the authorial intent—but also to situate that idea within the context of the big idea. Therefore, these sermons understood Paul's immediate context in light of the one-story plotline of Scripture which finds its fulfillment in Jesus.

I would like to express my heartfelt appreciation to Kent Hughes for inviting me to participate in this series. I've thoroughly enjoyed our friendship and partnership in the gospel these past few years, and praise God for the work he is doing in putting together such great pastoral resources. I want to express a deep sense of gratitude for Ted Griffin at Crossway for spending meticulous hours in editing this volume. For all their support and encouragement, I am indebted to my pastoral staff (Nameun, Ben, Andrew, Daniel, Tim) at Citylife Presbyterian Church for assisting me with their amazing editorial work. I would like to especially thank Justin Ruddy and David Cho for helping me to preach through this series. They are two young preachers whose preaching I greatly admire. Lastly, I would express my deep appreciation, love, and acknowledgement to my family for their constant grace and perseverance, particularly my wife, Kathleen, and my daughters, Noël, Adeline, and Charlotte. I am forever grateful to God for calling and equipping me to be a preacher of his.

1

Surprised by Encouragement

1 CORINTHIANS 1:1-9

WHEN APPROACHING A BOOK OF THE BIBLE it is not uncommon to sense a tangible difference between the ancient setting and our own context. While all of Scripture is clear and understandable, there are admittedly some portions that demand more of the reader than others. Unlike some of the more thorny passages of Scripture, the book of 1 Corinthians is one that presents the modern reader with numerous touch points. Yes, there will be interpretive questions to ask and cultural differences to comprehend, but on the whole 1 Corinthians presents us with an original context that looks strikingly like our modern-day setting. Here we meet a church that faces issues much like the ones we face. How are we to handle disagreements among God's people? What does a Christian sexual ethic look like when promiscuity is the cultural norm? In what ways does the gospel shape the institution of marriage? How should we relate to the cultural customs and practices of those with whom we disagree on matters of faith? How can the gospel tear down barriers that we have built between others and ourselves? We could go on.

The one who sets about answering these and other questions in the book of 1 Corinthians is the Apostle Paul (v. 1).[1]

He writes specifically "to the church of God that is in Corinth," and generally to "all those who in every place call upon the name of our Lord Jesus Christ" (v. 2). A little bit of digging reveals that the city of Corinth[2] shared much in common with the cities of our own time. So we'll find that Paul's explication and application of the gospel happens on the ground level. He's working out the implications of God's grace in the context of a pluralized, influential, cutting-edge city.

Corinth was an *aspirational* city.[3] Its citizens were looking to advance on the ladder of upward social mobility,[4] and they did this by aspiring to affluence[5] for the sake of establishing their own honor.[6] "The core community and core tradition of the city culture were those of trade, business, entrepreneurial pragmatism in the pursuit of success,"[7] and "perhaps no city in the Empire offered so congenial an atmosphere for individual and corporate advancement."[8] David Garland gives us a feel for the culture of the city and the way it overlaps with our own experience in the West:

> To use terms from American culture: schmoozing, massaging a superior's ego, rubbing shoulders with the powerful, pulling strings, scratching each other's back, and dragging rivals' names through the mud—all describe what was required to attain success in this society.[9]

Alongside the clamoring for affluence and honor, Corinth was also an *explorational* city. It was characterized by a cosmopolitan spirit and religious diversity. Being a center for trade, Corinth was occupied (and regularly visited) by a diverse group of people from all walks of life. As a result, "Corinthians were rootless, cut off from their country background, drawn from races and districts all over the empire."[10] It was a city that contained a variety of religious faith communities so that the everyday Corinthian had any number of potential options when thinking about which religion or belief system might fit him best. Garland states that "as a cosmopolitan city, Corinth was a religious melting pot with older and newer religions flourishing side by side"; in other words, "they could choose from a great cafeteria line of religious practices."[11]

As an aspirational and explorational city, Corinth looked much like the individualistic cultures in which many of us find ourselves in the twenty-first century.

The ideal of the Corinthian was the reckless development of the individual. The merchant who made his gain by all and every means, the man of pleasure surrendering himself to every lust, the athlete steeled to every bodily exercise and proud in his physical strength, are the true Corinthian types: in a word, the man who recognized no superior and no law but his own desires.[12]

It is into this context that Paul has occasion to speak. And in doing so he will address Christians who were being forced to ask many of the questions that we now find ourselves asking. Though the letter will go on to reveal significant issues within the Corinthian community, Paul begins with a note of profound, surprising encouragement. We'll consider this encouragement in three movements:

- The Truth of Encouragement
- The Tension of Encouragement
- The Basis of Encouragement

The Truth of Encouragement

Encouragement is a basic human need. Few people flourish in the absence of affirmation, approval, or some external declaration of worth. We long to be inherently valued—to have someone say, "I approve of who you are." We want to be respected for the contributions that we make (i.e., "I approve of what you do"). And we long deeply for assurance that the direction we are heading is one worthy of our investment and commitment (i.e., "I approve of where you are headed"). Paul will have to say some hard things to the Corinthians in the pages ahead; so he begins his letter with a surprising, well-rounded dose of encouragement.

Identity Encouragement

The apostle encourages the Corinthians in their identity in his opening salutation by addressing them as "those sanctified[13] in Christ Jesus, called to be saints[14] . . ." (v. 2). In this way he reminds them that they have been set apart by God—that they are important and unique because someone has declared them to be. In a city that measured one's honor by the importance of the patron[15] and friends to which a person was attached, to be set apart by God would have been the ultimate reassurance of one's identity. Though all the surrounding voices might tell them otherwise, to be sanctified in Christ—past tense—was to have already received the ultimate word of approval, acceptance, and identity encouragement. Similarly, the fact that they were "called to be saints" meant that their identity and purpose was externally bestowed upon them. Rather than working to build their identity or to self-manufacture a sense of purpose, they had received theirs by way of the gracious call of God.

Aptitude Encouragement

Along with being settled in their identity, Paul wants the Corinthians to know that they are well equipped to live into that identity. In our common experience, the thing that lies beyond the question of identity (i.e., "Who am I?") is the question of aptitude ("What am I to do?"). Aptitude is typically made up of the collection of gifts, skills, and abilities that you have been given,[16] combined with the steps you have taken to hone them. While still rooting their activity in the gracious activity of God, Paul speaks to the Corinthians as those who have been "enriched in . . . all speech and all knowledge"[17] (v. 5). They are able to speak clear, convincing words about the faith. They are also knowledgeable; they are not lacking in their grasp of the intellectual content of the Christian faith.

In a city and culture that placed an incredible amount of value on rhetoric[18] and logic, Paul's compliment about their speech and knowledge is an affirmation that they are not lacking in their culture's most marketable commodity. Furthermore, their speech and knowledge is not something they achieved by studying under the most prominent rhetoricians and philosophers, but they have been given them as gifts from God (v. 4). In this way both their identity and aptitude are secure because they have been externally bestowed.

Trajectory Encouragement

When you combine an identity with aptitude, you get forward momentum. We are all heading somewhere, and the questions that hang over our heads are: Where? What does my future hold? How can I know that my trajectory is worthwhile? Is it reasonable for me to be hopeful about my destination? Paul answers these questions for the Corinthians when he claims that Jesus "will sustain[19] [them] to the end" (v. 8). In essence, he tells the Corinthians that they are on the right trajectory. Their lives are worthwhile, and the path that they are on is clearly leading to the beautiful end that God has in store for them. This sure trajectory is rooted in the faithfulness[20] of God (v. 9) who called them and crafted them for his purposes.

We can imagine the substantial encouragement this would have been to readers living in a city where one's trajectory was perpetually insecure. In a meritocracy, one's future is only as secure as one's present success.[21] When your temporal future is only as certain as your ability to keep performing at a high level, the comfort of knowing that your eternal future has already been decided is the ultimate encouragement. In this way we can be encouraged that our futures are just as secure. We are not unfamiliar with the demand for high performance and the temptation of embarking on self-security projects, but the Scriptures assure us that no matter the uncertainty or precariousness of our present situation, our Lord Jesus Christ "will sustain [us] to the end" (v. 8), and we will enjoy life with him because we "were called into the fellowship[22] of his Son, Jesus Christ our Lord" (v. 9).

Surprising Encouragement

Can you imagine receiving a letter like this from a leader? Of course, when we read a letter from a superior or supervisor, we are hoping for encouragement, but we recognize that it is almost always attached to our level of performance. Paul avoids tying their identity, aptitude, and trajectory to their performance, opting instead to encourage them flat-out. He is essentially saying, "Regardless of what you bring to the table, God finds you incredibly valuable and worthy of investment. And on top of that, he is going to ensure that you are sustained and carried through to a joy-filled life with him in the future." Perhaps we expect to receive praise for a job well done, but no one expects to receive this kind of unconditional encouragement, particularly not when they were conducting themselves the way the Corinthians were. It's at this point that we are introduced to a significant tension in Paul's letter.

The Tension of Encouragement

In order to sense the tension in this text, we need to look ahead into the rest of the letter. If you are a first-time reader of the epistle, you may think that the Corinthians are doing an outstanding job of living into their God-given identity in Christ. Perhaps Paul will simply go on praising them. Perhaps this is what the original Corinthian readers might have hoped for. But the reality was that the church was profoundly, tragically flawed. As soon as we leave this section (vv. 1–9), we find a letter written to a church that is riddled with problems. The next heading in your Bible likely says something like "Divisions in the Church." The truth of the matter is that the Corinthians are the last people in the world who should be getting the kind of encouraging introduction that Paul has just given them. Let's consider the reality of what was happening in the Corinthian church.

Living Contrary to Their Identity

Although their identity is objectively settled as "sanctified" (v. 2), the rest of Paul's letter bears out that their subjective and experiential reality is far from saintly. Instead the idols of those within the church overlap with the idols of the city of Corinth. For example, the idolatrous aspirationalism of the culture dominates the church. While they ought to be defined by their primary identification with Christ, they are more concerned with aligning themselves to a particular Christian leader, and this has created stratification and factionalism (3:4–9). In their attempts to set themselves apart as honorable they have perverted the Lord's Supper, turning it into an occasion to separate the haves from the have-nots (11:17–22). The moral, ambiguous explorational-ism of the city is also vividly present. The fifth chapter makes it plain that the unrestrained passion and unbridled lust that was characteristic of the city was alive and well in the church. To their shame, they were engaged in things "not even tolerated among the pagans" (5:1).

Prideful about Their God-Given Aptitude

God had gifted the Corinthians with an identity, and he continued to pour out his blessings by enriching them "in all speech and all knowledge" (v. 5). But rather than seeing these gifts for what they were, the Corinthians began to take pride in them, mistakenly assuming that their aptitude was the actual basis of their identity. We can see this by looking at the sources of the divisions that unfold throughout the book. For instance, they are more concerned with eloquent speech than with grasping the true wisdom of God (1:18–31). And rather than finding unity in the knowledge they have received they have divided minds (1:10–17). They are overly concerned with pedigree and position, and as a result they are choosing to lead with competence in place of character—gifts in place of grace.

This happens each time we unhinge our gifts from their God-given source and neglect to use them the way he intends us to use them in community. Take an exceptional violinist. She may be heads above the others in her section and able to pull off amazing technical feats. However, if she becomes preoccupied with her gift and ignores her responsibility to accept the authority of the conductor, as well as the community of the orchestra, she will end up playing something that draws attention to herself but is out of tune with the rest of the orchestra. She has a phenomenal gift in isolation, but her pride in her gift has hindered her from using it properly. The end result of leading with aptitude instead of identity is communal disharmony.

On a Dysfunctional Trajectory

Though Paul is convinced that Jesus will "sustain [the Corinthian church] to the end" (v. 8), the rest of the book tells us that the church is severely unhealthy. In one case it is so bad that the apostle instructs the church to remove one of their members due to his flagrant sin (5:4, 5). While even that instruction is given with the purpose of ultimate restoration (5:5), the many issues we confront in the book of 1 Corinthians make us rightly question how this is all going to turn out for good. It would seem that the objective reality by which Paul encourages and commends them is being called into question by the subjective experience of the church. How is it possible that people who have received the grace of God and who will be preserved to the end could live this way?

If all of this is true, and if we see it reflected in our own lives and churches, how can we believe the content of Paul's encouragement? If our subjective experience is one of dissatisfaction and disharmony, then how is it possible to have confidence in believing that this encouragement is true of us? Is there a way to re-ground our identity, to rightly reevaluate our aptitude, and to live lives that are rightly aligned with the promised trajectory of perseverance?

The Basis for Encouragement

In short, the basis for Paul's encouragement to the Corinthian church is that their past, present, and future have been confirmed, declared, secured, enriched, and sustained in Christ. Take a look at our text again and see just how Christ-saturated it is:

> Paul, called by the will of God to be an apostle of *Christ Jesus*, and our brother Sosthenes,
> To the church of God that is in Corinth, to those sanctified in *Christ Jesus*, called to be saints together with all those who in every place call upon *the name of our Lord Jesus Christ*, both their *Lord* and ours:
> Grace to you and peace from God our Father and *the Lord Jesus Christ*. I give thanks to my God always for you because of the grace of God that was given you in *Christ Jesus*, that in every way you were enriched *in him* in all speech and all knowledge—even as the testimony about *Christ* was confirmed among you—so that you are not lacking in any gift, as you wait for the revealing of *our Lord Jesus Christ*, who will sustain you to the end, guiltless in the day of *our Lord Jesus Christ*. God is faithful, by whom you were called into the fellowship of *his Son, Jesus Christ our Lord*. (1:1–9)

All of the realities of Paul's surprising encouragement are grounded in Christ. The Christian's identity is not self-made or self-maintained. It is the result of an outside action of God on our behalf. We are sanctified not in ourselves but "in Christ Jesus" (v. 2). We are "called to be saints" not because we are inherently saintly but simply because we "call upon the name of our Lord Jesus Christ" (v. 2). The grace and peace we experience is delivered to us "from God the Father and the Lord Jesus Christ" (v. 3). The grace we experience was not earned but was a gift given to us "in Christ Jesus" (v. 4). Our speech and knowledge are "enriched in him" (v. 5). We are confident in our faith because God confirmed the "testimony about Christ" among us (v. 6). Our future hope is not in our manifold gifts or in the potential of our achievements but in "the revealing of our Lord Jesus Christ" (v. 7). In Christ, God sustains us to the end. He has promised to make us—the guilty— "guiltless in the day of our Lord Jesus Christ" (v. 8). And we are absolutely certain of this because "God is faithful," and he has called us into "the fellowship of his Son, Jesus Christ our Lord" (v. 9).

It may seem redundant, but Paul's laser focus on the work of God in Christ is meant to frame the entirety of his reflections throughout the book of 1 Corinthians. He wants the troubled church that he is addressing to know this: God's objective reality overrides their subjective experience. Christ's work on their behalf is more foundational to their identity than their ability to sully it with their failings. He is essentially saying, "Look, Corinthian church, you may be falling apart at the seams, but the God who called you has secured your past, present, and future. He is holding you together."

What does this mean for us? It means that our status as "sanctified" and "saints" is not based upon our work but upon the work of another. Our identity is sure because it was given to us by someone else. Our gifts are sure and sufficient because they were given to us by the gift-maker. And our future is secure because it has been prepared for us by the one who holds the future in his hands.

Because we live in a meritocracy, this sounds alien. The gospel is an anomaly in a culture that runs on self-definition, self-help, and self-realization. But for those who have reached the bitter end of identity building, competency maintenance, and future building, it is the greatest news imaginable. In the gospel, God declares us presentable before he ever even looks at our record. The gospel says, "Stop striving to build an identity; you have been given one free of charge because of the striving of another in your place! You no longer have to live in order to build an identity, but you can live into the identity that has been given to you."

2

The Appeal of Unity

1 CORINTHIANS 1:10–17

THE APOSTLE PAUL decides to speak into a completely factious Corinthian community that was full of arguments and disagreements. Paul recognized that it was a partisan spirit that led the church into disunity. Given this context, it is worth asking the following questions: What does Paul say to the Corinthians to express the importance of unity? How does Paul effectively and encouragingly communicate this message to them? This passage will be traced through the following three plot points:

- The Appeal for Unity
- Obstacles to Unity
- The Restoration of Unity

The Appeal for Unity (A Picture of Unity)

The undergirding human longing is for unity and not disunity, harmony and not chaos, integration and not disintegration. The desire is to be a unified, shalomic community of people who are able to sacrificially love one another. But in reality this is not the normative structure of communities. In most communities peace is difficult to find, and there is no shalom as the Bible describes it. But the Bible does mention the need for longing for shalom, and the evidence of that longing can also be seen in the human heart. Throughout the Old Testament prophets dreamed about that glorious day when all things that are corrupt and broken down would be rebuilt; the rough places would be made straight; there would be humility in the midst of arrogance; there would be peace among conflict and warfare; lambs could lie down with lions. This beautiful and almost unfathomable picture of reality is what the Bible describes as shalom. Plantinga defines shalom as "a universal flourishing, a wholeness, and delight."[1] In this Biblical shalom, God is introducing an unspeakable beauty that human beings are longing to find—a harmonious, shalomic state of unity. We long for a day when there will be no murder, envy, boredom, shame, racism, fear, stress, war, conflict, terrorism, snobbery, robbery, assault, and malicious gossip.

The Tone of Paul's Appeal (v.10)

> I *appeal* to you, *brothers*, by the name of our Lord Jesus Christ, that all of you *agree*, and that there be *no divisions* among you, but that you be *united* in the same mind and the same judgment.

Paul is very careful in how he handles the Corinthians in this situation. Note that he is making an "appeal." In other words, he doesn't begin with a demand, nor does he ignore the reality of the disunity in the church. He is operating by the gospel principle of speaking the truth in love. To leave them in their broken estate by ignoring the issue would be unloving, so he must speak the truth. But on the other hand, to crush them in their broken estate by coming with a heavy hand would be out of step with the truth of the gospel, so he must speak in love. His appeal is tender. Look at the way he chooses to use familial language: "brothers." He invokes their membership in God's family, and thus their filial relationship to one another. His appeal is also solemn. He appeals to them "by the name of our Lord Jesus Christ." Though this is a family matter, it is also a serious matter. Appealing "by the name of our Lord Jesus Christ" is to affirm the root of Paul's apostolic authority. The combination of a parental tenderness with a solemn authority is precisely what is needed in an instance where there is deep division. To be overly tender and ignore the issue is to pass over the truth; to be overly authoritarian and press the listener is to lose a hearing. Not only is Paul concerned about the tone,[2] but the very substance of his appeal speaks directly into the issue of division as well.

The Substance of Paul's Appeal

First, he instructs them to "*agree.*" Literally this means "to speak the same."[3] "Speak the same" was a term used to describe political parties that were free from factions. To speak the same, or to agree, is to be in harmony with one another rather than to talk past one another. Second, they must mend the fissures in their relationships—"no divisions." The Greek term here is *schismata*,[4] from which we get the English words *schism* or *schismatic*. Paul is appealing to them to find new methods of relating to one another. This is very relevant in today's context as well. We have trouble with people who are unnecessarily schismatic, always looking for an argument. Third, they are to communicate so that they can get on the same page. They are to be "united in the same mind and the same judgment." He's calling them to adjust their opinions and worldviews to be in line with the gospel that they have received. He is not looking for uniformity, but harmony about the basics of the faith. The upside-down content of the gospel is supposed to shape their mental framework, their "mind," and their worldview. And out of that mental framework they are to arrive at judgments and opinions that are in line with the truth of the gospel. So not only is the tone of Paul's appeal attractive, but so is the substance. Paul lays out a path toward unity:[5] agreement; mended relationships; and intentional, harmonious life together.

But Paul makes this appeal for unity precisely because the Corinthian church is coming apart at the seams. We all have a vision of what a restored, shalom-shaped world might look like. It is a good sign that each of us possesses an inherent desire for a reconciled life. But this can also be a source of division, discord, and dissonance—friction, feuding, and factions. Some think, *When you and I have different visions of the way the world is supposed to be, there is no room for unity.* This was exactly what was happening in Corinth.

Obstacles to Unity (The Vandalism of Unity and the Problem of Disunity)

The Corinthians had written a letter to Paul explaining some of the issues among them (spiritual gifts, problems surrounding the Lord's Supper, questions about the resurrection), but they had not given him all of the information. Paul then heard from another source that there were serious problems in the community. Chloe—who is most likely a prominent businesswoman[6] from Ephesus (where Paul wrote 1 Corinthians) with business interests in the city of Corinth—has had her people tell Paul about the issues that the Corinthian church did not want him to know about.

The Issue of Horizontal Factionalism (vv. 11, 12)

What we find in the Corinthian church is "*quarreling*" (v. 11) and there is a "party-minded spirit."[7] "Several factors contributed to a party-minded spirit: social stratification, personal patronage, philosopher/student loyalty, and party loyalties fostered by urban alienation."[8] They have adopted wholesale their culture's emphasis on *patronage*. Note that these are not theological divisions—Paul,[9] Apollos,[10] Cephas (i.e., Peter),[11] and Jesus[12] all preached the same gospel. They have divided themselves along stylistic and rhetorical lines (i.e., who was the most eloquent, who was the most impressive, who had the most pizzazz, etc.).[13] Despite Paul's teaching regarding security of identity in Christ, the Corinthians were trying to find their identity in union with another patron. They were looking for something that would give them ultimate meaning and enable them to be in a more privileged position than other people—patronage is an attempt at self-validation by means of another person's successes and status. In essence they are thinking, "I as the client will associate myself with a patron. The more elite, the more wealthy, the more upper class, the more honored my patron is, by my association with that patron I will also be honored, I will also be elevated, I will also be viewed as someone who is extremely important, valuable, worthy, and praiseworthy." Seeking validation in something outside of self is a very common phenomenon. People tend to attach themselves to individuals, causes, industries, and dreams that give them a vision of the world as they think it should be. There are identity attachments to schools, roles, jobs, etc.

In the world of educational credentials, there is always a desire to inform people (in an organic way) about our association with selective institutions and reputable scholars. Oftentimes people may hear, "I graduated from this institution, and I studied with this individual, and if anyone knows anything in this field, they'll know that he or she is one of the top five in this particular field." This happens everywhere. Why? It sounds as though we are praising the institution, but in essence we are praising ourselves. The institution is our patron. We are in union with the name of our institution, relationships, items, products, services, and individuals. These things falsely promise people that they would develop one's identity. This was the issue of horizontal factionalism—patronage for self-validation.

Patronage is our escapist fix to numb the suspicion and fear that there is something wrong with the world and that it might be us. We are looking to be a part of something bigger than ourselves, but we attach ourselves to things that cannot hold the weight and that ultimately crumble—creating walls between us and those who have attached themselves to other things. This is the reason we latch on to causes. They become our surrogate savior. We become fierce evangelists for political parties, diets, methods of parenting and education, etc. These things give us a sense of identity and purpose insofar as they make us different than or distinct from other people. Our patron-based identities necessarily build walls that destroy the shalom that we are seeking.

Christian leaders and churches also become means of building an identity that lead to the creation of shalom-inhibiting walls.[14] The Corinthians turned Jesus Christ himself into just another teacher among many, but Jesus isn't interested in being a patron—he is interested in being *the* Savior. The Corinthians adapted Christian doctrine to fit their mental framework (rather than allowing it to shape their worldview). They molded Christian doctrine to fit their culture and needs. They subsumed Christian baptism itself under the framework of patronage. Paul is saying that Christianity is the end of patronage; it is the end of self-identity building; it is the end of horizontal factionalism. We can end up building our identity on the forms and rituals of the Christian faith while lacking the substance. Factionalism is the symptom of a deeper issue.

The Root of Horizontal Factionalism = Vertical Fracture

When horizontal relationships are out of whack, it is a clear sign that there is a vertical disconnect—a vertical fracture. There is a tendency to be accepting toward other people only if their vision fits within ours. To unify various factions within a community, there needs to be a shalomic vision that is big enough for everyone.

Early in the book of Genesis, Cain, the older brother of Abel, ends up killing his brother. Cain's actions were driven by envy. He gave his vegetables as a sacrifice to God, and God seemed displeased. But God did not reject Cain's offering because he is a carnivore. God rejected his sacrifice because he did not give the firstfruits of his harvest, the best of his harvest. But Abel gave the best of his meat. What is evident here is that Cain's anger with God—the vertical fracture—stems from the fact that he had a different vision of the world than God had for him. This brings about horizontal factionalism and division. This is why there is a need for God's picture of a restored world. We need to latch onto the ultimate shalom. Ultimately we are out of line with God's vision of shalom because there is a fracture in our vertical relationship with God. We have decided that our shalom is better than his. We want to re-create and rule the world our way. This is the root cause of horizontal factionalism.

How can the vertical fracture that lies at the root of our horizontal factionalism be mended? How can there be true, holistic, satisfying, harmonizing, shalomic unity? How can we be brought to a place where God's word about our identity is the final word? How can we come to a place where we lay down our causes and attempts at self-validation? How can we come to a point where we no longer alienate people who are not like us and don't fit into our causes?

The Restoration of Unity (The Source of Unity)

The only way for unity to be restored is for us to give up our lesser visions of unity.

Although the human impulse toward patrons and causes is partially right, it gives us only a glimpse of our need for harmonious life in community. No cause or party or patron has the ability to bring about unity. Our vision of shalom must be greater than our own individual visions—it must ultimately come from the true source of shalom—God, himself.

Vertical Fracture Must Be Mended for Horizontal Fractionalism to Be Overcome

Horizontal factionalism must be eroded by the vertical condescension of God in Christ. Verse 17 says: "For Christ did not send me to baptize[15] but to preach the gospel,[16] and not with words of eloquent wisdom, lest the cross of Christ be emptied of its power."[17] In essence Paul is saying, "Christ didn't send me to create a faction of followers who look to me as their patron. He sent me to preach the gospel. The end of patronage! The end of grasping after security and identity and shalom! Your cause may produce good things, but it can't be crucified for you; it can't restore you in right relationship with God and others—that's what Christ has done." Paul is saying that the reason for going after patrons and causes is driven by the desire to be praiseworthy and honored. However, the picture of the cross is remarkably upside-down and counterintuitive. It is so different from the way the world evaluates everything. This must be the basis for a reconciled relationship. The vertical fracture in our relationship with God is mended by Jesus Christ who experiences and absorbs the vertical fracture on our behalf.

Restored Vertical Relationship Is the Basis for Reconciled Horizontal Relationships

On the cross Christ is divided in order that we may no longer be divided! His divided, crucified body establishes the spiritual unity of his body—the church. On the cross he is emptied in order that we may no longer be empty. Christ's self-emptying is the source of our fullness. No longer are we searching for identity in patrons, causes, or even spiritual rites and rituals because we have been filled with the fullness of God in Christ and a vision of the shalom toward which he is calling us. Horizontal divisions are now mended because Christ, who had the most intimate relationship with the Father, experienced division and fracture. Jesus experienced the breakdown of both vertical and horizontal shalom in order to secure for us the experience of restored vertical and horizontal relationships. Jesus gives us a new identity out of which we are free to embrace the other.

Practical Implications

A restored vertical relationship puts all good things in their proper place. Work is work; food is food; parenting is parenting. We will never ask something else to be the source of our identity and meaning. There won't be a need to create and manage our own individual visions of shalom because of God's ultimate vision and plan for shalom. Putting things in their proper place mends horizontal factionalism. The things that divide us become far less important. Ideological perspectives can take a backseat for the sake of the other rather than "otherizing" people in order to secure one's self in a particular cause. The church ought to be the place where this kind of horizontal harmony is on display. We are called to be an outpost of God's shalom in the present age.

This is the upside-down power of the cross of Christ. It does not come with words of eloquent wisdom, and it does not come with the kind of power that you would expect. But it comes in meekness and humility. This does not mean that it diminishes the majesty and greatness of Jesus Christ—it complements it! So what does this mean? To those who still undergo self-validation through different tangible and immediate patrons, Paul is saying that true validation comes through an upside-down picture of the gospel in which God prefers to use the unlikely, the weak, and the rejected. God is in the business of restoring and bringing about unity through these means.

This is possible because no one can ultimately give away true love that people long to have. The difference between true and fake love is rather obvious. Fake love can be easily spotted when somebody seems to be using us, making it seem as though they're interested in us. But at the end, they're all about self-interest and not self-sacrifice. Their commitment is conditional. True love is the opposite; true love is unconditional, sacrificial, other-giving, other-seeking. But no one is able to generate and provide this kind of love because people wrestle with their own patronage and validation. Because of our insecurity, we have to go to another source—to another individual who is not insecure, who does not struggle with his own identity. He's someone who understands true love, and he doesn't need to love us in order to understand what love is because he understands it within himself. When we get a hold of this picture of the gospel, we will know how to love people more and need people less. It will give us the substance that we so desperately long to have. We are in union with Christ, just as he is in union with the Father and the Spirit in the Godhead. People do not need to become objects for us to use for our own benefit. The wealth that we have in the gospel will empower us to give sacrificially without expecting anything in return. This power of the upside-down gospel will have a shaping power on our vertical and horizontal harmony.

3

Rewriting the Storyline

1 CORINTHIANS 1:18—2:5

IT IS OFTEN ASSUMED that there are only two ways for us to engage our cities, our culture, and the world. We tend to think that either we are going to become overly protective and separatistic, or we are going to assimilate and become just like the world. But Jesus tells his disciples in John 17 that we are to be in the world but not of the world (vv. 15–18). In other words, we are not called to under-contextualize (becoming evasive) or to over-adapt (becoming accommodating). Instead we are called to be a countercultural alternative society of God's people—to be a light to the world and salt to the earth. This was the very tension that the Corinthian believers faced in their own particular context—the dual dangers of separatism and assimilation, of isolation and absorption, both of which are equal threats to the gospel. So how can we avoid these pitfalls? We first need to understand the narrative of the context in which we live. We will do so under three points:

- A Common Cultural Storyline
- The Biblical Storyline
- Rewriting the Storyline

A Common Cultural Storyline: The Wisdom and Power of Man

The common cultural storyline of Corinth was a right-side-up view of wisdom and power. This was found generally in the Hellenistic world and specifically in Corinth. We see this clearly in verses 18 and following:

> For the word[1] of the cross is folly to those who are perishing,[2] but to us who are being saved it is the power of God. For it is written,[3]

"I will destroy the wisdom of the wise,
and the discernment of the discerning I will thwart."

Where is the one who is wise? Where is the scribe? Where is the debater of this age? Has not God made foolish the wisdom of the world? For since, in the wisdom of God, the world did not know God through wisdom, it pleased God through the folly of what we preach to save those who believe. For Jews demand signs and Greeks seek wisdom, but we preach Christ crucified, a stumbling block to Jews and folly to Gentiles, but to those who are called, both Jews and Greeks, Christ the power of God and the wisdom of God. For the foolishness of God is wiser than men, and the weakness of God is stronger than men. (vv. 18–25)

Paul is looking for a point of reference. In order to communicate the shaping power of the gospel for their community, he looks for language that will connect with them, that will address the deep issues of their hearts. For Paul, this letter is nothing short of a wrestling for the affections and allegiance of the Corinthians. The divisions among them indicate that they were chasing after other loves and were pledging themselves to other lovers. They had absorbed and adopted the reigning storyline of the surrounding culture. They were finding the purpose and value for their lives in the grand Corinthian cultural narrative.

Why should we be concerned about the Corinthian storyline? One reason is that there is significant resonance with the cultural storyline of most modern cities. And that is important because there is significant dissonance between this common storyline and the storyline of the gospel. Paul is helping the Corinthians to see their cultural blind spots as they relate to the gospel, things that they had unwittingly absorbed while swimming in their everyday cultural waters. To the extent that we can observe Paul pointing out the Corinthians' blind spots, to that extent we will have the opportunity to recognize some of our own blind spots.

The words "wisdom" and "power," along with their opposites ("folly/foolishness" and "weakness"), are used by Paul around twenty times in this short section (1:18 – 2:26). This word group functions as Paul's point of reference with the Corinthian community. He is touching a nerve. Issues of wisdom and power would have been at the forefront for the Corinthian Christians as they wrestled with their own affections and allegiances.

The Bible uses the word "wisdom" to describe skillful living[4] that is aligned with the things of God. So wisdom is the proficient application of Biblical principles to one's life, resulting from a Godward heart orientation. As one might guess, this was not the kind of wisdom that the Hellenistic culture embraced or embodied. When they thought of wisdom, they were primarily concerned with gaining intellectual knowledge that could be leveraged for the purpose of attaining influence and power. Wisdom, then, was viewed as a tool for achieving self gain. This constituted the Corinthians' right-side-up approach to wisdom and power. They were tempted to embrace a common cultural storyline that would put them in direct opposition to the upside-down storyline of the gospel.

Their Cultural Currency Was Intellect

The language of our passage reveals the cultural obsession with wisdom and rhetoric. Consider verse 20[5] "Where is the one who is wise? Where is the scribe? Where is the debater of this age?"[6] Here Paul makes reference to the experts who had purchased power with their rhetoric and sophistry, those who had procured status by way of education and intellectual gymnastics. This emphasis on wisdom was particularly prevalent in the Greco-Roman culture.

In verse 22 we see that it is the Greeks who are seeking wisdom as they consider spiritual things. It was thought that the way to the enlightened life was through contemplation, philosophy, and ornate speech. Buying into this right-side-up paradigm was creating division between the Corinthians and was ultimately keeping them from understanding the good news of the gospel.

Their Cultural Commodity Was Influence

The Corinthians had bought into the cultural paradigm of seeking wisdom because it was a means of achieving power. Remember that Corinth was not an aristocracy but a meritocracy.[7] Power, status, and position were not something you inherited, but something you had to merit. We see this in verse 26: "For consider your calling, brothers: not many of you were wise according to worldly standards, not many were powerful, not many were of noble birth." They were not noble by birth, and they didn't inherently possess power. Wisdom and knowledge were a means of achieving power and influence even if you did not come from a noble family.

Their Storyline Is Our Storyline

If you were to sum up the cultural story of a modern-day city, you might say something similar to what we've said about Corinth. Wisdom, knowledge, intellect, and education are the primary cultural currency in most of today's cities. We all want to make it—to have influence, to "make a difference"—and the way that we seek to accomplish this is through the accumulation of knowledge. Symbols of knowledge (academic degrees, institutional association, etc.) are symbols of latent power. Our culture places a high value on intelligence, thoughtfulness, and articulation. At the end of the day we respect those who have "made it"—whether by the ordinary channels of cultural ascension (Harvard, Yale, etc.) or by extraordinary entrepreneurial effort.

What is the one-word summary of your city's storyline?[8] We will obviously risk generalization in trying to pinpoint an entire culture like this, but it is helpful to try to hone in on the prevailing narrative of your town, your church, and even your own life. When I look at my own city, Boston, there is one word that continues to rise to the top: knowledge. Of course there are many other subplots, but one major storyline of my city is knowledge. Boston places a premium on wisdom, intellect, education, and expertise. It is believed that the more knowledge we have, the more we can achieve. The more degrees and educational prowess that we are able to attain, the more we will be able to neatly calibrate our worth.

Have you ever wondered why one of the top phobias or fears of our culture is public speaking? We are not necessarily afraid because we don't have the ability to speak well in public; rather, our fear is that we may be mistakenly perceived as inarticulate or less thoughtful than we actually are. In a culture that prizes knowledge, we do not want to be seen as unintelligent. This is especially true if our identity is wrapped up with the pursuit of knowledge, wisdom, and expertise. We want to avoid at all costs those situations in which people might see us as being beneath our actual dignity.

Spirit of Competition and Achievement

As we consider the context of Corinth, there are a few different broader cultural aspects that we need to keep in mind. First, as a Roman city, Corinth was affected by the cultural institution of the gladiatorial games—a life or death sport that separated the higher classes from those beneath them. The games emphasized the deep rift and separation between the patricians, on the one hand, and the plebeians, on the other.[9] Some individuals were viewed as being noble and consequential. These people who functioned as patrons had leverage, influence, and power. The plebians were the common folk who lacked prestige, and the necessary means of achieving it. Many of the plebians were purchased and placed into the gladiatorial games. Their only hope of survival and advancement was actually to be the best gladiator they could be. The best gladiators were able to fight their way out—some even becoming quite wealthy. In this way the gladiatorial games functioned as a micro-cosm of the ruthless meritocracy in which the Corinthians were embroiled.

Another expression of these dynamics can be found in what were known as "reciprocity conventions." Essentially, individuals would gather together for the purpose of finding ways of establishing reciprocal relationship. You scratch my back, and I'll scratch yours. They would gather together not only in a patron-client context, but also among their own friends for these reciprocity conventions.[10]

This is the transactional context in which "friendship" was understood. It is not coincidental, then, that Paul stays away from that reciprocal term in his letters, especially in his letters to the Corinthians. What language does he use? He employs familial language: "my brothers." He did not want them to think that he was a great patron-apostle. He did not want to be mistaken as the great patron-missionary of the Gentile world. In a context in which the Corinthians had said, "I follow Cephas, I follow Apollos, I follow Paul," he did not want them to think that the gospel was about patronage. The gospel does not fit well in a highly stratified social setting because it actually presents us with a completely different world altogether.

Mary Bell, a consultant to many high-level executives, says, "Achievement is the alcohol of our time." She goes on to say that

> . . . the more you achieve, the more you feel dynamite. These days the best people don't abuse alcohol; they abuse their lives. When you complete a project, you feel dynamite, or when you start something new and you're able to show your visionary entrepreneurial skills and you can be somebody who can start something from nothing, something that is so highly praised in our culture . . . There's a feeling of euphoria. And, of course, your self-esteem—the way you evaluate and form your identity—is on the line here. Remember? That we're so concerned about protecting our status and the reason why we are engaged in status anxiety is for this very reason, that somebody might actually find out that I might perhaps be a fraud. So, our self-esteem is on the line because we have been gathering our self worth externally. Living out your life dependent upon the judgments of the people outside of you.

She went on to say, "An achievement addict is no different than any other kind of addict."[11] Are we achievement addicts? Who are we? How do we calibrate our worth?

So what ends up happening? What does this look like horizontally? What happens when we achieve, when we perform, when we grab, when we pursue? It will ultimately bring us to a point where we end up becoming rank-conscious. While we may successfully avoid blatant sectarianism based on race, gender, etc., we will still make a primary distinction between "somebodies" and "nobodies."[12] While we may not diminish someone based on that person's race, we may still very well dismiss that person based upon his or her social rank. If we have achieved, if we have performed and earned a valued societal position, it will become easy for us to dismiss someone who is below us. The Corinthians were guilty of this mistake, as are many Christians today.

Much like the Corinthians, we unknowingly swim in the cultural waters of right-side-up wisdom and power. Our text creates a very uncomfortable tension for us when it offers a storyline that is different than the one that we have absorbed. Paul challenges us to consider the fact that God has a very different understanding of reality than we do.

The Biblical Storyline: Upside-Down Wisdom and Power— The Counterintuitive Wisdom and Power of God

The overall tenor of our text reveals that God has a different understanding of wisdom and power than the one revealed in the common cultural storyline. Paul uses a polemical approach to the language of the common cultural storyline in order to flip it on its head.

> For since, in the wisdom of God, the world did not know God through wisdom,[13] it pleased God through the folly of what we preach to save those who believe. For Jews demand signs and Greeks seek wisdom, but we[14] preach Christ crucified, a stumbling block to Jews and folly to Gentiles, but to those who are called, both Jews and Greeks, Christ the power of God and the wisdom of God. For the foolishness of God is wiser than men, and the weakness of God is stronger than men. (vv. 21–25)

Upside-Down Wisdom—Foolishness

The Corinthians have been tempted to abandon the message of the cross for more eloquent alternatives because they have recognized something true: *there is nothing particularly eloquent or attractive about the message of the cross.* The cross is not immediately philosophically compelling.

The cross of Christ—the wisdom of God—is "foolishness"[15] because it simply doesn't make sense within the reigning paradigm. The Greeks preferred to use reasoning and judgment to attain knowledge of God. Because their intellect was the main medium to perceiving God, they found it impossible to conceive of a personal God. No sane person is looking to embrace a wisdom that is going to land them on a cross, on death row, in the electric chair. Wisdom is supposed to do the opposite—wisdom is supposed to purchase power, to accumulate acclaim.

The gospel is not some new *sophia* (wisdom, or philosophy), not even a new divine *sophia*. For *sophia* allows for human judgments or evaluations of God's activity. But the gospel stands as the divine antithesis to such judgments. No mere human, in his or her right mind or otherwise, would have dreamed up God's scheme for redemption—through a crucified Messiah. It is too preposterous, too humiliating, for a God.[16]

Verse 24 says, "But to those who are called, both Jews and Greeks, Christ the power of God and the wisdom of God. For the foolishness of God is wiser than men, and the weakness of God is stronger than men." It's an upside-down wisdom, which appears to be foolishness to the world. While it is common for even nominal modern-day Christians to have positive associations when they think about the cross, the Corinthians would have no category for seeing the cross as positively inspiring or heartwarming. In the ancient world the image of someone being crucified was utterly and completely unacceptable. It was the form of capital punishment that was reserved for insurrectionists and terrible criminals.

The crucified Christ!? Christ is supposed to be the one who is going to come and deliver sinners from bondage. What do you mean by a crucified Christ? A Messiah on a cross? This is a contradiction in terms. To the Greeks who emphasized external strength and power[17] the cross is utter foolishness—a display of weakness. And for the Jews?[18] Deuteronomy 21:23 declares, "His body shall not remain all night on the tree, but you shall bury him the same day, for a hanged man is cursed by God."[19] How can the Messiah be crucified? This is not wisdom. This is folly. This is foolishness.

What this means is that God is not interested in the cultural currency of human eloquence and sophistication; it doesn't merit anything in his eyes. Status before God is not purchasable by means of erudition. In fact, what God is interested in is so different from our common conception of wisdom that when we see it rightly, the only category we have for it is "foolishness." Note that foolishness is not synonymous with stupidity, unintelligence, ignorance, or nonsense. Paul is happy to employ reason and argument in service of the gospel—that's what he's doing here! God's wisdom is only "foolishness" to the extent that it is viewed from within the reigning cultural storyline. If we are going to understand the wisdom of God, we are going to have to set aside the definition of wisdom that we have intuited and absorbed. God's wisdom is not about form but content, not about rhetoric but reality.

Paul is asking us to question ourselves, to put our own knowledge, wisdom, and presuppositions under the microscope. We need to doubt our doubts, to question our questions. God's foolish wisdom is this: we cannot reason ourselves to God. God is out of our reach—there is no "wising" up to God. Wisdom is giving up on our own wisdom. And if wisdom is our cultural currency, then that is the supreme foolishness.

The fear is that giving up on our own wisdom will leave us powerless and without purpose. But the Bible suggests that God turns power on its head as well. The Biblical storyline also introduces the subversive idea of an upside-down power.

Upside-Down Power—Weakness

> But God chose what is foolish in the world to shame the wise; God chose what is weak in the world to shame the strong; God chose what is low and despised in the world, even things that are not, to bring to nothing things that are, so that no human being might boast in the presence of God. (vv. 27–29)

God's view of power is upside-down. He is more interested in the weak than in the strong. He is more interested in those who recognize their low estate than in those who seek to prop themselves up in a lofty, powerful position. We even see this early on in verse 20 where it says, "Where is the one who is wise?" He's speaking directly into the heart of those Greeks and Gentiles who wanted wisdom and strength. And then it says in verse 20, "Where is the scribe?" The word "scribe" refers to the expert on the Law of the Bible. Paul is speaking to Greeks who did not necessarily have an understanding of the background of God in the Old Testament. But he is also speaking to a number of religious Jews who were well aware of that background. His point is that regardless of your cultural background, the cross will turn your concept of wisdom and power upside down.

This upside-down perspective on power is intended to have profound ramifications. We see an example of this in the ministry of Jesus. At one point he was passing through Jericho on his way to Jerusalem, and he encountered a blind beggar. Jesus went on to heal the beggar, and in the Gospel of Mark we actually learn his name—Bartimaeus. First, Jesus goes out of his way to encounter the beggar. Second, Mark goes out of his way to name the beggar. You see, one did not typically name beggars in history. This individual would usually be passed over, nameless, part of the anonymous conglomerate.[20] Only those with wealth or influence would be named in literary works, but in this case he is given the dignity of being named. The Bible generously represents the marginalized—the lepers, the prostitutes, the criminals, etc. They are deliberately attracted to Jesus, and Jesus was deliberately reaching out to them.

Malcolm Gladwell talks about the upside-down paradigm, and he finds evidence in history for it. In his book *Outliers*[21] he gives anecdotal, historical stories of how Jewish attorneys were able to advance at a particular moment in history. He calls this "the accident of time." Gladwell says the old-line Wall Street law firms, which were just made up of the majority culture, represented and handled taxes and legal work for those people who were in power. So they were involved in what they considered distinguished fields of securities and taxes. Hostile takeovers were disdained. Litigation? Those old-line Wall Street law firms did not participate in the "disdainful" work of litigation and proxy fights. So what ended up happening for those who were marginalized, like Jewish attorneys, was that they ended up doing work in litigation and proxy fights precisely because they were not able to be part of the distinguished field of taking care of securities and taxes. But in the 1950s to the 1980s everyone realized this was a very important field in the industry of law. We need legal representatives who will be able to protect us in proxy fights. So who was available? All those Jewish attorneys who had to form their own law firms because they were not invited into the old-line Wall Street law firms. They were now historically positioned to represent all of these companies and shareholders who needed their services. In the 1970s and 1980s, the amount of money involved in mergers and acquisitions on Wall Street every year increased by 2,000 percent, peaking at almost a quarter of a trillion dollars in revenues.[22] Gladwell calls this an "accident of time." It's not as though they had the foresight to go into that particular field.

In the year 1915, out of 3,000,000 total births, 30 out of 1,000 Americans were babies. In the year 1935 there were 2.4 million births but only 1.9% of the population were babies; that's 1.1% less than twenty years earlier.[23] Why? Because of these two amazing factors in society: the Great Depression and the Second World War. People were disillusioned, and they said, "We better not have a whole lot of children because there might be no future for them." So twenty years later, many people stopped having children, 600,000 less children. But the children who were born in 1935 had an economic advantage. There was less competition. And, again, if someone was born in 1935, even though he might have the same skills as someone who was born in 1950, Gladwell says that he would have had an advantage because of the "accident of time."

If we think that we don't have limitations, we're not going to understand the gospel paradigm of an upside-down framework. We're going to think that everything is right-side up. I'm achieving, I'm pursuing, and I will gain everything that I need to get. What ends up happening is that when there's a setback or failure, we don't have the resources to calibrate our worth because our value was tied up with our pursuits that are now crumbling.

From the perspective of human power-grasping, God's power can be called nothing other than weakness. There is no power in being crucified; that is the ultimate display of weakness, vulnerability, and frailty. God's "weak" power is a declaration of man's ultimate powerlessness as it relates to his relationship with God. Power is giving up one's own power—and if power is the ultimate cultural value, then this is nothing short of a scandal. And "scandal" is exactly what it was—Christ's being crucified was a "stumbling block" to the Jews—literally a *skandalon* (v. 23).

But there is tension because this sounds incredulous. Viewed from the common cultural storyline, this is ridiculous. In many ways it does not seem to be real or true to life. It would appear to play into the common criticism of Christianity (that it encourages mediocrity—i.e., it removes meritocracy and replaces it with mediocrity). If the wisdom I can gain and the power I can achieve are not true wisdom and power, then what's the point of engaging? Simply put, how can the foolish principle of the gospel be the dynamic for wise living? How can the weak principle of the gospel be the dynamic for a powerful life? Furthermore, how can those who are immersed in the common cultural storyline of right-side-up wisdom find themselves written into a new storyline?

Rewriting the Storyline: From Right-Side-Up to Upside-Down
The Cross as True Wisdom and Power

The cross is true wisdom because it is a call for intellectual humility and the admittance of human limitations from a God who chose to humble himself and experience human limitations. We know that the wisest individuals—those from whom we actually want to hear—are those who are aware of how much they *don't* know! True wisdom calls for intellectual humility, not rhetorical showiness. The best communicators are the ones who can take huge concepts and make them digestible for the average listener. True wisdom puts the emphasis of importance on the other; another's comprehension is more important than my gaining attention.

The cross is true power because it is a call to share the weakness of a God who subjected himself in order that he might share himself with others. We know that the most compelling exercise of power is when power is shared, and the cross is about power sharing, not power hoarding. True power calls for a self-giving, other-centric disposition, not tyrannical oppression. The power we long for is the one that willingly sacrifices itself for the weak. This is why Christianity has always spread like wildfire among the disenfranchised and the powerless—because it says to those who are of no account that God not only takes account of them but also is willing to become "of no account" on their behalf. But how does this upside-down wisdom and power actually break into the common cultural storyline in which we are so content to live? How can those who have absorbed the right-side-up story have their stories rewritten?

Jesus as True Wisdom and Power

If the common storyline is to be rewritten, it has to be done by someone who is outside of it. None of us is wise or powerful enough to rewrite the brokenness of this story. Jesus is the one from the outside—the Christ, who is "the power of God and the wisdom of God" (v. 24)—the one who enters the common cultural storyline to turn what is right-side-up on its head. Here is the ultimate scandal: in Christ, the God of the universe submits himself to our cultural storyline in all of its brokenness. In our "wisdom" we decided that we were smarter than Wisdom himself. In our "power" we decided that we were stronger than Strength himself. We sought to snuff him out, to write him out of his own story. The ultimate foolish wisdom and weak power is revealed in the fact that in this very act of giving himself over to death by means of the reigning paradigm Jesus overthrew the reigning paradigm and replaced it with a new one. The ultimately powerful one becomes the ultimately weak one. The ultimately wise one condescended to our level. By this great wisdom and power he has rewritten the storyline. He has redefined wisdom and power as we know them.

Living in This New Story

This "foolish wisdom" causes us to engender an intellectual humility. If it took the death of Christ to overcome our foolish blindness, then we will not quickly think of ourselves as the final arbiters of truth. It also causes us to be more concerned with truth than style because worldly wisdom is no longer the currency in which we are dealing. We are unimpressed by sophistication and flourish, but are concerned to know what is true and in line with the world as God defines it. This gospel wisdom causes us to listen to and value others because it begins with the premise that we do not know everything;

it puts us in the position of not only wanting to listen to others, but needing to listen to others.

Additionally, this "weak power" uncovers the abuse of power. Having seen self-giving power on display in Christ, it enables us to spot the abuse of power in our world. This subversive power inspires a power-sharing approach because we realize that power is not a zero-sum game. We get power precisely by giving it away and empowering others, and this changes the goal of the use of power. Power is not used to control situations in order to assert our own value. Because we are already valued by the ultimately powerful one, we use power as a means of valuing and caring for others. What Paul is trying to say is that the work of the cross is the most powerful expression of that upside-down picture.

> And I, when I came to you, brothers, did not come proclaiming to you the testimony of God with lofty speech or wisdom. For I decided to know nothing among you except Jesus Christ and him crucified. And I was with you in weakness and in fear and much trembling, and my speech and my message were not in plausible words of wisdom, but in demonstration of the Spirit and of power, so that your faith might not rest in the wisdom of men but in the power of God. (2:1–5)

The power of God was shown through weakness. The triumph of God was shown not through victory, but through loss. Jesus was the true Wisdom and Power of God. If the common storyline is to be rewritten, it has to be done by someone who is outside of us. When we as believers understand this, it completely frees us not to be performers or achievers. God uses hopeless, broken, and weak people. This is the picture of the cross.

4

A New Understanding of Community

1 CORINTHIANS 2:6–16

KNOWLEDGE IS POWERFUL. It has the ability to allow explorational and innovative minds to produce results that are extremely beneficial for human flourishing. One of the parallels between the city of Corinth and today's modern global cities is their emphasis on the importance of knowledge, understanding, and comprehension. Even though the word *knowledge* is not used, the idea is presented throughout this passage. When examining the value of the knowledge of this age, one must be careful not to demonize the whole pursuit of knowledge or conclude that there must be a separation between Christianity and the intellectual mind. Some Christians believe that they need to be anti-intellectual to be spiritual. They unnecessarily bifurcate the realms of the mind and heart. The Bible addresses the limitations of intellectualism and naturalism, but that certainly does not mean that there is no place for the mind in knowing God. In fact, knowledge serves as a tremendous tool for sharpening our knowledge about God. In this passage Paul discusses how one ought to properly approach the realm of knowledge and understanding. We will consider this under three headings.

- The Understanding of This Age
- The Understanding of God
- Gaining a New Understanding

The Understanding of This Age (Static, Nonpersonal, Informational)

The Understanding of This Age Is Incredible and Seems Almost Limitless

Much like the Corinthians, modern people greatly value knowledge. Our research institutions are doing some of the most cutting-edge work in the world. From the perspective of data and information, we know more about this world than any other culture that has preceded us. Tragically, Christians have often been among those who downplay the importance and even the veracity of scientific knowledge.

In an effort to uphold the Christian position that knowledge is not limited to that which is scientifically quantifiable, some Christians have dismissed the importance of science. In the process they have denied one of God's great gifts to humanity—the explorational mind. The sciences and philosophy are the result of God's mandate to cultivate and steward the world that he has given us. The Bible says that the mind is a gift to be cultivated and a means by which people can love and worship God. In this way God can affirm the legitimacy of work in finance, medicine, engineering, microbiology, philosophy, mathematics, education, and many other fields. Therefore, human research and knowledge are inherently valuable, God-glorifying pursuits. However, there is another side of this discussion that the Bible addresses as well.

The Understanding of This Age Does Have Its Limits

While static data, facts, and quantifiable understanding of the natural world are absolutely valuable and necessary, this passage suggests that they do not represent a comprehensive understanding of our world. Paul suggests that human knowledge[1] and understanding is limited in at least three ways.

Limited by Time (Temporal) (vv. 6, 7)

"Yet among the mature[2] we do impart wisdom,[3] although it is *not a wisdom of this age*[4] or of the rulers of this age, who are *doomed to pass away.*[5] But we impart a secret and hidden wisdom of God, which God decreed before the ages for our glory." Knowledge and understanding are obviously limited by time.

Currently, the Library of Congress houses eighteen million books. American publishers add another two hundred thousand titles to this stack each year. This means that at the current publishing rate, ten million new books will be added in the next fifty years. Add together the dusty LOC volumes with the shiny new and forthcoming books, and you get a bookshelf-warping total of twenty-eight million books available for an English reader in the next fifty years! But you can read only 2,600—because you are a wildly ambitious book devourer. . . . For every one book that you choose to read, you must ignore ten thousand other books simply because you don't have the time.[6]

This is not to say that our knowledge isn't valuable—it's simply admitting the reality that there are limits to knowledge and learning. Even with all the knowledge that is acquired, it is still limited by time because it will pass away—it does not endure forever.

Limited by Senses (Sensory) (v. 9)

"But, as it is written, 'What *no eye* has seen, nor *ear* heard, *the heart of man* imagined, what God has prepared for those who love him.'" Paul makes a reference to Isaiah 64:4[7] to indicate that some things are simply out of reach. There is no reason to think that our senses are not reliable means of perceiving and interpreting the world, but there is also no reason to suggest that the limits of our senses represent the limits of reality. It is rather presumptuous to claim that the only realities that are knowable are those that we can perceive. Paul is saying that many things can be perceived through the five senses, but certain things cannot be comprehensively perceived with our senses. There are certain things that God has to reveal.

C. S. Lewis contrasted the different qualities of life for the different types of living things—plant life, animal life, human biological life. He says that all three respond to a certain kind of stimuli, but they all have different ranges of sensations. A plant will respond to the sun through the activity of photosynthesis. But an animal has the ability to experience the five senses of seeing, smelling, hearing, tasting, and touching. Our pets have such ability, and their qualitative sense perception will be greater than that of a plant. For human biological life, Lewis went on to say, sense awareness is heightened even more. The quality of life that an average human being will experience is greater than that of an animal. In other words, the quality of life is radically different because a human person is able to experience certain realities that an animal cannot. Lewis then went on to say that there is another dimension of the quality of life. Spiritual life or eternal life is perceptively greater than mere naturalistic, biological life.[8] Similarly, Paul is saying that the understanding of this age can give an individual a certain amount of limited awareness, but only God can produce a supernatural, spiritual work in the human heart.

Limited by Access (Impersonal) (v. 11)

"For *who knows a person's thoughts* except the spirit of that person, which is in him? So also no one comprehends the thoughts of God except the Spirit of God."[9] Our understanding is incredibly limited by our inability to fully know anyone apart from ourselves. We can read an autobiography, but we can only know the individual to the extent that he or she is willing to be candid. While the Bible's acceptance of human wisdom and understanding within common grace could rub the religious person the wrong way, the Bible's honesty about the limits of human knowledge can rub the rationalist the wrong way. In this way the Bible holds human understanding in tension. It is remarkable, but it is not comprehensive. And in reality we already live in this tension. We do not inhabit the world as a collection of data that needs to be sorted or a spreadsheet of facts that need to be organized. We live within our limitations as personal, sensing, dynamic beings. What we need in order to live well is an understanding or a knowledge that is both intellectually rigorous and deeply personal.

The Understanding of God (Dynamic, Personal, Relational)

In contrast to the naturalistic understanding, the Bible presents a God who expands the borders of all understanding and comprehension.

The understanding of God is not temporally limited (v. 7): "But we impart a secret and hidden[10] wisdom of God, which God decreed before the ages for our glory."[11] "Before the ages" implies that God's wisdom predates timebound human existence. "For our glory" looks forward to the non-timebound future age. God's understanding and knowledge are said to be eternal. The understanding of God is not limited to sensory perception (v. 9): "But, as it is written, 'What no eye has seen, nor ear heard, nor the heart of man imagined, what God has prepared for those who love him.'" Paul quotes Isaiah 64:4 to communicate the idea that the understanding of God is not perceivable by eyes, ears, or the imagination. God's understanding is not limited by human categories of perception.

The Understanding of God Must Be Deeply Personal

... these things God has revealed to us through the Spirit. For the Spirit searches everything, even the depths of God. For who knows a person's thoughts except the spirit of that person, which is in him? So also no one comprehends the thoughts of God except the Spirit of God. Now we have received not the spirit of the world,[12] but the Spirit who is from God,[13] that we might understand the things freely given us by God. (vv. 10–12)

The idea of a personal God would have been almost impossible for the Corinthians to understand. In a sense it is equally difficult for us. And it is much easier to keep God at a safe distance. If he is just a set of data or a perceived lack of data, then we can treat him like an impersonal force. God becomes a decision that I need to make ("Do I believe in God or not?") rather than a personal reality with whom I need to reckon. On the one hand, understanding God personally is similar to understanding anything else. True knowledge cannot be obtained unless you learn it from the inside. This is the essential difference between knowledge and understanding. There is a difference between learning content and having a feel for something. It is the difference between rote memorization of vocabulary words and fluency in a language. Knowledge is different than wisdom; data distribution is different than understanding and comprehension. Nobody wants to be operated on by a medical student who has never been in an operating room—they may know the ins and outs of the problem, but they don't yet have a "feel" or sense for how it impacts reality.

On the other hand, understanding God personally is different than understanding anything else. One can understand Aristotelian ethics without knowing Aristotle. But Paul pushes it a step further and says that no one can really understand God until he begins to know God. In this way, knowing God is radically different than knowing about God.[14] Jonathan Edwards once said:

> There is a difference between having an opinion that God is holy and gracious, and having a sense of the loveliness and beauty of that holiness and grace. There is a difference between having a rational judgment that honey is sweet, and having a sense of its sweetness. A man may have the former, that knows not how honey tastes; but a man cannot have the latter unless he has an idea of the taste of honey in his mind. So there is a difference between believing that a person is beautiful, and having a sense of his beauty. The former may be obtained by hearsay, but the latter only by seeing the countenance. There is a wide difference between mere speculative rational judging any thing to be excellent, and having a sense of its sweetness and beauty. The former rests only in the head, speculation only is concerned in it; but the heart is concerned in the latter. When the heart is sensible of the beauty and amiableness of a thing, it necessarily feels pleasure in the apprehension. It is implied in a person's being heartily sensible of the loveliness of a thing, that the idea of it is sweet and pleasant to his soul; which is a far different thing from having a rational opinion that it is excellent.[15]

True knowledge is inner, personal understanding. And the same is true of knowledge about God. If we're going to give God a fair shake, it has to be on his terms. We have to enter into his world to see how he relates, how he defines himself. Paul understands this concept of true knowledge and polemically uses the language of his own culture to speak against it. He does it in such a way when he enters into the world and challenges it rather than simply dismissing it. He uses the language of wisdom and foolishness because the Corinthians worshiped the idea of wisdom. He uses the language of weakness because they loved power, strength, and glory. It seemed foolish for the Savior to die on a cross for people who had a right-side-up version of what they thought was real. An understanding of God is different from an understanding of this age because a relationship with God is dynamic and deeply personal.

A renowned French philosopher Luc Ferry confesses that there aren't enough compelling arguments by the New Atheists to convince him to consider becoming an atheist. Although he is more attracted to Christianity, he's not a Christian. But in his book *A Brief History of Ideas*[16] he essentially goes through the major intellectual moments in the history of humanity and shows how one particular worldview eclipses another. He starts with the Greeks and their emphasis on the *logos*—their admirable pursuit of finding order in the reality of the cosmos, their contemplation of the dimension of that which is real, reflecting primarily on the present. They wanted things to be orderly, reasonable, and logical, and therefore they would shun anyone who would become overly emotional. In light of this, it made sense for them to use the language of detachment or non-attachment.

One Stoic philosopher said, "So in this too when you kiss your child, or your brother, or your friend, never give way entirely to your affections." "Don't give yourself too much to that person." "Nor free rein to your imagination; but curb it, restrain it, like those who stand behind generals when they ride in triumph and remind them that they are just mere mortal men." "What harm is there while you are kissing your child to murmur softly, 'Oh, tomorrow you will die.'" The Greeks didn't want anyone to be overwhelmed by the circumstances of life. They actually wanted people to cope well with life, and this was one of their ways to do so: to think logically and rationally and to detach oneself from feelings, or even suffering in the world.[17]

Verse 10 clearly shows that God is not a detached, impersonal force: "... these things God has revealed to us through the Spirit. For the Spirit searches everything." If someone wants to know what's going on in the mind of a person, he would need to enter into that person's world. This is why God sends his Spirit. Informational knowing is not the same as personal knowing.

Gaining a New Understanding

At this point the reader of the text might conclude that to know God, we need to condescend and admit our limits. But this conclusion is problematic because we can't gain this new understanding on our own. There is no way for anyone to enter into the culture of the Godhead. We are limited and sinful, and he is beyond our reach. There is no way that we can go about getting to know God personally. We don't have the access or the means. How then can an individual enter into the life of God to actually know him? How can our knowledge of God become personal?

God's Graceful Condescension in Christ

We do not need to condescend to God and enter into his culture; he needs to condescend and enter into ours. The limited does not need to transcend its limits in order to reach enlightenment; the limitlessly enlightened one needs to enter the limitations of space and time in order to communicate himself. The only way to know God personally is to know that we have been known personally by God. God has already come for us and wants to know us and to be known by us. God's love for us is expressed to us in his initiating grace that does not wait around for us to show interest. And what are his terms? There are no terms.

God's Graceful Work through the Spirit

It is the Spirit who works within us. "For who knows a person's thoughts except the spirit of that person, which is in him? So also no one comprehends the thoughts of God except the Spirit of God. Now we have received not the spirit of the world, but the Spirit who is from God, that we might understand the things freely given us by God."[18] The Spirit knows the inner workings of God like a person knows the inner workings of himself—but even better. And it is this Spirit whom God gives to those who rest upon Christ and his self-substituting work of redemption. The Spirit gives us "the mind of Christ" (v. 16). He reconfigures the way we understand God, ourselves, others, and the world we inhabit. The Spirit gives us the eyes, ears, and imagination to know what God has prepared for those who love him (v. 9). This means that knowing God—gaining a new understanding—is actually God's work from top to bottom. This is not to say that having a humble approach to God is unimportant, but a humble approach to God hinges upon God's humble approach to us in Christ. And if there is a God who has done this, why wouldn't there be a desire to approach him on his terms, to be in a truly deep, personal relationship with him?

We may be simply looking at Jesus and analyzing him like Nicodemus did in John 3. There's nothing wrong with asking questions, but we'll never get our answers until we actually enter into the other person's life. This is true in our relationship with God also. God is not asking his people to adjust to God so they can understand the things of God; rather, he is providing himself by sending his own Son so that they might be able to understand what it means to have a personal relationship with God. For some of us, perhaps it is the personal nature of God that makes us afraid to get to know him. Maybe we don't want God to invade our privacy. But God's intention in providing a deep, personal relationship isn't to make us afraid; he desires to give hope to those who are in need. He is attached not to burden but to free those who are shackled by their own self-centeredness. And this is the kind of God who comes and says, "I'm going to adjust myself to you."

His terms are so radically refreshing and joyful! He enters into our lives and carries on a real relationship with us. If we want to know the mind of Christ,[19] then we will need to pursue this relationship in which God is actively involved in changing us from the inside out. Our identity is in the condescending, adjusting work of Jesus who died on the cross to give us hope, so that we have the mind of Christ.

5

God-Given Growth

1 CORINTHIANS 3:1–9

AGRICULTURE AND IRRIGATION METAPHORS are prominently used through-out this passage. These metaphors are vital for understanding Paul's descrip-tion of what it means to be involved in any sort of growth. Paul explains how he and Apollos participate in the growth process of believers that God ultimately controls and guides.

The Corinthians lived in a meritocratic society.[1] They were interested in being upwardly mobile. In some ways they lived to achieve, progress, and grow their portfolios. In the process of climbing the ladder, they were looking for an expression of Christianity that would serve them in their aspi-rational pursuits. They desired knowledge, rhetoric, and leaders that would set them apart as being wise, mature, and progressive. Paul speaks a difficult but gracious word into this context. The following three movements will be considered to deepen our understanding of this passage:

- Growth Desired
- Growth Derailed
- Growth Re-sourced

Growth Desired (vv. 1, 2a)

But I, brothers,[2] could not address you as spiritual people, but as people of the flesh, as infants in Christ. I fed you with milk, not solid food, for you were not ready for it . . . (vv. 1, 2a)

The desire for growth is innate. Paul speaks of this using a metaphor of natural, physical growth. He refers to the Corinthians in the early stages of their conversion as "infants." We have an innate desire for growth. We want forward movement and progression in our lives. Whenever we look at natural, physical growth, we assume that we ought to grow in other ways as well.

Natural Growth—A Sign of Physical Health

When things happen as they ought to, human beings progress through stages of physical growth—infancy, childhood, adolescence, and ultimately adulthood. Adults may long for the perceived innocence and carefree nature of their childhood, but they do not long for the physical stature and strength of their early childhood years. We tend to have a natural appreciation for the innocence of that age. When looking at kids and toddlers, we automatically think they have nothing to worry about. As a result, we reminisce about what it would be like to be in that stage of life again. But one thing we do not think about going back to is wearing diapers or crawling on the ground because we believe there is a natural trajectory for growth—natural, physical growth. Paul appeals to our desire for growth when he speaks about stunted spiritual stature by using a physical metaphor.

Personal Growth—A Sign of Mental Health

Market research claims that the self-improvement industry—which includes self-help books, seminars, and life coaches—is an $11.17 billion dollar industry.[3] We are obsessed with personal growth—finding fulfillment, happiness, and meaning. We are looking to be actualized, to become ourselves, to grow into the people that we believe we have the latent potential to become. The Corinthians were no different, and they viewed Christianity as a means of achieving their aspirational, progressive ends. But the innate desire for growth extends beyond the personal.

Cultural Growth—A Sign of Societal Health

Our modern society's narrative is one of progression, development, advancement, boundary pushing, and evolution. We want the newest, the fastest, the sharpest, the cleanest, the hottest, the touted, the praised, and the "must-have" commodities. To possess these symbols of our society is to assure ourselves that we have not grown stagnant. Behind our obsession with growth and progress lies the fear that when we stop evolving we will cease to matter or exist. In a culture where only the fittest survive, we are consistently fine-tuning our lives to display our ability to grow, adapt, and evolve. We want others to know that we are progressing into the kinds of people we aspire to be. This inherent drive for progress and growth is not all bad. Living things are supposed to grow! We should expect things that have life in them to display this life. Children are expected to grow; middle-school students are expected to advance to high schools; hard-working employees are expected to advance in their careers.

God created a world teeming with life that was meant to be cultivated. He designed human beings to flourish on every front—physical, mental, spiritual, interpersonal, and cultural (cf. Genesis 1:28). Growth and progress and flourishing are God's design. Stagnation and stasis call the vitality of life into question. No one is looking to simply maintain! When asked how we are doing, we never respond by saying we are simply coasting, maintaining the status quo, and trying to get by while doing as little as possible. Even if these were in our thoughts, we would not share them out loud because we do not want to appear as though we have given up or stopped making progress.

Now the only thing more fearful than stasis is regression, decline, and death. We go to great lengths to hide the ways in which we decline and regress. What is clearly known in the universe is that the principle of decay clearly exists. As it has been said, "Gravity isn't just physical, it's also historical." We hide physical decline via chemicals and anti-aging products; we hide personal regression with substances and medicine.

In verses 1, 2a Paul is attempting to appeal to the Corinthians' natural desire for growth. The Bible actually says that there is something very beautiful about growth; it does not promote anti-growth in the name of humility. Being humble and actively engaging in human progress are not mutually exclusive. Growth is a natural, Biblical, and spiritual reality. The problem occurs when growth is not only desired but also derailed. In this situation the Corinthians were likely expecting Paul to commend the ways in which they had grown beyond infancy. Because of this expectancy, it would have come as a great surprise and offense to the Corinthians when Paul claimed that their attempts to achieve growth had been derailed. They had been striving and trying to achieve spiritual growth—to latch on to some teaching or teacher that would make them mature,[4] but it had all been for naught. Paul is now telling them that they have not been progressing at all in the four years since they had come to Christ. Their worst fears are being realized.

Growth Derailed (vv. 2b–4)

And even now you are not yet ready, for you are still of the flesh. For while there is jealousy and strife[5] among you, are you not of the flesh and behaving only in a human way? For when one says, "I follow Paul," and another, "I follow Apollos," are you not being merely human? (vv. 2b–4)

Paul claims that they have made no progress in the faith—they are still acting according to the principles of progress and advancement of the broader Corinthian culture. The gospel has not hit home for them. On what basis does he make this claim?

Evidence of Growth Derailed/Delayed

The signs of regression are seen in factionalism, jealousy, and strife in the church. In Galatians 5:19, 20 Paul calls jealousy and strife "works of the flesh" on par with idolatry, sorcery, and sexual immorality. They are in direct contrast to the fruit of the Spirit. In this instance jealousy and strife had led the Corinthians to pit Christian leaders like Paul and Apollos against one another. In essence they had taken something that was beautiful, something that was good, and they had made it an occasion for division and discord.

The problem was the Corinthians were tapping into the wrong sources for growth.

We often end up searching for progress and growth in all the wrong places.[6] We look to things like clothing, travel, gourmet meals, and sophisticated culture to pull us forward toward our real selves—and we meticulously document our findings on social media for the world to see. We look to other individuals—romantic relationships, industry leaders, gifted writers, thoughtful celebrities, even influential religious leaders and pastors—to provide a sense of progress. This is what was going on with the Corinthians. In verse 3 Paul asks, "Are you not of the flesh[7] and behaving only in a human way?" He continues in verse 4, "When one says, 'I follow Paul,' and another, 'I follow Apollos,' are you not being merely human?" The word "human" in the Greek can be translated "carnal."[8] In other words, Paul is asking, are you being of the sinful nature—are you being fleshly? Paul's aim is to ask the Corinthians diagnostic questions so they will be able to make an assessment about what's going on inside. Paul is suggesting that the very root of the problem is that they are aligned with the wrong source. Ultimately the decision to seek growth in other things and other people is a turn inward. It is to trust one's self above all others to determine what growth looks like and how it is to be achieved. Growth is ultimately derailed when we search for it in ourselves.

During the second presidential debate in 2004, the moderator at the time asked President Bush a very difficult question. She asked, "President Bush, during the last four years, you have made thousands of decisions that have affected millions of lives. Please give three instances in which you came to realize you have made a wrong decision and what you did to correct it."[9] We do not like to admit our mistakes. That is why this was a terrifying and yet a good question. Questions like these help us self-assess and diagnose. Paul's pointing at the Corinthians and saying, "Your patron is your source of growth right now. But let me tell you where the true source of growth is and why until we get to that point we're never going to come to a clear awareness of where we are." God desires us to face tough diagnostic questions that are presented to us—he wants us to be self-aware. He doesn't want us to pretend to be someone we are not. These questions might be painful, but they are also merciful because God desires authenticity in us. He wants us to be genuine. He does not want us to miss the ultimate source of our growth. Growth is derailed because we search for the source of growth in ourselves or in others. When we say, "I follow Paul" or "I follow Apollos," Paul is urging us to say, "I follow God in Christ." But we often say "I follow _____" and insert our names there because we do not want to follow anyone else's authoritative rule even if it's a gracious one.

Is it true that following God in Christ is the proper source of growth? How can we know this? How does Paul want the Corinthians to find their ultimate source of growth?

Growth Re-Sourced (vv. 5–9)[10]

> What then is Apollos? What is Paul? Servants through whom you believed, as the Lord assigned to each.[11] I planted, Apollos watered, but God gave the growth. So neither he who plants nor he who waters is anything, but only God who gives the growth. (vv. 5–7)

Note what Paul does here: he depersonalizes both Apollos and himself when he says "what" instead of "who" (v. 5)—i.e., what are we supposed to do to make you grow? He de-pedestalizes[12] them both as well; "we're just servants," he says in essence (v. 5). He points to the source of their ministry—an "assignment" from the Lord.

True growth is always God-given. He doesn't dismiss the importance of the ministry he and Apollos had done ("I planted, Apollos watered," v. 6), but he points to the very source of the growth that the Corinthians had been looking for: "God gave the growth" (v. 6). Paul is saying to the Corinthians, "You ought to have been focused on the one who gives growth, but because you were hung up on the delivery method, you're still drinking milk! If you're starving for a drink of water, you shouldn't get hung up on the receptacle that you're drinking it out of! A man in the desert is not concerned about whether he is drinking from a glass or a bottle or out of a puddle in the sand; he's concerned to drink the water—the source of life!" The Corinthians had seized on the servants of God and had missed the point—the servants were just the messengers. God is the giver of growth, health, life, vitality, and flourishing.[13] If this is true, there are a number of stunning implications.

Implication #1

We don't need to strive to produce our own growth. If we know and believe that our growth is not something that we produce, then we can give up on all of our self-help, self-improvement, self-actualization projects. The gospel declares that salvation is by grace through faith (cf. Ephesians 2:8). It also declares that growth in Christ is by grace through faith. Growth is not going to come from reading the right book, or listening to the right preacher, or following a proper regimen of spiritual disciplines. These things are not unimportant—and God may very well use them just as he used Paul and Apollos! But that is not where growth is going to come from. Growth comes directly from God.

Implication #2

If God gives growth, we are able to place our differences in proper perspective. As Paul said, he and Apollos were simply "servants"[14] of Christ (v. 5). This means that there is no hierarchy. Though we are all different, no difference makes one qualitatively better than another. God affirms differences. Some plant, some water, some till the soil, some reap the harvest. Each Christian is equipped with gifts that are unique to his or her makeup, and each is uniquely and equally important to the body of Christ (cf. 12:19, 20). Difference does not imply division. A gospel-shaped community is one where there is unity in diversity: "He who plants and he who waters are one" (v. 8). The fact that they are different does not make them unique parties with divided interests. Note that Paul does not imply that there is any issue between him and Apollos. The Corinthians had invented a paradigm that created this division, but Paul says that he and Apollos are one. When we recognize that God is the source of growth, we are free to celebrate others when they flourish!

Implication #3

We need to place our obedience in proper perspective. Someone has to plant, someone has to water (v. 8a). In some sense the Corinthians would not have heard the gospel if Paul had not "planted" by preaching. Each servant is necessary. One can plant all day, but if there is no one watering, there will not be any growth. One can water all day, but if there is no one planting, there will not be any growth. Ultimately we can plant and water all day, but if God doesn't give the growth, there will not be any. While our obedience is necessary, it is not ultimate. We do not have to carry the ultimate weight of making ourselves or others grow because God has claimed that is his responsibility (v. 7). When we see ourselves growing stagnant, we can certainly do our due diligence in prayer, Scripture reading, and preaching the gospel. But it is God who ultimately gives growth.

How can we be sure that God will re-source growth? There is a gardener who created a world meant to thrive (creation). When his garden fell into disrepair (the fall), he didn't abandon it. He incarnated himself into the world he had created (the Incarnation) in order to take the fall for all of our sin, decline, regression, and death (the cross) and to create a new creational humanity through his defeat of death (resurrection). He has created a new people for himself who are called to be co-gardeners—servants in God's field (missional calling). And he has promised that in the end we will experience eternal growth, flourishing, and progression on all fronts (natural, personal, societal, cultural) as we live in a renewed, reconciled garden-city (the new creation). When we see the lengths to which this gardener has gone to assure us of the extent to which his promises reach, we can do nothing other than entrust him with our growth. The pressure is taken off of us to produce the growth. We do not need to ask the things of this world to produce it for us. Growth is given by God as we sink deeper and deeper into the meaty, sustaining realities of the gospel.

In John 15 Jesus says, "I am the vine; you are the branches. Whoever abides in me and I in him, he it is that bears much fruit, for apart from me you can do nothing" (v. 5). The growth cannot happen apart from the connection to the true vine. We need to be connected to the very source of growth—the true vine. Just as faith is utterly impossible, growth is utterly impossible. These are gifts given to us from God. Although there is no explicit mentioning of the cross of Christ, we need to understand Paul's message to the Corinthians in light of what he had said earlier in his letter: Christ sent him "to preach the gospel, and not with words of eloquent wisdom, lest the cross of Christ be emptied of its power" (1:17). Paul is arguing that when they look for power, strength, wisdom, light, and patrons, they are approaching all the wrong sources. But the paradigm of this alternate community is very subversive; it is upside-down. It is a community in which strength looks like weakness and wisdom looks like foolishness. The cross undergirds everything about this community. Apart from the very source of growth that is offered in the person of Jesus Christ, there is no way to attain growth.

When Mary Magdalene sees Jesus after his resurrection, she does not even recognize him. (cf. John 20). She sees him, but she doesn't see him, because she does not have the ability to create faith in herself. It wasn't until Jesus initiated and gave her the gift of faith and said, "Mary!" that she finally responded by saying, "Rabboni!" This is when her eyes were opened. This may sound uncomfortable initially because it would mean that both faith and growth cannot be acquired by one's effort. If this indeed is the case, what is the point of believing? And why do we need to grow when we do not possess the ability to grow ourselves? But what sounds troubling at first may be liberating after all. It is troubling if we work with the assumption that it is about what we can do for God and not what God can do for us. Attempting to create growth in ourselves leads to despair. But if we know there is an unconditional source that never changes, and if it is a source that actually gives us what we can't acquire on our own, then there is hope. We can avoid despair even when there are discouragements because we know that the ultimate source of growth does not come from our own efforts.

The good news of Christianity is that the very innate desire for growth can be properly celebrated and encouraged. Though there are enough reminders of discouragements in this world that diminish our hope for growth, we can find our ultimate hope in Jesus Christ. In him we find the resources to fight through growths that have been derailed. We no longer have to be enslaved by the wrong sources of growth because in Jesus Christ, and through the community of his people, we find an everlasting source of hope that can properly fulfill our innate desires for growth.

6

The Architecture
of Community

1 CORINTHIANS 3:10–23

IN THE EARLIER VERSES OF 1 Corinthians 3, Paul employed an agricultural metaphor to describe the Christian community, and in this chapter he uses an *architectural* one. In 3:1–9 he described the community as "God's field." With the transition statement in verse 9, the community is now referred to as "God's building." Remember that Corinth was a booming city. An agricultural metaphor may not have connected at a gut-level for some of the Corinthians, just like it might not for today's urban and modern people. According to David Garland, "The building imagery would be quite familiar to any urban dweller, and Paul beckons them to see themselves as a diverse group (some freeborn, some freedmen, some slaves) coming together with many different skills (some highly specialized—masons, carpenters, engravers—others unskilled labor) to construct an edifice."[1] In other words, Paul is contextualizing his message for a diverse, skilled, urban community. The architecture of community will be observed through the following three stages:

- The Construction of Community
- The Demolition of Community
- The Restoration (or Rebuilding) of Community

The Construction of Community (vv. 10, 11, 16)

Beautiful buildings speak for themselves. Their beauty naturally allows them to become destinations. Ugly and poorly constructed buildings also speak for themselves; they are the eyesores of our cities. Poorly constructed buildings are not only unimpressive in aesthetics; they are also dangerous. The news is regularly filled with reports of poorly constructed buildings around the world collapsing and thereby taking lives. Paul sees the potential for the same thing to happen metaphorically in the Corinthian community. He takes measures to instruct them about how to build their community in a solid, sturdy, beautiful way. Anything worth building is worth building well. This kind of preparation work is evident in the ways that we live our everyday lives as well. We get all of our ducks in a row when we "build" our careers, we read books about marriage and child-rearing, and we carefully scrutinize our financial portfolios. Why would we not do this with our spiritual lives? Our community?

The Necessity for Sound Construction

According to the grace of God given to me, like a skilled[2] master builder I laid a foundation,[3] and someone else is building[4] upon it. Let each one[5] take care how he builds upon it.[6] (v. 10)

Paul is the "skilled master builder" who combines the idea of an architect and an engineer. In that cultural context this was the role of the individual who oversaw all the various elements of a construction project from beginning to end. This puts Paul in a place of authority, responsibility, and personal interest. All of this is "according to . . . grace." He's not simply a hired hand, and he's not paying off a debt—he does his work "according to the grace . . . given." Paul is not a removed, outside observer, but is part of a co-construction project with the Corinthians. His initial role was to lay a foundation, and now others have come along to build on top of it.

The superstructure is a communal building project. Paul envisions all of the Corinthians being joined together as part of a highly skilled construction crew. Each member of the crew has particular responsibilities, and the soundness of the building will be dependent on the soundness of each member's contribution. Each is to "take care how he builds." So if the individual who is tasked with providing and positioning the support pillars decides to use cheap, flimsy wood instead of steel and isn't careful to ensure that the supports are placed in the right place, there will be a sagging floor—a hazard to anyone in the building. Each member has to be alert.

The foundation is ultimately what stabilizes and unifies. In the previous chapter Paul mentioned that he might have been the one who planted the seed, but Apollos watered it, and ultimately God made things grow. And in the same way Paul might have laid the foundation, but someone else (maybe Apollos or other leaders in the church) is building upon that foundation.

Paul is saying that the church is a communal building project. We need to all participate in building this with our respective responsibilities. Just as we are invested in building our marriages, relationships, friendships, and careers, we need to be equally—if not more—involved in building the church, a community of God's grace.

"For no one can lay a foundation other than that which is laid, which is Jesus Christ" (v. 11). The foundation provides unity because it is singular in nature. We are not invited to build on our own foundations. It is popular to ask, "What foundation are you building your life on?" But this question is misleading. According to the Bible, there is only one foundation: the person and work of Jesus Christ. This foundation is a stabilizing, unifying, unshakable, immovable force. In the context of 1:10—4:21, the Apostle Paul has in mind Jesus Christ and him crucified (cf. 2:2). Paul does not know anything about who Jesus is apart from what Jesus has accomplished through his dying work. Jesus Christ and him crucified is the singular foundation that establishes the unity for the community-building project and for all of life. It is a sure foundation that can guarantee and secure our greatest longing for unity, stability, and even our identity. Paul is saying that even though we might want to establish our identity on other things, we can be sure that the foundation for this building is Jesus and him crucified. And all of our participation in building is rooted and built upon that foundation.

This foundation is sure—it provides stability. All other foundations are non-foundations in comparison to Christ. In this way, if Christianity is true, it provides the foundation for two of the greatest longings of the human heart: First, the human heart longs for unity and reconciled relationships. No one wakes up thinking, "How can I create discord today?"—"How can I disrespect others and have them turn on me?" We long for shalomic, reconciled, harmonious, holistic relationships. Second, the human heart longs for stability that can withstand life's storms. No one wakes up thinking, "I hope life throws me a curveball that I can't handle today!"—"It would be great to experience a trial that will shake me to the core." We long for steady, normal, pleasant, secure lives. We long for identity; so we spend our lives constructing our own.

Identity Construction

Ultimately we are all looking for an identity that enables us to be secure in ourselves and meaningfully connected to others. We want to know who we are and to be honestly known. Paul claims that being God's "building" gives us this identity. Verse 16 says, "Do you not know that you are God's temple[7] and that God's Spirit dwells in you?" In a radical move Paul uses the term used to refer to the very sanctuary in which the presence of God dwelt (i.e., "temple") and applies it to the Corinthian community. He is saying that when the church joins together on the foundation of Christ, it is the very container in which God chooses to dwell on earth. This is reiterated when he says, "God's Spirit dwells in you." All individuals receive an identity as Christ-grounded community builders. All individuals relate to others as fellow Christ-grounded community builders. The result is that God's Spirit dwells among them. What other incentive do we need to work harmoniously together in community?

But there is a tension here that we simply cannot afford to ignore. Rather than functioning as unified constructors of God's superstructural community, the Corinthians were making the activity of building itself a cause for division, discord, destruction, and demolition. And we know that they are not unique in this. We see the same kind of destructive divisions at work in the church today.

The Demolition of Community (vv. 12–15, 17)

Churches are often the location where dysfunction and discord are most evident. Paul goes on to state in this text that there are several ways a community can be demolished.

One way a community is demolished is through a disregard for the foundation (v. 11). Though there are no other true foundations, many refuse to believe this and seek them anyway. Rather than recognizing that Jesus and him crucified is the only sure foundation, we consider our own foundations to be more reliable and more unshakable. We seek foundations in political causes, philosophical ideologies, consumerism, rugged individualism, etc. We can look like we're building, but when our work is out of accord with the foundation—the gospel—our building-like activity is actually destructive.

One popular foundation in modern culture is emotions. This is not to demonize emotions as a whole because people cannot just be cerebral and rational. There needs to be recognition that all people have an inherent personal nature, and therefore there is nothing wrong with having affection—in fact, we need affections. But when it comes to our foundation, we cannot merely rely on our feelings, as that will lead to sensationalism or emotionalism. If we rely on our feelings, that may explain why our lives seem to be too rocky. Something happens one day, and we feel great about ourselves. Then the opposite happens the next day, and our entire lives seem to crumble. Many have come to believe that our own conscience is now being determined by our own feelings and creation (intrinsic), rather than on something/someone that is apart from us (external), namely Jesus Christ. Consequently, we must admit that we are extremely fickle people. If we simply operate out of our own experience and our own feelings, we would be laying down our foundation on something that is very shakable rather than on the firm foundation of Christ.

The second way a community is demolished is through the use of shoddy building materials. Verses 12 and following state:

> Now if anyone builds on the foundation with gold, silver, precious stones, wood, hay, straw—each one's work will become manifest, for the Day will disclose it, because it will be revealed by fire,[8] and the fire will test what sort of work each one has done. If the work that anyone has built on the foundation survives, he will receive a reward. If anyone's work is burned up, he will suffer loss, though he himself will be saved, but only as through fire.

Note that Paul is not talking about salvific categories. He is simply talking about two sets of materials. One is imperishable (gold, silver, precious stones) and the other is perishable (wood, hay, straw). In essence, he is saying that to build a community with imperishable materials would be to live life according to the gospel as led by the Holy Spirit. Paul is urging the Corinthian believers to stay away from combustible materials like wood, hay, and straw—foundations that appear to work well for a time but are clearly finite because they will inevitably destroy the Christian and the church. In other words, the foundation of a truly healthy church must be the imperishable gospel of Jesus Christ. So how can we be sure that we're not using shoddy materials but are instead building on the sure foundation of Jesus? Paul tells us that the final judgment will make this plain: the materials we build our lives with that are not imperishable will be "burned up" or "consumed" at the end (*katekaio*, v. 15; cf. Matthew 3:12; 13:30, 40), revealing shoddy building materials. But if we are building on the foundation of Christ with materials of imperishable integrity like the gospel, the fires of judgment will reap an imperishable reward at the end. Thus, the person and work of Jesus Christ is both the foundation *and* the building materials for every healthy Christian person and Christian community. Therefore, these building projects, as it were, built on and built with the materials of the gospel, have intrinsic value both in the present and the future.

The third way to demolish the building of God is to demolish yourself.

If anyone destroys[9] God's temple, God will destroy[10] him. For God's temple is holy, and you are that temple.

Let no one deceive himself. If anyone among you thinks that he is wise in this age, let him become a fool that he may become wise. For the wisdom of this world is folly with God. For it is written, "He catches the wise in their craftiness," and again, "The Lord knows the thoughts of the wise, that they are futile." (vv. 17–20)

God takes his dwelling place, his building, his people very seriously. He reserves destruction for those who oversee the destruction of his temple, his people. God has called his people to be craftsman, to build, cultivate, and craft his temple, but he will catch "in their craftiness" and "destroy" those who work against this plan, according to their own wisdom. Though they might think themselves wise, it is the height of foolishness, because they are actually working against themselves.

"If anyone destroys God's temple, God will destroy him. For God's temple is holy, and you are that temple. Let no one deceive himself." Paul is basically saying that if an individual turns on his community, he is really turning on himself—and it is conceptually irrational to do. We cannot expect someone to thrive in isolation. We must be part of the building to receive the benefits of the foundation. One brick cannot say to another brick, "I don't really like being so close to you; it's making me uncomfortable!" The building will only stand because they stick together. They must be unified, meshing, and interdependent. Being a rugged individualist will only lead to self-cannibalization. In other words, any push for independence from the community is really a push toward one's own demise. Furthermore, there is already a foundation and a blueprint. To deviate from the foundation (Christ) or the blueprint (Scripture) is to create a faction that ultimately brings destruction to God's temple. We must see ourselves as co-builders, determined to maintain unity, not foremen with competing ideas of how the project ought to be developed.

We need to recognize that we are part of a bigger cause. If we are only driven by self-fulfillment and self-authentication, then we can never be a helpful co-builder. We would only be concerned about our own bricks, our own building blocks, and we would not be concerned about the rest of the building. When it comes to buildings, temples, walls, the bricks are usually layered on top of one another. We cannot all of a sudden say, "I don't want to be next to this brick. I don't like this brick" because the reality is, the bricks are cemented together. Everyone is cemented to the wall.

We cannot be isolated Christians. If we live in isolation, we are living a life that is not natural. We are violating our nature. But we also need to see that beyond violating our nature, without community we will have no accountability or intimacy systems in our lives. Some might say, "That's why I don't go into community. I don't want accountability." But if we do not want accountability, then we will never have intimacy, and therefore we will always complain about being lonely. And we will not have people to speak the truth in love in our lives at moments when we need it. We were not built to be isolated bricks. Paul uses this architectural or structural metaphor because if we are hurting or if we need protection, then we would go into a building, behind high walls to receive help and/or protection. But how can one be in isolation, weathering the storm, all by himself or herself? The Apostle Paul is saying that the Bible does not support that sort of Christianity.

The trouble is that we are all prone to disregard the foundation, to build with shoddy materials, and to turn on ourselves as we turn on the community. What hope is there? How can the unity, structural solidity, and architectural beauty of God's temple, his people, his church, be restored and maintained?

The Restoration (or Rebuilding) of Community (vv. 18–23)[11]

> So let no one boast in men. For all things are yours, whether Paul or Apollos or Cephas or the world or life or death or the present or the future—all are yours, and you are Christ's, and Christ is God's. (vv. 21–23)

Notice here that Paul doesn't tell them what they must do and who they must become in order to make the transition away from their community demolition project and go back to their calling for community construction. He reminds them what they already have and who they already are.

Do You Know What You Have?
The Corinthians were looking for a foundation that would provide them with an identity. As we have seen in previous chapters, they sought to build upon the foundation of various Christian leaders—"I follow Paul, I follow Apollos, I follow Cephas." In this text Paul makes it very clear that none of these leaders were ever meant to function as foundations. We already have *an identity-forming foundation*, which is Christ. Christ laid the foundation in his death and resurrection, and it is unshakable. People may forget the foundation, take it for granted, maybe even ignore or disregard it, but the truth remains unchanged: Christ is the one sure foundation upon which a life and a community can be built. We already have "all things." God has given "all things" to his community through Christ. So rather than saying,

"I belong to Paul," they ought to have been saying, "Paul belongs to us—he is a servant-leader who has been given to us as a gift." In Christ the Corinthians already have everything for which they've been striving. They don't have to divide over leaders because all of their leaders are gifts from God. They don't have to demolish themselves in pursuit of the world because "the world" is already theirs. "Life" is not something to be achieved or earned; it is already theirs. "Death" is not something to be dreaded; it has already been demolished. The present and future can be fully embraced without anxiety, worry, or alarm—they are already ours! On top of all this, we have the Spirit of God dwelling in us. "Do you not know that you are God's temple and that God's Spirit dwells in you?" (v. 16). The very Spirit of God—the one who searches the depths of God—dwells in our midst to ensure that the building holds together, filling it with the life and beauty of God.

Do You Know Whose You Are?

Verse 23 says, "and you are Christ's, and Christ is God's." The certainty of our reconstruction lies in this: we are Christ's, and Christ is God's. We belong to him. We are his possession. We are his treasure. He purchased us with his blood. We do not have to fear that the temple will be ultimately destroyed because the temple has already been destroyed.

> So the Jews said to him, "What sign do you show us for doing these things?" Jesus answered them, "Destroy this temple, and in three days I will raise it up." The Jews then said, "It has taken forty-six years to build this temple, and will you raise it up in three days?" But he was speaking about the temple of his body. When therefore he was raised from the dead, his disciples remembered that he had said this, and they believed the Scripture and the word that Jesus had spoken. (John 2:18–22)

The judgment has already been passed. The temple has already been demolished. God's ironic wisdom is this: it was the very destruction of the temple/Christ's body that would become the foundation of the temple of God the Holy Spirit's building, the church (we, God's building). God is so committed to this reconstruction project that he gave up his own life to lay the foundation, ensuring that all things are ours—life, death, even the world itself.

Let me conclude with an illustration from sports. If we are playing for a championship caliber team that has a shot at winning it all, we must each play our parts. We would have a similar identity: we are all part of the same team. But we would also have our individual roles, focused on each person's particular gifting. We would have harmonious interaction: everyone does what he or she needs to do in a way that builds up others. We would have our identical goal: because of the same vision in view, we work together. But the difference here is that in Christ we have already won the game. The victory is already ours, so we can enjoy the spoils of Christ our Victor!

7

A Proper Evaluation

1 CORINTHIANS 4:1–13

IN THE SPRING OF 2013 a debut crime fiction novel from a writer by the name of Robert Galbraith hit the shelves. The book received generally positive reviews but experienced modest sales. Over its first three months it sold 8,500 copies. By the summer of 2013, sales had dipped significantly. During the week of July 7, the book sold just forty-three copies. How then did *The Cuckoo's Calling* make the sudden jump to the #1 best-selling book in the US and the UK? How did it jump from forty-three copies during the week of July 7 to 17,662 copies during the week of July 14? How did a book that was sitting comfortably at 4,709th on Amazon's best-seller list immediately jump to first place? It was revealed that Robert Galbraith was a pseudonym for J. K. Rowling, the best-selling author of the Harry Potter series. Rowling was upset. She sued the law firm that had revealed her name and demanded that the law firm make a sizable donation to charity for their slipup. We would like to think that our world is fair and does not evaluate people on the basis of their name, status, or position. But evaluation is a many-layered, multifaceted, almost impenetrable thing. What is the difference between Galbraith and Rowling? Absolutely nothing but a name and a reputation.

We are all evaluators, and we are all evaluated. We judge people, places, and cultural commodities by a diverse web of standards that we have weaved together over the course of our lives. Others evaluate us by the same or similar standards. We relish evaluating others, but greatly fear being ranked by others. We do this naturally, and the hardest thing to do is to undertake the risky task of stepping back to evaluate our own evaluation.

Paul wanted the Corinthians to evaluate their own evaluative frameworks. Here are the three different ways one could evaluate:

- A Common Evaluation (Standard, Right-Side-Up)
- A Desired Evaluation (Exceptional, Upside-Down)
- An Alternative Evaluation/Evaluator (Gospel)

A Common Evaluation (Standard, Right-Side-Up) (vv. 1–5)

Human beings are evaluators. There is no getting around it. We evaluate the world around us. We fancy ourselves as amateur (or semipro) critics with an unimpeachable perspective on everything from food to film, athletes to news anchors. We are particularly fond of evaluating other people. We talk to friends about what our other friends post on their social media profiles — there are those we look up to and those we look down on. We are also prone to evaluating ourselves and, paradoxically, hold in tension an overinflated evaluation of ourselves and a gnawing suspicion that we don't measure up in the eyes of others. Evaluation is brutally cyclical. We have an overinflated self-evaluation, but we fear that the evaluation of others will uncover our swollen self-evaluation. In self-defense we evaluate and overanalyze others, but the scrutiny to which we subject others is not something that we ourselves can bear. So we start the cycle over — self-inflating and other-deflating through various evaluative techniques. Our text pulls us toward the freedom of giving up the charade by evaluating our own evaluation. But it does so by way of an author who is caught in the middle. Paul is being subjected to this cycle of evaluation by the Corinthian church, and he has been laboring over this in the last three chapters in an attempt to get them to snap out of it. We find that the Corinthians' methods and approach to evaluation reflect the most common methods still seen today.

A quick glance at verses 1–4 gives us the context. Paul is challenging their means of evaluation and is prescribing a more accurate approach for them (i.e., "This is how one should regard us," v. 1).[1] The Corinthians are judging Paul according to a criteria that falls right in line with the common cultural criteria: "It is a very small thing that I should be judged by you or by any human court" (v. 3).[2] And verse 5 shows us the kind of common evaluation in which the Corinthians were involved.

It was *premature*. They were making snap judgments before having all of the relevant information: "do not pronounce judgment before the time."

They had a *"know-it-all" posture* : ". . . before the Lord comes, who will bring to light the things now hidden in darkness and will disclose the purposes of the heart" (v. 5). There are things we cannot know or see, particularly as they relate to human heart motivations.

It was *short-lived with limited praise*. They were accepting temporary, performance-based commendation over something more lasting: "Then each one will receive his commendation from God." Again recall verse 3: "It is a very small thing that I should be judged by you or by any human court."

All of these issues are derived from *self-appointed authority*, viewing oneself as the ultimate authority on an issue and failing to recognize that evaluating authority lies elsewhere ("before the Lord comes," v. 5). Paul claims that there is an authority that is bigger than any individual and bigger than any justice system ("human court"). There is a cosmic evaluating authority, and unless an evaluation of others and of oneself is done in light of this cosmic authority, it is going to be out of alignment with reality.

This sums up our common experience of evaluation—premature judgments made by self-appointed authorities who possess limited knowledge of the situation and whose opinion holds no true weight. However, once placed into the evaluative cycle, these evaluations feel as if they hold all the weight in the world. If we buy into the cultural storyline of glossy magazines, high expectations, striving, achieving, grabbing, climbing, ascending, conquering, these evaluations become our bread and butter, or they tragically become our poison. The Corinthians had bought this evaluative storyline hook, line, and sinker: verse 8 shows us that they were intensely self-inflated. Listen to Paul's hyperbolic sarcasm: "Already you have all you want! Already you have become rich! Without us you have become kings! And would that you did reign, so that we might share the rule with you!" They fancied themselves as being rich royals. And they proceeded to judge Paul accordingly.

But we must admit that we buy the evaluative storyline ourselves. How do we evaluate others? Does it have anything to do with pedigree, style, position, influence, power, production, output? Often it does! Even though we live within the evaluative cycle, we are tired of it, and we long to break out. Deep inside we know there must be another way. The cycle is good to us in those few moments that we are performing at a high level and we feel accepted, but it is impossible to maintain. We end up being paralyzed by other people's judgment of us. The survival of the fittest may be workable as a textbook philosophy, but it is an unworkable approach to life. We cannot bear the crushing weight of the microscope of the evaluative storyline. We are dying for someone to wade through the mess in order to see and accept us for who we really are—no performance necessary.

Tullian Tchividjian has written a new book entitled *One-Way Love: Inexhaustible Grace for an Exhausted World*.[3] Tchividjian states that Richard Lahey, a prominent psychologist and an anxiety specialist, says that an average high school student today has the same level of anxiety as the average psychiatric patient in the early 1950s. The *New York Times* reported in 2011 that 30 percent of American women admit to taking sleeping pills before they go to bed. Tchividjian says, "The news of God's inexhaustible grace has never been more urgent because the world has never been so exhausted. In our culture where success equals life and failure equals death, people spend their lives trying to secure their own meaning, worth, and significance." We are exhausted because we are living out our lives in front of a watching but critical world. We sometimes shrink under that watching eye. This is the type of evaluation that is commonly found, but what type of evaluation do we actually desire? What is the longing that we have within our own hearts? Paul gives us a glimpse of the kind of evaluation that we desire.

A Desired Evaluation (Exceptional, Upside-Down) (vv. 1–7)

The Corinthians are working within a common paradigm of evaluation, but Paul says there are cracks in their perspective. Paul then gives us a glimpse of the kind of evaluation we desire:

Patient Assessment Instead of Premature Evaluation

Paul urges that they withhold judgment until the proper time has come. We don't want to be judged on snapshots and sound bites—we want to be evaluated on the sum total.

Recognizing Personal Limits Instead of Assuming a "Know-It-All" Posture

Paul challenges their know-it-all approach and appeals to the fact that there are some things beyond our reach. There are things hidden in the dark and heart motivations that we cannot measure. Sometimes there is a J. K. Rowling behind the Robert Galbraith, and we do not have the necessary information needed to judge properly.

Valuing an Ultimate Commendation over Short-Lived, Limited Praise

We cannot stand it when athletes betray their long-term team for bigger money elsewhere. We love athletes who take a home-team discount to play for the team that brought them up in the system. We desire an evaluation that takes our long-term trajectory into account rather than our ability to produce quick, shallow results.

Self-Giving Service That Trumps a Self-Appointed Authority

Paul is the church-planting apostle par excellence. If anyone is deserving of acclaim, it is Paul, but he tells the Corinthians to regard him *as a servant of Christ—a steward of the mysteries of God* (v.1). He is a servant[4] doing his master's bidding and a steward—like the manager of an estate—distributing goods that are not his.

He is to be *judged not on production but on faithfulness* (v.2). If any apostle could have been judged based on production, it would have been Paul—he worked harder and saw more results than any other apostle. But verse 2 indicates, "Moreover, it is required of stewards that they be found faithful."

Recognizing Any Authority as a Gift, Leading to Humility.

Verse 7 says, "For who sees anything different in you? What do you have that you did not receive? If then you received it, why do you boast as if you did not receive it?" The Corinthians saw themselves as unique and worthy of being in the position of evaluating. They were parading their Christian identity and position as if it were something they had earned, but Paul says that anything we have is a gift. This perspective should allow all individuals to judge themselves and others rightly. If all that has been given is actually a gift—not something that was earned or achieved—then one's self-evaluation and evaluation of others must change radically. An external gift has the power to break this brutal cycle of evaluation.

A New Self-Evaluation

Verse 4 says, "For I am not aware of anything against myself,[5] but I am not thereby acquitted. It is the Lord who judges me." Paul was not saying that he is above reproach—he's saying that even if he is above reproach, it does not matter if he thinks so because another's evaluation is ultimate. The Lord's judgment trumps our judgment and self-evaluation. Even if we can't find fault within ourselves, *that* does not justify us!

The Biblical approach to evaluation is attractive because it appeals to the more human parts of us. It is more human to die to oneself, to give for the needs of others, and to make sacrifices. When there is humility and deference—when there is praising of others rather than stripping down and attacking others—then the upside-down nature of the gospel is trumping and moving the human heart. There is always greater appreciation for the humble over the arrogant, and this is evidence of our longing for the upside-

down. Why is it that this different approach to evaluation is what we long
for? And why is it that even though it is our default longing, it is never our
default posture? Paul is pointing us to the fact that the universe itself is cruciform at its core. He explains this in the following verses:

> For I think that God has exhibited us apostles as last of all, like men sen-
> tenced to death, because we have become a spectacle to the world, to angels,
> and to men. We are fools for Christ's sake, but you are wise[6] in Christ. We
> are weak, but you are strong. You are held in honor, but we in disrepute. To
> the present hour we hunger and thirst, we are poorly dressed and buffeted
> and homeless, and we labor, working with our own hands.[7] When reviled,
> we bless; when persecuted, we endure; when slandered, we entreat. We have
> become, and are still, like the scum of the world, the refuse of all things.
> (vv. 9–13)

Malcolm Gladwell, in his book *David and Goliath*, takes the story of
David and Goliath and reveals a universal life principle. There is a chapter
in the book entitled "The Disadvantages of Advantages and the Advantages
of Disadvantages." He interviewed a handful of successful Hollywood stars
and was surprised to find out for one of the individuals that he had a very
unexpected upbringing—he grew up extremely poor in a mixed neighborhood in Minneapolis. His father owned a scrap metal business, and he was
taught from a very early age what it meant to work extremely hard and not
delight in the work that he was doing. When he was young—around twelve
or thirteen—he raked leaves for money, and he mobilized other kids on the
block to create a business. When he was in college he ran a laundry service,
picking up and delivering dry cleaning for his wealthy classmates. And after
he graduated from college, he found work in Hollywood, which led to various doors of opportunities for work. This all somehow led him to a place
where he would one day be interviewed by Gladwell, relaxing at his palatial
home in Beverly Hills with a Ferrari in the garage. And what he went on to
say to Gladwell was: "I understood money growing up because I received
a thorough education from my father. We were impoverished. Whenever I
would be lazy and not shut off the light in the hallway, my father would
come and show me the electric bill. 'I am now paying more money for elec-
tricity because of your laziness. Now if you need more light to study that's
fine, but not for your laziness.'" So he understood what it meant to work
extremely hard.

But he finally got to his point in his interview with Gladwell when he
explained that he had children whom he loved very dearly like any other par-

ent, and he wanted to provide for them and give them more than what they had. But he had created a giant contradiction in his own life. He was successful because he had learned what it meant to find fulfillment that comes from making his own rules for his own world. But because of his success it would be difficult for his children to learn those same lessons. He went on to say, "My own instinct is that it's much harder than anybody believes to bring up kids in a wealthy environment. People are ruined by challenged economic lies, but they're also ruined by wealth as well because they lose their ambition, they lose their pride, and they lose their sense of self-worth." The point is this: it is hard for a rich man to be successful in raising his children as that man's father had done in a mixed neighborhood in Minneapolis. This is an important point because we often think that more is better, and therefore we study more, sacrifice more, and work harder. Many of those who are still in their twenties are constantly aspiring for more because we work with the common evaluation that more is better. Gladwell is trying to argue for a cruciform expression of reality. We tend to think that the greater wealth accumulation, the greater we will be, and Gladwell concludes by saying: ". . . we have always been told that the kind of things that wealth can buy always translate into real world advantages . . . they don't."[8]

We all assume that being bigger and stronger and richer is always in our best interest, but it isn't. The universe is cruciform at its core. That is why at times when we long for the upside-down paradigm we see glimpses and have moments of what is truly right with the world.

An Alternative Evaluation/Evaluator (Gospel) (vv. 8–13)

Here Paul is talking about the upside-down character of the Christian faith. He is talking about the paradoxes of the gospel. The way down is the way up. The way of weakness is the way of strength. The way of poverty is the way of riches. Why is Paul so convinced that this way of evaluation is actually superior to the common paradigm of evaluation? How can Paul labor and strive, serve, and give to and for these people who are so trapped in the brutal cycle of evaluation? In short Paul has received a cosmic evaluation from the one who follows this alternative pattern, and it has radically transformed his life. The most important thing is that this paradigm is the fingerprint of a person. This is why an upside-down, paradoxical model feels right. Everything that Paul says in this text can only be said because Christ said it first. "God has exhibited us apostles as last of all, like men sentenced to death, because we have become a spectacle to the world, to angels, and to men" (4:9). This is a picture of people who are being carted into the Colosseum to be devoured by wild animals. It is talking about what it means to be a gladiator, being ushered to one's own demise. God has exhibited all of these things that he wants us to understand in the person of Jesus Christ because it was a reality in the person of Jesus himself. Jesus was the great apostle (Hebrews 3:1) who was not only sentenced to death but also experienced it! He was exhibited as a spectacle to and for the world!

And so, "We are fools for Christ's sake, but you are wise in Christ. We are weak, but you are strong.[9] You are held in honor, but we in disrepute" (4:10). Christ was the wisdom of God that was considered foolish by men. He became weak and in that very weakness exhibited his greatest strength. He was subject to the ultimate disrepute that sinners might receive the ultimate honor! It is almost as if Paul is giving a description of Christ that we might hear in the Gospels: "To the present hour we hunger and thirst, we are poorly dressed and buffeted and homeless, and we labor, working with our own hands" (4:11, 12)

And in perhaps the most amazing, jarring statement of the paradox of the gospel anywhere in Paul's letters, our minds are drawn again to Jesus: "When reviled, we bless; when persecuted, we endure; when slandered, we entreat. We have become, and are still, like the scum[10] of the world, the refuse[11] of all things" (4:12, 13). Paul sinks to the bottom of the metaphorical barrel to press his point home. He picks words that have been variously translated as "trash," "mud," "garbage," "excrement." Paul says that the treasures of the kingdom are the trash of the world, which offers great hope to anyone who does not measure up. The trash of the world is made into the treasure of the kingdom because Jesus, the ultimate treasure, became "like the scum of the world, the refuse of all things."[12]

The gospel says that our evaluation is not ultimately based on what we think of ourselves or what others think of us, but what God thinks of us. And God ultimately evaluates sinners on the basis of what they think of Jesus. This changes the way individuals think about themselves—it turns failures upside-down.

J. K. Rowling gave a commencement speech[13] at Harvard in 2008. The title of her speech was "The Benefits of Failure." You may know her background. She went to college but wasn't a great student. She studied classics and Greek mythology. She came from an impoverished background, and all she wanted to do was write. She shared in her speech that what she feared the most was not poverty—even though she grew up in poverty—but failure. "Passing exams was the measure of my success." She went on to describe how seven years after she had graduated from college, she had a divorce, she was unemployed, and she was a single mother reaching the point of poverty. She explains:

So why do I talk about the benefits of failure? Because failure means the stripping away of the non-essentials. I stopped pretending to myself to be anything than what I was. It is impossible to live life without failing at something, unless you live so cautiously and take no risks that you might not have lived at all, in which case you fail by default. Failure taught me things that I would never have learned any other way. You will never truly know yourself or your ability to survive or the strength of your relationships unless both have been tested by adversity. Such knowledge is a true gift for all that is painfully won and has been more precious than any qualification that I have ever earned. Personal happiness in life is not acquisition, achievement, qualifications, or your CV. These are not your life although many of us confuse the two. Life is difficult and complicated and beyond anyone's total control, and the humility to know that will help you to survive this world's vicissitudes. As is the tale, so is life. Not how long it is, but how good it is, is what really matters.

Even J. K. Rowling realizes that life is cruciform at its core. Why? Because we can all realize that there is a longing deep inside of us as we see through the finished work of Jesus who laid down his life for us—and this is what life truly is about. Gospel life is about deferring, about elevating others, about pursuing someone else's interests, about being humble and not being arrogant, about giving and not always receiving, about wealth distribution and not wealth accumulation, about leveraging one's power and influence for those who are powerless. Only the inverted, upside-down, ironic paradigm of the kingdom of God through the person of Jesus Christ will help us to be noble and heroic in the true sense of the term.

Gladwell too acknowledges this upside-down nature in life:

> What about Jesus? Where might he fit in your narrative? He does fit. Here is one of the most revolutionary figures in history. He comes from the humblest of beginnings. He never held elected office. He never had an army at his disposal. He never got rich. He had nothing that would associate with power and advantage. Nonetheless, what did he accomplish? An unfathomable amount. He is almost a perfect illustration of this idea that you have to look in the heart to know what someone's capable of.[14]

This is the paradigm of grace: the way up is down; to be first one must be last; to be a leader, one must follow; to gain glory, one must know suffering; to be elevated, one must be humble. If we were to embrace this paradox, we would be completely fine without getting all the credit. We would be fine lifting up other people as long as the team wins. We could make a meaningful contribution without necessarily having to be noticed along the way.

8

The Indispensability of Authority

1 CORINTHIANS 4:14–21

THE WORD *authority* raises all kinds of red flags in our culture. R. R. Reno states that our culture views authority as "something to be grimly endured or simply overthrown."[1] The bumper sticker "Question Authority" first appeared in the 1970s and was popular in the 80s and 90s, yet one hardly ever sees it today because it now represents the default position in our culture. One can't even imagine a bumper sticker that would say the opposite: "Don't Question Authority." But the very reaction against authority implies that authority itself is inevitable and indispensable. There is no such thing as a state of non-authority. There is never an authority vacuum. Even if someone overthrows authority, that person becomes the new authority by virtue of overthrowing the preceding authority. Nevertheless, our allergy to authority is very real. This is why people today become uncomfortable when they encounter Paul in this passage. Paul claims the position of a father (v. 15), calls on the Corinthians to imitate him (v. 16), and warns them about the possibility of being disciplined (v. 21). It is important for us as modern people to acknowledge our resistance to authority and to whatever extent it is possible to anesthetize our understanding of authority so as not to commit chronological, cultural, or geographical snobbery. There are many throughout history and around the world for whom the West's rampant individualism and radical anti-authority posture would be almost incomprehensible. To avoid this, it is first important that we understand *what authority is not*.

Authority is not authoritarianism. Authority is the *ability to influence others*—the right to give orders and make commands with the good of others in view. Authoritarianism is enforcing strict obedience to authority at the expense of personal freedom. It is "showing a lack of concern for the wishes or opinions of others; domineering; dictatorial."[2] Authority is having a supervisor who seeks his or her staff's good in harmony with the good of others, leading to personal and social flourishing. Authoritarianism, however, is having a supervisor who demands strict obedience and crushes both individual and social flourishing for the purpose of maintaining control. The problem is that all of the uneasy feelings associated with authoritarianism (which are good and proper!) have been imported into the conception of authority. If we read the Bible incorrectly as an authoritarian document, we will buck it because we view it as being against us. If we read the Bible rightly as an authoritative document, we will delight in it because we view it as being for us and for our flourishing. The same is true of this passage. One can either wrongly view Paul as a dictator or rightly view him as a God-given authority for the Corinthians. The Corinthians are in rebellion. Yet Paul still comes to them with fatherly care. He wants them to respond to his stern warnings and follow his example to prevent having to use his authority to discipline them. Discipline is not inherently wrong either. When carried out properly, it is for the good of the individual and the community. We will consider three points:

- The Inevitability of Authority
- The Issue with Authority
- The Ideal Authority

The Inevitability of Authority

Authority is necessary for human flourishing. The more free we become, and the more gifted we become as individuals, the more we will need thoughtful and careful authority to help us flourish.

Gifted orchestras are wonderfully talented—totally free in their creativity—and they can play anything they want. But if they want to play Beethoven's *Eroica*, they will have to submit themselves to the authority of the score, and then to the authority of the conductor. Numerous interpretations of the score are possible, so all musicians must freely submit to the conductor's interpretation. The musicians flourish both as individuals and as a community when they submit to an authority that seeks to leverage power for each individual's good as well as for the common good.[3] This is exactly what is happening in Corinth. Paul sees the Corinthians playing off the score. There's a cacophony of messy human relationships, and he's calling them to relocate their vision back where it belongs. He's using his authority to bring them back to an estate of flourishing in relationship to God and one another.

Authority is inevitable. It's something that hardly needs explaining. A world without authority is completely unlivable. If a child never has someone with influence over him or her who uses that influence to help him or her grow, learn the ropes, and blossom into a fully realized human being, something is clearly wrong. Hands-off parents raise tyrants and miscreants. Everyone depends on others being in roles of authority and leveraging their influence for the greater good (government, public servants, etc.). Sometimes we even elect to submit ourselves to authority because we see that it's beneficial for us—to a personal trainer, life coach, professor, supervisor, etc.

Again there is no such thing as a state of non-authority. There is never an authority vacuum. There is either good authority or bad authority. Every single human being, whether he or she is religious, Christian, or a skeptic, ultimately believes in authority structures. But the question is whether he or she believes in an internal, intrinsic authority structure or in some sort of an external, extrinsic authority structure. One cannot believe in a non-authority. This is why people get somewhat uncomfortable when they encounter Paul in this passage when he says in verse 15, "For though you have countless guides in Christ, you do not have many fathers. For I became your father in Christ Jesus through the gospel."[4] Paul is assuming a position of authority.[5] First, he says, "I am your spiritual father." And secondly, he calls on the Corinthians to imitate him ("I urge you, then, be imitators of me," v. 16).[6] Thirdly, in verse 21 he warns them about the possibility of being disciplined: "What do you wish? Shall I come to you with a rod?"

Upon a closer look at Paul's statement in verse 15 ("For though you have countless guides in Christ, you do not have many fathers"), the reader recognizes that the reference to a guide carries a slightly stronger meaning than a mere travel guide or a tour guide. The word here is "guardian." This word in the first-century Hellenistic world meant a trusted slave in charge of providing care and protection for a child, usually a son, and generally supervising his conduct (although his authority was somewhat derived and less authoritative than that of a parent). Therefore Paul is saying that Christians ought to imitate him, as he says in 11:1 ("Be imitators of me, as I am of Christ"). He is saying, "Imitate me because I am your spiritual father." One might read this and think that Paul simply wants the children to imitate him in some generic way. Such an interpretation is reflective of the culture we live in—that is, a ruggedly individualistic culture where independence is a badge of honor. Unlike our modern Western culture, however, in every other pre-industrial culture and in many non-Western cultures today, it is expected for a child to imitate the father in the sense that the child would essentially adopt the father's vocation. So, for instance, if the father were a baker, the child would be a baker. If the father were a sheepherder, the child would be a sheepherder. So a much stronger authoritative picture is being communicated by this analogy.

As modern people it is important to acknowledge our allergy to authority. There are many throughout history and around the world for whom the West's rampant individualism and radical anti-authority posture would be incomprehensible. So everyone ought to be respectful of different cultures. No one should place himself in a position within a non-Western culture that may be just as technologically and industrially developed as his own country and argue for how someone ought to understand authority. Of course, Westerners should not do that anyway because doing so would go against their philosophy of tolerating other cultures.

Once we anesthetize authority and realize that it's both necessary and inevitable, we ought to be okay with it, right? Unfortunately, we still have issues with authority.

The Issue with Authority (We Don't Like It, but We Know We Need It)

Authority is inevitable and necessary, perhaps even good, and yet no one likes it. Why don't modern people like authority? C. S. Lewis, speaking of his pre-conversion self, said,

> What mattered most of all was my deep-seated hatred of authority, my monstrous individualism, my lawlessness. No word in my vocabulary expressed deeper hatred than the word "INTERFERENCE." But Christianity placed at the center what then seemed to me a transcendental Interferer. If its picture were true then no sort of "treaty with reality" could ever be possible. There was no region even in the innermost depth of one's soul (nay, there least of all) which one could surround with a barbed wire fence and guard with a notice No Admittance. And that was what I wanted; some area, however small, of which I could say to all other beings, "This is my business and mine only."[7]

No one wants an external rule defining what he or she is allowed to do. No one wants to be admonished (v. 14). Paul is calling, warning,[8] and reprimanding them. Everyone wants his or her own way, and nobody wants someone else to step in. No one wants to be "urged" (v. 16). We often consider other people presumptuous when they have an opinion about the way we run our lives. We buck any authority that tries to get us to shift directions.

No one wants an external criterion for belief and behavior (v. 16). Paul calls them to imitate him as he imitates Christ (11:1). No one wants any standard outside of himself or herself to tell him or her how to behave—let alone another person! Certainly no one wants to be judged or disciplined (v. 21). Paul is going to come and make an authoritative decision about the Corinthians. He's not merely going to offer his opinion for consideration, but he's going to decide whether they are in or out.

But the ironic truth about authority is that ultimately people like authority. We like authority, but only when we are the ones wielding it. Everyone loves authority when it belongs to them (internal) rather than someone else (external). We are fine with authority when we are exercising it, but we don't like it when others exercise it over us. We are fine with authority when we possess it, but not when we feel like an outside authority possesses us. We are fine with authority when we are in control. But when we are not in control, we feel as though we are being controlled. The problem with the human heart is that it wants to play God. Everyone wants to sit on the throne of his own life, calling the shots, judging those who stand before him (whether they be passersby or family members), and ensuring that there are no legitimate threats to the kingdom of self. It's not true that we don't like authority. But we only love authority as long as it is ours. And this is exactly why we are suspicious of authority on the whole. Human beings use and abuse the authority given to them for their own selfish desires.

Authority quickly becomes authoritarianism when one uses it to achieve one's own ends. Everyone's primary experience with authority is that it is a tool used for self-exaltation at the expense of others. People tend to react to authority in one of two ways (and there's a bit of both approaches in each and every one of us): they either pursue it vigorously by any means necessary or reject it vigorously by any means necessary. Some seek to achieve it by brute force, intellect, or ladder-climbing. This is the cerebral man—authority structures make sense, so they do their best to work within them and end up at the top. Secondly, people seek to be free of authority by brute force, instinct, denial, alternative lifestyles, etc.,—the visceral man. Authority structures can be stifling, so men and women do their best to make sure they are not enslaved by them. They avoid becoming pawns at all costs. Everyone either over-embraces authority or under-embraces it, but the one thing we all dread is that it would embrace us.

But even as we dread the embrace of authority, we long for it. Paul calls on the image of fatherhood in verse 15 because he understands that true authority is not about brute force, truth-speaking, or laying down the hammer;

true authority is about a filial and fatherly affection that longs to see a child flourish. When a child is running into oncoming traffic, it is the responsibility of the parent to authoritatively grab the child to ensure that he or she is not injured or killed. This is simultaneously the most authoritative and loving thing that can be done. This is what Paul is doing with the Corinthians, and this is what we must often do for one another. While playing God in our own lives, we are prone to run headfirst into oncoming traffic. The most loving thing that can be done is for someone to authoritatively and lovingly stop us. Everyone ultimately longs for an external authority that balances grace and truth—that against our will and for our good lovingly stops us from running into oncoming traffic. Where does one find this kind of external authority? Oddly enough, one needs only to look at his or her internal propensity to want to play God.

Friedrich Nietzsche in his book entitled *Thus Spoke Zarathustra* gives a profound analogy regarding the different metamorphoses of the human spirit. He refers to the first stage as camel, the second as lion, and the third as child. The camel essentially represents traditional culture, the lion represents modern culture, and the child represents the postmodern culture. The camel is one who kneels down to assume a burden, to carry its weight. And here the camel represents moral humanity. Nietzsche goes on to suggest that through the different life stages of the metamorphoses of the human spirit, people must evolve from the stage of being a camel ultimately to a lion. And in the final stage the lion wants to capture freedom and to be born. It struggles for victory over the great dragon. The great dragon is represented by moral humanity. And so the lion comes and wants to slay moral humanity, the traditional culture. The dragon, and moral humanity, says, "Thou shalt, thou shalt, thou shalt." And of course the lion's worldview is "I will. I will. I will." But Nietzsche goes on to say that that's not good enough for one to go from the traditional culture, because he recognized the limits even of the influence of the Kantian revolution of the scientific method. He understood that there are limitations even to the totalizing discourse of modernity. So he goes on to say that the last stage—where we ultimately want to be—is the stage of the child who was, as one commentator put it, "the third and the last metamorphosis. The child is the new beginning, humanity is truly self-created. The spirit now wills its own will. And the child is the superman."[9]

Arguably one of the great iconic figures of this generation for innovation and technology is Steve Jobs. Many might not be aware, but for Jobs technology was not one of his idols. He had a very healthy understanding and view of technology. His idol, however, according to the authorized biography by Walter Isakson, was food.[10] Jobs was obsessed with food from a very early period. So his entire life was dominated by an attachment to food. It's ironic because the symbol of Apple is also a fruit. Moreover, it affected all of his decisions. He had unusual diets that were influenced by the broader exploration of Eastern spirituality. Jobs had an eating disorder, and he had no problem stating it that way. In October 2003 he was diagnosed with pancreatic cancer. What many might not be aware of is that Jobs had a rare type of pancreatic cancer, islit cell cancer. This form of cancer is slow-growing and is in most instances curable with prompt surgery to remove the tumor from the pancreas. But Jobs's idolatry of food took control. "To the horror of his friends and wife, Jobs decided not to have surgery to remove the tumor, which was the only accepted medical approach. 'I really didn't want them to open up my body so I tried to see if a few other things would work,' he told me years later with a hint of regret. Specifically he kept to a strict vegan diet, with large quantities of carrot and fruit juices."[11] "To the regimen he added acupuncture, a variety of herbal remedies . . . he found on the internet or by consulting people around the country, including a psychic." "For awhile he was under the sway of a doctor who operated a natural healing clinic in Southern California that stressed the use of organic herbs, juice fasts, frequent bowel cleansings, hydro therapy, and the expression of all negative feelings." The point is that Jobs ultimately depended on his own control and obsession with food. For Jobs food was his life. As one commentator put it, "Every idol makes two simple and extravagant promises: you shall not surely die and you shall be like God." The problem with Jobs was both his unwillingness to submit to an external authority and his desire to trust his own internal approach.

No one likes authority outside of himself or herself because no one wants anything to control him or her. Sadly, however, whatever becomes our life, whatever becomes our obsession, our ultimate value, or our personal center—for Jobs it was food—will ultimately lead us not to human flourishing but to human diminishing. This is because everyone wants to play God. Even if one dreads the full embrace of authority, everyone longs for a certain sense of it.

Paul calls on the image of a father in verse 15. He discusses a sort of authority that comes not with coercion, not in an oppressive, tyrannical way, but with an authority that is filial, fatherly, and affectionate for his children whom he loves. It is an authority that compels a parent to grab a child to ensure his or her safety and prevent injury when the child rides his bicycle through a busy intersection.

The most authoritative and loving thing that anyone can do for someone is to speak the truth in love, that is, to admonish in love and gentleness. That is exactly what the Apostle Paul is doing. How ironic that someone such as Jobs, who wanted to be independent and autonomous, was ultimately controlled by something. Everyone is submitting to some system of authority. And the only way that anyone's heart can be liberated from that is to look at the ideal authority.

The Ideal Authority (Where Do We Find the Kind of Authority for Which We Long?)

Paul is displaying an authority that is based upon everything he's said to this point in the epistle.

> What Paul expects the Corinthians to imitate are those things that will end the boasting and factionalism in Corinth. Garland explains: "They are to welcome being regarded as fools for Christ, and as weak and dishonored. . . . They are to recognize that all that they are and have comes to them as a grace-gift from God (3:10) and that they are not inherently extraordinary (4:7). They are to think of themselves as no better than menial field hands (3:5) and servants (4:1) awaiting God's judgment to determine if they were trustworthy (4:5). They are to rid themselves of all resentments and rivalries with co-workers so that they can toil together in God's field (3:5–9). They are to resist passing themselves off as wise or elite by using lofty words of wisdom or aligning themselves with those who do and to rely instead on the power of God that works through weakness, fear, and trembling (2:1–4)." These actions and attitudes constitute the pattern of Paul's life both in the present and as he had lived it out before the Corinthians. In short, Paul is a model of the wisdom of the cross.[12]

The ideal authority is the wisdom of the cross, and Paul modeled that. "I do not write these things to make you ashamed, but to admonish you as my beloved children.[13] . . . For I became your father in Christ Jesus through the gospel" (v. 14, 15b). We also read in verse 21: "What do you wish? Shall I come to you with a rod, or with love in a spirit of gentleness?" Paul says in Ephesians 4:15 that Christians need to "speak the truth in love." He says, "I became your father through the gospel" (v. 15). And this refers back to 1:17: he was sent "to preach the gospel, and not with eloquent wisdom, lest the cross of Christ be emptied of its power." The Apostle Paul, even though he may not specifically make reference to the cross, knows that whenever he uses the word *power*, he's referring to Christ and him crucified. When he says, "I want to remind you of my ways in Christ," he is summarizing the upside-down picture of the cruciform reality of what Jesus has done for us.

Behind all of Paul's authoritative and loving care for the Corinthians lies the authoritative and loving care of Christ for his church. The ideal authority is the subversive kingliness of the cross. The ultimate authority of the universe lays down his authority in order that others might flourish. God "plays God" in the most unexpected way imaginable at the cross. He plays God exactly in the way man does not. Whereas we grasp for power and use it against others to advance our own self-absorbed agendas, the God of the universe lays his power aside for the sake of others. His agenda is redemptive and cruciform in nature. Andy Crouch puts it this way:

> Like life itself, power is nothing—worse than nothing—without love. But love without power is less than it was meant to be. Love without the capacity to make something of the world, without the ability to respond to and make room for the beloved's flourishing, is frustrated love. This is why the love that is the heartbeat of the Christian story—the Father's love for the Son and, through the Son, the world—is not simply a sentimental feeling or a distant, ethereal theological truth, but has been signed and sealed by the most audacious act of true power in the history of the world, the resurrection of the Son from the dead. Power at its best is resurrection to full life, to full humanity. Whenever human beings become what they were meant to be, when even death cannot finally hold its prisoners, then we can truly speak of power.[14]

Only as a result of having received this self-giving, self-sacrificing authority can Paul approach the Corinthians with a combination of boldness and humility. Not like a boss but like a father. Not as a demolisher but as a cultivator, a gardener. The cross is where mercy and justice, truth and love, strength and weakness, boldness and humility, durability and delicacy meet.

These are the results of receiving the ideal authority. We can cease to be the ultimate authority of our life and stop playing God. We are freed to give up the burden of both chasing after and running from authority. But once we stop playing God, we get to start "playing God"[15] in the proper sense. We get to be imitators of Christ, seeking to cultivate culture and help humanity flourish in line with the cultural mandate. Once we are embraced by God's authority of grace, we are free to use our gifts, talents, and resources in the ways that we were intended to use them. This puts all sub-authorities in their proper place. One is able to submit to authorities when they are functioning as they should (government, church, etc.). We do not have to live in fear of authority (boss, judge, etc.) because we have received the embrace of a greater authority. We can spot authoritarianism and call it out (i.e., because we are embraced by God's authority we can fight against oppression and injustice, and we are free to wriggle out from under the thumb of oppressors). The authority of grace is what we've been longing for.

In John 13:3 one reads, "Jesus, knowing that the Father had given all things into his hands . . ." This means that Jesus had all authority on earth and knew that he had come from God and was going back to God. John says that Jesus knew all this—that he knew that he had received all authority and had come from God. He had all the authority, all things from God. So what would one then expect to see in the very next verse? That he would perform some miraculous sign? That he would heal someone? That he would part the Red Sea? That there would be some act of transfiguration? It says in verses 4, 5: He "rose from supper. He laid aside his outer garments, and taking a towel, tied it around his waist. Then he poured water into a basin and began to wash his disciples' feet." This is incredible. This is the ideal authority of somebody who had all authority at his disposal, "all things." He had come from God. Yet he did not manipulate or wield that power and authority in a coercive, tyrannical, oppressive, or authoritarian way. What did he do instead? He laid down his life. He showed what it means to be self-giving. He showed what it means to be self-sacrificial.

In this passage one finds a picture of admonishing and speaking the truth in love that is a narrative of the authority of grace, which is not coercive but generative, not repressive but emancipatory.[16] What does this look like for us? Some of us want to pursue power, authority, influence, and excellence. Some of us are close to being there. The Bible doesn't necessarily speak against power. The Bible shows that God is the ultimate example of power. He is the Creator of all things, and we are his image-bearers. Furthermore, we have been given responsibility from a derived authority, which comes from God, to be able to pursue individual and social human flourishing. But the human heart is prone to being shaped, influenced, attracted, and tempted by other preoccupations and other desires. And therefore man's heart becomes enslaved by them. Paul is teaching about this paradoxical authority so we will know that Jesus Christ gave himself up for us, although he was full of authority.

What does this paradoxical authority look like? If someone has people within his or her community and wants both their flourishing as well as his or her own flourishing as part of that community, then he or she must admonish and exercise that authority out of a spirit of love and gentleness. Everyone must speak the truth in love. Many people don't want to admonish or speak the truth in love. Many are hesitant to demonstrate any authoritative influence or shaping power into another person's life. Many would rather stay out of the way and let others live their lives the way they want. This is one reason why Christians receive a bad reputation, but this is not unique to Christians. This is what every human being does. It always depends on the level of intimacy in the relationship.

The problem for everyone is that no one can control himself or herself. Everyone struggles with a tendency toward abrasiveness. And everyone allows his or her powers to corrupt. We all have this tendency to be coercive, so we speak the truth, but we become obnoxious and abrasive. That is why we need this beautiful picture of the paradoxical combination of authority and meekness, boldness and humility. Everyone must go and speak into his or her own heart and speak into others' hearts by doing what Richard Sibbes recommends: "To take the soul to task and to deal roundly with our own hearts and to let conscience have its full work and to bring the soul into spiritual subjection unto God, this is not an easy matter, because the soul, out of self-love is loathe to enter into itself, lest it should have other thoughts of itself than it would have."[17] "Take the soul to task." If you have a friend whom you love, if you have a wife, brother, or friend whom you love, then you need to—especially in the context of a loving, gentle, safe, secure relationship—take that person's soul to task. However, this means admonishing with love and a spirit of gentleness.

Keller puts it another way.[18] It is a paradoxical kingliness of Jesus who was majestic and meek, holy and humble, bold and sweet, brave and meek, lamblike and lionhearted, courageous and compassionate, all at the same time. But it is only paradoxical to the world. It is real royalty to humanity. In Jesus Christ one sees the combination of infinite power and complete vulnerability, unbounded justice yet unending mercy, transcendent highness and exquisite accessibility and nearness. It's mighty and powerful, yet perfectly under control. The attraction is deep. It's lordliness. It's a loyalty. It's a kingliness that everyone longs to have.[19] This is the kind of person to whom we are attracted. Somebody that is not afraid to speak difficult truths into our lives because he or she ultimately love us. Moreover, they do it in such a gentle, sweet, meek, loving, and compassionate way. And the only way anyone will be able to have this paradoxical authority is to be able to look at the ideal authority—the authority of grace. Not forfeiting authority, but being able to see an individual who is actually harder on sin and the Law, but at the same time is far more extravagant in his expression of grace than offering mere tolerance. This is the picture of a paradoxical combination of the ideal authority that the believer has in Jesus. The Christian does not need to be timid or coercive because he has the gentleness and the sweetness of the Spirit of love that shows what it means to speak the truth in love.

9

The Grace of Discipline

1 CORINTHIANS 5:1–13

CHURCH DISCIPLINE is not a topic that comes up very often in Scripture. It's also not something that happens all that often in the church, at least not on the scale that's happening in this passage. But talking about discipline is actually more reasonable *and* relevant than most people might first think. The word *discipline* typically stirs up only negative images in people's minds—vindictiveness or judgmentalism. But this is precisely what Biblical discipline is not.

There is cultural aversion to discipline. We're *comfortable* with the idea of self-discipline—bringing ourselves into line with a certain standard in order to reach a long-term goal like weight loss, eating healthily, or earning an additional degree. We even refer to different branches of knowledge or fields of study as "disciplines" because we understand that it takes sustained focus, hard work, and self-discipline to grasp them. However, we are *uncomfortable* with the idea of being disciplined by an external force—someone or something outside ourselves. And the reason for this is because of rampant individualism. Jonathan Leeman says, "[for] the average person in Western culture today: every attachment is negotiable. We are all free agents, and every relationship and life station is a contract that can be renegotiated or canceled, whether we are dealing with the prince, the parents, the spouse, the salesman, the boss, the ballot box, the courtroom judge, or, of course, the local church. I am principally obligated to myself and maximizing my life, liberty, and pursuit of happiness. . . . I retain power to veto *everything*."[1] But in reality we understand that discipline is healthy and necessary.

In cities where education is highly valued, a heavy emphasis is placed on the value of institutional authority and even discipline. In order to graduate from an institution, everyone needs to submit himself to the external *authorities*, follow the protocol, and meet the requirements. There are clear *boundaries* between those who graduate from an institution and those who don't. If someone claims the name, the identity, of a school, then we expect that person to have graduated from that institution. There should be strict *disciplinary action* taken for those who cheat and plagiarize (unless of course we happen to be among those who bend the rules!). It's the same in the workplace, in politics, and in the courtroom. It would seem that the only place that we don't want the principles of discipline to apply is in the church. But that's not entirely accurate. Discipline is the means by which we try to carefully, graciously, and with great conviction manage our own house, so to speak. If discipline is functioning properly in the church, there will be a self-correcting ecosystem, and the glaring examples of hypocrisy that we see would be greatly reduced, if not eliminated.

Discipline is done, not to harm each other, but to help each other—because the church is so committed to the community's good that it can't do anything else. This actually happens in every healthy community. There is a certain set of standards that make it internally coherent and, in turn, consequences when that coherence is compromised. One of the things that is hated the most is hypocrisy, isn't it? Discipline keeps us from that. It keeps us real, and it keeps us authentic. But it also keeps us healthy. Because when the church is in community, its actions always have social consequences. What an individual does affects someone else, and what that person does affects the other individual. So when there's a disruption or when someone is wronged, the question simply can't be, "Should there be discipline?" but rather, "Will the discipline be done well?"

The passage considered in this chapter helps us do precisely that, by showing us three important things about discipline.

- The Grounds for Discipline
- The Goal of Discipline
- The Grace in Discipline

The Grounds for Discipline

> It is actually reported that there is sexual immorality among you, and of a kind that is not tolerated even among pagans, for a man has his father's wife. And you are arrogant! Ought you not rather to mourn? Let him who has done this be removed from among you. (5:1, 2)

In order to understand Paul's plea, we need a bit of historical background. There was a man who "ha[d] his father's wife." It's important to note that Paul's focus is not on the case of sexual immorality itself, but on the church's response to it.[2] Sexual immorality is in the background, while the church's response or lack of response is in the foreground. What was going on here was both more surprising and less surprising than what appears to be happening on the surface. When these verses are first read, people probably envision a man sleeping with his own mother, but that's probably not the case. The phrase "his father's wife" is most likely referring to a stepmother.[3] In ancient times women married young; so it is likely that this woman was actually closer in age with the son than she was with the father. This is much *less* surprising than you might first think. And yet at the same time it's also far *more* surprising. These days if you did something like this, it might land you on an episode of a reality TV show, but not necessarily in jail. But in ancient times a relationship like this was against both Jewish and Greco-Roman law,[4] not just because of its abnormality, but because of the harmful social effects it could have on a family. And yet while all of this was going on, the Corinthian church simply stood idly by.

The question that needs to be asked is, why? There were a couple of reasons. First, this man had a great amount of wealth and prominent social standing, clout, and influence within the community.[5] So the Corinthians were simply afraid to say anything that would ruffle his feathers. But second, they had found a way to rationalize away what he was doing. "We're free in Christ," they said; "so we're no longer bound by the Law. We will take suggestions, but in the end we're going do whatever we see fit!" Does this sound familiar? In a few chapters we're going to look more intently into the issue of human sexuality, but I need to say here that you probably won't be tempted to "[have your] father's wife" any time soon. But how do we respond to the Biblical witness generally in the area of human sexuality? Do we balk at the thought of no sex outside of marriage? Do we even go so far as to rationalize it away? Verses 2, 6 are pertinent here for us if we do: "Ought you not rather to mourn? . . . Your boasting is not good."

On the other hand, to some who are investigating the faith, it's not that Christians don't care enough about sexual relations, it's that they seem to care too much. Some have felt judged and condemned because of that. Christians need to apologize if they have dismissed and dehumanized and have not loved their non-Christian neighbors who have a different sexual ethic. Notice in verses 12, 13 that Paul goes out of his way to tell Christians that's exactly what they should *not* be doing.

> For what have I to do with judging outsiders? Is it not those inside the church
> whom you are to judge? God judges those outside. (vv. 12, 13a)

But we've gotten it the other way around! We judge the world, but then soft-pedal the issue in-house. We don't say hard things to people on the inside because we're afraid of making things awkward. So we just condemn those on the outside, because it's just easier that way. But there's more.

> I wrote to you in my letter not to associate with sexually immoral people—
> not at all meaning the sexually immoral of this world, or the greedy and
> swindlers, or idolaters, since then you would need to go out of the world.
> (vv. 9, 10)

Not only are we to keep ourselves from judging the world, we are supposed to get close to it and win it over with love. The problem is that we've made it the other way around. We don't get close to the world, we run away from it. Instead of loving it, we smugly condemn it from the outside. We have gotten it tragically wrong! Consider again Paul's words in verses 9–13a:

> I wrote to you in my letter not to associate with sexually immoral people—
> not at all meaning the sexually immoral of this world, or the greedy and
> swindlers, or idolaters, since then you would need to go out of the world. But
> now I am writing to you not to associate with anyone who bears the name
> of brother if he is guilty of sexual immorality or greed, or is an idolater,
> reviler, drunkard, or swindler—not even to eat with such a one. For what
> have I to do with judging outsiders? Is it not those inside the church whom
> you are to judge? God judges those outside.

Notice the dichotomy that he sets up: there is the danger of being separatistic—removing ourselves from the world. Separatists turn church discipline upon the external world—they judge the world for its sin and remove the entire world from their midst—creating subcultures in which they can feel comfortable, removing themselves from the world and removing the world from their midst. Accommodationists eschew discipline entirely, welcoming the world into the church and living in the world as though there were no distinctions inherent in a Christian identity. Paul casts an alternate, balanced, credible approach. Stop "disciplining" the world by attempting to force Christian ethics upon them. Instead enter into the world fully as witnesses. Remove the sinful aspects of the world from our midst and be in the world not of it! And when it comes to discipline within the church, a credible church will never abuse its disciplinary responsibilities, but will always have the Biblical end of restoration in view.

But maybe it's not so much this condemnation and judgment that has rubbed us the wrong way, but constant preoccupation with sex. It seems that all Christians want to do is harp on what they call "sexual sin." How we handle sex is *extremely* important regardless of our faith commitment because deep down there's something within all of us that knows that sex isn't *just* sex. As Lewis Smedes put it, it's "never casual, because it's not something anyone can just take out at night and put away until he wants to play with it again . . . you can't go to bed with someone and leave your soul parked outside."[6] So to think about sex, to evaluate its rightness is something that everyone needs to do.

In verse 10 Paul lists two other important things that need to be considered—greed and swindling. Now the word for greed[7] meant more than just the love of money, and swindling meant more than just theft. New Testament commentator David Garland said that from these two words the reader is supposed to

> get the picture of those who enrich themselves unfairly, the rapacious, the grasping, the have-mores whose insatiable hankering after more causes them to disregard completely the have-nots, to kick them down the ladder and to trample their rights and ignore their needs in order to advance upward at any price. The church has more readily condemned those guilty of sexual sin, [but] Paul regards this kind of unjust acquisitiveness to be no less nefarious, to be in the same boat.[8]

How Christians handle sex is absolutely important. But it's not exclusively so. Christians are to fight as unceasingly for justice as they do for sexual purity. And if they did that, they'd be more faithful to their faith and probably more credible too.

The ground for discipline, very simply put, is any moral wrong—whether it be sexual or social, immoral or unjust, done by someone who claims to be a Christian and refuses correction and change.

The Goal of Discipline

Throughout this passage there's some pretty harsh language. We're told that this man needs to be "removed from among you" (v. 2), to be delivered over "to Satan for the destruction of the flesh" (v. 5), to be cleansed out (v. 7); the church is "not to associate with . . . not even to eat with" him (v. 11), and he needs to be purged from among them (v. 13). But it sort of makes sense—it's discipline, it's not supposed to be pleasant. We do ourselves a disservice if we defang the teeth of this passage too quickly. But at the same time, we might bring a lot of baggage to this passage—ideas that we import that Paul didn't intend at all.

First of all, when he says in verse 11 not even to eat with folks under discipline, he's *not* saying you can't go to out to dinner with them anymore. He's talking about a very different meal here. In the early church, Christians would typically gather in homes, not in church facilities, to worship and to celebrate the Lord's Supper.[9] And because this was the case, the Supper wasn't just a sliver of bread and a shot of wine. It was a supper, a full-blown meal. And Paul is saying *this* is what you can't do anymore. Why? The purpose of the Supper is to wake up the spiritually sleepy person from his numbness to his wrong,[10] give him grace to overcome it, and then restore him and the community at large. But folks under discipline are by definition those who have dug their heels into the ground and said, "I don't want a warning, nor do I want grace. And I don't care about how my actions affect others either." For someone like that, not only has the Supper ceased to do its work *in* them, but it's also ceased to be grace *for* them. Instead it's a threat. Over and over we see in the Scriptures that when a person gets near God, things get dangerous. But get near him with a spirit like that, and it's fatal. Discipline is meant to protect. There's grace in it.

Second, when Paul warns the Corinthians "not to associate with" those under discipline in verse 11, he wasn't saying they should give them the cold shoulder or cut off all ties. The image is that of a vine weaving around and attaching itself to the trunk of a tree. And *that's* what is to be avoided. Because when relationships get that intertwined, it's hard to see clearly, it's hard to see objectively, no matter how objective one thinks he can be.

Lastly, Paul says in verse 5, "you are to deliver this man to Satan for the destruction of the flesh, so that his spirit may be saved in the day of the Lord."

Here he's not saying that this man should be killed in order to save his soul. The word "flesh" here isn't talking about the physical body; it's talking about a person's stubborn orientation—a settled, resolved opposition to correction and change. Some say, "What I'm doing is wrong, but I don't care!" If you have people in your life telling you that something isn't a good idea, and you don't want to take it to heart, you still just want to do what you want to do, you're just inches away from this. And that's a scary place to be. This is why the language here is so harsh. It means doing whatever we can to wake up the individual from his spiritual anesthesia, everything in our power to break the spell that sin and stubbornness has over the person. When something gets to the point of discipline, we're not just saying, "We don't think what you're doing is such a great idea." We're saying, "If this doesn't change, we fear for your soul." And in all of this we see what the goal of discipline is. It's not condemnation or judgment but rather *restoration*—"that his spirit may be saved in the day of the Lord" (v. 5).

Furthermore, it's the restoration not just of the individual but of the community at large. Notice what Paul says in verses 6, 7:

> Your boasting is not good. Do you not know that a little leaven leavens the whole lump? Cleanse out the old leaven that you may be a new lump, as you really are unleavened. For Christ, our Passover lamb, has been sacrificed.

Paul uses the metaphor here of leaven[11] or yeast[12] to capture the social consequences of wrongdoing. Yeast doesn't stay in one corner of the loaf; it permeates the whole. In fact, even a very small amount of it will gradually expand and work its way through the entire loaf. The same is true with sin or social wrong because the community is all one loaf. What one person does impacts another. What happens to me affects you, and what happens to you affects me. So any wrong, whether it's sexual or social, immoral or unjust, has social effects. It can never be treated as if it were only a private matter. Take this man and his stepmother. Their relationship couldn't just be something "between you and me." It affected the father, the family, and the community at Corinth. For someone who has felt condemned by Christians, that's not just "between him and those particular Christians," is it? It has significantly colored how that individual feels about all Christians in general. What we do is never a private matter. It can never be! And discipline understands that. So its goal is restoration—of both the individual and the community.

The Grace in Discipline

> For Christ, our Passover lamb, has been sacrificed. Let us therefore celebrate the festival, not with the old leaven, the leaven of malice and evil, but with the unleavened bread of sincerity and truth. (vv. 7b, 8)

Here Paul is talking about the Lord's Supper, or Communion. It might seem a bit strange that he would do this while he is talking about discipline, but it's not as strange as it appears. Here's why: the Supper is basically discipline in miniature form. It's intended to provide mini-spurts of warning every single time a Christian takes the elements. In fact, no one is supposed to come to the Table without first examining himself or herself, as Paul says in chapter 11. The church has grown far too casual with this meal.

Here are some of the questions that should be asked: are we teachable, humble, correctable, or do we have a stubborn resolve that refuses to change when confronted with wrong? If it's the latter, then the Supper needs to challenge us and wake us up.

It's also intended to cause us to ask difficult questions about our relationships. In verse 7 Paul calls Christians "a new lump" or a new loaf—in other words, a body that's united as one. Is this evident in our lives—unity or reconciliation in the fullest sense? If we have wronged someone, have we done everything we can to make things right, or do we just not care? If someone has wronged us, have we confronted him gently, or is it more important to us that we avoid the awkwardness of broaching the issue?

A healthy church is a self-correcting ecosystem. Rather than experiencing formal, corrective discipline, in community we willingly submit to one another and receive informal, formative discipline. In the context of the church we should experience spurts of informal discipline every time we gather. We should regularly admonish one another to confess sins. We should preach the necessity of a life lived in step with the gospel. In the context of the Lord's Supper we are regularly challenged to consider the weight of being members of the body of Christ. We are regularly self-correcting. When individuals are heading down a destructive path, members of their community ought to speak up and remind them to live in accordance with the identity that is theirs in Christ. "Be what you are!" "Work out what Christ has worked in you." Speaking the truth in love is admittedly uncomfortable in our cultural context, but it's absolutely necessary. In fact, it is the only way to truthfully love. In a healthy community you will rarely see formal discipline because there is a self-correcting ecosystem of regular, gracious, informal discipline happening all the time. When the ecosystem breaks down, measures must be taken to maintain the internal purity, health, and integrity of the church. The situation that Paul is addressing in the church is out of control—it is like a wound that hasn't been treated and is now festering. Drastic measures need to be taken to prevent the spread of the impurity. Paul's solution is that the offending individual should be purged from their midst (v. 13).

Are we intentionally seeking life together with people who are different from us, striving to have relationships that are more just, or are we simply surrounding ourselves with folks like us, perpetuating our privilege and maybe even holding on to a quiet suspicion of those of a different race or class or educational pedigree? The Supper is intended to wake us up from all of that, to break the spell of our own stubbornness and sin. This is why we say time and again that we need to be at peace with God and neighbor to take this meal.

And lastly, the Supper is also designed to make us ask difficult questions about our commitment to Christ's body. Paul uses the imagery of bread to describe the church at Corinth. There is a reason he does this. Only the body of Christ is supposed to take the body of Christ. This is why churches often say something like, "If you're not a baptized member of a gospel-preaching church, and if you haven't made yourself a part of a local church body through baptism and membership, then you should not take the bread, symbolizing Christ's body given for you." The body of Christ is for the body of Christ.

Now up to this point one might be thinking that there have been more challenges than grace in discipline. Where's the grace? It's important to first recognize that everyone has issues. I don't think that anyone can say they are doing all of those things that were mentioned before without blemish or shortcoming. There are broken relationships that need to be put back together, divisions and injustices that need to be mended. Yes, the Supper is designed to wake up the sleepy from their indifference. But it's also supposed to empower growing Christians to overcome their issues as well. Verse 8 tells us to celebrate the festival with "sincerity[13] and truth." Notice it does *not* say "*perfection* and truth." We don't have to be perfect to take this meal, or else none of us would be able to. It's not about having no issues; it's about knowing that we have them and that we need help overcoming them. If we have a spirit that says, "I don't care," we need to think twice, not only about taking the Supper, but about how we're doing with God. But if we're saying, "I know I have issues, and I need help—that's precisely why I'm coming to this Table—that's why I'm coming to God," then the Supper is for us. Take it, and find grace in it. Celebrate the festival.

Paul says in verse 7 that "Christ, our Passover lamb, has been sacrificed" for us. What he's doing here is deliberately bringing us into another world, the one that surrounds this meal. Thousands of years ago, a people was groaning under the weight of the oppression that was laid on them by their stubborn and unjust captors. To make matters worse, they were obstinate and oppressive themselves, unwilling to change or seek help. But in spite of all of this, someone intervened with a plague of death that would strike their captors and set them free. But there was a problem. This plague was sent to swallow up the stubborn, the oppressive, the unjust, but that wasn't just for their captors, but for the very people themselves. So what could they do? The blood of a sacrifice, painted on the lintels and doorposts, would cause this plague of death to pass them by.[14] The blood of another, a substitute, would protect them from danger and save them from death. And now, thousands of years later, this very same tale would play itself out yet again. There was a plague of death for the obstinate, the stubborn, the unjust—you and me. But again, someone would intervene with the blood of another, a substitute, a sacrifice that would protect us from danger and save us from death—Christ our Passover lamb. His body and blood challenge us, it's true. But his body and blood save us and change us because we can't do that for ourselves. And that's why we can come and celebrate this meal, even though we are not perfect.

If we are in Christ, we don't have to fear the ultimate judgment of God. God will discipline us, but he will not destroy us. Christ has absorbed the full, final judgment of God. We can embrace the spurts of informal discipline because they are God's grace to us, preserving us from formal judgment. Knowing that we are secure in our union with Christ, we partner together to live in deeper communion with him. The church can strive to create an edifying ecosystem where mutual correction is offered. This is not always easy or comfortable, but it is truthful and loving. God's people are welcomed in by grace and are sustained by grace, and even in the extreme case of formal discipline it is grace that calls them home. We all need the Passover lamb! It is not about being better than someone else. There are no levels in the household of God—there is in and out, and in is only by grace. We only have to acknowledge that we can't meet God's requirements, but one has met the requirements in our place.

If our relationship to the church is currently one where discipline could not happen to us (i.e., non-membership), then our relationship to the church is different than the ideal one laid out in Scripture. We need to be accountable to a community in which we can receive informal, mutually-correcting discipline—and in the worse case scenario, we need people to hold us accountable when we are running off the tracks. We need to recognize the grace of the spurts of informal discipline. When we see the church functioning as a self-correcting ecosystem, we need to thank God for his work among us. When a fellow believer lovingly confronts any of us, we need to receive it as grace.

We need to understand that we all have a vital role to play in the grace of discipline. Each member has committed to maintain and pursue the purity and peace of the church—seeking opportunities to do this actively—and not as a witch hunt! Rather we are to look for ways we can support and encourage our brothers and sisters in Christ. Be grateful for the ways in which

God's gracious community is unlike any other institution. We are a part of God's community because of grace. We are sustained in that community by grace. May our churches be self-correcting ecosystems of grace, in which we support one another by speaking the truth in love and thereby come to understand the grace of discipline.

In all of this, we see the grace that is in discipline. The goal of discipline is restoration, and in that we see grace. We see it too even when it excludes, because it's protecting us from danger when our spirit has grown stubborn. But we see grace most clearly in the body of Christ broken for us and in the blood of Christ shed for us—not only to wake us up or protect us, but ultimately to save us and change us because we can't do that for ourselves. There's grace in discipline in every way.

10

Grace and Grievances

1 CORINTHIANS 6:1–11

THE PROBLEMS OF THE Corinthian community continue to stack up one after the other.

This chapter considers h*ow believers are to relate to one another when someone has been wronged.* How does a gospel-shaped community handle disputes and grievances between believers? Much like what has already been discussed in previous chapters, the book of 1 Corinthians provides us with a very good example of how *not* to respond!

Before we begin we need to explore the background of our passage. There are things that likely pop out to us—perhaps the list of transgressions in verses 9, 10. While Paul does address a wide variety of issues, the main thrust of this passage is an address to the community about how they are to handle internal, family disputes, when a member of the community has a grievance against another member. Rather than handling the issue internally, the church has allowed the problem to escalate, and the church members are now going at it in the public square via a nasty lawsuit. While it may initially be hard for us to relate ("I've never taken another Christian to court. I've never even been to court!"), we'll see that Paul's response to this situation has wide-reaching effects on how we understand ourselves, our community, and our interpersonal relationships, regardless of the legal character of a given situation.

Paul instructs the church to handle these standard issues internally. This instruction does not imply that all things that happen within the church are necessarily in-house issues. Throughout history churches have made the mistake of trying to handle issues in-house that require the intervention of the authorities. If this had been an issue like embezzlement, abuse, sexual misconduct—any matter with actual legal ramifications—Paul would have called for the intervention of the authorities. The scope of the passage is limited to intra-church disputes that don't need to be elevated outside the community. Following Paul's logic in the passage, we're going to look at this case in three movements:

- The Consideration of Identity
- The Crisis of Identity
- The Recovery of Identity

The Consideration of Identity (vv. 1–4)

The first four verses revolve around a number of questions that Paul poses to the Corinthians in order to get them to consider their identity. Despite the fact that there are serious issues in the church, Paul sees them no less as set apart by God, and he wants to remind them of their identity as God's community. It is only from this perspective that they will see the absurdity of what's happening between the family members.

Identity as God's "Saints" (v. 1)—Set Apart—Holy Ones

Verse 1 says: "When one of you has a grievance against another, does he dare go to law before the unrighteous instead of the saints?" God has set the Corinthian believers apart and made them holy. The church is to be God's community that conducts its family affairs in ways that are not shaped by the brokenness of the culture in which it exists. Identity as God's saints means that we are to display an alternate way of doing life. God's justice system runs differently than the world's, and the church is the one place where it supposed to be on display.

Paul wants them to consider what their identity is—who they are in Christ as they contemplate an intra-church issue about handling disputes and grievances. And he says, "You are saints." First Corinthians 1:2 says: "To the church of God that is in Corinth, to those sanctified in Christ Jesus, *called to be saints* together with all those who in every place call upon the name of our Lord Jesus Christ." So from the very beginning he is reminding us that we are sanctified. Believers are called out as part of the church. That's what the word "church" in the Greek means, "to be called out." We have been set apart; we are holy ones. Not holy in the sense that we are morally perfect, but in the sense that we have been objectively settled as people set apart to be his saints (although we struggle with our own experience of being subjectively flawed). The Apostle Paul is saying that the Christian's identity as a saint is that of someone who has been set apart.

Identity as God's Future Community (vv. 2, 3)—Final Events

Secondly, Paul wants them to consider their identity as God's future community. In verses 2, 3 he says: "Or do you not know that the saints will judge the world? And if the world is to be judged by you, are you incompetent to try trivial cases? Do you not know that we are to judge angels? How much more, then, matters pertaining to this life!" Paul gives us a mysterious glimpse into the future—the way things will be at the end of time. When God sets the world right—when he balances the scales of justice—he will include those whom he has made right (those he has justified) in the process. Although it is not entirely clear what this means,[1] at the very least it means that justice in the church—the way we deal with our issues—should be superior to the system of justice in the world. Sadly, this is rarely the case. Christians are notorious for their infighting, their backstabbing, their gossiping, their slandering, etc. These are all denials of the reality of God's work in our midst and are out of accord with the beautiful, shalomic[2] future to which he has called us. Christians have a shared identity as God's future community that will be given rights and responsibilities to judge the world. When it says "judge" here it simply means to assess and evaluate with the scales of justice; it doesn't mean being judgmental.

Identity as God's Present Community (v. 4)—Called to Be Gospel-Shaped

Paul is talking also about identity as God's present community in verse 4: "So if you have such cases, why do you lay them before those who have no standing in the church?" A family ought to be able to handle its own business. When a brother brings suit against another brother, it is a sign that something has gone tragically wrong. Paul is not calling for anything radical; he is just calling for the church to handle its own business in line with the gospel. They are individuals who have been made right with God—as a result, they ought to make things right with one another.

Despite the fact that God has given this identity to his church, we are prone to live in ways that are counter to our identity. God views us one way, but we choose to reshape our own identities around the things that please, comfort, and excite us. There is a crisis of identity—a case of gospel amnesia—which leads to us acting like non-saints/unrighteous.

The Crisis of Identity (vv. 5–10)

> I say this to your shame. Can it be that there is no one among you wise enough to settle a dispute between the brothers, but brother goes to law against brother, and that before unbelievers? To have lawsuits at all with one another is already a defeat for you. Why not rather suffer wrong? Why not rather be defrauded? But you yourselves wrong and defraud—even your own brothers!
>
> Or do you not know that the unrighteous will not inherit the kingdom of God? Do not be deceived: neither the sexually immoral, nor idolaters, nor adulterers, nor men who practice homosexuality, nor thieves, nor the greedy, nor drunkards, nor revilers, nor swindlers will inherit the kingdom of God.

We are not given any information on the grievance, but we are led to believe that it is not actually a serious matter that should have ended up in court. Paul views the plaintiff's actions as "wrong[ing]"[3] and "defraud[ing]"[4] a brother in Christ (v. 8). The matter is an internal family dispute. Paul shames the parties by pointing out the fact that they are "brothers" (v. 8). Rather than handling a family matter in-house, they've taken it to the law court of the city in the center of the marketplace. Essentially they are displaying to the entire city of Corinth that they do not believe the gospel has the resources to overcome grievances. Here is the irony: in chapter 5 we encountered a community that was unwilling to deal with the internal issue of incest in their midst, and they avoided judging a prominent member *inside* their community, even while judging those *outside* the community. Ironically, in chapter 6 we find the Corinthians being completely inconsistent in how they handle their issues. Now they are judging a member *inside* their community, but rather than handling it inside they are turning the case over to those *outside*! A multifaceted gospel-identity crisis is taking place.

Individual Identity Crisis

The questionable nature of the lawsuit calls the individuals into question. Why would the case have ended up in court? The legal system in Corinth was not used so much to seek justice as to establish one's status, honor, and position in society.[5] The courts were often used by the fortunate to tread upon the less-than-fortunate. The court was a quick way to move up the ranks and to establish one's supremacy over another. The reason that this situation is so shocking is not simply because it is a legal dispute—it is shocking because one brother in Christ is seeking to get a leg up in the "unrighteous" world by means of treading upon another brother in Christ. The plaintiff is willing to wrong and defraud the defendant—his brother in Christ—for some gain in the eyes of the world. The plaintiff has forgotten his identity in the gospel and is seeking to build his identity along Corinthian culture's lines—honor, wisdom, strength, etc. He has forgotten the gospel, and he is working against the grain of the gospel in an attempt to attain what only the gospel can really give him.

The court was a quick way to move up the ranks and to establish one's supremacy, honor, status, and position. Remember patronage? This is what they were doing. They even used the legal system in this way. And the Apostle Paul is saying it is appalling and shocking that they would do this.

In 1982 Warren Buerger, the chief justice of the United States at that time, said, "One reason our courts have become overburdened is that Americans are increasingly turning to the courts for relief from a range of personal distresses and anxieties."[6] He added, "Remedies for personal wrongs, that once were considered the responsibility of institutions, other than the courts, are now boldly asserted as legal entitlements. The courts have been expected to fill the void, created by the decline of church, family, and neighborhood unity."[7] These issues should be resolved within the context of the church, within the context of the family, within the context of the neighborhood. But we don't do this because we believe that we have certain legal entitlements, and rather than trying to take care of an intra-neighborhood, intra-family, intra-church grievance or dispute—by speaking the truth in love, by keeping others accountable but responding to them graciously—we bring it to the courts and abuse the legal system in the process.

The associate Supreme Court justice Antonin Scalia has made this observation:

> I think that this passage [1 Corinthians 6; I'm grateful that some Supreme Court Justices actually look at the Bible] has something to say about the proper Christian attitude toward civil litigation. Paul is making two points. Paul says that the mediation of a mutual friend, such as the parish priest, should be sought before parties run off to the law courts. . . . I think we are too ready today to see vindication or vengeance through adversary proceedings, rather than peace through mediation. . . . Good Christians, just as they are slow to anger, should be slow to sue.[8]

This is helpful for everyone, regardless of faith commitments, Christians or not. Everyone can use the wonderful principles that Jesus has outlined for us in Matthew 18, namely, do not simply take somebody to court immediately, but rather engage in private discussions; speak the truth in love, maintain accountability, admonish with the spirit of gentleness because we're seeking welfare and reconciliation. Isn't it interesting that our legal system imitates what Jesus taught in Matthew 18—both mediation and arbitration?

So the church can actively encourage forgiveness and promote reconciliation by accepting what we have done wrong, whereas the adversarial process will encourage us to focus on what we have done right. If we take it to the legal level, our advocate or our attorney will tell us that we need to emphasize what we have done right and what the other person has done wrong. But that often leaves both parties with a distorted view of reality. They begin to think, "I've always done right, and I've never done wrong. And that person has always done wrong and has never done anything right." But in contrast the church can point people to Christ, through whom we are able not only to talk about awarding money damages or transferring property or enforcing a contract, but are able also to resolve disputes by encouraging one another to develop creative solutions. This is what one person has said in his book on peacemaking.[9]

We do this every time we take a brother or sister to the court of public opinion. All of our divisions are based in selfish attempts to get a leg up, to shore up our identity, status, and to show superiority by any means necessary.

Communal Identity Crisis

The very existence of the lawsuit calls the entire community into question. Paul implies that rather than living like a community of saints, the Corinthian church is living just like the surrounding culture. He makes this clear by issuing them a stark warning in verses 9, 10: "Or do you not know that the unrighteous will not inherit the kingdom of God? Do not be deceived: neither the sexually immoral, nor idolaters, nor adulterers, nor men who practice homosexuality, nor thieves, nor the greedy, nor drunkards, nor revilers, nor swindlers will inherit the kingdom of God." Note that these are not simply actions these people commit; they are their very identities! Now some of those sins pop out to us more than others—Christians have ceased to view sins like greed and reviling as serious offenses, but Paul knows nothing of a hierarchy of sin. The things that will bother us the most in this list are those relating to the way we use our bodies. This is because Christians generally have a gnostic approach to spirituality in which the body can be used for whatever is desired. Paul lists sexual immorality, adultery, and homosexuality as some examples. Sexual immorality is heterosexual behavior that is out of accord with God's design for sex within the context of marriage between a husband and a wife. Adultery is the breaking of the covenant that represents God's design for sex. And lastly Paul mentions the sin of homosexuality.

When you find your identity in any idol—whether it is your money, your work, your relationships, the things you consume, or even your own sexuality or your sexual ethic—it will lead to personal and communal breakdown. Paul is calling the Corinthians to live lives in step with the identity they have been given in Christ.

The Core Issue: Gospel Amnesia (or Gospel Forgetfulness)

Ultimately the Corinthians are conducting themselves as though their God-given identity is of no importance. They are forgetting the gospel. They are failing to be what they are. They are saints, but they are acting like non-saints. They are righteous, but they are living as though they were unrighteous. The result is that their community, which is to be a present glimpse of the future community that God intends for the world, has nothing to offer—they have no means of displaying the way a gospel shapes a community.

How do you overcome a gospel identity crisis? How do you get over gospel amnesia? Where do you find the resources to be able to handle family grievances in the context of the church?

The Recovery of Identity—Acting Your Identity—
Gospel Memory (vv. 7b, 11)

Remembering the Beauty of the Gospel

When we lapse in our identity, the answer is not to learn a new one, but to relearn who we already are. Our identity is not ours to form; it has already been formed for us and given to us as a gift. In what is our identity grounded? Our identity in Christ allows us to absorb the blows because Christ absorbed them on our behalf. Verse 7b says: "Why not rather suffer wrong? Why not rather be defrauded?" This only makes sense if you have nothing to lose, if "suffer[ing] wrong" is not an ultimate threat to you, if being "defrauded" is not a loss to you. Suffering wrong and being defrauded are not ultimate grievances because Christ bore the ultimate grievances in our place. He endured the wrong that we ought to have endured. He was defrauded of what was rightfully his in order to give us what we never deserved. If Christ absorbed all of our wrongs, if he absorbed all of our attacks, if he absorbed all of our rejection, then when others do the same to us, we can practice gospel memory in place of gospel amnesia, which will give us the resources to absorb the blows of others. And that's what forgiveness is about. That is what the Christian pursuit of reconciliation is all about. Suffering wrong and being defrauded are not ultimate grievances because Christ bore the ultimate grievances in our place. He has pursued reconciliation and brought the perfect balance of being able to demand justice and hand out grace all at the same time.

This changes everything about the way we understand justice and reconciliation. Our courts function on justice. We do not want grace to invade the Supreme Court. And yet we long for grace. We love when people get what they don't deserve because of grace. How can the two ever come together?

Grace and justice are perfectly balanced in the heavenly law court. We don't simply demand justice, and we don't simply hand out grace. Because of the work of Christ, justice and grace meet perfectly. The mystery of the gospel is that God is both perfectly just and perfectly gracious in forgiving sinners. The church ought to be the one place on earth where people can glimpse this beautiful balance at work.

Grasping the Resources of the Gospel

We were washed, and the filth of sin has been removed. We are cleansed. We can stop trying to hide our sin and brokenness because it has been objectively dealt with. Christians have the essential fuel for honest reconciliation. We were sanctified. The grip of sin has been released. We are freed. We don't have to live under the illusion that sin ultimately wins the day. We are free to pursue joyful obedience by the power of the Spirit. The essential perspective for Christian growth is that we were justified. The identity of sin has been replaced. We are accepted.

But not only does he want us to remember. He also wants us to grasp the resources of the gospel. Look at verse 11: "And such were some of you. But you were washed [past tense], you were sanctified, you were justified in the name of the Lord Jesus Christ." "You were washed"; that is, the filth of sin has been removed. "You were sanctified"; the grip of sin has been released. "You were justified"; the identity of sin has been replaced. So what does this mean? What are the implications for an individual who has been wronged? Forgiveness, even though this is not what Paul is emphasizing here, is costly. When somebody has wronged you, you can either choose to forgive or you can exclude. Whether it's through elimination, abandonment, assimilation, rejection, or whatever, we can exclude, or we can embrace.[10] And if we're going to embrace, we can only embrace that person if we remind ourselves of the gospel—that those who ought to have been excluded were embraced by the saving work of Jesus Christ. Jesus forgave us and embraced us and brought us into the fold, into the family of God; even though we were children of wrath, he made us brothers and sisters and brought us into the presence of God the Father. That is what forgiveness is. Either we're going to reject that person and make him pay, or *we* are going to forgive and *we* are going pay. Those are the only two options we have. We will either make that person pay, or we can forgive him. How do we make others pay? We slander them, gossip about them, shift blame onto them, we go to the court of public opinion and make our case there, or we end up being cold to them.

We don't have to live in fear of the judgment that others make of us, and we can have a right self-assessment because God has already made his final statement about where we stand in relation to him. This is the essential foundation for life with God and life in community.

Living out the Implications of the Gospel

We can absorb the cost when we've been wronged because a wrong done against us does not touch our identity unless we fail to believe the gospel. If we have been financially wronged, we need to know that our net worth doesn't define us. If we have been relationally wronged, we need to know that our ultimate relationship is secure. Christ endured every imaginable wrong in order to win for us every imaginable right. Because of this, we can be the ones to absorb, to forgive, to pursue reconciliation, even when it's counterintuitive. The wrongs that we commit against others become things that we freely confess and of which we sorrowfully repent. The extent to which God went in order to save us (the death of Christ) shows us the extent of our sin. If we believe the gospel, then our default position will not be one of being in the right. Instead we are open to the possibility that we may be wrong. We will not pursue self-protection and ignoble gain. Instead we will admit our weaknesses and our propensity to drop the ball.

The Christian community takes sin seriously but handles it graciously. Also, we do not overlook when wrong is done. We are called to be a community that reflects God's good, shalomic intentions for the world. This means that we never pass over wrongdoing in our midst. But we also do not crush people for wrong they've done. The church is a court like no other—justice is served when grace is extended. Repentant perpetrators are forgiven. Radically broken individuals are restored. We fight gospel forgetfulness and identity crises by pressing one another into the gospel. In every aspect of the life of our churches we confront ourselves with the realities of who we are in Christ. When we consider the identity that we have in Christ, even the most drastic identity crisis cannot cause us to forget who we are. The Christian life is a process of remembering our true identity and striving to live in line with it by way of the resources provided in the gospel.

Have we been cold to some friends? Are there certain people in our hearts we don't want to forgive? That means there's gospel amnesia and we're not embracing those others but are excluding them or eliminating them. The Apostle Paul is appealing to us to remember. There needs to be gospel memory. If there are to be living implications of the gospel working in our lives, if the default position is forgiveness rather than rejection, we need to remember the gospel and what Jesus has done for us.

So here's an application Christians need to consider: is there somebody with whom we have a grievance, a dispute, or an issue? Forgiveness is felt before it is practiced. In other words, we must know it in our hearts. The human heart needs to have a propensity and an inclination because of the embrace of God the Father who loved the sinner through his Son. If a sinner has been cleansed, justified, and sanctified in Christ, then that heart should be moved to want to forgive. Is there somebody who needs our forgiveness? We might not even know that we haven't forgiven. Those who need our forgiveness are to be sought out and forgiven. May our hearts be warmed by what Jesus has done.

11

Sex

1 CORINTHIANS 6:12–20

CHRISTIANS HAVE NOT DONE the best job of handling the issue of sex, especially in the public square. They are known for condemnation and hate. "It's wrong, and there's simply no excuse for it." But what needs to be seen is that when Christians act in this way, it's not because they are being faithful to their faith, but precisely because they're *not*. Sexual sin is sin, but it is *not* the unforgivable sin, and Christians need to stop treating it as if it were. On the other hand, we are not to let the failings of Christians stop us from hearing what the Bible has to say about sex.

The Bible *will* rub against our cultural sensibilities on this issue. No one human culture has cornered the market on truth, and so everyone would expect the Divine Word to affirm every culture on some points, but challenge them on others. And this is precisely what the Bible does. It crosses our wills on the topic of sex, but when it comes to forgiveness and love, it's the wind in our sails. It would be cultural arrogance for anyone to presume that he or she has it all figured out. So everyone must learn to be open to all of his or her cultural assumptions being challenged, even their most beloved ones. In this passage Paul's major overarching point challenges us—he says that sex isn't as casual as people have made it out to be, that everyone must take their bodies and what they do with them seriously. Why?

- Because We're Free
- Because We Matter
- Because We Were Bought by Someone Who Gave All to Have Us

Because We're Free

In verse 15 Paul addresses the issue of prostitution. Prostitution in the ancient world was a much more culturally acceptable sexual practice than it is today.[1] Temple precincts would frequently host dinners, after which prostitutes would be presented and offered to guests. It wouldn't have been out of the ordinary either for a man to end a hard day's work with a visit to a brothel. A man's wife was for bearing heirs, for securing strategic political and social alliances, but not so much for sexual pleasure. Visiting prostitutes was a culturally and socially accepted practice among the people of that day.[2] It was so customary that the Corinthian Christians had done everything they could to justify its acceptance. This reflects in many ways our current modern experience. The prevailing sentiment these days is that sex outside of marriage is normal. It's just something everyone does, and if one does not, it's because he or she is strange. What's more, many today have convinced themselves that it's okay and have done everything they can to explain it away. Our cultural moment isn't all that different from ancient Corinth, and the passage at hand is surprisingly relevant. Upon closer look one notices that Paul engages the issue by going back and forth between an argument made by his readers and then his response to that argument. In verse 12 Paul writes, "All things are lawful for me."[3] He is essentially saying, "I'm free of inhibitions, of restraints!" This is the basic mantra of our sexually progressive day.[4] And there's actually a good deal of truth to what it's saying, and because it's true, everyone is free! Christianity has this terrible reputation for being sexually stuffy, but nothing could be further from the truth. The book of the Song of Solomon is filled with explicit content that would make some of the most erotic literature out there today blush![5] And that's because sex is a good thing[6] — it's something God made and gave to everyone to be enjoyed freely within the context of a lasting commitment![7] It's a beautiful thing! But take notice, it's a powerful thing too. Sex has the potency not only to please, but also to control. Anyone who's wrestled with sexual addiction can testify just how powerful it is. But this is true not only for the sex addict but for everyone. Sex has a stronger grip on us than we know. For many, when they hear the Biblical witness against sex outside of marriage it rubs them the wrong way. So much so that they just can't stand to listen because it offends them so much. In such cases there's a good chance that they've been dominated by sex, and they don't even realize it. In fact, if there's anything they're not willing to be challenged on, anything of which they say, "You can't cross my will on this," it's evidence that it has a grip on them that's stronger than they know. So they're not really free![8] "All things are lawful for me, but I will not be dominated by anything" (v. 12b).

But some may not be that adamant about it. Some people don't have this resolved commitment to sexual progressiveness, but just want the physical pleasure or emotional connection that sex affords. Most often when a person sleeps with someone without making a lasting commitment to him or her, its almost never the case that the person is not looking to help him or her but is simply looking to personal interest. They just want to get what's theirs,[9] whether physically or emotionally, and they're not really free. Free people serve, free people help others, because free people need people less, and so they can love people more. But when anyone has sex outside of a lasting commitment, he or she is not loving the other person. He or she needs the other person to get something for himself or herself. And thus they're not really free. It's popular these days to say, "I love her" [or "I love him"], but why do I need to marry her to prove it?" But if a man *really* loves a woman like he says he does, why *wouldn't* he marry her? Could it be that he *needs* her more than he *loves* her, that it's not so much that he doesn't *have* to, but it's more that he doesn't *want* to, because he's not free enough to do what might be helpful for someone else? "All things are lawful for me, but not all things are helpful."

Wendy Shalit is a feminist writer who has written a number of provocative books calling women to recover their sexual modesty as a protest against a world that has objectified them. Perhaps her most controversial work was a book entitled *Return to Modesty*. This book caused an uproar among those who labeled it as sexually regressive and oppressive to women. But surprisingly it caused a parallel stir among many women who had become disenchanted with the sexual revolution and the whole new set of oppressions that came along with it. In that book Shalit basically argues that the sexual revolution has told women that modesty is oppressive because it impinges on a woman's right to be sexually free. "Why should boys get to have all the fun?" But, as Shalit argues, it is precisely this revolution that has actually made women *less* free. And it has done this in two ways. First, "there's a certain misogyny [Shalit writes] behind the sexual revolution. Yes, dear . . . you can sleep around as much as you want, and you can pretend to be a man, but you're not allowed to be *this*."[10] "You'd better be having many hook-ups—or else! Shyness will not be tolerated! Go on Prozac! Lose your curves! Stop being a woman."[11] "A woman [these] days cannot 'opt' to be [what she wants to be], she is *put* on Prozac, she has her new persona assigned to her and then [is] celebrated as the hallmark of true liberation. Ours is supposed to be a time of great freedom. Yet [we] have just ended up letting others dictate our choices."[12]

Upon first reading, this might sound more like oppression than freedom. But a modest woman, as Shalit goes on, "may be conveying to the world by her bashfulness, I have my own compass, thank you. I have my own sense of what is good and what is right, and it's not always what everyone else says."[13] She's free. But second, the sexual revolution has not only dictated to women who they have to be, but it's actually restrained them even further by putting them at the mercy of men. Ever wonder what happened to chivalry, why men don't treat women the way they used to? Well, quite frankly it's because they don't have to. It's because they're in the driver's seat. And the sexual revolution has put them there. Back when modesty was more sexy, it was sort of a woman's blue chip of power. It commanded respect and dignity, it empowered and protected her from the sleaze of the earth. But "being [promiscuous] far from making women [free], put them at the mercy of men. Today we're taught that this 'every woman is a lady' idea was sexist, that it made [them] into property, but it seems as if abandoning it has made [them] all the more [so]. Maybe [modesty] wasn't subordinating or oppressive to women after all. Maybe it was liberating [because] it made [them] powerful."[14] It was a woman's natural bodyguard, her support in her decision to say no.[15] As Rousseau predicted, if we seek to raise our daughters like men, "the men will gladly consent! The more women want to resemble them, the less women will govern them, and then men will truly be their masters."[16] What the sexual revolution actually achieved was not a great deal of liberation for women, but "a great deal of legitimacy for male [power]."[17] She's absolutely right. "All things are lawful for me, but not all things are helpful. All things are lawful for me, but I will not be dominated by anything."

So the first reason why everyone needs to take their bodies and what they do with them seriously is because they're free. But there's a second reason.

Because We Matter

In verse 13, Paul writes, "'Food is meant for the stomach and the stomach for food' — God will destroy both one and the other."[18] Here Paul was quoting another prevailing sentiment of his day, which was shaped by the philosophy of Plato who said it didn't really matter what you did with your body, because your soul was the only thing that really mattered.[19] Now this very sentiment has not only survived throughout the centuries, but it has been subtly codified into the very air we breathe. Sex, many argue, is just something someone does with his or her body, but his heart, her soul — that's with God, and that's all that really matters. But this is precisely what the resurrection of Jesus showed is *not* true. Paul says in verse 14 that "God raised the Lord and will also raise us up by his power." One's body and what he or she does with it matters eternally because it won't be destroyed—God will raise it, just as he raised Jesus![20] In fact, one's body is so important that God would even go so far as to make it his home and on top of that call it his own. Verse 19 says our body is a temple of the Holy Spirit, and in verse 15 that it's a member of Christ! What Paul is saying is absolutely revolutionary! Absolutely radical! Our bodies are the place where God has chosen to live and the very thing he has chosen to make a part of himself! He's bound himself so tightly to us, even our bodies, because he wants to be with us—for us to be his and for him to be ours—forever! No other religion would ever dare say anything even remotely close to that. Gods live in temples, not in human bodies. Gods keep their distance; they don't wrap themselves up with people, especially not their bodies. But this One does! Our bodies have tremendous value, and they cannot be treated casually because they matter eternally!

But that's true not just of one's body, but of the whole person. In reading this, one might think that the picture that's been painted so far is a rather dramatic one. Sex doesn't have to be about all of that. It can be casual, without all of the baggage coming along with it, some say. Can it really? Paul says in verse 16 that in sex "the two . . . become one flesh." What Paul is getting at here is the fact that there's an inevitable uniting effect that happens when you have sex. Lewis Smedes, a Christian ethicist and theologian, put it really well when he wrote, "There is more to sex than meets the eye—or excites the genitals. There is no such thing as casual sex, no matter how casual people are about it."[21] "No one can take sex out at night and put it away until he wants to play with it again, nobody can go to bed with someone and leave his soul parked outside."[22]

> Afterward, the two people seldom feel the same way toward each other again. They may love each other as never before; they may resent each other; they may only feel comfortable with each other. But after intercourse, the relationship is not what it was before. [And that's because] what we do with sex shapes what we are; what we do with our bodies, we do with ourselves. Sexual intercourse is a personal life-uniting act [and so] the demand for continence is not a killjoy rule plastered on the abundant life by antisexual saints. It is respect for reality as we know it.[23]

Something happens in sex. As much as one would like to, he or she can't ever go to bed with someone and leave his or her souls parked outside, as Smedes said. This was Paul's point in verse 18b when he said, "Every other sin a person commits is outside the body, but the sexually immoral person sins against his own body." He's not saying there's nothing else that involves your physical body, because it's obvious that a slew of other things do. He's saying there's nothing else that involves *us*—all of us, including our bodies, everything we are—quite like sex does.[24] With sex, we're all in; with sex, we give ourselves—all of ourselves—away. And that's the second reason why one's body and what one does with it matters—because our body matters, or maybe more importantly, because *we* do.

It matters because we're free. It matters because we matter. But there is one last reason.

Because We Were Bought by Someone Who Gave All to Have Us

In verse 13 when Paul writes, "Food is meant for the stomach," he is quoting a prevailing thought of the day, which went something like this: just as food is intended for the stomach, and in turn the stomach for food, so sex is intended for the body, and in turn the body for sex. Sex, in other words, is natural. It's what human bodies were made for; and because that's true, sexual desires shouldn't be frustrated but should be fulfilled.[25] The ancients were much more modern than people today give them credit for. Sex is indeed for the body—it's a good thing, and it's supposed to be enjoyed. But the other half of that statement must be called into question. Paul says in verse 13 that the body is meant not for sex, but "for the Lord, and the Lord for the body." But what does that mean? It sounds like something someone's mom would say to her child before he or she went off to college. What is your body and ultimately sex for? Yes, pleasure. Yes, to love and to serve the one to whom you've committed yourself forever. And yes, to conceive children. But ultimately, beyond and beneath all of that one's body and what one does with it is intended to be a reflection of one's commitment. Yes, to the one you love, but maybe even more deeply to the one who gave all to commit himself to you forever. Verse 17 tells us that God joined man to himself, making man one with him. God is not a tyrant who makes arbitrary rules to kill man's joy. He's a Lover who wants to be one with the love of his life—to have us—all of us, not just our soul.

There's a great story in the Old Testament about God telling one of his prophets to marry a girl whom he knew would absolutely break his heart. She was a girl with a spotty past and a fickle heart, who would time and again spurn his love and seek solace in the arms of other lovers. The story, as you may know, sort of comes to a head when the woman finds herself on a bidding block, destitute and dejected and with no other options to dig herself out of the debt she has incurred. So she stands there on that block, naked under the scrutinizing gaze of her bidders, awaiting the verdict that would decide her fate forever. But as the auction begins, something strange happens. She hears faintly, yet unmistakably, a voice in her ears. "Five shekels." It's one she knows all too well. "Ten shekels." But why would he do this? "Fifteen shekels." "Sold." She's been bought by the man she had spurned, the man whose heart she had broken time and again. As she's trying to make sense of what had just happened, it suddenly dawns on her, and her heart sinks because she knows there's only one reason why he'd do this. He'd have his revenge. So she lifts her head, bracing herself to get what's coming to her, but what comes next is perhaps the biggest surprise of all because she's greeted not by indignation, but by a kind smile and a warm embrace that seems to say, "I love you more than you'll ever know. Let's go home."[26]

Romantic dramas, eat your heart out. But as incredible as this story is, it's but a faint echo of the Great Drama that has animated our entire world—and each of our lives. The one in which that Great Lover who, despite our spotty pasts and fickle hearts, whose love we spurned and whose heart we broke, didn't just bid to get the love of His life back, but gave all—body and soul—to have us as his own once more. And when we lift our heads and look at the cross, we know for sure that he's not out for revenge, because we're greeted not by indignation but by a kind smile and a warm embrace that says, "I love you more than you'll ever know. Let's go home." "You were bought with a price," verse 20 says, and "you are not your own" (v. 19). But why would you want to be when the One who has bought you loves you like that? This might be the most compelling reason to take our bodies and what we do with them seriously. Not just because we're free, or even because we matter, but also because we were bought by someone who gave all to have us.

In conclusion, people are free, and they matter. They were bought with a price. So glorify God in your body by taking it and what you do with it seriously.

12

The Beauty of Marriage

1 CORINTHIANS 7:1–16

THE COMEDIAN CHRIS ROCK OFTEN SAYS, "Do you want to be single and lonely, or married and bored?"[1] Unfortunately, we tend to think those are the only two options. Dana Shapiro, commenting on the film *Monogamy*, says that a monogamous marriage relationship is intractably difficult.[2] The reason he said that was because he believes that a really intimate, committed relationship in which there is deep devotion is essentially going to smother or stifle one's autonomy and independence. So whether it's from a public thinker like Shapiro or a comedian such as Chris Rock, modern culture has all sorts of negative impressions about what marriage is. And sadly, some Christians' principles have been borrowed from what is found in the culture rather than what is found in the Bible.

The Corinthian culture was essentially hedonistic.[3] Paul has already addressed the topic of sexual immorality in the context of the local church.[4] Some members of the community were visiting prostitutes because prostitution was socially acceptable and was more of a norm than an exception.[5] The Corinthian culture believed that marriage was not the place where one could experience sexual fulfillment. Some Christians in Corinth reacted to this by being overly ascetic. It was right to react to the hedonism of the culture, especially in light of the fact that it was creeping into the church, but they overreacted. According to verse 1, some were saying, "It is good for a man not to have sexual relations with a woman."

There are similar issues in our day. The broader culture is extremely libertarian and hedonistic in its approach to human sexuality. Religious people have often been criticized of being extremely prudish and ascetic in their approach to human sexuality. Against these two extremes Paul gives us an incredibly balanced and humanizing view of sexuality. Hedonism essentially says, "Have sex with anyone you want. The body is a morally neutral zone. As long as the adults are consenting, there are no moral implications." This view ultimately dehumanizes the participants by removing the soul from the picture of sexuality, thereby animalizing human beings. Asceticism, on the other hand, says, "Don't have sex with anyone! The body is a morally evil zone." Even within the context of marriage, sexuality is viewed as a weakness and potentially a sin. This view ultimately dehumanizes individuals by rejecting an essential part of their humanity—the body. Asceticism overspiritualizes human beings.

Biblical sexuality, on the other hand, promotes an individual having sex with an individual of the opposite gender within the context of marriage. It declares that the body is good. God has given us bodies to steward for his glory and our enjoyment. Sexuality is healthy when it is expressed in the context for which God designed it. It ultimately humanizes individuals by affirming both the body and the soul. Biblical sexuality is the only view of sexuality that can properly account for the body *and* the soul.

Culturally speaking, marriage is at an all-time low. For all the cultural debate about marriage, the numbers show that marriage has seen better days. "In 2011, the Pew Research Center found that *51 percent of Americans* were married, compared to 72 percent in 1960. *Rates of cohabiting couples* are rising. . . . less than half a million couples were cohabiting in 1960, compared to 7.5 million in 2010."[6] Divorce rates continue to astound everyone. The 2009 US Census shows that "1 out of 2 first marriages [is] estimated to end in divorce." This has led many to give up on marriage altogether. Cohabitation is at an all-time high. More than half of all first marriages begin with unmarried cohabitation. Some have grown up in contexts where there was no marriage to speak of, just single mothers or single fathers. The wreckage of a broken marriage, parents having split up when the children were very young, is way too common. Even the most "functional" family is dysfunctional. Even if the parents are still together, one can often observe the uglies of marriage. Others know the uglies from firsthand experience. Some have personally experienced the pain of divorce. Others are married, but have had a very difficult experience in their marriages up to this point. There is no shortage of the brokenness of marriage on display in the world and in our own personal lives. For this reason we need an outside perspective to recover the beauties of marriage. Here the Apostle Paul shows the church:

- The Beauties of Marriage
- The Uglies of Marriage
- The Archetype of Marriage

The Beauties of Marriage: What Marriage Was Intended to Be

Oneness

Our text does not explicitly teach the idea of oneness, but it implicitly assumes it. Paul's vision of marriage is dependent upon the teaching of Jesus, which has its foundation in the Genesis account of creation. Mark 10:6–9 says, "But from the beginning of creation, 'God made them male and female.' 'Therefore a man shall leave his father and mother and hold fast to his wife, and *the two shall become one flesh.' So they are no longer two but one flesh.* What therefore God has joined together, let not man separate." Marriage is a one-flesh union and is intended to be a literal melding of identities, i.e., an abandonment of autonomy. All other aspects of our identity take a backseat to the oneness that we now share with our spouse. This is the normative relationship that forms all other relationships. Relationships to one's family, friends, the opposite sex, and even oneself change. The Bible views human sexuality within the context of marriage as the primary illustration and picture of this oneness. We see this in Paul's description of the sexual relationship of a husband and wife in verse 4: "For the wife does not have authority over her own body, but the husband does. Likewise the husband does not have authority over his own body, but the wife does." In a healthy marriage there is a beautiful giving up of one's autonomy to the other. Ultimately the oneness of a couple is intended to be drawn from and point to their mutual *relationship to the Lord*. In other places in Corinthians,[7] Paul qualifies Christian marriage as something that is only to be done "in the Lord" (7:39—"A wife is bound to her husband as long as he lives. But if her husband dies, she is free to be married to whom she wishes, only in the Lord."). How is this oneness maintained and fostered?

Service

The general witness of Scripture is that a beautiful marriage is maintained when a husband and wife put each other's needs before his or her own and this is expressed through selfless service. Paul says clearly in Philippians 2 that we should be concerned about the other person's interests before our own. In 1 Corinthians 7 the discussion of self-giving service is in the context of talking about sex. Husband and wife are to complement one another, to serve the other in his or her weaknesses. Here the discussion of self-giving service revolves around sex. Verses 2–4 say: "But because of the temptation to sexual immorality, each man should have his own wife and each woman her own husband. The husband should give to his wife her conjugal rights, and likewise the wife to her husband. For the wife does not have authority over her own body, but the husband does. Likewise the husband does not have authority over his own body, but the wife does." Notice the beautiful balance on display in this other-serving relationship.

In a patriarchal society where male sexual dominance was part and parcel of maintaining one's status and position, where the needs and desires of women were rarely considered,[8] Paul's teaching was radically progressive. Paul is claiming that women and men have equal rights in the marriage bed. Paul envisions sex as a means of serving one's spouse. Ascetics who claim that the Bible's perspective on sex is limited to its pro-creational function aren't reading this text. Paul acknowledges that human beings have sexual passions, and he envisions a healthy marriage relationship in which these passions are exercised regularly. To the ascetic who views frequent marital sexual activity as being less than holy, Paul's counterargument is that married couples should have regular sex in order to remain holy. It is only on the rarest of occasions that a couple should temporarily forgo sexual relations. Verse 5 states: "Do not deprive one another, except perhaps by agreement for a limited time, that you may devote yourselves to prayer; but then come together again, so that Satan may not tempt you because of your lack of self-control." The reason married individuals have sex is in order to please God, which points to the ultimate goal of selfless service. Ultimately, selfless service in a marriage relationship is intended to spur both partners on in their devotion to the Lord. The greater end of sexual pleasure in a marital relationship is to live a life that is pleasing to God. This is the aim of marriage even beyond a couple's sex life. God calls us to be kind and gracious sanctifying agents in the lives of our spouses. Now we know there's a difference between lust and love. C. S. Lewis puts it this way in his excellent book *The Four Loves*.[9] Lust is going after the body. Love is going after the person. If an individual is passionate about someone just for her body, that means he doesn't love that person—he just wants the body. The Bible shows that sex is a beautiful gift given to humanity by God to be enjoyed as a blessing within the context of a faithful, monogamous marriage relationship between a husband and a wife.

Commitment

Verses 10–16 contain Paul's instructions on how Christians ought to approach the extreme difficulties of marriage. Is divorce ever permissible? How should someone who comes to know Christ respond when his or her spouse is decidedly not a Christian?[10] Though these verses are dealing with negative and difficult cases, the underlying teaching is in regard to the beautiful commitment that lies at the heart of marriage. The Bible's seemingly strict views on divorce are derived from its even higher view of marriage. The marriage commitment is an *objective* reality that should not be altered. Paul makes it clear in verses 10, 11—"To the married I give this charge (not I, but the Lord): the wife should not separate from her husband (but if she does, she should remain unmarried or else be reconciled to her husband), and the husband should not divorce his wife"—that marriage is not to be interrupted by separation or terminated by divorce. The marriage commitment *subjectively* works itself out in steadfast love that is not determined or altered by emotions or changes in oneself or one's spouse. Now some singles might quickly make a false connection at this point. Some might say, "There must be some principle that is going to allow me as a Christian single woman to marry this non-Christian man who's willing to come to church." The Bible is clear. If a Christian is to marry, he needs to marry "in the Lord" (7:39—"A wife is bound to her husband as long as he lives. But if her husband dies, she is free to be married to whom she wishes, only *in the Lord*"). But in a culture where marriage can be incredibly difficult and where divorce, which appears to be an easy way out, is rampant, we have to willingly confront the uglies of marriage.

The Uglies of Marriage

For some this section of Paul's letter is difficult to read because, despite the deep longings, many are not married. Another chapter[11] will deal much more directly with the issue, and hopefully it will answer some of the questions more directly. But this particular passage does address those who are single, and Paul highlights a few things. Singleness is an *ideal* (v. 6: "Now as a concession, not a command, I say this"). Alongside marriage, Paul views singleness as a *gift* (v. 7: "I wish that all were as I myself am. But each has his own gift from God, one of one kind and one of another"). For some, perhaps even many, singleness is a calling. Those who are currently single are currently called to be single. In this particular season the call is to seek to live a Biblically single life in anticipation of God's provision. At the same time Paul knows that singleness can affect anyone negatively at the deepest level—often there are passions that burn deep inside of us (v. 9), whether relational, emotional, or sexual, and when they are unmet it can be tormenting. This is part of the ugliness of marriage. Sin has so twisted marriage that for many unmarried people it seems impossible to live without being married. On the other hand, sin has so twisted marriage that it seems impossible to live within marriage for many married people.

We now turn to some specific uglies of marriage.

Divided

Practically speaking, many couples are living separated lives. It is possible to be objectively one (e.g., there is a marriage license), but to live subjectively as two (e.g., separate beds or separate bank accounts). There isn't a shared vision for life. There are two people in the marriage, but they have never really understood what it means to be one. Division often gets expressed via sexuality. That is, there is division via ascetic withholding. Paul is speaking to Christians who were withholding their bodies from their spouses because of a twisted sense of spirituality. Something like this happens regularly in modern marriages—intentional withholding, keeping oneself from one's spouse to get what one wants or to get the upper hand. There can also be unintentional withholding—allowing one's passion for one's spouse to disintegrate—"we're more like good friends." It's like a commercial business transaction. There is a withholding of the benefits, namely the gift of sex, which is getting leveraged in order to manipulate the relationship. Division can also manifest itself via hedonistic exploration. Elsewhere in the Corinthian letter we have encountered individuals who were letting their sexuality get them into all kinds of morally reprehensible situations—committing incestual adultery with one's stepmother[12] or visiting prostitutes.[13] Modern marriages are victim to such hedonistic exploration too. There is adultery and pornography (the temple prostitution of our day), along with other anonymous, quick, easy, culturally acceptable ways to get sexual satisfaction from someone besides your spouse. The source of the division in our marriages is self-service.

Self-Serving

Our approach to marriage is self-serving rather than selfless other-serving.[14] Tara Parker-Pope wrote a *New York Times* article entitled "The Happy Marriage is the 'Me' Marriage."[15] "The notion that the best marriages are those that bring satisfaction to the individual may seem counterintuitive. After all, isn't marriage supposed to be about putting the relationship first? Not anymore. For centuries marriage was viewed as an economic and social institution, and the emotional and intellectual needs were secondary to the survival of the marriage itself. But in modern relationships people are looking for a partnership. They want partners who make their lives more interesting, who help each of them attain their respective value goals. So marriage is supposed to be about "us," but in our modern culture it has become about "me." It's all about me.

In the 2002 National Marriage Project, Barbara Defoe Whitehead wrote an article entitled "Why Men Won't Commit." This was her conclusion: ". . . many men said that they wouldn't marry until they found a perfect soul mate who was perfectly compatible with them."[16] If people think, "I need a perfect, compatible soul mate . . ." this can be a problem. This is different from people who think, "I want to have a friend I can have deep friendship with." Timothy Keller summarizes it this way: There are two key factors for having this so-called new idealism. The first is *physical attractiveness and sexual chemistry*. In other words, the other person has to be extremely physically attractive. Secondly, *compatibility*. Compatibility means "they wanted someone who has the willingness to take you in as you are and not to change you." Oftentimes there is resentment when one person in a relationship wants to change the other. Men want a woman who fits into their lives, who will be truly compatible with them, and who will not want to change them. If that's what people want in a relationship, they will remain single for a long time. A deeply devoted loyal relationship requires a surrendering of one's independence.[17]

Many people might agree that the traditional approach to marriage — e.g., being committed, loyal, faithful, monogamous, and dutiful — is oppressive and that the progressive view toward marriage is liberating. The irony is that it is the complete reverse because the so-called new idealism (i.e., the notion that there is a perfect person out there who is going to be able to fulfill every need) is utterly enslaving. What reality shows us is that this is an unrealistic set of expectations that we have placed on the other person. Of course, this is not only true for men; it is a struggle for women as well. John Tierny wrote an article entitled "Picky, Picky, Picky." He draws attention to how people might be in denial of their desire to find that perfectly compatible soul mate, a person who does not exist. Keller says, "[Real marriage] requires two completely well-adjusted individuals, with very little in the way of emotional neediness of their own character flaws that need a whole lot of work."[18] That's the kind of person everyone desires, a perfectly compatible soul mate who is well adjusted and not emotionally needy but rather is full of emotional wealth and is attractive. But even if that person — who doesn't actually exist — was found and pursued until a new relationship was formed, it's still not going to be a match made in Heaven. Once that relationship is established, it's broken immediately because the individual pursuing this relationship brings with him all sorts of issues and problems.

Stanley Hauerwas, a university ethics professor says, "Destructive to marriage is the self-fulfillment ethic that assumes marriage and the family are primarily institutions of personal fulfillment necessary for us to become whole and happy. The assumption is that there is someone just right for us to marry, and that if we look closely enough, we will find the right person. This moral assumption overlooks a crucial aspect to marriage. It fails to appreciate the fact that we will always marry the wrong person."[19]

As Ernest Becker, a Pulitzer Prize author, says, this is apocalyptic romanticism. This is a desire for the divine ideal in the other person, but the other person doesn't have the goods. Any husband doesn't have the goods to be his wife's savior, let alone her husband. In the same way, any wife doesn't have the goods to be her husband's savior. The only reason anyone might have the goods to be a positive spouse is due to the archetypal picture of what marriage is all about.[20]

If marriages begin with a self-serving purpose, then when a spouse can't meet certain expectations, that self-serving posture gets even more amplified. This self-serving approach twists and distorts the sex life within a marriage. In verses 3–5 Paul shows a beautiful balance of a mutually self-giving and other-centered expression of service.

> The husband should give to his wife her conjugal rights, and likewise the wife to her husband. For the wife does not have authority over her own body, but the husband does. Likewise the husband does not have authority over his own body, but the wife does. Do not deprive one another, except perhaps by agreement for a limited time, that you may devote yourselves to prayer; but then come together again, so that Satan may not tempt you because of your lack of self-control.

Sex, within the context of marriage, ceases to be what it was meant to be when it becomes about the other person meeting your needs. The current sexualized culture places too much pressure on highly sensitized sexual experiences, and the beauty of ordinary sex gets drowned out. The ascetic needs to realize that sex is ordinary and that it is not wrong, gross, or abnormal. The hedonist needs to realize that sex is ordinary—it is not ultimate, there is not some experience out there that will be fulfilling. Sex becomes extraordinary when we recognize the power of ordinary, other-centered, monogamous sex between a husband and a wife—everything else is a distortion and imitation.

When those who are one start acting like they are two, and when those who are called to serve one another are more interested in serving themselves, it leads to breakdown.

Breakdown

Though there's a call to commitment, the values of being autonomous and self-serving will ultimately lead to a breakdown at some level. There is a progression to this sort of breakdown. Even though marriage is objectively in view, it might function more like a divorce. Every marriage feels varying degrees of this dynamic. So how is it possible to cultivate the beauties and not mortify the beauties?

The Archetype of Marriage

The beauties of marriage begin to overcome the uglies of marriage when marriage ceases to be the most important relationship in one's life. However, things become difficult if marriage continues to be the center of one's life. There is nowhere to go because that person has become the object of apocalyptic romanticism, and everything starts falling apart. That is why resources from outside that relationship—outside of that center—are necessary and will be able to fuel a potential for a marriage to soar. So if there's a loss of money and that is already the center, that's an example of apocalyptic materialism. And if sex is the center, then that becomes apocalyptic. But the main emphasis here is one of apocalyptic romanticism. What Paul is trying to say is, "Your marriage is meant to be a type of the archetypal marriage." The archetypal marriage is Jesus' relationship with his bride. Jesus is the bridegroom. He's the husband, and he has a relationship with his bride, the church.

Though marriage is a blessing, a gift, a calling, and a place where Christians can find deep satisfaction, it is not the source of ultimate satisfaction. Expecting marriage to satisfy one's longing or to bring happiness will smother the other person, which oftentimes causes resentment. On the other hand, this view can also stir resentment toward others for their inability to satisfy one's desires. All of this is a result of asking marriage to do something that it was never intended to do. Marriage is not meant to be turned in on itself—it is not ultimately about the two individuals. Marriage is meant to be a type of the archetypal marriage. Human marriage is penultimate, because there is an ultimate marriage that will outlast it. The New Testament tells us that this archetypal marriage is the marriage between Christ and his church:

> Husbands, love your wives, as Christ loved the church and gave himself
> up for her, that he might sanctify her, having cleansed her by the washing
> of water with the word, so that he might present the church to himself in
> splendor, without spot or wrinkle or any such thing, that she might be holy
> and without blemish. In the same way husbands should love their wives
> as their own bodies. He who loves his wife loves himself. For no one ever
> hated his own flesh, but nourishes and cherishes it, just as Christ does the
> church, because we are members of his body. "Therefore a man shall leave
> his father and mother and hold fast to his wife, and the two shall become
> one flesh." *This mystery is profound, and I am saying that it refers to Christ
> and the church.* (Ephesians 5:25–32)

Human marriage finds it purpose in referring to Christ and the church. Christian marriages are fulfilling their purpose when they display the "profound . . . mystery" of Christ's love for his bride. How do the beauties of marriage begin to break through and overshadow the uglies? There needs to be a constant rediscovery of gospel memory—that is, rehearsing the gospel and practicing the gospel in the heart. If the institution of marriage is about a greater marriage, then it is vital to get the instructions for how marriage works from the reality that Christians are being called to image and reflect. It's the profound mystery of Jesus Christ, the only perfect person. Nobody out there is the right person for anyone. Only Jesus is the right husband. And he lays down his life for us through his sacrificial life and death. When he sacrifices all that he has, when he gives up his rights and does not exploit or take advantage of them, he empties himself in order to meet the needs of an adulterous, sinful bride.

Look at the marriage of Christ and the church.

The Unbreakable Commitment of Christ Overcomes the Breakdown

Though humanity had broken its commitment and created the breakdown, Christ committed himself to the church as his bride. This commitment came when believers were at their ugliest. As in the story of Hosea and Gomer, the love of God pursues an adulteress wife to the very end. There were no requirements attached to his commitment. There was no behavioral regimen that had to be maintained in order for him to commit himself to the church. This is utterly shocking. God has covenantally committed himself to an adulterous wife—and the church is the adulterous wife![21] God's covenantal commitment to his people is steadfast, unflagging, unshakable. It is only when the church sees herself for what she is (adulterous) that she will come to know the freedom of the grace of God. The radical grace of God to us is the source we need to be radically gracious to our spouse. When a person in the marriage is content to see it break down and disintegrate, the other one can remain steadfastly committed because of God's steadfast commitment to the church. This is also what lies behind Paul's command that a believer who comes to faith after having been married ought to stay in the marriage (vv. 12, 13). Marriage is not about the benefits one can receive from his or her spouse, but rather the commitment that can be made to that spouse. It is possible to remain faithful to one's commitment because of the resources made available in the ultimate commitment that Christ has made to the church.

The Selfless Service of Christ Overcomes Our Self-Serving

How does Christ display his covenantal commitment to the church? He seals it through utterly giving himself away. He is not self-serving but selfless. He places the needs of his spouse above his own. He is completely other-focused. He keeps no record of wrongs. In fact, he sacrifices his own life to erase the record of wrongs. He doesn't even hang on to his record of rights, but gives them over to the church so that she is spotless, clothed in robes of his righteousness. Being the beneficiary of Christ's death-defeating, selfless service helps us to no longer keep track of wrongs. Christians can now stop standing in judgment over their spouses because Christ absorbed the judgment they deserved. And they can selflessly serve their spouses because Jesus, the ultimate husband, selflessly served his bride, the church.

The Union-Establishing Work of Christ Heals the Relational Divide

Christ has mended and resewn the torn fabric of the believer's relationship with God. The Old Testament actually describes the rift between God and Israel as a divorce. The sins of Israel were piled so high that God finally sent his adulteress wife away with "a decree of divorce" (Jeremiah 3:8). Israel was exiled in Assyria because of her adultery, but Jesus was exiled on the cross because of *our* adultery. Jesus experienced ultimate division from the Father in order to secure our ultimate oneness with him. Because of our union with Christ, the one who experienced the divorce of the cross, we never have to fear being divided from the love of God. Christ's marital vows to his bride are eternally unbreakable because they are sealed with his blood. In the church's marriage to Christ, it is not "until death do us part"; it is "my death ensures that we will never be apart." This is the foundation for oneness in a marriage that is divided. The indissoluble union that the church has with Christ is the foundation for the union between a husband and wife.

The marital devotion of Christ ought to stir hearts. Marriage is beautiful, and it is meant to image the profound mystery of Christ and the church. But even the most beautiful marriage relationship ever witnessed is a mere shadow of the reality that is objectively found in Christ. His commitment, his selfless service, and his union-securing death turns uglies into beauties. That is the profound mystery of the gospel.

Where do we get the resources to tolerate fickleness, irritability, and an unforgiving heart? It comes from gospel memory and from being reminded of the profound mystery of what it took for that perfectly right husband/person who came and chose a perfectly wrong person. And once this profound mystery is understood, anyone can look across and see that perfect wrong person who is her husband, that perfectly wrong person who is his wife, and be able to resolve in his or her heart, "This marriage is not about one individual. It's not about me. It's about us." It's about meeting her needs. It's about meeting his needs. Not about our own individual needs. But does this mean that personal freedom is being forfeited? No! Here's the beauty: when an individual is pursuing his spouse's happiness and holiness, the spouse is going to get her happiness, and that husband's happiness will increase. Also the holiness of God will be evident because that individual is trying to sanctify his spouse through his character and the memory of the profound mystery of what Christ has done. But when individuals pursue their own happiness, they will get neither their own happiness nor their spouse's happiness, and certainly not the holiness of God. And perhaps those people will wonder over and over again why they always get stuck in marriage, why there are more uglies than beauties, why can't seem to soar. It's because they are stuck in self-service.

Consider the profound mystery of what Christ has done for his people. With this immense resource, it's possible to pursue nothing but the needs of our spouses. And because of the emotional well of the profound mystery of Christ, there's no need to complain. The only way someone can look at the wrong person in his or her marriage and for that person to become the right person in his or her marriage is to be able to know that the perfectly right person has come for the wrong person—for all of us.

13

On Calling

1 CORINTHIANS 7:17–24

IF ANYTHING IS CLEAR from the preceding passages, it is that Christianity has far-reaching implications for all of life. Allegiance to Christ is a whole life allegiance. It has implications for life goals and our conception of community, authority, marriage, sexuality, etc. Many Corinthian believers were naturally asking, "What does Christ have to do with my vocation?" "How does the gospel shape my sense and practice of calling?" The question of calling is incredibly important for modern people. Christian or not, most people will likely spend the majority of their waking hours working. Between the years of twenty-five to sixty-five years of age, an average person will spend about 96,000 hours at work. Therefore, it is essential to step back and ask: What am I doing? Why am I doing it? How am I doing it? Who am I doing it for? What is my motivation for work? What are the guiding principles for work? Is my work largely self-serving or other-serving?

Christians typically have not been very helpful in sorting through these questions. Two erroneous, unhelpful views are: 1) an overspiritualized view of one's calling or 2) an underspiritualized view, often represented by a cultural Christianity that encourages individuals to seek their perfect niche calling (as though God has an almost indecipherable calling on our lives that, should we find it, will lead to an ultimate, abiding sense of purpose and fulfillment). Much like there is no "Mr. Perfect" in marriage, there is no perfect vocation or calling. Work is not meant to provide ultimate fulfillment. More experiential, mystical movements within Christianity have a tendency to overplay pietistic spiritual devotion, and therefore work is viewed as something that *has to be* done in order to support the "more important" work of the church.

In contrast to this view, the Bible teaches that all work is inherently valuable. God intends for his people to take joy in their work, to leverage their influence for the common good, and to mirror him as they care for and cultivate creation and culture. Per usual, Paul demonstrates a remarkable balance in his perspective on vocation and calling. On the one hand, his view is not overly spiritual: he highlights the call to live ordinary, faithful lives in whatever vocational field we find ourselves. On the other hand, his view is not underspiritual: he suggests that ordinary callings are invested with immense value because of the end to which they point. In 7:17–24 the following three plot movements provide helpful guidelines for understanding Paul:

- The Reason for Living as We Were Called
- The Difficulty of Living as We Were Called
- The Power for Living as We Were Called

The Reason for Living as We Were Called

"The average worker today stays at each of his or her jobs for *4.4 years*, according to the most recent available data from the Bureau of Labor Statistics, but the expected tenure of the workforce's youngest employees is about half that. Ninety-one percent of Millennials (born between 1977–1997) expect to stay in a job for less than three years. . . . That means they would have 15–20 jobs over the course of their working lives!"[1] Why are people hopping from one career to another at this rapid pace? The answer lies in the confusion between one's fundamental identity and vocational calling. Millennials have been told "you can be whatever you want to be." The implicit assumption behind this statement is that happiness can be achieved and fulfilled when "you can be whatever you want to be." Boomers learned to find their security, comfort, and identity in work that often left them unfulfilled. They passed on to Millennials the idea that work provides security, comfort, and identity, but they added the idea that work should provide ultimate fulfillment and satisfaction as well. The result is a generation of individuals who are seeking their identity and fulfillment in their work, but who lack the kind of steadfast commitment that might actually afford them some level of proper satisfaction in their work.

Nathan Hatch, the president of Wake Forest University, noted that there are a disproportionate number of students who are majoring in finance, law, and medicine.[2] Hatch notes that this reality is reflective of a belief that vocational fields in finance, law, and medicine will guarantee a high salary, reputation, prestige, and success. So instead of asking, "Which jobs will help other people flourish?" many are now asking, "Which jobs will will help me flourish?" This is reflective of our views on marriage as well. Marriages are no longer about "us" but "me." We are constantly asking our partner, "What can you do for me in this relationship?" No wonder there is so much dysfunction in marriages today. This self-centered orientation can be found in our approaches to both relationships and vocations.

This is not an entirely modern phenomenon. The Corinthians and the other churches dealt with the same problem. This is why Paul has to instruct them. Verse 17 states: "Only let each person lead the life that the Lord has assigned to him, and to which God has called[3] him. This is my rule in all the churches." The Corinthians had their identity and their vocation mixed up. They began to think, "Now that my identity has changed as a result of Christ, my vocational calling must change too." This is essentially works-righteousness being played out on a horizontal level. They were not necessarily seeking to change their behaviors to please God, but were looking to make shifts in their identities to please man.

Paul speaks into both their fundamental identity and their vocation using the lens of calling. According to Paul, every Christian has *two callings*. The first calling is a fundamental identity calling (a vertical calling): every time the word *calling* or a form of it shows up in this passage (with one exception, in verse 17), it is in reference to the Christian's fundamental identity calling. God's saving grace is spoken of as a "call" in verses 18, 20, 21, 22, 24. This is the unshifting, foundational core calling for the Christian. This identity is the wellspring out of which everything else flows. This is where believers are intended to derive their identity, fulfillment, security, comfort, and hope. This call is primarily vertical because it has everything to do with how one relates to God.[4] Then there is the supplemental vocational calling (a horizontal calling). This calling is mentioned in verse 17: "Only let each person lead the life that the Lord has assigned to him, and *to which God has called him*." This is a secondary call. Though there are elements of enjoyment, excellence, and contribution to the common good, this secondary call is not designed to function as a source of identity, fulfillment, or security. This call is primarily horizontal. While God cares deeply about it, it has everything to do with how one relates to the world at large.[5] One historian writes concerning Martin Luther's view of these two callings: "Luther understood that the Christian is genuinely bi-vocational. He is called first through the Gospel to faith in Jesus Christ and he is called to occupy a particular station or place in life. The second sense of this calling embraces all that the Christian does in service to the neighbor not only in a particular occupation but also as a member of the church, a citizen, a spouse, parent, or child, and worker. Here the Christian lives in love toward other human beings and is the instrument by which God does His work in the world."[6]

Note that the two callings are not unrelated. They are vitally connected, but only one is instrumental. An individual's fundamental identity calling (salvation by grace) shapes one's supplemental vocational calling (work in the world). It is never the other way around. What is the reason for living as we were called? A vertically derived identity gives horizontal *freedom*. Verses 18, 19 say: "Was anyone at the time of his call already circumcised? Let him not seek to remove the marks of circumcision. Was anyone at the time of his call uncircumcised? Let him not seek circumcision. For neither circumcision counts for anything nor uncircumcision, but keeping the commandments of God." A secure identity makes vocational decision-making far simpler. No one needs to fret about work because there is no need for it to provide more than it can produce! This gives hope to those who do not love their jobs, because our jobs are not designed to define who we are in our fundamental identity. But this also gives a proper foundation to those who do love their jobs, because our fundamental identity won't fall apart if we were to lose our jobs.

Ernest Becker, as mentioned earlier, has written about making the other person or the relationship itself to be the ultimate thing in life. In other words, one's happiness or satisfaction in life is fully dependent on the condition of the partner's love or the health of the relationship as a whole. If these were to crumble down, one's hope in life would evaporate immediately and entirely. This is why Becker called this phenomenon (i.e., making romance an ultimate thing), apocalyptic romanticism. The same concept can certainly be applied to the understanding of work and vocation. If we make our supplemental vocational call ultimate, we will find ourselves stuck in apocalyptic careerism or vocationalism. Our supplemental vocational call is indeed important, but we do not want this be the source of our fundamental identity and ultimate hope.[7]

In some senses, vocational calling is as simple as just doing something! The problem is that this perspective on the two callings can often lead to serious problems for modern people.

The Difficulty of Living as We Were Called

The primary difficulty of settling into our vocational callings is that we live in a state of perpetual uncertainty about our identity calling. As a result, we seek our identity in vocation. The Corinthians were wrestling through the same issue as well. "Was anyone at the time of his call already circumcised? Let him not seek to remove the marks of circumcision. Was anyone at the time of his call uncircumcised? Let him not seek circumcision. For neither circumcision counts for anything nor uncircumcision, but keeping the commandments of God" (vv. 18, 19). The Corinthians were seeking social works-righteousness. They wanted to gain acceptance from their peers by changing the externals. One group was Judaizing, claiming that for their identity to be fully Christian an external change in appearance needed to take place. Another group was reverse-Judaizing, claiming that circumcision was so unimportant that if anyone happened to have been circumcised one ought to seek a reversal. Paul claims that both groups miss the point. One's identity is not secured by making an external change. A Christian needs to live out the identity that he or she has already been given. We do want to affirm that wisdom is needed regarding what is externally portrayed, but Paul is simply trying to communicate that it is not ultimately about the external marks.

Paul gives another illustration in verses 20, 21: "Each one should remain in the condition in which he was called. Were you a bondservant when called? Do not be concerned about it. (But if you can gain your freedom, avail yourself of the opportunity.).". Later in verse 23 Paul states, "You were bought with a price; do not become bondservants of men." Some of the translations might read "slave"[8] instead of "bond-servant."[9] "Slave" is a legitimate rendering of the Greek, but "bondservant" helps us recognize the categorical difference between slavery in the ancient world and slavery in the pre-modern and modern world. The Bible nowhere condones slavery and consistently sets up social conditions under which slavery will inevitably fail (1 Timothy 1:10). Nevertheless, there are difficult passages in the Bible dealing with the language of slavery that must be dealt with.

It is important to note the differences between the modern understanding of slavery and the slavery Paul is referring to in 1 Corinthians. The modern understanding of slavery is largely about hard labor; in the ancient world it covered all vocational levels. A slave could run a business, be a teacher, or even manage a household, etc. Slaves in Corinth would not have been laborers. Modern slavery was about forced labor; in the ancient world that labor was optional. Many would sell themselves into slavery for economic and social advantages. Modern slavery was race-based; in the ancient world, slavery was non-race-based. Anyone could become a slave. Modern slavery was permanent, whereas in the ancient world it was temporary. Slaves were able to purchase their own freedom. Ancient slavery was oftentimes (but not always) much more like indentured servitude than the oppressive, coercive, forced slavery we see today.[10] Even with all of these qualifications, Paul still sets conditions that will lead to the end of slavery when followed to their logical conclusions. In verse 21 slaves are encouraged to gain their freedom, and in verse 23 non-slaves should not sell themselves into slavery, no matter the perceived potential advantages. Elsewhere Paul uses the gospel to urge Philemon to free his slave. This clarification that comes from disinfecting the issue of bond-service is much needed for properly interpreting Paul's instruction to people dealing with less-than-ideal vocational circumstances. The security of the identity calling should make the situation of the vocational calling less than ultimate. Dignity and identity are not ultimately derived from or threatened by vocational circumstances.

But the point that Paul is trying to communicate even through this example of slavery is that the security of one's identity calling makes one's vocational calling less than ultimate. How, then, can people know if they are consuming their identity with their vocation? This works itself out in two primary ways: it can cause a person to be *unhealthily aspirational* or *ambitionless*. Being unhealthily aspirational makes an individual an opportunist. He is future-focused and consistently dissatisfied. He is never able to exist in the present, and therefore never able to exist in *this* place. He takes risks for all the wrong reasons—to attain power, to accumulate wealth, to achieve false security, to amass creature comforts. One of the worst expressions of this can be expressed through upward social mobility by using or abusing others. In an ancient culture this would have included owning slaves—something that Paul views as antithetical to the gospel. In a modern context this includes abusing power, pulling rank, preying on the needy, and ignoring the impact (or lack of positive impact) that your work has on the marginalized or less-privileged.

Another unhealthy expression is being ambitionless, being entrenched and having a sense of martyrdom, or simply accepting the status quo. This person focuses primarily on the past, and he is consistently hunkering down, settling, or remaining risk-averse. He refuses to take vocational chances that would put him in a position to steward his resources for the sake of others. This is different than not engaging in selfish ambition. The worst expression of this identity confusion is settling for what is comfortable and readily achievable. In an ancient culture this might have expressed itself by selling oneself into slavery for all of the perceived benefits. The Biblical perspective on vocation is one of faithful ambition—neither overly focused on the future, nor always sedentary. Christians should not be stuck in the past as traditionalists, always shying away. But we should have a faithful presence in the present by being aware of our present calling. And, ironically, because we are no longer investing our resources in striving for identity, we may even actually be more productive in our vocational calling. So how does one walk a tightrope between identity and vocation?

The Power for Living as We Were Called

> For he who was called in the Lord as a bondservant is a freedman of the Lord. Likewise he who was free when called is a bondservant of Christ. You were bought with a price; do not become bondservants of men. So, brothers, in whatever condition each was called, there let him remain with God. (vv. 22–24)

The gospel speaks a word of grace and challenge to everyone who hears it. The gospel tells those who are aspirational that they are bound—they are slaves of Christ because they have been bought with a price. Their new master is not simply a shareholder; he owns 100 percent of their identity, and their vocational calling is his to do with as he pleases. They are not as free as they think they are, and this ought to breed humility. On the other hand, to ambitionless, "bound" individuals, the gospel says that they are actually free. They are set free in Christ because they have been bought with a price. No other master has a claim on them; they belong fully to Christ. They are much more free than they think they are, and this breeds in them a greater boldness.

The Christian is free from enslavement to the social status quo in order to be a bondservant of Christ. Now we need to remain where we are and to be faithful. Christ diffuses the tension between identity and vocation.

In 2 Kings 5, Naaman the Syrian general, essentially the prime minister, second in command to the king of Syria, comes to Elisha to be healed from leprosy. Elisha tells Naaman to go dunk himself seven times in the River Jordan. Naaman does as he was told, and it seems as though he gets converted. At the very end Naaman comes to Elisha and tells him that he is willing to give a lot for compensation. Elisha politely refuses, telling him that he does not need anything. He could have gathered a pretty nice offering at that time. The text does explicitly state that Naaman commits himself to worshiping the Lord as a result of his miraculous healing (2 Kings 5:17). But it is worth noting here that even as a changed man, Naaman still dealt with his responsibilities as a commander of the army of the king of Syria (2 Kings 5:18). It wasn't as though he completely dropped his work because of his newfound allegiance and worldview. He was essentially committing himself to serving his nation, but he was no longer going to worship his nation. Likewise, even though we may be in a workplace where there is not much clarity and certain things do not seem too favorable, it does not necessarily mean that the only option for us is to then leave our work because of circumstantial difficulties. Naaman was able to go back to his workplace as a changed man with different allegiances and commitments even though the situation was not ideal. He was entering into the temple of Rimmon, but he was not worshiping Rimmon. He was serving his king by doing all of the duties that he was called to do. He was serving his nation, but he wasn't worshiping his nation.[11]

The gospel gives us a declaration of freedom. It is an act of liberation. This is where we can understand the idea of practicing the Sabbath. This is a very difficult practice for some contemporary people. But when we adopt the work-rest cycle properly, we are essentially saying that work doesn't define us, because we are resting. Those who cannot adopt this into their lives easily feel as though they are losing their sense of meaning; they feel out of touch with reality because they have defined their fundamental identity with their vocational call. For many, busyness and personal worth go hand in hand. Some people like to be busy because it gives them a sense of worth and significance. But in situations like these, we must remember that ultimately the work of securing our identity with God has already been finished. That is where our true rest lies. Our true rest lies in the already finished work of Jesus Christ.

Are we mistaking our vocation for our identity? Are we asking our work to provide that which only Christ can provide? Are we unhealthily aspirational? Have we embraced our work as being apocalyptic? Are we looking for that perfect future role in which our whole life will snap into place? Or are we functionally ambitionless? Are we stuck because we've pursued comfort and success above all else? Are we entrenched and unwilling to budge? Look ahead. Wherever we are, we need to be faithful (vv. 20, 24). Where we are right now, that is our call at this moment, and we need to remain and be faithful. Our present is loaded with significance because God is with us.[12]

14

Singleness

1 CORINTHIANS 7:25-40

THE ANCIENT CITY OF CORINTH was remarkably similar to the modern city of Boston (where I pastor). So for me and my church this letter is remarkably relevant today. And the same holds true of the topic in the passage we will now study, because for the first time in human history, the majority of Americans actually find themselves single.[1] People marry later than they used to, and live longer. Women no longer need men; in fact a lot of times they do better without us! Cities give us not only the space but also the savvy to fly solo. And all of this, of course, is undergirded by good old-fashioned American individualism, which tells us the best thing we can do is take care of ourselves. In this passage Paul basically argues that when it comes to singleness, we have an incredible amount of freedom. But he argues that there's also a certain kind of freedom that we need in order to handle it all well. We will consider all of this under three points:

- The Freedom You Have to Be Single
- A Freedom You'll Need to Handle It All Well
- The Freedom You Have When You Are Single

The Freedom You Have to Be Single

"Now concerning the betrothed,[2] I have no command from the Lord, but I give my judgment as one who by the Lord's mercy is trustworthy. I think that in view of the present distress it is good for a person to remain as he is. Are you bound to a wife? Do not seek to be free. Are you free from a wife? Do not seek a wife. But if you do marry, you have not sinned, and if a betrothed woman marries, she has not sinned" (v. 25–28a). Now go down to verses 36–38:

> If anyone thinks that he is not behaving properly toward his betrothed, if his passions are strong, and it has to be, let him do as he wishes: let them marry—it is no sin. But whoever is firmly established in his heart, being under no necessity but having his desire under control, and has determined this in his heart, to keep her as his betrothed, he will do well. So then he who marries his betrothed does well, and he who refrains from marriage will do even better.

There's a lot going on in these verses, and we'll do our best to tease out as much of it as we can throughout this study. But what I wanted to do to get us started is to look not so much at the details of Paul's argument, but rather to hover over it with a bird's-eye look. Basically his argument goes like this: when it comes to singleness—and to marriage for that matter—*you're free to choose what you want* because there's no "command from the Lord" (v. 25). Now this might not be earth-shattering for us today, but it absolutely would have been for Paul's original hearers. Remember, in the ancient world an ultimate premium was placed on marriage, especially for women. And that's because your family was not only your economic security, but your meaning in life too. A woman without a family during this time would have been a social outcast, her singleness the sign of her social failure. Some of us still feel this today, don't we? We feel a stigma has been placed on our singleness; we're frustrated because people always assume there's something wrong with us if we're alone, and sometimes we even begin to believe that ourselves. But Paul completely shatters this paradigm by presenting singleness not only as a *valid* option, but maybe even the better one! He says in verse 38, "So then he who marries his betrothed does well, and he who refrains from marriage will do even better."

But at the same time he renders marriage legitimate. "If you do marry, you have not sinned" (v. 28); "let them marry—it is no sin" (v. 36). I think we need to hear this too, because although traditional cultures elevate marriage at the expense of singleness, modern cultures are beginning to do just the opposite. Singleness is becoming not a sign of social failure but of social success—a mark of liberation from the traditional paradigms of living. But Paul refuses to go to either extreme. He recognizes that it's legitimate to be single, but that it's legitimate to be married too.[3] It might be better, practically speaking, as we'll see later on, to be single (v. 38), it might be best to stay as you are—whether married, single, or even widowed (v. 39), but through it all *you're free to choose*. "I say this for your own benefit, not to lay any restraint upon you" (v. 35a).

And I think we would do well to take Paul's lead and strike this balance ourselves. For those of us who are married, we need to stop treating singles like they have a disease. "When are you getting married? You're not getting any younger!" "You're still single? Maybe if you lost some weight or cleaned yourself up." But remember, "he who refrains from marriage will do even better." On the other hand, those of us who are single need to hear the very same thing, just from the other side. "If anything is a disease," we say, "it's marriage! Needy people pairing up with each other because they just can't make it on their own." Really? And it certainly doesn't help when people ask you insensitive, asinine questions about when you're going to get what they have. It's frustrating, I know. But remember, "he who marries . . . does well."

There's just one last thing I'd like to consider here before we move on. Back in 2008 Lori Gottlieb wrote an article for *The Atlantic* summarizing the insights from her book *Marry Him: The Case for Settling for Mr. Good Enough*. This book caused all kinds of controversy, and when I read the article, it wasn't hard to see why. I found myself conflicted while I was reading it, nodding my head, but shaking it at the same time. I was really confused, until suddenly it dawned on me—if both singleness and marriage are legitimate, then this is precisely how we should feel! It also enabled me to see this issue we're about to address from both sides. For those of us who are married, when we look at our single friends we just want to shake them and say, "You need to stop being so picky and just settle." But if singleness is legitimate, why are we pressuring our friends to do this? Why would we want what's second best for them in marriage when they can have what's best for them in singleness? But now, for those of us who are single, we need to consider the other side. Gottlieb is a woman in her forties, but what she has to say applies to both women *and* men, regardless of age. Here's what she writes:

> What I didn't realize in my thirties is that while settling seems like an enormous act of resignation when you're single, once you take the plunge and do it, you'll probably be relatively content. [That's because] what makes for a good marriage isn't necessarily what makes for a good romantic relationship. Marriage isn't a passion-fest; it's more like a partnership formed to run a very small, mundane, and often boring nonprofit business. And I mean this in a good way. It's not that I've become jaded to the point that I don't believe in romantic connection. It's just that as your priorities change from romance to family, the so-called "deal breakers" change. Some guys aren't worldly, but they'd make great dads. Or you walk into a room and start

talking to this person who is 5'4" and has an unfortunate nose, but he "gets" you. I bet there are plenty of these men in the older, overweight, and bald category (which they all eventually become anyway). Part of the problem is that we grew up idealizing marriage, thinking that [it] meant [finding] the man of your dreams (who by the way, doesn't exist, precisely because *you dreamed him up*) and so we walk away from relationships that might make us happy in the context of a family. Those of us who [are looking for] a soul mate are almost like teenagers who believe they're invulnerable to dying in a drunk-driving accident. We lose sight of our mortality. We forget that we, too, will age and become less alluring.[4]

Beauty, wealth, ambition, success, character—those are good things, but they'll all wear out on you. So don't look for them. Look instead for someone who grasps grace.

The Freedom You Have When You Are Single

I think that in view of the present distress it is good for a person to remain as he is. Are you bound to a wife? Do not seek to be free. Are you free from a wife? Do not seek a wife. But if you do marry, you have not sinned, and if a betrothed woman marries, she has not sinned. Yet those who marry will have worldly troubles, and I would spare you that. This is what I mean, brothers: the appointed time has grown very short. From now on, let those who have wives live as though they had none, and those who mourn as though they were not mourning, and those who rejoice as though they were not rejoicing, and those who buy as though they had no goods, and those who deal with the world as though they had no dealings with it. For the present form of this world is passing away. (vv. 26–31)

Here, as well as in the four verses that follow, Paul traces the various freedoms you have when you're single. Now before we get to that, we need to address something very important that will help frame our conversation the rest of the way. There's been much debate over what "the present distress" in verse 26 actually was.[5] Many have said that Paul was talking about the end of the world, which is why he says in verse 29, "the appointed time has grown very short" and in verse 31 that "the present form of this world is passing away." But I'm not so sure that that's what he was saying because the word translated "short "in verse 29 would probably be better rendered "critical."[6] "The time has grown not short but critical." Here's why. Thousands of years ago God came down from Heaven to be with us, to die for us, and to rise from the dead to set us free. And in light of that, *everything* changed. A whole new paradigm emerged, one that didn't render the world and the things in it unimportant, but that put all those things in their proper place. Paul says in verse 29, "From now on, let those who have wives live as though they had none, and those who mourn as though they were not mourning, and those who rejoice as though they were not rejoicing, and those who buy as though they had no goods, and those who deal with the world as though they had no dealings with it." Notice he does *not* say, "Stop having a wife, stop dealing with the world," but rather to live *as though* none of those things were everything.[7] Not to renounce them, but to relativize them.[8] Love your spouse, mourn, rejoice, do business, engage the world—but don't do any of those things as if they were everything.

Okay, but then why does he say explicitly in verse 31, "For the present form of this world is passing away"? The word for "form" was one that was used in the broader Greek culture to describe a mask an actor would wear in the theater.[9] "For the present mask of this world is passing away." But what does that mean? Everything we have, as we said before, is good. The problem is, it parades itself around as ultimate, promising to give us everything our hearts desire. But it's all a charade. And now that Christ has come, the jig is up. Everything is slowly but surely being unmasked for what it really is—good but not ultimate, not everything.[10]

Okay, fair enough. But if Paul wasn't talking about the end of the world here, then what was he talking about? Life.[11] He's just saying life is hard. It's distressing and taxing, and it gets even more so the more people you add. And the reason that's the case is because people have problems. Put one person with problems with another person with problems, and you don't get fewer problems, you get more. It's really just simple math! Now, it's not that if you're single, you don't have difficulties. But you have them for one instead of two. The same goes for anxieties.[12] Paul says in verse 32, "I want you to be free from anxieties." Whenever I travel alone, Sharon gets anxious. Will I miss my flight? Will I touch down and arrive safely? She worries. And whenever I'm out late at night, I'm anxious about her. Will she be able to sleep? Will someone break in while I'm not there? But when you're single, you're free from this—from the anxiety, the worry, the distress that marriage brings.

But if you're single you have another freedom. Verse 32 says, "The unmarried man is anxious about the things of the Lord, how to please the Lord. But the married man is anxious about worldly things, how to please his wife, and his interests are divided." Now Paul is *not* saying that it's better to be single because then you can *really* please God, as if having a spouse and pleasing God were at odds. In fact, anytime we see a sharp divide between "spiritual" and "worldly" things, it's because we're bringing baggage to the text that doesn't belong there. But what did Paul mean? Think about it this way. One thing that pleases God is when we care for others—and not just our families.[13] And when you're single, you have a certain freedom to do this that you don't have when you're married. When you're married, you can't make unilateral decisions anymore. Paul said in 6:19, "You are not your own," and that applies to your schedules too! Let's say a friend calls me with a crisis, but I'm with my wife. I can't just say, "Honey, I have to go. My friend needs me." I can't just get up and leave, because I have obligations to her that I have to consider. Now this doesn't mean that when you're married, you don't have to love your neighbors. Too often married folks hide behind their families so they don't have to do this. And when you're single, it's not that you don't have any obligations, but you have one less. Your interests aren't divided, at least not here. You are uniquely free to care for others outside of your family, and that pleases God!

I think this was Paul's point in verse 34, too, when he said, "And the unmarried or betrothed woman is anxious about the things of the Lord, how to be holy in body and spirit." Often we've taken Paul to be saying that single women can be more holy because they don't have sex, which, as we all know, is dirty. But again that's baggage *we* bring to the text. So how should we read that? The phrase "in body and spirit," as you may know, was basically Biblical shorthand for saying everything, every area of life[14]—the body referring to the public dimensions, and the spirit to the private.[15] In fact, scholars have noted that Paul had in mind the incredible synergy you can have between the two when you're single—to cultivate yourself *so that* you can serve more effectively in the public sphere; to grow personally *so that* you can do more good for your neighbors. You're free to do this because you don't have any of the restraints or pressures that marriage brings.

Eric Klinenberg, a professor of sociology at NYU, has written a compelling book entitled *Going Solo*. In it he traces the rise of singleness and sociological factors that have contributed to it. He also teases out the various social benefits, as well as some implications for a society whose landscape has shifted dramatically because of this rise. One of the arguments that he consistently makes is more or less what Paul was saying here. Here's how Klinenberg put it: "Today there is an abundance of pop sociology that associates [solitude] with the rise of loneliness, the collapse of civil society, and the demise of the common good. [But] I find this line of reasoning to be worse than misleading."[16] "De Tocqueville found [in solitude] an abiding moral code that binds citizens to each other in civic organizations. Durkheim argued that the private time that individuals spend on their own allows them to preserve energy and build an appetite for social participation."[17]

Transcendentalists such as Emerson and Thoreau shared a similar vision. They argued that being alone was necessary not because solitude grants us freedom from the burden of intimate social ties but because it allows us the freedom to cultivate ourselves, develop original ideas, and make a productive return to the world. [Solitude], for them, always preceded a return to society, and the insights born of [it] were meant to promote the common good. In fact, most of the leading figures in that movement—Emerson, Thoreau, as well as Bronson Alcott, Elizabeth Peabody and Margaret Fuller—were deeply engaged in civic and political life.[18]

"[Even today], the rise of living alone has produced some significant social benefits. We have seen, for instance, that young and middle-age singletons have helped to revitalize the public life of cities, because they're more likely to spend time with friends and neighbors, to frequent bars, cafes, and restaurants, and to participate in formal social activities such as civic groups. People who live alone become more socially active than those who live with others, and cities with high numbers of singletons [are] enjoying a thriving public culture."[19] And that's because of the freedom you have when you're single.

So we've seen the freedom you have to *be* single, as well as the freedom you have when you are.

A Freedom You'll Need to Handle It All Well

But whoever is firmly established in his heart, being under no necessity but having his desire under control, and has determined this in his heart, to keep her as his betrothed, he will do well. So then he who marries his betrothed does well, and he who refrains from marriage will do even better. (vv. 37, 38)

We said before that the ancient world placed an ultimate premium on marriage. Maybe it was an act of protest, but in Corinth that was almost completely reversed. Corinth was a very ambitious city, and many were arguing that marriage simply got in the way of personal aspirations. So the Corinthian Christians were facing strange conflicting pressures—to get married from one end and to stay single from the other. You know exactly what that's like, right? And Paul's response is basically, don't stay single or get married—in fact, don't do anything *just because* everyone is telling you to do it. Why? Because when you succumb to social pressure, you're under "necessity" (v. 37), and that's never a good way to make decisions. If you want to navigate the ropes of singleness and marriage well, you're going to need freedom from this.

But you not only need freedom from what everyone else is saying, but also from yourself—from *your own voracious desires.* In verse 37 Paul says that we have to get our desires under control. If you're staying single because you want the freedom to love your neighbors, you have a pretty good reason. But if you're doing it because you just want to focus on your career, or because you hate the thought of being obligated to someone else or of someone better coming along—if any of that describes you, you don't have a good reason. Because in each case you're just out to get more of what you want, and you don't have your desires under control. In fact, they have you under theirs. Or let's take the other side. If you're looking to get married because you want to give yourself away, then you have a good reason. But if you're doing it because you can't live without it, because being single just kills you—you can't bear the thought of being alone, and when you are, you don't even know who you are anymore—then you don't have your desires under control, and you will absolutely crush your spouse because of that. No human being can bear the kind of weight that you're asking, no human being can complete you like that.

And they never were intended to! Only one person was. Only one person can. Paul closes in verse 40 by saying, "And I think that I too have the Spirit of God." Paul, you see, had found the final answer. And it wasn't himself, but it wasn't a spouse either. It was neither singleness nor marriage. It was the One whose love was better than both, who would free him from everything that would control him, including himself. Both singleness and marriage parade themselves around as ultimate, promising to give you everything your heart desires. But it's all a charade. And now that Christ has come, the jig is up. They're both being unmasked for what they really are—good, but not ultimate, not everything. They'll always let you down. But he will never do that to you. Even when he was staring death square in its dark face, he refused to let you go, He refused to let you down. And when you know a love like that, it gives you a freedom to handle it all, to handle anything that comes your way.

Some of you are single, and there's nothing you want more than marriage. I wish I could tell you that it'll happen for you someday. But I can't. People say that if you don't want to be single, then you don't have the gift. But I don't think that's true. We live in an imperfect world where our deepest desires are often left unmet. And sometimes you get a gift you wouldn't have chosen for yourself. Maybe you have a knack for cooking, but you hate the kitchen. Things like that happen sometimes. I'm not going to tell you that you're going to get everything you want, because you might not. I'm going to tell you something better. I'm going to tell you that you're going to get the chance to be satisfied—whether solo or with a spouse, because you have a love that's better than both. A love that will never let you go. A love that will never let you down.

But some of you are single, and it's not that there's nothing you *want* more than marriage, it's that there's nothing you *fear* more than marriage. Losing your freedom. Missing out. Being let down. Maybe you were burned in the past, and you've grown cynical and suspicious of others. Or even worse, you're terrified of being seen to the bottom of who you are and then rejected. But remember, there's a lover who refused to do that to you, who's seen you to the bottom and chose to stick around. So you don't need to be afraid of being rejected or of losing anything and missing out. One of the women Eric Klinenberg interviewed said, "We fell in love once, and then twice, and it didn't work. Once that happened, the whole myth of romantic love as salvation came to an end."[20] And the same is true of the other side. "I've heard so many people say," another put it, "that they love living alone because it allows them [to do] whatever, whenever and wherever they want, but [this] turns out to be a false god. It can't answer your deepest questions or give you everything you're looking for."[21] That's because these things were never meant to do that. They were never meant to be gods. They were meant to be gifts.

Conclusion

Learn to see them for what they are, and treat them that way. Not to make them everything, but to use them to love not just your family, but your neighbors too. And you can do that because you have come to know a greater love that frees you to handle it all well.

15

The Right Use of Rights

1 CORINTHIANS 8:1–13

THOSE WHO APPROACH a text like this might say, "This is my primary problem with Christianity and the Bible. It's so encultured that it has no connection to my lived experience." "What do I care about food sacrificed to idols?" "The religious squabbles of antiquity have nothing to do with me." Caution needs to be taken in order not to fall into two subtle errors that plague the modern West. 1) *Geographical snobbery.* There are many around the world for whom the issues this text addresses are still quite real. It is dangerous to stay in a position where an individual cannot learn from these issues. 2) *Historical elitism.* The questions and solutions of the past are a treasury of wisdom. Only the most arrogant thinkers believe that nothing can be learned from different historical contexts. Once the Christian admits that he is not inherently more intelligent than people from other places and times, he will be able to start reading the text with humility.

Our text asks a key question: How should the members of a gospel-shaped community exercise their Christian liberties and privileges? What is the right way to exercise our rights? The language of "rights" refers to liberties or privileges, and not to modern-day "human rights."[1] We will again pursue our discussion around several key points.

- The Essence of Rights—What Are Our Rights?
- The Aim of Rights
- The Realignment of Rights—How Can We Rightly Exercise Our Rights?

The Essence of Rights—What Are Our Rights?

How does the world perceive rights, privileges, and liberties? The cultural sea that this generation swims in emphasizes the individualization of rights. It is a firmly held belief that an individual has the right to do anything at all that he would like to do so long as another human being is not endangered or harmed.[2] "If I want to eat meat sacrificed to idols, who cares if another person has a hard time with it—let them deal with it. It's my right." Self-expression and self-actualization are the ultimate goods, so anything that would hinder that right is seen as inherently bad.

Because all individualized rights are justifiable, it is rarely a question of "should" or "ought." "Should I purchase this? Should I consume this? What are the personal and social implications of this decision?" When was the last time anyone asked those questions when making a decision? Instead it is always a question of "can" (which carries an implied "should"). "Can I purchase this? Can I consume this? What are the personal implications of not doing this or owning that?" Many of the Corinthians were asking the same questions that modern people ask and were seeking every opportunity to justify their individual rights and privileges.

There were two parties in the Corinthian church, those representing the permissive party (progressive) and the restrictive party (conservative). These groups had different concerns. The primary concern for the progressives was personal freedom, whereas the conservatives pursued personal morality. These concerns when carried out to their extreme ends led to licentiousness for one party and legalism for the other. In our passage Paul is directly addressing the permissive party. He will address the restrictive party in passages to come.

> Now concerning food offered to idols: we know that "all of us possess knowledge." This "knowledge" puffs up, but love builds up. If anyone imagines that he knows something, he does not yet know as he ought to know. But if anyone loves God, he is known by God.
> Therefore, as to the eating of food offered to idols, we know that "an idol has no real existence," and that "there is no God but one." (vv. 1–4)

The progressives who saw no problem with eating meat sacrificed to idols had written to Paul with a theological explanation in expectation that he would back up their position. The phrase "all of us possess knowledge" (v. 1) is a reference to members of this party.[3] They understood that because there is only one God, there is nothing of substance in or behind an idol. This knowledge had led them to embrace the common cultural practice of eating meat sacrificed to idols, and even eating meals in the pagan temple on occasion.

The restrictors are expecting Paul to pounce, but he actually affirms the progressives' desire to support their rights and privileges as Christians. In verse 8 he affirms that what one eats doesn't really make a difference because "food will not commend us to God." A person is not worse off if he does not eat, and no better off if he does.[4] Because all things are created and given by God (v. 6), ultimately no material thing is evil in and of itself. In 10:23 Paul puts it this way: "'All things are lawful,' but not all things are helpful. 'All things are lawful,' but not all things build up."

Christians who properly understand the gospel and God's ownership of the world are not moralistic and rigid. If an individual has encountered a Christianity that is primarily about measuring behavior, about tracking morality, about what he can't do, then that individual has been given an incomplete and distorted picture of Christianity. When the gospel transforms our life, it uncovers former idols for what they were—lifeless, being-less, substance-less frauds. Christians cannot find ultimate fulfillment and satisfaction in the consumption of sumptuous food. However, once people understand this, they are able to fully enjoy food for the creational blessing that it is. Similarly, Christians cannot find a life-giving storyline in cultural artifacts like films, novels, and music. So whether it's consuming food or alcohol or certain cultural artifacts such as art, music, and film, it is not supposed to become the focal point or the center of one's Christian experience. Paul is saying, "You absolutely have liberties to exercise your rights in all of these areas." Our rights and privileges in Christ are far greater than we could ever imagine. In that sense it's kind of scary. We have all kinds of freedoms. Paul says in Galatians 5 that we have been set free because we are no longer under the bondage of slavery.

Once we understand this, we can properly consume the stuff of culture as something that points us to the gospel. Our rights and privileges in Christ are far greater than we can ever imagine. We are so free that it ought to make us nervous, and it should cause us to properly think of ways to use our freedoms for God's glory.

The Aim of Rights

If our rights and privileges in Christ are so astounding and if he sets all created things in their proper places for his glory and our enjoyment, then what is the source of the consternation in Corinth? What is the source of the consternation in the modern-day church over so-called gray areas?[5]

Though the progressives had their theology right, they were completely missing the point when it came to their practice. They were misapplying their understanding of the gospel and so were living lives that were antithetical to the gospel. According to verses 1, 2, their knowledge—which was true in theory—had puffed them up.[6] The permissive party was saying, "Hey, all of us possess knowledge," but Paul was saying to the progressives, "Your knowledge puffs up, but love builds up." The use of the verb "to know" or "to be known" comes up multiple times (e.g., "But if anyone loves God, he is known by God," v. 3) which shows that the members of this party were highlighting the fact that they had much "knowledge." But Paul speaks to this by saying, "You need to know the aim of your rights, and you need to know the purpose for why those rights were given."[7]

If our rights and privileges in Christ are so astounding, then why was there a whole lot of consternation? Because even though they had right theology, in the sense that they said, "all of us possess knowledge" and "an idol has no real existence" (vv. 1, 4), their problem was that their good theology was not working deeply into their hearts. The Corinthians unfortunately ended up becoming puffed up with their knowledge rather than understanding that the aim of their rights were supposed to bend toward love.[8]

What is the church to do with gray areas? Meat was not nearly as common in the diet of an ancient Corinthian as it is in a modern city. It was a delicacy—only the rich would have been able to afford to eat meat regularly. Nearly all edible meat would have begun its journey to the plate as a sacrifice to an idol. Some of it was apportioned to the priests, some eaten in the temple, and the rest sent to the market for purchase. For the poor, the only time they would have eaten meat would have been at an idol festival. Essentially the restrictive Christians in our text, whom Paul describes as having a "weak" conscience, were likely poor individuals who had recently converted to the faith. They would have been unable to dissociate the consumption of meat associated with the worship of false gods from Christian liberties. The permissive Christians were likely more seasoned in the faith (relative to the restrictive group) and were more financially secure (i.e., they ate meat more regularly). They "knew" that because there is only one God, there was no reality behind the idols of the temple. They viewed the consumption of meat from idol worship as an expression of Christian liberty.

This is not talking about moralistic people who have a strong preference for not eating or drinking. This is talking about individuals who will actually be tempted to worship other gods and revert to their old pre-Christian lifestyles. The issue is that the progressives have completely missed the aim of their Christian freedom, namely *to build one another up in love*. Christian rights and liberties are meant to be bent toward love![9] This is not what's happening with the "stronger" brothers. Paul has to point out their error in verse 7: "However, not all possess this knowledge. But some, through former association with idols, eat food as really offered to an idol, and their conscience, being weak, is defiled." And again in verses 9–11: "But take care that this right of yours does not somehow become a stumbling block to the weak. For if anyone sees you who have knowledge eating in an idol's temple, will he not be encouraged, if his conscience is weak, to eat food offered to idols? And so by your knowledge this weak person is destroyed, the brother for whom Christ died." The progressives were pressing their freedoms without considering the social impact of their actions.

This is not simply an ancient phenomenon. *The exercise of personal freedom is never simply personal.* Though people would love to believe that their actions do not affect those around them or the society as a whole, to believe this is to be naive. Culture is the result of countless individuals exercising their personal rights for good or ill. No one cannot exercise his rights in a bubble. David Brooks shares an insightful thought on self-expression: "Many of the people who led the social and political movements of the sixties and the eighties naively assumed that once old restrictions were removed and individuals liberated, better ways of living would automatically appear. But in life things are not that easy. If we start up-ending obsolete social norms, pretty soon we will notice that valuable ones, like civility and manners, get weakened too. By dissolving social ties in order to unleash individual self-expression, valuable community bonds are eroded as well. . . . If the sixties and the eighties were about expanding freedom and individualism, [we] are now left to cope with excessive freedom and excessive individualism."[10] If nervousness sets in when an individual thinks about freedoms that he might need to give up for the common good, that is a clear indication that he is enslaved by his entitlements.

It is interesting to find verse 6 in the middle of this discussion. It is one of the highest Christological statements in the Bible, emphasizing the deity of Christ: "Yet for us there is one God, the Father, from whom are all things and for whom we exist, and one Lord, Jesus Christ, through whom are all things and through whom we exist." The prepositions "from" and "for" are attributed to the one God the Father, and the object of the preposition "through" is the one Lord Jesus Christ. New Testament scholar Richard Bauckham says, "God is not only the agent or efficient cause of creation ('from him are all things') but he's also the final cause and the goal of all things ('to him are all things') but also the instrumental cause ('through him all things')."[11] So Paul is taking what Bauckham calls "the instrumental cause ('through him are all things')," which has always been given to God, and is now applying it to Jesus. In other words, Paul is not interested in just associating Jesus as an agent or as a really high, intermediary figure. This expression goes to the heart of Jewish monotheism, whose God was the one true God. As we see in Deuteronomy 6:4 over and over again—this is what the Jews recite twice every day—"the Oʀᴜɢ our God, the Oʀᴜɢ is one." The words, "Oʀᴜɢ," "God," "our," and "one" ("us") are all found in 1 Corinthians 8:6: "for *us* there is *one God*, the Father, from whom are all things and for whom we exist, and *one Lord*, Jesus Christ, through whom are all things and through whom we exist." Paul brings this up because he's saying that God is sharing his divine identity with the Son, Jesus Christ. And in a similar way Jesus shares his glory with his people—the community of God. The mutual interior deference, love, and sharing within the community of the Trinity between God the Father and God the Son has now become the basis for the community of God's people to share their rights and to revolve around others' needs rather than standing statically and expecting others to orbit around them.

This leads us then to the question, how do we realign? If the aim of our rights is to bend toward love, then what is the realignment? How can we get to a point where we use our rights for their intended purposes? How can our overindividualized understanding of rights be communalized? How can our inward-bent use of rights begin to bend outward toward love? How can we be freed from our slavery to our so-called freedoms?

The Realignment of Rights—How Can We Rightly Exercise Our Rights?

Christians are able to enjoy freedom because someone sacrificed his freedom on their behalf. Their rights are the result of Christ laying aside his claim to any and all of his rights.[12] Our liberties are ours because the ultimate stronger brother gave up his liberty to secure the liberties for his weaker brothers, namely us!

A true knowledge of the gospel recognizes two things: First, the privileges we have are shared privileges. "And so by your knowledge this weak person is destroyed, the brother for whom Christ died" (v. 11). Christ did not die to save the solitary individual; he died for his bride, his collective people, his church. Rights are never exercised in isolation, because they always have a bearing on those around us. We must never miss the sociological implications of the cross. It's not a question of what one can or cannot do.

It's a question of how to serve others and live a life that makes the gospel compelling.

Secondly, a lack of care for Christ's bride is a lack of care for Christ. When one sins against one's brother, he or she sins against Christ. "Thus, sinning against your brothers and wounding their conscience when it is weak, you sin against Christ" (v. 12). Jesus' teaching that whatever is done to "the least of these" has also been done to him (Matthew 25:40) does not only apply to those outside the church—it applies to those inside as well. How do we know whether or not we recognize the deep implications of the cross? When we give up our rights for the sake of loving our brother.[13] To the degree that we keep laying down our life down and sacrificing our rights for the weaker brother, to that degree we are understanding Paul's application of the gospel.[14] "Therefore, if food makes my brother stumble, I will never eat meat, lest I make my brother stumble" (v. 13). We are only truly free if we can set aside our freedoms for the sake of others. It is not a question of what we can get away with—it's a question of how we can best use our liberties for the sake of others.[15]

Our unity is meant to reflect the unity of the Godhead. ". . . there is one God, the Father, from whom are all things and for whom we exist, and one Lord, Jesus Christ, through whom are all things and through whom we exist" (v. 6). All things are ours in Christ; therefore all things are meant to be used in service to and worship of Christ. Only the gospel tells us that we are so free that we can give up our rights for the sake of another. Our identity is not bound up in self-expression—it is bound up in the ultimate self-expression of a God who is characterized by self-giving love. The Son gave voluntarily; there was voluntary self-renunciation and self-abasement. The most entitled person gave up his rights for us. That is powerful.

16

The End(s) of Entitlement

1 CORINTHIANS 9:1–18

EACH SUNDAY Christians from all traditions gather together to listen to words read and preached from the Bible. But when they encounter God in his Word they don't find what they might expect. One of the most amazing things about the Christian Scriptures is just how gritty they are, how this-worldly and real they are. It's not that there aren't some mysterious passages, some other-worldly bits here and there. After all, we're dealing with God. But on the whole the Bible happens on the human level. It's written in plain language, it's about ordinary people living ordinary lives and trying to cope with a God who keeps breaking into the midst of the mundane. We read there about people who are dealing with doubt and grief and pain and anger. There is relational turmoil—lovers betrayed, friendships on the brink of collapse, churches about to split. The Bible doesn't present a God who simply helps or who overlooks or transcends the difficulties of everyday life; it presents a God who meets people in the middle of the difficulties of everyday life.

So, whether the reader is a confessing Christian, a confessing skeptic, or simply ambivalent to the whole deal, the Bible is a book that happens in his world—in our world. The Corinthian church is in the middle of a real mess. And one of its biggest issues is that it has very little respect for its founding leader, Paul.

In short, the Corinthians believe that they are *entitled* to a certain kind of leader, and Paul doesn't quite measure up. They feel that the world should spin on the axis of their desires, preferences, and tastes. They *deserve* a different scenario than the one in which they are living. They feel as though Paul *owes* it to them to adapt his personality, his style, and his ministry methods to their liking.

This passage zeroes in on a sense of entitlement that can be observed in these ways

- The Dangers of Entitlement
- The Realities of Entitlement
- The Ends of Entitlement

The Dangers of Entitlement

This present era has been dubbed "the Age of Entitlement."[1] Of course, there are the horror story examples of sixteen-year-olds who complain about the color of the new car they've just been given by their parents. One author remarks, "Go to the mall or a concert or a restaurant and you can find them in the wild—the kids who have never been told no, whose sense of power and entitlement leaves onlookers breathless—the sand-kicking, foot-stomping, arm-twisting, wheedling, whining despots whose parents presumably deserve the company of the monsters they, after all, created."[2] Now that seems a bit harsh, but it gets at something that everyone has all experienced. Not simply in other people but within ourselves.

In a *Huffington Post* article Tim Urban asked the question, "Why Are Generation Y Yuppies Unhappy?" Urban invents a new term for yuppies in the Generation Y age group: Gen Y Protagonists & Special Yuppies, or GYPSYs. Now, his acronym is a bit unfortunate because the word gypsy is properly used to refer to an actual ethnic group, but leaving that aside, Urban claims that "a GYPSY is a unique brand of yuppie, one who thinks they [sic] are the main character of a very special story." GYPSYs have a sense of "optimism and unbounded possibility." They were told by their parents that they could be whatever they wanted to be, which instilled this special protagonist identity deep within them. As a result, "each individual GYPSY thinks that he . . . is destined for something even better" than everyone else around him. "GYPSYS consider a great career an obvious given for someone as exceptional as themselves."[3]

When people view themselves as the protagonist in their own special life narrative, they end up running on a sense of entitlement. "Well, *of course* I'm supposed to get into that school. This is my story after all. Of course my hard work pays off in the end. Of course I get the promotion. Of course I get the girl. I get the home. I get the picturesque family. I get the kids who end up being even more self-absorbed and narcissistic than I am. *Of course*. This is my story." The trouble comes when the bubble pops. And it always pops.

Look at what Paul says in verses 1–3:

Am I not free? Am I not an apostle? Have I not seen Jesus our Lord? Are not you my workmanship in the Lord?[4] If to others I am not an apostle, at least I am to you, for you are the seal of my apostleship in the Lord.
    This is my defense to those who would examine me.

Verse 3 paints a picture of what is going on. "This is my defense to those who would examine me." The original language behind the translation uses legal terminology.[5] Paul is being put on trial. Paul is being examined. He's been backed into a corner, and now he has to defend himself.

Everyone knows how to put other people on trial. When someone doesn't fit into our special life narrative, we examine them, we scrutinize them with surgical precision. We pore over every word of the emails they send. We read into every line. Every text message is like a bomb threat. Every personal encounter is a tense, awkward, forced-smiles affair. Why do we relate to this person through a filter? It is because we have put them on trial for not fitting into our story.

In essence legal filters are used to filter them out of one's life. The Corinthians are trying to filter Paul out. What are they attacking? What are they nitpicking? Verses 1, 2 give us an idea. "Am I not free?" As we'll see, they are attacking his ministry methods. "Am I not an apostle?" They are attacking his vocation and calling, "Have I not seen Jesus our Lord?" They are attacking the veracity of his words and the grounds for his ministry. "Are not you my workmanship in the Lord?" They are on their way to ignoring or denying the instrumental role that Paul played in bringing them the good news about Jesus.

To What Do They Feel Entitled?

Why are they putting Paul on trial? In short, they feel that they are entitled to a particular kind of leader and that they are entitled to control the situation in order to get the kind of leader they want.[6] What they want is a strong, articulate, impressive, showy, culturally acceptable leader. They want to identify with someone who is respected, well-known—someone who can go toe-to-toe with the philosophers in town, someone with the charisma and rhetorical flourish of the popular speakers who have recently passed through. Paul did not have any of this, and their message to the apostle was essentially, shape up or ship out—start fitting into our special life narrative, Paul, or it's over.

How Did They Want Paul to Change?

Interestingly enough, and this may be hard for us to grasp because of the cultural distance and difference, they were upset at Paul because he wouldn't take their money.[7] The strong, popular, culturally palatable leaders and rhetoricians of the day made their living by collecting money and staying in the homes of their hearers. This gave wealthy individuals leverage and sway in their relationships with their leaders. It was a means of creating relational debt—of ensuring that even though an individual's leader was leading, he was ultimately dependent upon the "sponsor" for his livelihood/well-being.[8]

So the Corinthians are looking for a win-win. They want a respectable leader to identify with, whom they can also control. But with Paul, they're in a lose-lose situation. Frankly, he's not a very flattering leader to be associated with, and they have no means of controlling him because he won't take their money! In accordance with entitlement, then, they need to manipulate the situation in order to filter Paul out of the story.

Modern people, even Christians, are not strangers to this kind of entitlement. Of course we deserve a raise. Of course we deserve the respect of our peers. Of course we deserve a spouse that acts this way and doesn't act that way, especially not in public. Of course we deserve attention and affection and love and a sense of meaning and purpose. We deserve the thrill of travel—to eat at the best restaurants, to get tons of likes on my Instagrams of my food. This is what we deserve. This is what the world owes us. Doesn't everyone else know that this is my special life narrative?

The summer after I graduated from college I was doing an internship at a church that was an hour and a half from my home. So about three times a week I was driving to the church. Very quickly I began to feel entitled. This isn't how my story was supposed to go. Do these people have any inkling of how much I'm sacrificing to serve them? A few weeks into the internship a sweet couple whom I had known for a few years finally started to see things from my perspective—how could they not?—and they made a proposition. "We need to get away. You need to commute less. You can stay at our place for a week, watch our dogs, and just breathe easy. There's plenty of food in the fridge. You'll love it." I thought, *Thank you, Lord, for finally getting it right for once. I can kick back, watch TV, and even make a few bucks on the side.*

Well, to put it bluntly, it was the week from Hell. Their dogs were humungous greyhounds or some other gigantic breed. Wherever I was they needed to be near me. If I went in another room and closed the door they went nuts. They barked all night. They needed to be walked multiple times a day, which consisted basically of them dragging me around. And I won't even tell you about how one of them got away in the middle of the night and I ran around in my pajamas in the rain for an hour and a half trying to track him down.

When the relaxed and rested couple finally returned home, I put on my best "it was a great week" face and kept the escaped dog story under wraps. And then I waited and waited for something more than a thank you, an envelope or a card or something that could possibly contain some cash or a check for what I deserved, for what I'd earned. Of course they would give me something! Even a measly $100 would do. But nope. Nothing. Nada. Zero. As I drove away I realized that we had never discussed money, and then I began to seethe. Those ungrateful . . .

They were on vacation while I was forced to live with those mongrels. How dare they take advantage of me that way. I was entitled to something more than what I currently had! This situation did not fit my special life narrative!

I tell you this to illustrate the threefold danger of entitlement.

First, *it distorts our perception of reality.* An inflated view of the self puts us in a position of deserving, and it puts everyone else in our debt. This is precisely what is happening at Corinth. They can't see straight. They think they deserve a certain kind of leader, and Paul owes it to them to either adapt or depart.

Second, *entitlement impairs our ability to receive gifts.* I was given free room and board for a week! I saved on gas money and travel time. But all I could see was what I *didn't* get. The Corinthians have been given the gospel and one of the greatest leaders in the history of the church, but their sense of entitlement overshadows the gift that they have in their leader. They are incapable of experiencing or expressing gratitude.

The third danger of entitlement is that *it turns us against the world and against the ones we love.* These dear sweet people who were simply trying to help out a sorry intern became the villains in my story. They became the enemy. This happens in marriages and friendships and work relationships. I believe that I am entitled to this. You owe it to me to be this person, to play this role, to act this way, to talk to me in this tone at this time. Here's your script, and if you don't follow it I'll just find someone to replace you. Entitlement is the bane of relationships. And it's certainly the bane of the Corinthians' relationship with Paul. He's not following their script. They've turned on him and put him on trial, and now it's time for Paul to make his defense, which brings us to our second point.

The Realities of Entitlement

The Corinthians' sense of entitlement has given them a skewed perspective on Paul. They're unable to see him as the gift that he is, and they're out to get him. As Paul offers his defense, he cuts through the Corinthians' *sense of entitlement* by appealing to the *substance of entitlement*. Take a look at verses 4–7:

> Do we not have the right to eat and drink? Do we not have the right to take along a believing wife, as do the other apostles and the brothers of the Lord and Cephas? Or is it only Barnabas and I who have no right to refrain from working for a living? Who serves as a soldier at his own expense? Who plants a vineyard without eating any of its fruit? Or who tends a flock without getting some of the milk?

Paul says, "So you would like to talk about entitlements? You want to talk about rights? About what is deserved? Okay. Let's get down to it." The gloves come off, and the first thing he says is, "I agree with you." "I have every right to take your money. In fact, let me develop your argument for you just to show you how right it is." And from verses 4–14 he makes an extended argument for why he has every right to make money in the course of doing the work of the ministry.

Commentators such as David Prior have found five different tiers of Paul's argument.[9] We'll look at them very quickly. First, in verses 4–7 he appeals to *ordinary practice*. Soldiers don't serve at their own expense. Viticulturists don't refrain from eating grapes and drinking wine. Shepherds don't have to pay for the milk produced by their flocks. In the same way, Paul, who guarded the Corinthian church like a soldier, tended it like a vineyard, and cared for it like a shepherd, had every right to make his living as a minister. Ordinary practice almost demanded it.

The second tier of his argument is found in verses 8–10, where we see that there is *Scriptural precedent* for Paul's rights as a minster.

> Do I say these things on human authority? Does not the Law say the same? For it is written in the Law of Moses, "You shall not muzzle an ox when it treads out the grain." Is it for oxen that God is concerned? Does he not certainly speak for our sake? It was written for our sake, because the plowman should plow in hope and the thresher thresh in hope of sharing in the crop.

Here Paul appeals to Deuteronomy 25:4 to show that laborers, even non-human laborers, have a right to derive their sustenance from their work.

In verses 11, 12a he appeals to *common sense*: "If we have sown spiritual things among you, is it too much if we reap material things from you? If others share this rightful claim on you, do not we even more?" Paul is saying, "Your logic makes sense. You're right. I am entitled to your money. That's the way that the world works. You put in your time, you get paid."

But on top of ordinary practice, Scriptural precedent, and common sense, Paul appeals to *religious custom*. "Do you not know that those who are employed in the temple service get their food from the temple, and those who serve at the altar share in the sacrificial offerings?" (v. 13). Pick a religion, any religion, Paul says. Go to the Jewish temple, or take a walk around downtown Corinth to the temple of Apollo or Octavia, and you'll find the same thing. Priests make their living being priests.

And if that were not enough, in verse 14 Paul backs up his argument with the words of Jesus himself: "In the same way, the Lord commanded that those who proclaim the gospel should get their living by the gospel." Paul likely has Matthew 10:10 in view. The point is, Paul agrees with the Corinthians!

He has a right to receive their money. Ordinary practice, Scriptural precedent, common sense, religious custom, and even Jesus himself all back him up.

So there is substance and reality to entitlement. As human beings we all have basic, inalienable rights, and society can only function when we abide by them. We have the rights of the nation in which we live. We have the entitlements of the law. We deserve not to be enslaved. We deserve not to be lied to. We deserve not to be cheated. We deserve to earn a decent wage for work that we do.

But before we get too excited about our entitlements, we have to recognize that they cut the other way too. People deserve to be punished for lying. They deserve to be censured for cheating. They deserve to be fired when they get paid for work that they didn't do. In other words, the world of rights and entitlements feels safe because it offers us balanced scales, but it also feels dangerous because it offers us balanced scales.

The economy of entitlement only truly works if the scales are perfectly balanced. We have a right not to be lied to, and so does everyone else; so if we lie to others, we deserve to be punished. Now, of course people get away with all kinds of breaches of protocol. Little white lies pass under the radar all the time. But if people take the principle of entitlements to its natural end, see it all the way through, balance every scale, and use every right that they have, they will need to punish every wrong.

From one angle this might sound like justice, but from another perspective it sounds like prison. If we live life according to the realities of entitlement, we will find ourselves handcuffed by our own worldview.

People desperately desire to live in a world where it's not about keeping score, one-upping, checks and balances, tit-for-tat, owing, earning, or deserving. People want to live in a world where they don't constantly have to shore up their reputation and cover up their mistakes with a creative, revisionistic, autobiographical knife because they're scared to death of being put on trial. We all want to live in a world where we don't put oppressive demands on our friends, family, and leaders to conform to the script we've written for them. We want to stop filtering people out of our lives. We want people to stop filtering us out!

But, to put it flatly, *that world will never exist if our principal approach to life is one of rights and entitlements.* That world can never exist if we are all the protagonists at the center of our own individual special life narratives. That ideal world, which we might describe as peaceful, flourishing, harmonious, fulfilling, and beautiful, can never exist if life is primarily about what I want, what I need, what I deserve, what I am entitled to, what I have a right to demand of others.

The only world that is really free—the world that we want to live in—is the one where we are free from ourselves. Free from the ceaseless scorekeeping, the incessant card counting, the criteria meeting, the accomplishment amassing, the credential checking world that we have built for ourselves. In our attempt to hold on to our rights and our entitlements, we've written scripts for ourselves that we can't measure up to! And we can't measure up to the script others have written for us, and if others hang around us long enough, they'll be looking for a way to write us out.

Our rights and entitlements have gotten us in quite a bind. Is there a way to break free? Is there an alternate universe where people don't have to cling to their rights? Where we can love others even when they're unlovable? Where others will love us even when we're unlovable? Where we can give to others even when they don't deserve it? Where others will give to us even when we don't deserve it? Where we can forgive the people who trampled on our rights? Where others can forgive us for trampling on their rights?

Paul points the way forward, and we'll consider his approach in our concluding point.

The End(s) of Entitlement

Paul has just finished his five-tiered defense of his right to make a living by preaching the gospel. The amazing turn comes when Paul says that even though he has every right, he would rather not exercise his rights. He says in verse 12: "If others share this rightful claim on you, do not we even more? Nevertheless, we have not made use of this right, but we endure anything rather than put an obstacle in the way of the gospel of Christ."

If anyone is actually entitled in this passage, it is Paul;[10] yet he's the very one who says he's not interested in entitlement. He has rights, but he's not interested in using them. In other words, he's done with leveraging his position and title and pedigree for gain. He's been there, done that, and it left him wanting. He is far too interested in the work he has to do (namely, preaching the gospel of Christ) than any perks or fringe benefits that may accompany it, including financial compensation.

What happened to Paul? How did he get this free? He is actually turning down money. He is working with a new paradigm, one that is almost impossible to get our heads around. Verses 15–18 will help us understand just what is happening with Paul:

> But I have made no use of any of these rights, nor am I writing these things to secure any such provision. For I[11] would rather die than have anyone deprive me of my ground for boasting. For if I preach the gospel, that gives me no ground for boasting. For necessity is laid upon me. Woe to me if I do not preach the gospel! For if I do this of my own will, I have a reward, but if not of my own will, I am still entrusted with a stewardship. What then is my reward? That in my preaching I may present the gospel free of charge, so as not to make full use of my right in the gospel.

In verse 15 Paul makes it clear that this whole spiel has not been an underhanded attempt to get the Corinthians to give him money. In fact, he claims that he would rather die than take their money. Verses 16, 17 lay out Paul's calling as an apostle. He has been entrusted with "a stewardship." Someone else has given him a treasure that he is responsible to protect, invest, and steward. This treasure is the gospel. He *has* to preach the gospel out of necessity. He has no choice. In verse 16 his language recalls that of the Old Testament prophets when he pronounces a "woe" over himself.[12] "Woe to me if I do not preach the gospel!" For Paul, preaching the gospel—his calling, his vocation—is not optional.

However, what *is* optional to Paul is the exercising of his rights and entitlements. And what is it that has allowed Paul to set this aside, to break out of the economy of entitlement, to work free of charge, to abandon the pageantry of the powerful, eloquent leader in favor of being himself? Simply put, *he has found something better than rights and entitlement.*

He has discovered a new paradigm where he is no longer at the center of the solar system. He has set aside his special life narrative and all of its attendant demands in favor of a new narrative where someone else is at the center. Verse 18 gives us Paul's reason for throwing out his self-centered script: "What then is my reward? That in my preaching I may present the gospel free of charge, so as not to make full use of my right in the gospel."

Paul has found a reward more valuable than rights. He is exhilarated by the freeness of the gospel. "It's free," he's shouting. "Your whole world runs on purchasing, paying, earning, deserving, and entitlement. The gospel doesn't run on any of that—it's free. And I want you to know that so badly— I want you to experience this good news for yourself so much—that I will live my life in a way that calls your whole system into question. I'm going off script, and that's going to frustrate you, but you have to see that the game of entitlement is a joke!"

What kind of news leads a man to work for free? What words would we have to hear to give up the act? What would need to be said for us to lay down our entitlements? What kind of message would we need to hear in order to tear up the script that we've written for our spouse, kids, family, friends, coworkers? What would it take to knock us out of the director's chair of our special life narrative? That's what we need! We need someone to forcibly knock us out of the silly little director's chair that we've set up every morning in order to get the world to spin our way.

What kind of gospel would we need to hear in order to give up our sense of entitlement? This is what we would need to hear: we can stop trying to achieve, purchase, and deserve everything we've been after. "Here. Take it. It's free."

That sense of security we've been trying to achieve, the one that made us buy into the special life narrative, "Take it, it's free." That love and affection that we've been trying to buy with our carefully chosen words, with sheer romantic willpower, "Take it, it's free." That respect and dignity that we so desperately desired that it drove us through graduate school and has us at work 70 hours a week, "Take it, it's free."

These are outlandish claims, but they are the outlandish claims of the free-of-charge gospel that we encounter in the Scriptures. There we learn that Jesus Christ, the ultimately entitled one, mysteriously and graciously chose to write himself into the script of our world. He came preaching freedom from the special life narrative. He came preaching freedom from entitlement and self-absorption. And what did we do? We put him on trial. We examined him and found him guilty. We filtered him out; we wrote him out of the script. Such a threat was he to our entitlement economy, our individual solar systems, that we had to snuff him out. We erased him. We edited him out. And at the moment when he could have exercised his rights and climbed down from the cross, at the moment when he could have actually directed the universe to work in his favor, he submitted to our deletion.

And yet—mystery of mysteries, wisdom of wisdoms—as the Bible would have it, ironically it is our worst directorial moment, the moment when we killed the Son of God, that God uses to rewrite the script of history. And in the resurrection of Jesus he proves once and for all that we are not actually the ones writing the story. We never were. We've been deluded, duped, deceived into thinking that we run the world. But in Jesus Christ the one who runs the world has broken in to announce that the jig is up. And this just happens to be the best news that we will ever hear.

The jig is up. The game is over. Everything you've been trying to purchase is available for free. "Come, everyone who thirsts, come to the waters; and he who has no money, come, buy and eat! Come, buy wine and milk without money and without price" (Isaiah 55:1). It's a free-of-charge gospel.

And it's this free-of-charge gospel that sets us free from the grip of entitlement. We are free to give up the director's chair. Which means that we will begin to perceive the world properly, without an inflated sense of self or a sense of entitlement. We are free to stop writing scripts for the people in our life because we no longer need them to play a certain role to fulfill us. We can free them to be them. We can enter into a relationship with them instead of guilt-tripping them and pressuring them into the version of them that we wish they would be.

This free-of-charge gospel allows us to stop putting the world on trial. We can forgive and find room for the people whom we once attempted to write off and write out. Ironically, it is in giving up our entitlement and rights that we are placed in a position of being able to care about the rights and entitlements of others. We can fight for justice, not for ourselves but for others. We can put our directing skills to use for our neighbor because we've acknowledged that we were never really directing our life anyway.

And the free-of-charge gospel allows us to receive life itself as a gift—as an undeserved, unearned, unpurchasable, unentitled, given thing.

I pray that this profound, absurd, free-of-charge gospel would stop us dead in our tracks, that we would see Jesus stepping onto the trading floor of entitlement and hear him announce, "The jig is up. It's all free."

17

An Effective Witness

1 CORINTHIANS 9:19–27

THE PASSAGE AT HAND is one that the reader may know well, given that it's *the* quintessential passage concerning Christian witness in the world. If an individual identifies himself as a Christian, and since he most likely was schooled on the importance of being a witness, he might believe there's nothing more important for him to learn. Times have changed, and our cultural moment now is vastly different from what it was even a decade ago.[1] And given this difference, much of what was learned to be true about witness has to be reevaluated. And this passage is helpful in doing precisely that. On the other hand, for a mildly curious skeptic the topic of Christian witness doesn't seem so much unhelpful as unreasonable. Witness reeks of coercion and imperialism, which is one of the things many modern people can't stand about religion. There has to be an admission that coercion and imperialism have absolutely no place in civil discourse. But the good news is that's precisely the kind of witness the church is *not* talking about. The kind of witness Christians are after is about persuasion, not coercion,[2] cultural immersion, not cultural imperialism, and both persuasion and cultural immersion are foundational blocks in a pluralistic society. Witness—at least the kind that we're after here—is important for all to consider, regardless of one's faith commitment, because it's the way in which we should interact with one another in the world. So we would do well to think through how to do it well. The passage presents three approaches or realities that need to be considered if witness is going to be done well.

- The Agility to Go In
- The Discipline to Stay In
- A Goal to Keep Us Going

The Agility to Go In

Paul says in verses 19–22,

> For though I am free from all, I have made myself a servant to all, that I
> might win more of them. To the Jews I became as a Jew, in order to win
> Jews. To those under the law I became as one under the law (though not
> being myself under the law) that I might win those under the law. To those
> outside the law[3] I became as one outside the law (not being outside the law
> of God but under the law of Christ) that I might win those outside the law.
> To the weak I became weak, that I might win the weak. I have become all
> things to all people, that by all means I might save some.

Basically there were these two groups of people—"those under the law" and
"those outside the law" who lived in the city of Corinth at the time—Jews
("those under the law") and non-Jews, mainly Greeks ("those outside the
law"). These two groups were very different from one another. They had
vastly different hopes and aspirations, different questions and troubles with
the gospel that had taken their city by storm. And because of these cultural
differences, Paul had made it his central priority not only to understand these
two respective worlds, but also to enter into their lives and immerse himself
deeply within them. In fact, he had become so entrenched in both Jewish and
Greek culture that they had become a part of him and he a part of them to the
point that he could see things from the inside. I think this is what Paul meant
when he said in verses 20, 21, "To the Jews I *became* as a Jew"[4] and to "those
outside the law" (the Greeks) he became as a Greek.[5] He didn't just understand them; he *became* one of them. He didn't just learn *about* their culture,
he became a part of it, and it became a part of him. "I have become all things
to all people, that by all means I might save some" (v. 22). Now it certainly
required a tremendous amount of agility to do that. But that's precisely what
Paul resolved to cultivate within himself.

Are Christians cultivating this kind of agility, immersing themselves so
deeply in their respective cities that they can see it from the inside? Do they
feel the deepest hopes and aspirations of their neighbors? Do they know the
questions they're asking and what troubles them about Christianity, and can
they speak in ways people can actually understand? Or have Christians become so entrenched in their little Christian enclaves, so detached from their
city and culture that they have no clue what its hopes are, so they struggle to
articulate truth without the crutch of Christian jargon?

Here's why it's so important for this to be considered. When the famous
twentieth-century British missionary Lesslie Newbigin left for India, Chris-

tianity had risen to ascendancy and had essentially asserted its dominance within British culture. And because it had, the hopes and aspirations of that broader culture were essentially Christian, questions and troubles with Christianity were virtually nonexistent, and Christian jargon was the lingua franca of the day. But upon his return to England decades later, Newbigin found that the ground beneath him had shifted dramatically. He could no longer assume a Christian public. The hopes and aspirations had changed, questions and troubles with Christianity had emerged, and Christian vocabulary had become more or less unintelligible to the average person—"the ranting of ignorant foreign barbarians," as Timothy Richard put it.[6] And as all of this was going on, the British church didn't budge. She continued with business as usual, and Christianity became more and more privatized, more and more detached from the broader culture as a result. In response to this, Newbigin argued tirelessly for change—for what he called "a missionary encounter" with the broader culture so the gospel would engage that culture once again.[7]

This missionary encounter is precisely what is needed today. We live in a post-Christian culture where the ground has shifted dramatically and where we can no longer assume a Christian public. The church needs to have a healthy contextual approach that neither assimilates to the host culture nor under-adapts from its home culture. Business as usual won't cut it anymore. Because the landscape has changed so drastically, there's a good chance that any paradigm that's familiar to us, any paradigm we're comfortable with and that just feels right to us, is unintelligible to the average person, "the ranting of ignorant foreign barbarians." The church needs to make adjustments. We must learn the hopes, the questions, and the language of our neighbors without overcontextualizing. We need the agility to go in.

One quick clarification is necessary when engaging in a discussion about agility and cultural immersion. Agility does *not* mean blind adherence to the cultural status quo, and immersion does *not* mean inculturation to the point that one can't critique the culture at all. In fact, if a person is really an insider he should be able to evaluate his culture *more* effectively precisely because he can see things from the inside. This is what Paul was doing when he said in verse 20, "To those under the law I became as one under the law" and in 21, "To those outside the law I became as one outside the law." As an insider he is critiquing both Jewish and Greek culture. The Jews had placed such a strong emphasis on the letter of the Law that they'd lost sight of the spirit of it.[8] The Law all along was designed to foster love, but strict adherence to its rules somewhere along the way had become primary. And that generated division and hostility between those who kept it and those who didn't—

which is the very opposite of what it was intended to breed! It had become a law without love. On the other hand, Greek culture swung the pendulum almost completely in the opposite direction. What had become central for the Greeks was freedom from the Law and anything else that would restrict.[9] It was a love without law. But here's the thing. A love without law isn't really love at all. Because the Law sets the necessary social conditions for everyone to flourish, for there to be justice and equity, apart from which there can be no real love. Without the Law one might have sentiment cloaked in a thin veneer of love, but one does not have love. And Paul knew the danger of both of these pitfalls. So he basically says, "I refuse to be slavishly under the Law like the Jews [v. 20], but I also refuse to be stubbornly outside of it like the Greeks [v. 21]. Instead as an insider of both of those cultures, I'm going to argue for a third way—not a law without love or a love without law but a law *of* love that gives people every freedom in the world, but also leads them to use those freedoms for the good of others. "For though I am free from all, I have made myself a servant to all, that I might win more of them" (v. 19).

So we've seen that if we want to witness well, we are going to need, first, the agility to go in. But second, we will see that we are going to need the discipline to stay in once we get there.

The Discipline to Stay In

In verses 24–27 the Apostle Paul says, "Do you not know that in a race all the runners run, but only one receives the prize? So run that you may obtain it. Every athlete exercises self-control in all things. They do it to receive a perishable wreath, but we an imperishable. So I do not run aimlessly; I do not box as one beating the air. But I discipline my body and keep it under control, lest after preaching to others I myself should be disqualified." These verses are very well known and are typically used to talk about how we need discipline in order to run the race of the Christian life. That is certainly true, and we ought to be concerned about that, but this wasn't Paul's point. His point was that discipline is absolutely essential not to our progress in the Christian life, but to our *witness in the world*.

Here's the reason why. It's so much easier for a Christian to retreat to his safe enclave instead of staying in the world. It takes a lot of work and intentional focus to know one's neighbors and the broader culture—to feel their hopes and to discern their questions. It's even harder to be able to do all of that without the safety net of our subcultural jargon. It takes work and intentional focus. *It requires discipline.* Paul compares it to the rigorous training to which an athlete would subject himself. A Christian can't expect to witness well without a tremendous amount of effort, any more than he could expect to be an effective athlete without that. The discipline to stay in takes rigorous training and voracious effort.

But given this particular cultural moment, this will take a certain *kind* of discipline. Along with the cultural shift has come an increasing amount of suspicion as well. Because this is the case, the church cannot expect people to take the gospel at face value anymore. Christians have to make a compelling case for it—to make the gospel not only intelligible but *intellectually credible* as well.

John Nicol Farquhar, a Scottish missionary to India, noticed something about Indian culture that was pretty much identical to our contemporary world. Basically Farquhar had arrived in India on the heels of the missionary giants Alexander Duff and William Miller. Duff and Miller had both done important work, and as a result of their efforts Christianity had risen to ascendancy within the broader culture. But after a while, as it had done in Britain, the ground shifted. But along with this shift came an increasing amount of suspicion as well. Cultural elites had initially flocked to Christianity because of its modernizing influence, but now found they could be modern without it. What's more, Christianity was beginning to be seen as culturally intrusive as many bristled at its westernizing influence while craving a return to their own cultural roots. As a result the gospel lost credibility, and a compelling case needed to be made for it again. To that end Farquhar emphasized rigorous intellectual and cultural training. Now some were saying, "Why are you wasting your time with that stuff? Just preach the gospel. Show them how they can know God." But the problem was, he couldn't simply do that because the gospel was no longer plausible or intellectually credible to the broader culture. Its veracity had almost completely eroded away, and so business as usual just would not cut it anymore.[10]

This is virtually identical to our cultural moment. So many questions have to be addressed before folks can even begin to take Christianity seriously. How do you reconcile Christianity and science? A loving God with pain, Hell, and the terrible track record of the church? Are the Bible and the resurrection of Jesus historically credible? What do we make of Christianity's exclusive claims in a relativistic world?[11] What impact does the gospel have on civil society in a pluralistic one—on politics,[12] economics,[13] peacemaking,[14] neighboring,[15] and the public sphere?[16] These are the issues that need to be addressed winsomely and apologetically; otherwise people will have difficulty taking Christianity seriously. Unless these are addressed, many things Christians say and do, no matter how well intentioned, are simply exercises in "aimless running" and "beating the air" (v. 26). Are we thinking deeply about them, and are we listening and learning to communicate in ways people can understand? It's tough to do this without help. Tim Keller's *The Reason for God* can be very useful. Not only does he raise a lot of the right issues, but he also speaks in ways people can understand.

Now it's true that we don't *have* to do any of this. We're free not to. We're free to keep doing business as usual. An athlete doesn't *have* to subject herself to rigorous training. She's free to reach for that slice of cake instead of an apple or to skip that morning session for an extra hour of sleep. But she doesn't't[17] because there's something that's more important,[18] something worth the discipline. The same is true with our witness. Sure, we're free to do it on our terms. We're free to ignore the deepest questions of our neighbors and to speak in ways that are easier for us. But we don't because there's something that's more important, something worth curbing our freedom for.

And that's love. If a Christian is unwilling to discipline himself then something has gone terribly awry. It means that he might have something that might look like love but is really just sentiment cloaked in a thin veneer. This was the thing that Paul fought with all of his might to avoid. He says in verse 27, "But I discipline my body and keep it under control, lest after preaching to others I myself should be disqualified." The word translated "disqualified" literally means "to be shown counterfeit."[19] And this is precisely what will become of our love if we're not willing to do the hard work of training ourselves. Our love will be shown counterfeit, a charade, a façade if we don't discipline ourselves to stay in.

The agility to go in—the discipline to stay in—but now thirdly and finally . . .

A Goal to Keep Us Going

Throughout the passage Paul uses some off-putting language. Over and over he says he's out to win the Jews, the Greeks, the weak, to save them, to win over more and more of them. This sounds a whole lot like imperialism, which we see far too much of today. Witness that is intrusive, that tries to box another person into a corner to win the argument, or that treats him as a prize to be won rather than a person to be loved, shouldn't happen. Any form of witness marked by imperialism like that runs counter to the very nature of the gospel, which tells believers that the God of Christianity wins not by conquering but by dying, not by bringing the sword but by bearing the cross. And any witness that calls itself Christian has to do the same.

This was Paul's point when he said in verse 23, "I do it all for the sake of the gospel, that I may share with them in its blessings." But it seems like Paul's saying just the opposite here. It seems like he's saying, "I do it for the blessings—winning rewards, converts, arguments!" This seems to be giving credence to the kind of witness that disturbs us so deeply. But if we look a little closer, we'll find that's not the case. Verse 23 literally reads, "I do it all for the sake of the gospel, that I might share with them in *it*." Not in its blessings, but in the gospel itself, in its *nature*.[20] But what does that mean? What is the nature of the gospel? The gospel foundationally is about a witness who came to us by becoming one of us—an insider who felt our deepest hopes and aspirations, who learned the questions we were asking and the things that troubled us. It's about a witness who immersed himself deeply in our fallen world, speaking and giving, living and loving in ways we could understand—sharing everything *with* us, but even more, giving his life away *for us and our sin*, becoming weak, losing it all—because he had a goal that kept him going.[21] That goal was you. It was me.

And when we see him doing all of that for sinners like us, it gives us a goal of our own—not only to share this gospel with others, but to share in its *very nature* as we do that. Why do we listen and why do we learn the hopes and questions of our neighbors and to speak in ways people can understand? Why do we keep going when the rigor of intellectual and cultural training and loving our neighbors gets hard? We keep going in order to share not only *what* God has done for us but *how* he did it for us too. The goal that keeps us going isn't winning souls or arguments. It's not about amassing converts, rewards, or all the knowledge in the world. It's about standing side by side with our neighbors and sharing in the nature of this gospel that has saved us, even as we learn to show it more and more to one another through our words and through our love. "I do it all for the sake of the gospel, that I may share with them in it."

Conclusion

Believers should be encouraged to cultivate their cultural agility, to discipline themselves intellectually, but through it all to keep the goal in mind—sharing not only the gospel with others, but also sharing in its nature as we do that.

18

Escaping Idolatry

1 CORINTHIANS 10:1–22

IN THIS PASSAGE Paul outlines the history of humanity as a history of idolatry. What is idolatry?[1] In Romans 1:25 Paul argues that we will worship and serve either God or a created thing, namely idols. In other words, idols are anything more fundamental than God for our happiness, meaning, and identity. They are inordinate desires for even good things such as material possessions, a career, family, marriage, achievement, work, independence, political cause, financial security, human approval, romance. All of these things are good in and of themselves. But what ends up happening for many people is that these created things become ultimate things.[2] And when this takes place, they become functional masters, over-desires, and ultimately idols in man's heart. Most believe that once their hearts are captured by these things, then finally their lives would be much happier. So idolatry is always the reason people ever do anything wrong. In other words, it is the shaping power that is underneath human impulses, human behavior, and the motivational cause for why there is any desire to do anything.

First John 2 lists the triad of lusts—the lust of the flesh, the lust of the eyes, and the pride of life or pride in possessions. It's worth noting that lust doesn't simply mean sexual lust. When the Bible uses that particular word, it actually means an over-desire or an inordinate desire.[3] Destructive thoughts, ideas, and actions are not merely horizontal; they are connected vertically to a relationship that all humans have either with an uber desire[4] erected in their hearts or with God. It is at the same time operating horizontally and vertically; therefore, a behavioristic symptom will reveal what the human heart is trusting and worshiping at that particular time.

So there are three things worth attention in this passage.

- Recounting Idolatry (Historical)
- Experiencing Idolatry (Personal)
- Escaping Idolatry (Historical)

Recounting Idolatry (Historical) (vv. 1–10, 18–22)

In this passage there are two histories at play: Israelite history and Corinthian history. In reality these are two examples of a common human experience, that is, idolatry. Both histories speak about people who had been delivered by God (vv. 1, 2)—the Israelites from Egypt, the Corinthians from sin and death. Both histories speak about people who had been sustained by God (vv. 3, 4)—the Israelites by spiritual (and literal) food and drink, the Corinthians by spiritual food and drink (the Lord's Supper). Both histories also speak about people who, in spite of deliverance and sustenance, were drawn to other gods.

These passages speak primarily about God's judgment and discipline in the lives of his people. Though the Bible condemns idolatry as a whole, it does not point its finger only at the world but also at the church. In other words, this passage does not consist of moral instruction aimed at those outside of the believing community, but rather to those within it. One of the things that skeptics and nonbelievers tend to abhor is hypocrisy. One may have great tolerance for someone who is consistent in his belief and actions, but he might have a hard time with people who don't live up to their own standards. The Bible actually abhors this too.

These two histories of idolatry confront individuals who claim to believe one thing while doing something contrary to their confessed belief. Verse 5 points out that despite God's providence and provision, the Israelites responded in a way that displeased God. Verses 7–10 give a number of examples about how this is played out. The first example (v. 7) is Israel and the golden calf. "Do not be idolaters as some of them were; as it is written, 'The people sat down to eat and drink and rose up to play.'" Here, Paul is quoting from Exodus 32:6. This is the classic scene: Moses is meeting with God on Mt. Sinai, and in the meantime the Israelites are melting down all of their gold in order to build an idol for themselves. Note that what they do is rather ordinary; they knew from their time in Egypt that idol building was a common cultural practice. They desired a visible representation of their God. Idolatry affected them at the level of ordinary practices—eating, drinking, playing, culture-making (idol-crafting).

Their actions themselves were not the only sinful activity, but they were twisted by a desire for a providential provider other than the one who had rescued them from Egypt. There is always something helpful even in our understanding of idolatry. The word comes from two Latin words, one meaning "idol, image, or icon" and the other denoting the worship of that image. The impulse to worship is healthy. Humankind has been created to worship. The problem here is that idolatrous worship is fixed toward an icon instead of toward the one true God. They desired a god they could craft and control to their liking.

Because God knows that idolatry is a dead-end, he takes action. One finds this in the second example in verse 8: Israel yoked himself to Baal of Peor. "We must not indulge in sexual immorality as some of them did, and twenty-three thousand fell in a single day." Paul recalls an episode in Numbers 25 when the Israelites began to intermarry with devotees of another religion. Again the deepest desires of the heart show up in the most ordinary aspects of life—marriage, sexual relations, and eating. "While Israel lived in Shittim, the people began to whore with the daughters of Moab. These invited the people to the sacrifices of their gods, and the people ate and bowed down to their gods. So Israel yoked himself to Baal of Peor. And the anger of the Orug was kindled against Israel" (Numbers 25:1–3). By pursuing their own desires, they ended up "yoking" themselves with another god. From their perspective, this was all ordinary! People intermarry with people from other religions all the time. But Yahweh calls for undivided allegiance—a singularity of focus. The result was a plague upon the people of Israel, which only repentance and decisive communal action could stop.

The third example comes from the Israelite history of idolatry. In verses 9, 10 one reads of the rejection of providence and provision: "We must not put Christ to the test, as some of them did and were destroyed by serpents, nor grumble, as some of them did and were destroyed by the Destroyer." In Numbers 21:4–9, the Israelites were impatient with God, and they began to grumble and complain about food and drink. God afflicted them by sending serpents into the camp, but he also gave them a means of escape. They failed to trust him, so he sent a trial into their lives to show them that the only means of escape is to trust in him.

Corinthian idolatry, much like Israelite idolatry, had to do with ordinary stuff—eating food sacrificed to idols in temple sacrifice.[5] In Corinth the temple functioned as a central, communal gathering place. The temple courts included tables for regular feasting; so the temple functioned something like a modern-day restaurant. There would be nothing out of the ordinary about attending a brief sacrificial ceremony and then joining friends for a nice meal afterward. This wouldn't necessarily have been accompanied by a religious feeling either. The priests were doing their thing, and there were some devoted believers, but many would have felt rather indifferent to the whole process. It was a social, communal gathering. The Corinthians were used to going to the temple for these meals, and now that they have realized that the idols don't have any substance, they have begun to visit the temples again.

Paul calls on them to stop attending these feasts for a number of reasons. First, one's desires and affections are shaped by the way one lives his or her ordinary life. There is a shaping liturgy to one's life, a rhythm, an order of worship. As James Smith suggests in *Desiring the Kingdom*, "Our heart's desires are shaped and molded by the habit-forming practices in which we participate daily."[6] One's desires are shaped and transformed by his or her habits, actions, and relationships. One might think this or that is neutral, but Paul is saying that everyone's actions have a shaping effect. The Corinthians' acceptance of and participation in the temple practices made them susceptible and less-than-suspicious about the dangerous effects of idolatry.

Secondly, there are spiritual realities that man does not fully comprehend. While it is true that the idols in the temple have no substance, there is a spiritual, idolatrous, shaping system that stands behind them. Paul claims that it is contradictory to simultaneously buy into the system of the old world order and the new creational world order that is put forward in the gospel. "What do I imply then? That food offered to idols is anything, or that an idol is anything? No, I imply that what pagans sacrifice they offer to demons and not to God. I do not want you to be participants with demons. You cannot drink the cup of the Lord and the cup of demons. You cannot partake of the table of the Lord and the table of demons" (vv. 19–21).

In verses 6, 11 Paul claims that these histories are examples for us, but in what way? What do the histories of Israel and Corinth have to do with us?

Experiencing Idolatry (Personal) (vv. 11, 12)

In verses 11, 12 Paul writes, "Now these things happened to them as an example, but they were written down for our instruction, on whom the end of the ages has come. Therefore let anyone who thinks that he stands take heed lest he fall." Idolatry, as noted earlier, happens on the level of one's desire. Consider what we read in verse 6 as well: "Now these things took place as examples for us, that we might not desire evil as they did." The Apostle Paul is not so concerned here about a particular situation. He's trying to give a bigger framework for understanding how one can make wise choices in all the little decisions that are part of the mundane things in life.

Idolatry happens in ordinary life. It is tempting to read the accounts of Israelite and Corinthian idolatry and absolve ourselves from any danger, but this is a misread. Dick Keyes writes:

> A careful reading of the Old and New Testaments shows that idolatry is nothing like the crude, simplistic picture that springs to mind of an idol sculpture in some distant country. As the main category to describe unbelief, the idea is highly sophisticated, drawing together the complexities of motivation in individual psychology, the social environment, and also the unseen world. Idols are not just on pagan altars, but in well-educated human hearts and minds. . . . The Bible does not allow us to marginalize idolatry to the fringes of life . . . it is found on center stage.[7]

Idolatry happens beneath the level of action; it happens on the level of appetite and desire. Idolatry shows up in the subtle twists of ordinary desires and activities—eating, drinking, playing, marrying, and having sex. These activities and desires are often not ends in and of themselves, but are means to another end (personal fulfillment, comfort, security, power, control, etc.). Whenever we take a created thing and put it to use in such a way as to meet a need or fulfill a desire that only the Creator can ultimately fulfill, we are committing idolatry. When we use food or substances or sex to fulfill or numb our deep desires, we are engaging in idolatry. Idolatry ultimately spoils life, because we aren't able to enjoy things for what they actually are.

Idolatry is in the air that we breathe, and it's rarely explicit. Most people don't know it's happening. They're not saying, "I want this instead of Christ"; they're saying, "I want Christ *plus* this." To get at the idols of one's heart, one has to step back and consider the way one's desires shape his or her life. What drives us to work (or not work) the way we do? What causes us to eat and drink (or not eat and drink) the way we do? What desires lie behind the way we relate (or don't relate) to our spouse? What do we daydream about? Fantasize about? Long for? Do we often say, "If only I had this . . ." or "If only I were like this . . ."? What is our desire pointing at? What is our affection pulling us toward? What is our end goal? Answering these questions will help one discover some of the layers of idolatry in one's own heart.

Tragically, idolatry inevitably leads to living a double life. The Corinthians' deepest desire was to find a way to serve Christ and still remain acceptable in the public square. They wanted the benefits of the new creational order while still participating in the old creational order. They did not want to stand out. They didn't want their faith in Christ to threaten their ordinary lives. They wanted to participate in the shaping liturgy of the church, while maintaining the shape of the liturgy of the surrounding culture. As a result, they ended up trapped between two different versions of themselves. They were leading double lives. Idolatry isn't a choice between two gods; it is the attempt to serve many gods at the same time. Idolatry is syncretism. Or put another way, idolatry is adultery.[8]

So a man still loves his wife, but there's something over here that he wants. In many cases, when a man is caught cheating, he could potentially be legitimately remorseful. He will claim to love his wife. In some sense he may actually think he loves his wife, but he has lived a life that says otherwise. We tend to think, "I'm not a bad idolater," but every time we look at or bow down to something besides God we are cheating. Idolatry is insidious, ordinary, mundane, subtle, and almost normal. Functionally speaking, we have many lovers besides God. We have given ourselves over to our desires. Idolatry is a sharing, a fellowship, a participation, a yoking with something alongside of our relationship with God, and Paul says this simply can't be. As a result, we find ourselves living double lives. We lack purity of heart and intention; we are duplicitous. We are double-minded with divided hearts.

Genesis 31 tells the story of Rachel, the wife of Jacob. It says in Genesis 29 that she was beautiful in form and appearance. Her older sister, Leah, the text reads, "had weak . . . eyes" (29:17). Rachel was the one who was beautiful, and every suitor was coming to the house of Laban and asking for Rachel and not Leah. Jacob eventually marries both women, but he loved his wife Rachel but didn't love his wife Leah. However, Leah is the one who is now able to bear children and to provide Jacob with their first four sons: Simeon, Reuben, Levi, and Judah. Meanwhile, Rachel is barren. She is the one who has everything—beauty and the love of her husband. Yet because her older sister is having all the children for Jacob, she says, "Give me a child, or I shall die!"(30:1). Jacob is trying to quickly leave the household of Laban, and he is trying to take all of his possessions and go out quietly because Laban had not treated him fairly.

While Rachel's father, Laban, is out in the field, what does she do? She goes into his living quarters and discreetly finds all his idols and his gods and brings them along on the trip. The reader can see that idolatry takes place in her heart before she steals the gods from her father. It was in her heart when she started to think, "Give me a child, or I shall die!" Her over-desire, her liturgy, her commitment, and her preoccupation had to do with finding her meaning through childbearing and through her children.[9]

If anything is desired too much, if it becomes an over-desire, if there's anything in our hearts where we say, "give me this or I will die," we're being double-minded. We're living a double life. We're being adulterous at that very moment.

This is exactly what we *don't* want! We want to be characterized by integrity, sincerity, authenticity, and genuineness. Idolatry impedes our ability to be fully human. Our text communicates that one can be an individual whose life is somewhat shaped by the gospel, who participates in Christ when symbolically we eat his body and drink his blood at the Supper and who participate in the liturgy and life of the church, and yet if we are bound by idols, we are still worshiping other gods. Many of us are in adulterous relationships! We are cheating on God. And he's saying that he wants a monogamous relationship with us. He wants all of the idols out of the picture. If we check out when we hear that—if we think, "that's not me!"—we must carefully heed the words of Paul in verse 12: "Take heed lest [you] fall"— we're being lulled into a false sense of security. How, then, can we escape the grasp of idols that have invaded our lives at the level of ordinary desires?

Escaping Idolatry (Historical)

The true God meets us in the ordinary. In Christ he entered into the fullness of ordinary life. The true God, unlike the idols that we think can fulfill our desires, actually understands our desires because he has experienced them for himself. He wrestled with everything that humans wrestle with, and yet was without sin. He never caved in to idolatry. And because of him, God continues to meet us in the ordinary. How do we participate in Christ, according to Paul? One way is through the Lord's Supper. "Therefore, my beloved, flee from idolatry. I speak as to sensible people; judge for yourselves what I say. The cup of blessing that we bless, is it not a participation in the blood of Christ? The bread that we break, is it not a participation in the body of Christ? Because there is one bread, we who are many are one body, for we all partake of the one bread" (vv. 14–17). It is not a mistake that God makes the sacraments ordinary, physical signs and seals. He feeds us.

The true God meets us at the level of desire. He understands our weaknesses and need for rescue. "No temptation has overtaken you that is not common to man. God is faithful, and he will not let you be tempted beyond your ability, but with the temptation he will also provide the way of escape, that you may be able to endure it" (v. 13). The phrase here to be highlighted is "the way of escape."[10] Even though God brought about the judgment, he provided a way out. Jesus, in the same way—in the midst of our trials, tests, temptations, and adulterous idolatry—provides an escape. He always creates a way of escape from idolatry. Often he uses trials to bring people to the end of themselves—to reveal the emptiness of their idolatry and to cause them to put their trust in him.

The Israelites in the wilderness looked upon God's sign of lifted-up judgment as the means of escape. Looking to Christ, lifted up, receiving the judgment on our behalf, is our means of escape. Jesus is the only one in history for whom no escape was provided. He had nothing for which he needed to repent, no sin of which he was guilty. And yet he suffered the consequences of *our* sin. He chose not to escape in order that we might escape by looking to him. Jesus is our escape from idolatry.

The true God overcomes our adultery with his fidelity. Paul's words can be troubling to those with sensitive consciences. How does one know if he or she is in Christ? How does one know if he or she is escaping idolatry? You may think, "I have had such a difficult fight—I have an adulterous heart!" Here is gospel comfort: we place our trust in the fidelity *of* Christ, not in our fidelity *to* Christ. "For they drank from the spiritual Rock that followed them, and the Rock was Christ" (v. 4).[11] Jesus is the Rock of our assurance. He is the Rock—a sure foundation. He is the Rock that accompanies and follows. He accommodates himself to us in our need and meets us even in our rebellion. Every day God extends himself to his people in the gospel. He has not changed the terms since yesterday. He still gives himself to us in the Lord's Supper; he is not about to temporarily halt the distribution of Communion. The gospel is a once-for-all declaration of free grace. Jesus meets us in the midst of our ordinary life. He meets us on the level of desire, and he shows us fidelity even when we prove to be adulterous. We must flee from idolatry. We must cling to Christ because he clings to us.

19

The Glory of God and the Good of Neighbor

1 CORINTHIANS 10:23—11:1

IN THIS PASSAGE Paul wants to help the Corinthians wisely navigate through the gray areas of life—particularly in the area of food sacrificed to idols. Notice here that Paul does not address the issue on the axis of what an individual should or shouldn't do. He addresses the issue based on what is best for one's neighbor and what will bring the most glory to God. The key to the gray and controversial areas in life is the law of love. Paul's idea of glorifying God through loving our neighbors can be explored in the following three points:

- The Glory of God
- The Good of Neighbor
- The Grace of a Glorious God

The Glory of God (What Does It Mean to Glorify God?) (10:31)

So, whether you eat or drink, or whatever you do, do all to the glory of God.[1]

The idea of the glory of God, or glorifying God, can be slippery. It's a concept that religious people throw around a lot, but one that is rarely reflected upon. In some sense it is hard to make it unslippery because there's no place in our culture where the word *glory* maintains its proper usage. Typically it is used in a negative sense: "That film glorifies violence." "That is a glorified sense of self-importance." It is also used in a self-directed way: "No guts; no glory." "Those were the glory days." *Glory* properly defined is "public praise, honor, and fame." To glorify something is to give glory to it. To glorify is also to light something up brilliantly.[2] Paul suggests that Christians are to live all of their lives, starting with the most ordinary things like eating and drinking, in such a way that God is publicly praised, honored, and made famous. He is indeed weighty and glorious in his being. Paul tells us that all of our desires should ultimately be aimed at making God gloriously known for who he is. Our daily activities, as simple and ordinary as they may be, should be aimed at his glory. The shape of our lives is meant to make the beauty of God light up brilliantly to those around us.

However, people often make the crucial mistake of confining glory-aimed activity to devotion and public worship. Evangelicals have often made the mistake of compartmentalizing their lives and worship. They have neglected the glory-aimed potential of the ordinary because they have focused almost exclusively on matters of piety and explicit praise. As such, they have tended to downplay the importance, significance, and potential for all of life to be glory-aimed. While God does want our piety—our public worship, our spiritual disciplines, etc.—he wants more than that. We need to see the clear connection in the integration of faith and work, God and science, faith and justice, etc., making ourselves available as citizens pursing human flourishing and common good.

It is important to understand that giving glory to God is not simply vertical (between the individual and God) but also horizontal (between the individual and neighbors/communities). God's glory is designed to be gained comprehensively. If this is indeed the case, then what exactly is the nature of the relationship between our doing good to our neighbors and giving glory to God?

The Good of Neighbor (How Does Doing Good to Neighbor Glorify God?) (vv. 23–30)

The call is to think about the choices and decisions we make in light of what is good for our neighbors. In the context of discussing the matter of food sacrificed to idols, Paul is asking, "What are the far-reaching implications for your neighbor?"

Struggling to Love Neighbors (vv. 23–26)

"All things are lawful," but not all things are helpful. "All things are lawful," but not all things build up. Let no one seek his own good, but the good of his neighbor. Eat whatever is sold in the meat market without raising any question on the ground of conscience. For "the earth is the Lord's, and the fullness thereof." (vv. 23–26)

There are two groups within the Corinthian church that Paul is addressing. One can be categorized as *licentious*.[3] He addresses them in verse 23: "All things are lawful." They were using the theological truth of the liberty of the gospel as license to do anything and everything they wanted with little regard for those who disagreed. Then there is the *legalist* whom Paul addresses in verses 25, 26: "Eat whatever is sold in the meat market. . . ." They did not fully understand the liberty they had in the gospel and were applying their scruples to the community at large, thus improperly binding the consciences of their brothers. Paul answers their error by quoting Psalm 24:1 — "The earth is the Orug's, and the fullness thereof" — a verse that was invoked in Jewish mealtime prayers.

In today's church there are both types of people — publicly legalistic people who are privately licentious, and publicly ascetic folks who are privately hedonistic. The word to both groups is the same: "Let no one seek his own good, but the good of his neighbor" (v. 24), The legalists sought their own good and ignored the way their approach bound the conscience of their neighbors. The licentious ones sought their own good and ignored the way their approach scandalized the conscience of their neighbors. The word to both is, "Stop seeking your own good. Seek the good of your neighbor, thereby giving glory to God."

There are three potential approaches to God and neighbor (vv. 27–30). The legalistic pietist was attempting to glorify God without loving his neighbor. "If one of the unbelievers invites you to dinner and you are disposed to go, eat whatever is set before you without raising any question on the ground of conscience" (v. 27). In this view, loving neighbor is unnecessary, but it could be a nice accessory or an add-on to one's devotion. God doesn't actually get glory because it is refracted. This approach would be either robbing God of his glory by ignoring his desire or choosing our desire for self-directed spirituality over God's desires. Consider this example: A typical legalist is invited to a home of an unbeliever. The non-Christian offers meat, which would have been a delicacy at that particular time.[4] Now the legalistic individual is thinking, "Was this meat offered up to those pagan gods?"[5] Rather than simply receiving the offer and giving thanks to God, the legalistic individual hesitates and ultimately refuses the offer. This is not being a good neighbor. For this legalistic individual, doing good to a neighbor is an accessory, not a necessity. Paul wants to steer people away from being privatized moral conformists because they would end up being imperialistic and rigid.

On the other hand, the libertarian individual was attempting to love his neighbor without glorifying God. "But if someone says to you, 'This has been offered in sacrifice,' then do not eat it, for the sake of the one who informed you, and for the sake of conscience — I do not mean your conscience, but his. For why should my liberty be determined by someone else's conscience?" (vv. 28, 29). Paul is addressing those who are more concerned about their own freedom than the good of their neighbor. Paul does not negate Christian liberty, but calls on the believer to give it up for the sake of his brother. The Corinthians were attempting to love their neighbor without directing the act toward the ultimate source of love (i.e., God). In this view, loving one's neighbor is necessary, but it is an end in itself. The self gets glory because it is reflected back. It is robbing God of his glory by ignoring him and by choosing one's desire for self-generated good works over God's desires. A variant of this approach is manifested in apathy toward both God and neighbor. The libertarian individual can also be sectarian against the legalist who wants to restrict his or her rights. This is also prevalent in our contemporary context. Modern-day toleration can become intolerant toward the intolerant, namely the legalists. "Progressive" individuals think religious people are intolerant, so they end up becoming intolerant toward them. This particular modern individual may be saying, "I can be open-minded and recognize the rights of everyone else, but not the religious." Modern-day tolerance can be self-negating and inconsistent.

But there is another way to approach this issue, a third way, namely the gospel-centered approach. This Pauline approach loves one's neighbor in order to glorify God. The love of neighbor is a means of glorifying the God who first loved us.[6] In this view, loving one's neighbor is necessary, but it is not an end in itself — the glory of God is the end to which all means are directed. God gets glory because he receives it by the means through which he has asked to receive it. We are called to give God the glory he deserves in the way he receives it. We must allow God's desire to shape and direct all of our activity to his glory. Through this gospel-centered approach, others become necessary but not sufficient (i.e., there is not a one-to-one correlation between loving God and loving neighbor) and necessary but not exclusive (i.e., there are other ways to glorify God, including the spiritual disciplines, etc.).

The problem is that we are not actually all that interested in loving our neighbors. We wonder, "What's in it for me?" When loving our neighbor is about what we do or do not get out of it, we are not really loving our neighbors — we're simply using them! We are not ultimately interested in giving glory to God; we end up becoming glory thieves. Even when we can objectively acknowledge that God is the supreme being who is ultimately worthy of all glory, we're still looking for a piece of the glory for ourselves.

In his famous sermon "The Weight of Glory," C. S. Lewis writes: "If you are to ask the modern person what is the highest of all virtue, that person would say 'unselfishness' or selflessness. The ancients of old would not have responded that way. That's how the modern person responds. What is the highest virtue of all virtues? The ancients of old would have responded not with unselfishness but they would have responded with the virtue 'love.'" Lewis continues, "The negative ideal of unselfishness carries with it the suggestion not primarily of securing good things for others, but of going without them ourselves as in so far their absences and not their happiness is the important point."[7] It is quite possible to think about love in a negative sense that is too self-referential—it's about selflessness and not really about love. And one can also think of glory in the same manner.

How can a Christian individual move beyond the self-centered cycle? How do we move past the dangers of pietism and legalism? How do we move past the dangers of activism and licentiousness? How do we love our neighbors as ourselves and so bring ultimate glory to God?

The Grace of a Glorious God (10:32—11:1)

> Give no offense to Jews or to Greeks or to the church of God, just as I try to please everyone in everything I do, not seeking my own advantage, but that of many, that they may be saved. (10:32, 33)

The call for Christians is to have an other-centered, self-giving love on a mission. It is to have more concern for the needs and interests of others than for one's own needs (cf. Philippians 2). It is also to be self-giving—not seeking one's own advantage. Paul is calling upon the Corinthian believers to open up by allowing themselves to be disadvantaged for the sake of others. It is love on a mission: "that they may be saved" (10:33). Paul can give out this call because he himself has lived out this call in his own life. This statement is a purpose clause. It is through our other-centered, self-giving posture that we can be good neighbors because we are concerned about their ultimate good, namely their salvation. Though this need not and cannot be the exclusive aim in the way we relate to our neighbors, it must be the primary aim. God is glorified when our love for our neighbors leads them to embrace him. Paul offers himself as a model of this kind of love. His ministry is a model for how one can adapt to all kinds of different settings in order to make the gospel of Christ compelling. But his model is based on the accomplishments and example of one who is even greater. The only way we can be moved out of our self-interest and self-centeredness and live lives of other-centered, self-giving love on a mission is to see that we are the recipients of God's other-centered, self-giving love on a mission in Christ!

"Be imitators of me, as I am of Christ" (11:1). Paul says, "Let no one seek his own good, but the good of his neighbor" (10:24). And Jesus says in essence, "I did not seek my own good but the good of my enemies!" Jesus—the one who was ultimately glorified—in a sense became de-glorified in order that we, his enemies, might be recipients of his love. Jesus was the only person in history who perfectly loved his neighbor (and his enemy) for the glory of God. He fulfilled the Law even while avoiding the trap of legalistic pietism—he never attempted to avoid his neighbors in his glorification of God. He secured and exercised freedom even while avoiding the trap of hedonistic activism—he never attempted to use his neighbors to gain glory for himself. Christians can love their neighbors for the glory of God because Jesus loved us—his enemies—for the glory of God. We can disadvantage ourselves for others because Jesus ultimately disadvantaged himself for us.

How does receiving the other-centered, self-giving love of God on a mission in Jesus change the human heart? Our spiritual capital is no longer invested in trying to get God's love but in demonstrating the love that we have been given. Tullian Tchividjian states:

> [W]hen we understand that everything between God and us has been fully and finally made right—that Christians live their life under a banner that reads "It is finished"—we necessarily turn away from ourselves and turn toward our neighbor. Forever freed from our need to pay God back or secure God's love and acceptance, we are now free to love and serve others. We work for others horizontally because God has worked for us vertically. The Christian lives from belovedness to loving action. His love for us begets love from us. . . . Because everything we need, in Christ we already possess, we're now free to do everything for others without needing others to do anything for us. We can now actively spend our lives giving instead of taking, going to the back instead of getting to the front, sacrificing myself for others instead of sacrificing others for myself.[8]

This sort of truth protects Christians from being concerned about the verdicts people place on them. Every day we desire to hear the kind of verdict that declares that we are good, competent, and worthy. So we walk around daily performing because we know that we are always on trial. Our lives are fixated on other people's responses. Paul's solution to this insecurity is to know that the trial is over. There's no longer any condemnation for those who are in Christ Jesus (Romans 8:1). It is immensely encouraging to know that because Christ has gone to trial for us, we are no longer on trial. As a matter of fact, the court is adjourned. We are free to love our neighbors and to glorify our God. We're no longer in the courtroom. We are newly motivated lovers because our affections have been steered by the beautiful picture of Jesus going to trial in our place and giving us all the advantages that he had. He gave up his rights so that we might utilize our rights not to be sectarian and to abuse or to ignore other people, but rather to lovingly serve them and to be disadvantaged for their good. We now can live a life of freedom that doesn't abuse our liberties but instead uses them for the glory of God by loving our neighbors.

In John 21 Jesus confronts Peter who had betrayed him, and he asks him three times, "Do you love me?" Peter is broken, completely shattered, but he also loves Jesus. Jesus does not give Peter a recovery program; instead, in the midst of his brokenness, Jesus tasks him with one thing: "Feed my sheep"—care for my people. What Jesus is trying to do for Peter at that very moment is to help him understand that loving God means loving one's neighbor. Likewise, glorifying God means doing good for one's neighbor. Like Peter, we too are broken in our sin—we deny Christ and rob God's glory with our self-centered lives. But God tells us that even though we've betrayed him, he reinstates us. We need to reflect on this radical, restoring love and share it with others.[9]

20

Issues in the Worshiping Community

1 CORINTHIANS 11:2–16

THIS TEXT REPRESENTS A thought transition in the letter. Paul has been talking about how the members of the church were exercising their rights and liberties in the world—outside of the context of worship. Here Paul begins to talk about how the members of the church should exercise their rights and liberties within the church—in the context of worship. There is a shift from the life of the church in the world to the life of the church in the church. In chapters 11—14 Paul addresses a number of different issues in the life of the church such as head coverings, the Lord's Supper, spiritual gifts, prophecy and tongues, and orderly worship.[1]

Verses 2 and 16 clearly set the passage in this context: "Now I commend you because you *remember me* in everything and *maintain the traditions* even as I delivered them to you" (v. 2). They remember Paul's apostolic office and Paul's apostolic teachings (i.e., "the traditions" that he had passed down). "If anyone is inclined to be contentious, we have *no such practice*, nor do the churches of God" (v. 16). The Corinthians are encouraged to conform their worship practice to that of the universal church. Thus, the primary thrust of the passage is about how the church can please God in worship. Paul is calling the church to evaluate its worship practices to ensure that all due attention is being drawn to God and no undue attention is being drawn to the members of the church.

God asks us to consider three things in the context of corporate worship and the propriety of worship:

- The Scandalous Freedom of Worship
- The Scandalous Order of Worship
- The Scandalous Reality of Divine Love

The Scandalous Freedom of Worship

Dispelling Misconceptions about This Passage

First, it is very likely that readers today, Christians or not, bristle when they read or hear this text. There is a significant cultural distance between us and the Corinthian church. Some of the things that were common to them seem strange to us; of course, much of what is common to us would be incomprehensible to them. But there is significant overlap between us as well, particularly on the level of principle. Though the application of Biblical principles can take various forms in different cultures, the principles stand.

Second, the text is not simply addressed to women. There is actually structural balance between women and men in the passage, with only one verse addressed to women that doesn't have a parallel addressed to men (v. 10).

Third, the text does not leave individuals with only two interpretive options. Some liberal camps seek to dismiss Paul's words and intention altogether. Some conservative, traditionalist camps pursue a strict adherence to the letter of Paul's words, missing the underlying principle and spirit. There is a third-way: "liberated traditionalism."[2]

Setting the Stage by Considering the Background

The issue at hand was attire in Christian worship. "Every man who prays or prophesies with his head covered dishonors his head" (v. 4). Some men were wearing head coverings and/or growing their hair out in a way that reflected the attire worn by pagans in idolatrous worship. It was an attempt to assimilate idolatrous culture. This scandalized the church. ". . . but every wife who prays or prophesies with her head uncovered dishonors her head, since it is the same as if her head were shaven" (v. 5). Some women were eschewing the common cultural practice of wearing their hair up and/or wearing a covering of some sort on their head during worship. In the freedom of worship they allowed their hair to hang down on their shoulders. This implied that they were "available."[3] It was an attempt to move past cultural norms. This scandalized the culture. Paul's remarks only make sense when the reader understands that . . .

The Church Was a Progressive Cultural Institution

The freedom afforded to the members of the congregation in worship was scandalous in that culture. Women were encouraged to pray and prophesy.

Verse 5 assumes this: "every wife who prays or prophesies." This was in contrast to Jewish synagogue worship where women were not considered full members and were required to sit behind a veil. In the Christian church, women were to be full congregational participants in the worship service— unheard of.[4] Christianity recognizes the full equality and interdependence of the sexes. Both were made in the image of God. Genesis 1:27 tells us: "So God created man in his own image, in the image of God he created him; male and female he created them." Paul calls on the Corinthians to recognize this interdependence in verses 11, 12: "in the Lord woman is not independent of man nor man of woman; for as woman was made from man, so man is now born of woman. And all things are from God."

This understanding of interdependence and equality would have been scandalous and unheard of. It was a challenge to a hierarchical society in which women were understood as less than. The equality and interdependence of the sexes afforded the Corinthians scandalous freedom in worship. Christians today enjoy this same freedom as they worship God in a diverse, unified community. Together Christians approach him without regard to age, ethnicity, class, or gender. However, it is possible that an overemphasis on liberality may threaten "traditions" (i.e., apostolic, Biblical teaching; v. 2). It is possible to embrace these Scriptural truths and yet ignore some of the clear teaching of Scripture. That is what the Corinthians were doing—they were neglecting the scandalous order of worship.

The Scandalous Order of Worship

Paul's purpose is not to cause the Corinthians to abandon their freedoms and liberties, but to direct them in the way they can best exercise their liberties to the glory of God in corporate worship. It is at this point that many begin to bristle. Consider verse 3: "But I want you to understand that the head of every man is Christ, the head of a wife is her husband, and the head of Christ is God." The liberality that God's grace engenders is paradoxically character- ized by order.

Rooted in the Trinitarian Order

"The head of Christ is God." Whatever Paul means by "the head of a wife is her husband" can't be understood to denigrate, downplay, or threaten her stance as an equal because Christ also has a head. The Son joyfully chooses to submit himself to the Father. Paul is not saying anything about one's es- sence. The beauty of this passage here is that he roots this in the Trinitarian order. He is saying that in the Trinity the Father, the Son, and the Spirit are equal in being and essence, but they willingly choose to fulfill different functions and roles for the purpose of communicating communal love. In other words, looking at Jesus and recognizing his willingness to subordinate himself to the will of the Father in the Trinitarian economy is a sign of humility and strength and not weakness. I believe that looking at the husband and wife relationship from that lens frees us to be able to see the beauty of it.

Displayed in the Creational Order

The heart of Paul's prohibition is essentially this: "Do not unintentionally scandalize the order of creation." God created human beings in his image — male and female, and the members of each gender have the privilege to uniquely display God's image. Even though they are completely equal, there is an order to creation: "For a man ought not to cover his head, since he is the image and glory of God, but woman is the glory of man. For man was not made from woman, but woman from man. Neither was man created for woman, but woman for man" (vv. 7–9). Paul is not stating anything new. Genesis tells us that Eve was created in light of Adam's lack of a suitable mate.[5] When he finally laid eyes on her he said, "This at last is bone of my bones and flesh of my flesh" (Genesis 2:23). When God looks at man, he sees his own image. When man looks at woman, he sees his image.

When Christians display this creational order in worship (and in marriage), God is pleased. Gender distinctions are not a curse to be covered, but a blessing to be celebrated.

Paul is essentially saying, "Everyone willingly submits to something. Don't conduct yourself in a way that would dishonor the one to whom you are submitting." Men, don't dishonor God by adopting idolatrous dress in worship. Women, don't dishonor God and your husband by adopting dress that calls your marital status into question. Paul is insinuating that some women were skewing the common cultural practice of wearing their hair or wearing a covering of some sort on their head during worship. They felt as though they had freedom in their worship, which they did, and they allowed their hair to hang down on their shoulders. We must understand that the cultural norm, whether in the church or even in the Greco-Roman world, was for women to wear not necessarily a full veil but a shawl to cover their heads.

This strange issue of course is confusing in our modern culture. In fact, it would seem odd for a woman to wear a shawl, veil, or some sort of head covering in corporate worship. But in that particular culture not to wear a shawl meant that the woman was essentially saying, "I'm not too concerned with the relationship with my husband," because for a married woman to take her shawl off and let her hair loose like that and not be covered by a head covering would have meant she was saying, "I am available."

One commentator says: "The only woman who did not wear them were the *hetairai*, who were the 'high-class' mistresses of influential Corinthians. Also, slaves had their heads shaved, and the same practice [was] enacted as punishment for convicted adulteresses"; that is, they would shave their heads.[6] So apparently in the excitement of worship, certain women were tempted to throw back their hair, and Paul is saying, "That's probably what you ought not to do in this context, as important as it is for you to be able to recognize the freedom of worship."

A Part of the Cultural Order

Another aspect of Paul's instruction is that he doesn't want the Corinthians to do anything that will unnecessarily scandalize the cultural order. "Judge for yourselves: is it proper for a wife to pray to God with her head uncovered? Does not nature itself teach you that if a man wears long hair it is a disgrace for him, but if a woman has long hair, it is her glory? For her hair is given to her for a covering" (vv. 13–15). Paul may be addressing an overemphasis on tradition that threatens personal liberty. Paul makes a direct appeal to "nature," by which he means "the way things are." He obviously knows that men can have long hair (Nazirite vows), but he appeals to common practice to buttress his case. His argument does not strike us as airtight because our cultural context makes this much less self-evident.

Note on Contextualization

One has to get to the principle (creational order) and determine how that applies in the present cultural order. Obedience to this section of the Word of God in this day and age more likely means *not* wearing head coverings because the culture would be needlessly scandalized in an overemphasized view of legalistic practices. God desires Christians to reflect the Trinitarian and creational orders in such a way that we do not unnecessarily scandalize the cultural order. If the danger of freedom is that one can express liberty at the expense of the apostolic tradition, the danger of order is that individuals can fall into the error of hierarchicalism and traditionalism that chokes out liberty. The nuance we're looking for is: liberated tradition.[7] The trouble is that individuals tend to lean toward one or the other. Although there are still pockets of unchecked traditionalism, many tend toward unchecked liberalism. The call is for expressing one's freedom within the order God has set out in creation, an order intended to lead to maximum human flourishing. But how can one trust that God actually knows what is best for human flourishing?

The Scandalous Reality of Divine Love

Kathy Keller writes:

> Justice, in the end, is whatever God decrees. . . . So whether or not you are able to see justice in divinely created gender roles depends largely on how much trust you have in God's character. . . . If trust must be earned, hasn't God unequivocally earned our trust with the bark on the raw wounds, the thorns pressed into the brow, your name on the cracked lips? [And if God can be trusted, then] gender roles, with all of God's gifts to human beings, are to be rejoiced in and enjoyed, not endured and resented.[8]

The Trinitarian reality allows the reader to understand our place within a liberating tradition. Whatever prescribed order one finds in creation is a result of God's good design and is intended to reflect his very nature. The Son did not have to submit to the Father for any reason besides redemption for humanity. He was not forced or coerced; he willingly submitted in order to secure our salvation. Personal deference and self-giving are a part of the fingerprint of the one who made us. Yes, our attempts at reflecting this are fallen, broken, etc. Yes, there are abuses. But the loving submission that the reader sees on display in the Trinity offers individuals a window into what redeemed human relationships might look like. Seeing the relationship of the Father and the Son enables individuals to disinfect their views of differences in role or function. The relationship that Christ has to the Father is the ultimately enviable/desirable relationship, and it takes the shape of willing submission. This allows one to see that submission is not a denigration but a beautiful expression of love.

This is ultimately seen in a sacrificial reality that allows us to take our place within the liberated tradition. Ultimately Christ, though he is the head, laid down his life for the church.

> Wives, submit to your own husbands, as to the Lord. For the husband is the head of the wife even as Christ is the head of the church, his body, and is himself its Savior. Now as the church submits to Christ, so also wives should submit in everything to their husbands.
> Husbands, love your wives, as Christ loved the church and gave himself up for her, that he might sanctify her, having cleansed her by the washing

of water with the word, so that he might present the church to himself in splendor, without spot or wrinkle or any such thing, that she might be holy and without blemish. In the same way husbands should love their wives as their own bodies. He who loves his wife loves himself. For no one ever hated his own flesh, but nourishes and cherishes it, just as Christ does the church, because we are members of his body. (Ephesians 5:22–30)

All roles in Christian marriage are informed by Christ's relationship with the church. There is nothing regressive, dictatorial, or heavy-handed about Christ's relationship with the church. He gives himself up to and beyond the point of death in order to save his bride. He gives himself up to beautify his bride. Husbands are to give themselves up. They are to love their wives as their own bodies. Wives are invited to be recipients of and responders to the sacrificial giving of their husbands. When one's marriage fails to reflect this beautiful, artistic balance, there is abundant grace. Individuals are equal and interdependent, and they function in relationships of mutual self-giving.

And all of this is from God the Father (the head of Christ) and from Christ who is the head of his church. This grace drives us to live lives that reflect God's good creational order in a way that compels (rather than unnecessarily scandalizes) the culture. The relationships of Christian men and women become the mystery that displays the gospel to a watching world.

21

Discerning the Body

1 CORINTHIANS 11:17–34

FEW ACTS are more expressive of companionship than the shared meal. . . .
Someone with whom we share food is likely to be our friend, or well on the
way to becoming one."[1] In an ideal world the dinner table is far more than a
functional space where human beings mechanistically refuel by themselves.
The dinner table is a place where community is created and sustained. The
dinner table is a place where hospitality is extended and conversation experienced. It is also a place where communal dysfunction or breakdown is seen
and felt.[2] Meals carry values; they tell stories about the people who have
prepared them, the people who partake of them, and even about the people
who are excluded.

In the city of Corinth a meal was "an occasion for gaining or showing
social status. . . . It [was] in many regards a microcosm of the aspirations and
aims of the culture as a whole."[3] A dinner party would have been one of the
primary places where one could observe intense social stratification.[4] The
Lord's Supper was designed to demonstrate something radically different.
It was intended to create, sustain, and display an alternate community—an
upside-down social order. The Lord's Supper is the meal, the dinner table,
the food, and the sustenance of a gospel-shaped community. Today some
Christians rely on retreats and special conferences to gain gospel renewal
in their lives. While these special occasions and venues may be helpful and
even important, what believers in the church need to understand is that God,
through the Lord's Supper, is able to regularly tune our hearts to him. When
we experience this vertical attunement with him, it affects the ways we relate
to other people socially and horizontally. Paul is asking Christians to shift

their focus to the communal, sociological implications of the Lord's Supper. His thoughts can be traced through the following three points:

- The Beauty of the Lord's Supper in Community
- The Challenge of the Lord's Supper in a Fractured Community
- The Grace of the Lord's Supper for a Fractured Community

The Beauty of the Lord's Supper in Community

The Lord's Supper as a Vertical Means of Grace

This subject has raised many theological questions throughout church history.[5] Many approach this text through a personal and theological lens. The following views[6] are presented to guide our thoughts concerning the Lord's Supper.

The Supper as Memorial

Christ is understood to be subjectively present in the mind of the believer. Communion, then, is mostly about a person's ability to focus upon, think through, and remember the death of Christ. The problem is that the grace of Communion is dependent on one's ability to recall. If one is broken and can't focus, it leaves no consolation. What happens if an individual doesn't want to recall, or there is gospel amnesia or forgetfulness, or a heart is not inclined to wanting to remember what Jesus Christ has done? There is no consolation for the one who cannot remember or recall if the Supper is simply a memorial.

The Supper as Ritual

Christ is objectively present in the bread and cup. Communion is mostly about a mechanistic, mystical process whereby bread and wine are transformed into something that must be ingested to fulfill religious duty. The problem with this approach is that it is impersonal. It "works" regardless of one's relationship to Christ. Unlike the first view, where the emphasis heavily lies on the subject (the person), this view focuses on the importance of the object (the bread and cup).

A Third Way: The Supper as Spiritual Communion

"The cup of blessing that we bless, is it not a participation in the blood of Christ? The bread that we break, is it not a participation in the body of Christ?" (10:16). The objective reality of Christ's work is subjectively appropriated by the work of the Spirit. Christ is really spiritually (but not physically) present—but not in a mechanistic sense. The Christian's subjective experience is important—but not in an instrumental sense. In the Lord's Supper, Christians commune with God in Christ through the Holy Spirit. In the language of the Westminster Catechism, readers "feed upon his body and blood, to [our] spiritual nourishment and growth in grace."[7] Paul asks the reader to move beyond theologizing to consider the function of the Supper in the life of the church.

What should the Lord's Supper do in the believer's experience? What are the horizontal realities of this meal? This passage presents an inverted picture of how grace is supposed to function in community. ". . . when you come together it is not for the better but for the worse. For, in the first place, when you come together as a church, I hear that there are divisions among you" (vv. 17, 18a). The "better" that the church is supposed to display is the common divisions of society (social status, race, class, wealth, gender, etc.) being overcome. However, the Corinthians are divided. Paul sees this as being somewhat inevitable but not pardonable. ". . . And I believe it in part, for there must be factions among you in order that those who are genuine among you may be recognized." While the anti-gospel divisions are inexcusable, at the very least God can use them to reveal genuinely gospel-shaped Christians. "When you come together, it is not the Lord's supper that you eat. For eating, each one goes ahead with his own meal. One goes hungry, another gets drunk" (vv. 18b–21). Christians are intended to share one common meal. The broken body and spilled blood of Christ eradicate divisions that would be present elsewhere in the city's culture. Whereas most groups divide up along the lines of rich/poor and free/slave, the church is to be the one institution where things get flipped upside down.

The church is also the place where people approach God's creational gifts (such as food and wine) with an orderly, God-glorifying enjoyment. But the Corinthian believers are overindulging. They are doing it at the expense of other believers who have nothing to drink or eat. When Christians eat common bread and drink from a common cup, it is a symbol, a visual representation, of the common divisions and disunities of our world being conquered in Christ. We tend to marginalize others who are different than we are. We tend to alienate people as "the other" because they are not like us. Therefore, rather than being concerned about their interests, we place ourselves at the center and ask everyone else to revolve around us. But the beauty of the Lord's Supper is that there is a common bread and a common cup. It is a visual representation of the fact that the common divisions and the disunities of our world are overcome in Christ.

The Challenge of the Lord's Supper in a Fractured Community

Corinth was a fractured community, and this was evident in their gatherings. Blomberg explains the setting of this fractured community in the following way:

> Once again Paul refers to "divisions." But here he is not thinking of the rival parties that possibly separate various congregations but of the gulf between the rich and poor within a given house-church. The minority of well-to-do believers, including the major financial supporters and owners of the homes in which the believers met, would have had the leisure-time and resources to arrive earlier and bring larger quantities and finer food than the rest of the congregation. Following the practice of hosting festive gatherings in ancient Corinth, they would have quickly filled the small private dining room. Latecomers (the majority, who probably had to finish work before coming on Saturday or Sunday evening—there was as of yet no legalized day off in the Roman empire) would be seated separately in the adjacent atrium or courtyard. Those that could not afford to bring a full meal, or a very good one, did not have the opportunity to share with the rest in the way that Christian unity demanded.[8]

Paul isn't so much interested in the elements or the distribution—this is a social justice issue. There is "a marked social stratification."[9] The irony here is that the very thing that was supposed to ground their unity (the sign and seal of Christ's work) had become the place where their divisions were expressed. The thing that was supposed to eradicate their divisions was exacerbating them. Rather than reflecting the self-giving love of Christ, they were accumulating for themselves. "When you come together, it is not the Lord's supper that you eat. For in eating, each one goes ahead with his own meal" (vv. 20, 21a). It is no longer the Lord's Supper—they have made it their own meal! They have profaned it to the point that it is unrecognizable. They have twisted the sacrament from being about Christ's accomplishments to being a "sacrament" of their own accomplishments. It no longer reflects their need; it reflects their prominence and importance.

Paul is essentially saying, "You may be carrying out the ritual, but your life shows evidence that it's not sinking in!" They were gorging themselves and getting drunk in the dining room, while the people in the atrium were starving with nothing to eat. This is exactly what was going on in Corinth. Whether they did it by design or by default, the majority of the people who were poor were alienated and excluded. They were considered second-class citizens in their participation. "For in eating, each one goes ahead with his own meal. One goes hungry, another gets drunk. What! Do you not have

houses to eat and drink in? Or do you despise the church of God and humili-
ate those who have nothing?" (vv. 21, 22a). This is a picture of communal
breakdown. Paul's response is only natural: "What shall I say to you? Shall
I commend you in this? No, I will not" (v. 22b).

Paul is saying that this cannot be the picture of the church. Lucian, an
ancient writer, vividly describes this painful picture: "You eat oysters, fat-
tened, from the lake, while I suck a mussel through a hole in the shell. You
get mushrooms while I get hog funguses. Golden with fat, a turtle dove
gorges you with its bloated rump, but a magpie that has died in his cages
is set before me."[10] This is the reality of a fractured community. Nobody
deserves the leftovers. No one in the Christian community should get the
scraps. The beauty of the gospel of Jesus Christ must be alive and active to
overcome all of the barriers in a fractured community.

If the broken reality of this world repeatedly shows up in the Lord Supper, should we abandon it altogether because it has not yet created the community that we are called to be? Absolutely not! We must dig deeper into the
reality of grace that is offered in the body and blood of Christ.

The Grace of the Lord's Supper for a Fractured Community

There is *historical grace* (vv. 23–25), looking back to Jesus' historical work
on our behalf. "For I received from the Lord what I also delivered to you,
that the Lord Jesus on the night when he was betrayed took bread, and when
he had given thanks, he broke it, and said, 'This is my body which is for you.
Do this in remembrance of me.' In the same way also he took the cup,[11] after
supper, saying, 'This cup is the new covenant in my blood. Do this, as often
as you drink it, in remembrance of me'" (vv. 23–25). The Supper is a sign
and seal of Christ's redemptive work on behalf of a fractured community.
Christ, the ultimately loyal one, was betrayed so that Christians, the great
betrayers, might receive the steadfast, loyal love of God. It is rooted in the
history of what has happened to God's people throughout Israelite history. In
the Lord's Supper we see the fulfillment of the Passover meal.[12] The Passover
meal had certain notable elements. The four cups were to remind the partici-
pant of Exodus 6, where God makes four promises concerning the Israelites'
deliverance and freedom.

Jesus was there as the presider of the Passover meal, completely revolu-
tionizing people's mind-sets. A typical Jewish understanding of the Passover
would have reminded them of the sacrificial system. But Jesus interrupted
this typical Passover meal by saying, "This is my body." He is essentially
saying, "I am the bread of life" (John 6:35). He was revealing to the watch-

ing world that he is indeed the fulfillment of all that was symbolized in the Passover meal. To ensure that sight is not lost, the one continuing sacrament that he set up is centered upon his death on our behalf. The breaking of his literal body binds Christians together in his mystical body. Communion together is based upon his relentless grace. Christ's blood removes every barrier — socioeconomic, racial, class, gender, age, etc.

There is also future grace, looking forward to Jesus' return on our behalf. "For as often as you eat this bread and drink the cup, you proclaim the Lord's death until he comes" (v. 26). The Lord's Supper calls Christians toward the future when Christ will return to make all things right. Though our present situation may be dire, the Lord's Supper causes us to look forward with hope. Participating in the Lord's Supper is a "proclamation" that Jesus is our sustenance in this world — the sufficiency of his death is proclaimed for our salvation and hope.[13]

Then there is *personal grace*, looking through self-examination in light of Jesus' work. "Whoever, therefore, eats the bread or drinks the cup of the Lord in an unworthy manner will be guilty concerning the body and blood of the Lord. Let a person examine himself, then, and so eat of the bread and drink of the cup" (vv. 27, 28). Note that Paul says "unworthy manner," not "unworthy individual." He is not concerned about whether or not the reader deserves to approach the Lord's Table. It is a question of whether one is approaching with indifference or an unrepentant heart.[14] If one is afflicted by sin, the Supper is comfort. If an individual is comfortable with sin, the Supper is affliction. Paul is calling the Christians to examine themselves, not to find reasons they are unworthy, but to find evidence of a repentant heart — evidence that grace is at work. If a believer has a repentant heart, he or she should be coming to the Table. Paul wants believers to examine themselves not for perfection, but for recognition of their need of Christ's perfection on their behalf. The only time Christians should refrain from the Table is when they find hardened apathy within themselves about their relationship with God and/or others. God provides a regular portion of his grace for sinners at the Table, so they are encouraged to relish it, celebrate it, enjoy it, and feed on Christ. The key is to keep solemnity and celebration in tension. We can look toward solemnity because of its significance and to celebration because of what Christ has done.

There is also *communal grace* (vv. 29–34), looking around to "discern the body." "For anyone who eats and drinks without discerning the body eats and drinks judgment on himself" (v. 29). Paul is calling people to look around them. "Discern the body" is a reference to the church. Jesus' body is broken for believers so they can be whole. Division within a Christian body is not a faithful proclamation of the gospel. Christians are to consider their relationships with other members as they rejoice in healthy and fruitful relationships. If there are ways in which the community is encouraging social, racial, or economic stratification, then the members need to repent. The grace of God needs to permeate our relationships, to put us around those who are unlike us. Christians need to seek to dismantle systemic disunity. When we realize that Christ was torn up and broken for us, we can then begin to pursue gift distribution rather than personal accumulation. "So then, my brothers, when you come together to eat, wait for one another—if anyone is hungry, let him eat at home—so that when you come together it will not be for judgment" (vv. 33, 34a). "Wait for one another" means to put others' needs before our own because Christ put our needs before his. We can refrain from gorging ourselves because Christ refrained for our sake.

Don Carson in his book *Love in Hard Places* writes, "[The church] is made up of natural enemies. What binds us together is not common education, common race, common income levels, common politics, common nationality, common accents, common jobs, or anything else of that sort. Christians come together because they have all been saved by Jesus Christ and owe him a common allegiance . . . they are a band of natural enemies who love one another for Jesus' sake."[15]

There's a beautiful picture of this in the early church. In Acts 16 we read about the membership of Lydia's house church. One historian observes that the three converts in this passage represent different races. Lydia was Asian, the slave girl was probably Greek, and the Philippian jailor was Roman. But they also came from different economic classes. Lydia was white-collar, the slave girl was poor, and the jailor was from the working class. They come from different cognitive styles too. Lydia was rational, the slave girl was intuitive, and the jailor was concretely relational. The gospel led them to embrace one another, referring to each other as "brothers" and of course sisters (Acts 16:40). In the ancient world a common prayer could have been said something along this line: "God, I thank you that I'm not a woman, a slave, or a Gentile." What we find in Acts 16 is a community that is comprised of different types of people—marginalized people who were saved by the relentless grace of God. The Lord's Supper reveals the vertical aspects of what it means to be in union with God through the Lord Jesus Christ, but there are also horizontal and social implications for what it means to put others' needs first.

22

A Gift-Giving God

1 CORINTHIANS 12:1–11

THE LAST CHAPTER addressed the socioeconomic stratification and the divisions between the rich and the poor that were evident in the life and practice of the church at Corinth. Paul was shocked. The lifestyle of the church and the way it mirrored the division of the broader culture were antithetical to the gospel of grace that the Corinthians had received. In our current passage Paul addresses spiritual status stratification. The members of the church are looking at one another and are placing value judgments on one another based on performance, competence, and charisma. Some members have more "impressive" talents, skills, and gifts than others, and the Corinthian obsession with power and status is causing them to overvalue some members' contributions and to undervalue the contributions of others. In this context Paul is looking to level the playing field—to underscore the inherent equality of all of the members and what they bring to the community.

This passage represents another thought transition in the letter, as Paul begins with, "Now concerning spiritual gifts . . ." (v. 1). The word *pneumatikon* here is different than the word for gifts in verse 4 (*charismata*). The word in verse 1 is probably best translated "spiritual things." The Corinthians have written a letter to Paul, and they are interested in learning about "spiritual things," and Paul says, "I do not want you to be uninformed." This indicates that what Paul wants them to take note of is an important subject.[1] Paul's logic on the important matter of "spiritual things" will be examined in three different movements:

- The Givenness of Gifts
- The Reception of Gifts
- The Giver of Gifts

The Givenness of Gifts

Paul's discussion of "spiritual gifts" may sound odd to some, especially skeptics. What in the world are spiritual gifts? Does God actually endow Christians with gifts, talents, and abilities that he doesn't give to others? "Spiritual gifts" is a common category for the kinds of things that individuals do not quite understand. Individuals misunderstand "spiritual gifts" when they understand them as being primarily miraculous in nature. According to D. A. Carson, "spiritual gifts" can also be translated as "grace gifts."[2] Spiritual gifts are not something on top of grace or better than grace, but are manifestations of God's grace to his people. At their core, spiritual gifts are *gifts*; they are given things. One cannot merit or earn a grace gift. It is something that is given that one does not deserve.

This is difficult for individuals to understand because of the achievement-focused cultural context in which we live. Although people understand the language of *gift*, they do not live in a culture where a pure gift is an operative category. Even celebrations that include gifts typically reflect attachment to the economy of achievement. "Gifts" are given to people to mark out their achievements. Children receive "gifts" at Christmastime for being nice as opposed to being naughty. Graduating seniors get "gifts" to mark their success in completing a program. "Gifts" are given to mark occasions of cultural advancement (wedding, promotion, retirement). Acts of kindness that are not attached to achievement are rare and strikingly beautiful. Meaning is found in what is achieved, won, and earned, and achievement gives individuals a sense of accomplishment, and winning assures them that they are special. What earning does for individuals is that it assures them they have rights and entitlements. Because lives are filtered through an achievement-centered culture, even encounters with gifts are marred by performance-ism. "Gifts" are seen as things that can be achieved or earned. Wish lists are elaborately created for loved ones to consult. When one receives a "gift" that he or she does not like, he or she returns it or regifts it. Individuals believe they have earned the right to pick and choose even the gifts that they receive. Have you ever felt cheated when you bought a nicer gift for your spouse than he or she bought for you? Doesn't your act of "gifting" earn for you the right to receive an equally valuable and desirable gift?

I was once speaking with one of my church members who is a faculty member of an elite university in Boston. He had received a very selective, prestigious research grant for which he had applied. Then he started to receive polite emails from all of his colleagues who said, "We're proud of you, and it is well deserved . . . well deserved . . . well deserved." He appreciated the fact that others were saying "well deserved," but he was challenging that whole notion by saying, "Did I really deserve this?" It was a very keen moment of awareness for this man because most people tend to think, "Of course I deserve it. I've worked hard for this. I'm where I am because of all that I've achieved."

An achievement mentality is poisonous. It pollutes self-understanding. One thinks he deserves a better life than the one he currently has, and he thinks he can procure it for himself if he expends the effort. We thus are unable to see the givenness of all of life. In the midst of an achievement culture Paul calls for a paradigm shift. He wants us to think of our identity as a gift. "You know that when you were pagans you were led astray to mute idols, however you were led. Therefore I want you to understand that no one speaking in the Spirit of God ever says 'Jesus is accursed!' and no one can say 'Jesus is Lord' except in the Holy Spirit" (vv. 2, 3). In this pluralistic world, individuals pride themselves on making informed, intellectual decisions about religion and worldview. While Paul never downplays the importance of engaging the mind, asking good questions, or expressing and addressing doubts and issues, he does make the radical claim that there is no such thing as becoming a Christian by achievement! The fundamental identity of a Christian—defined by the confession of faith "Jesus is Lord"—is not something that can be achieved, earned, or arrived at via self-exertion. The confession of faith can only be made "in the Holy Spirit." Faith is given; it is a gift. This removes all pride and ego because an individual's abilities and skills are all gifts.

Amazingly, Paul makes the claim that much of what Christians conceive of as temperament and natural ability is actually a "gift." The fundamental and practical identities are given things. Gifts (v. 4),[3] services (v. 5),[4] and activities (v. 6)[5] are all given because God "empowers them all in everyone" (v. 6). This is a direct challenge and threat to an achievement-oriented culture and the idea that I am what I do/earn/obtain. Furthermore, the things that we have been given are not first and foremost for the purpose of investing for self-gain or selfish return. The purpose of gifts is for giving. "To each is given the manifestation of the Spirit for the common good" (v. 7). Gifts are given in order that a believer might contribute to "the common good."[6] The end goal of one's identity and abilities is not the building up of self but the building up of others. An intended dynamic of gift-giving is meant to be at play.

Admittedly, it is difficult to conceive of one's identities and abilities as gifts. Individuals have a hard time determining what their gifts are precisely because they view so much of who they are as something they have created or earned. Many others may think, "I'm not gifted" or "I don't know what my gifts are." This is a common thought, and we can sort it out briefly in our second point.

The Reception of Gifts

Everyone has received a gift (or gifts) from God. "To each is given the manifestation of the Spirit for the common good" (v. 7). In this second point the attention will be on the "to-each-ness" of gifts. This is a great comfort to anyone who has ever wondered, "Am I gifted?" "Do I have anything to contribute?" "What do I have to bring to the community?" "What are my gifts?" Every single believer has received a gift that is intended to be used "for the common good." Individuals do not need to be in doubt about their giftedness. Gifts are not worked up to, but are lived into. They are not things that one earns, but things that one is. Spiritual gifts are grace gifts, and anyone who has experienced the grace of God in Christ can be certain that they have received a grace gift that is intended to be used for "the common good." That is the encouragement. But here is the challenge: If Christians are not exercising and using their particular gifts, whatever they might be, for the common good, they are depriving the rest of the body. They are withholding and being stingy with their gifts. Every Christian has a responsibility to bless the rest of the community with his or her gift matrix or gift mix. Many tend to think, "I can't bless anyone," but Paul says, "Of course you can! Because *to each* is given . . ."

A grace gift is uniquely fitted to each individual. And there is amazing variety to the gifts that God gives. "For to one is given through the Spirit the utterance of wisdom,[7] and to another the utterance of knowledge[8] according to the same Spirit, to another faith[9] by the same Spirit, to another gifts of healing[10] by the one Spirit, to another the working of miracles,[11] to another prophecy,[12] to another the ability to distinguish between spirits,[13] to another various kinds of tongues,[14] to another the interpretation of tongues" (vv. 8–10).[15] Though there is not enough space here to address each of these grace gifts, the great variety that is present should be observed. This is not a comprehensive list. This leads the reader to believe that the Scriptures' lists of grace gifts are not necessarily comprehensive. It is reasonable to believe that specific spiritual gifts extend beyond the lists that one finds in Scripture, although the types or categories of gifts are listed. Furthermore, these gifts are to be differentiated from natural abilities.

All human beings have been blessed and given all sorts of talents, competencies, and abilities at the level of creation through God's common grace. Everyone has been given the opportunity to beautify the world through common grace. But that sort of competency, ability, or talent is not the same as encouraging someone spiritually through a grace gift. Through a grace gift a Christian is essentially asserting the reality that Jesus is Lord over every dimension of life. And not everyone can do that merely with natural, creational competencies and gifts. So grace gifts have been given for a believer to faithfully steward and cultivate the resources of the gift matrix that God has given. Tim Keller has stated, "No one is merely a consumer of services, but everyone is a distributor." A Christian ought to be a distributor of grace gifts and not just a consumer of services.

Once it is recognized that God gives grace gifts to all believers and that there is a great variety to the gifts he gives, how does one identify the gift(s) that God has given to him or her? Here are some helpful categories for thinking through the paradigm of spiritual gifts that is encountered in the Bible. All of the gifts are listed in a "tri-perspectival" way—that is, they fit into one of the three messianic categories of prophet, priest, and king.[16]

Prophetic gifts are "abilities based on understanding and articulating truth." These include "the utterance of wisdom" (v. 8), "the utterance of knowledge" (v. 8), prophecy, tongues, and interpretation (v. 10), distinguishing between spirits (v. 10), and other examples in the New Testament such as evangelism (Ephesians 4:11), teaching (12:29), and speaking (1 Peter 4:10, 11). Utterances of wisdom and knowledge are essentially communicating God's truth with precise clarity. If a person shares her troubles and trials but is indecisive about how to navigate through some of her difficult moments, and a friend with this gift is able to speak a word of wisdom or utterance of knowledge, asserting with precise clarity that Jesus is Lord, then that friend has this gift. These gifts are often exalted in the church because they are public in nature. But if these gifts are understood as given, they will never be a source of pride. They are not inherently better or more valuable than other gifts.

Priestly gifts are "abilities based on understanding and supplying basic needs."[17] These include encouragement or exhortation (Romans 12:8), pastoring (Ephesians 4:11), serving (Romans 12:7), sharing (Romans 12:8), mercy (Romans 12:8), helping (12:28), and healing and working miracles (vv. 9, 10). All of these gifts are self-evident, but one needs explanation. The reference to this particular grace gift does not say *gift* of healing. Both Greek terms are in the plural; literally it's saying "gifts of healings." In other words, anyone with this gift can be used as an instrument in which he can provide emotional, spiritual, or even physical healing. But the focus is not on the individual who has a special gift of healing but on his willingness to be a conduit of the givenness of the gift because God is the ultimate healer who will use the gift in a variety of ways.

Kingly gifts are "abilities based on understanding direction and group needs."[18] Faith (v. 9) is "the ability to envision a goal clearly." Other kingly gifts include founding gifts (apostle/planter) (Ephesians 4:11) or having an apostolic posture toward multiplication, leadership (Romans 12:8),[19] and administration (12:28).[20] Paul is not referring to salvific faith, or even faithfulness, but rather the ability to envision a goal clearly.

This is the beautiful variety that is seen in grace gifts, and there is reason to think that the list might be even larger. A quick guide to determining what one's spiritual gift(s) might be is to ask questions concerning one's affinity (what do you love?) and ability (what are you good at?).

The problem arises when rather than seeing all of these gifts as given and finding one's place in the community for the common good, some individuals jockey for position and engage in gift-grabbing. Others jockey out of position and engage in gift copout (or justification). These members decide that they have one gift and therefore do not need to serve the common good through other means. Could the addiction to an achievement-obsessed culture sabotage an individual's ability to appreciate the Bible's emphasis on cultivating a gift culture? Absolutely because this approach threatens the desire for self-actualization. How do we break out of the cycle of achievement, competition, and one-upmanship? How do we come to a place where we can receive and give life as a gift?

The Giver of Grace Gifts

The answer to the problems of both gift-grabbing and gift copout is a fresh encounter with the gift-giver. "Now there are varieties of gifts, but the same Spirit; and there are varieties of service, but the same Lord; and there are varieties of activities, but it is the same God who empowers them all in everyone" (vv. 4–6). It's not coincidental that Paul sets up a very clear parallel when he says, "varieties of gifts . . . the same Spirit," "varieties of service . . . the same Lord," and "varieties of activities . . . the same God." He's trying to emphasize the inner life of the Godhead: the Spirit gives, the Son serves, and God the Father energizes his people with great power to serve the common good. The Son sends the Spirit; the Father sends the Son; the Spirit gives life and also gives gifts. So it's no longer about gift-grabbing because Jesus Christ did not consider his gifts or his abilities something to be held onto tightly. He wasn't involved in gift-grabbing, gift-grasping, or gift-exploiting, but he gave up his life. After Jesus Christ sacrificed his life through his service to sinners, the Spirit gave grace gifts to each member of Christ's church.

God is a giver by nature. The Father gave the Son to redeem us. God did not have to give. If anyone deserved to be given to, it was him! But he looked at us in our sin, our hoarding, our non-giving, and freely gave of himself.

The Son accomplished and achieved redemption. Jesus perfectly achieved what sinners never could, so that they are free to receive the gift they could never deserve. He overturned the culture of achievement and created the culture of giving.

The Son sent the Spirit. Just when one would think he had given everything, Jesus ascended to Heaven and gave more. He poured out the Spirit! And the Spirit gives life. The Spirit applies all that Christ achieved, namely his grace. But he does not stop at this one-time gift of salvific grace; he gives perpetually. The Spirit also gives gifts. God is in a perpetual state of self-giving; he "apportions [gifts] to each one individually as he wills," "empowering" those to whom he gives his gifts (v. 11). God himself overcomes our achievement-centered culture by giving himself away. Our identity itself is a gift to be received. This allows sinners to give up their attempts to earn status and position. This also allows sinners to view others as inherently valuable regardless of status or position. One's abilities, skills, and gifts are all the result of grace—they are given. This allows Christians to be humble. We did not earn what we have. This also allows Christians to invest because our gifts are for the purpose of the common good. Individuals no longer gift-grab because they have been given all they need. Individuals no longer gift copout because they have been given all that they have for the express purpose of using it for the common good. The exercise of our gifts is the result of the empowerment of the Spirit. While exercising our gifts with diligence and intention, the power source for our activity is the perpetual self-giving of God through his Spirit. Christians can be confident that they have the necessary resources for using their gifts for the common good because the God who gives gifts also empowers them to use them.

The community of God's people are intended to reflect the self-giving nature of God. The exercising of gifts is a way that builds up the body (not for personal advantage). Gifts are conduits through which the community is supposed to stick together and commune with God together. The reason why improper use of gifts is so destructive is that it breaks down communion with God and with one another. In order to achieve unity, members of the body need to engage in the passive act of receiving and the active act of sharing. The economic principle is to pay it forward. When a donor invests, the recipient doesn't simply say "thank you" and forget about the gift; he needs to respond by investing what he has received. The instrumental, generative work of the Spirit empowers and enables the church to be able to share its gifts. It is grace that always leads to the use of gifts rather than one's gifts earning God's grace.

The animated movie *Frozen*, based on the great Hans Christian Andersen story, has quietly become one of Disney's best movies of all time. When I first heard about the story, my thoughts were similar to others. "Not another Disney movie about self-indulgence and finding salvation through romantic love and being true to oneself with a heroine who's going to sing a song about independence and autonomy—'I don't want constraints, I don't want any restrictions, I'm going to be true to myself'—at the end of the movie." But this movie was surprisingly different. The beautiful thing about it was that it actually introduced moral consciousness and challenged the shallow culture of self-indulgence that we often find in Disney movies. The theme song actually is about self-discovery, but it needs to be interpreted in light of its context to the rest of the storyline. The song is situated not during the end of the plotline of self-redemption when she is a great heroine, but rather in the moment of her personal fall when she goes out into the mountains to erect a castle as a monument of isolation.

> The wind is howling like this swirling storm inside
> Couldn't keep it in, heaven knows I tried!
> Don't let them in, don't let them see
> Be the good girl you always have to be
> Conceal, don't feel, don't let them know
> Well, now they know!
> Let it go, let it go
> Can't hold it back anymore
> Let it go, let it go
> Turn away and slam the door!
> I don't care
> What they're going to say
> Let the storm rage on,
> The cold never bothered me anyway!
> It's funny how some distance
> Makes everything seem small
> And the fears that once controlled me
> Can't get to me at all!

It's time to see what I can do
To test the limits and break through
No right, no wrong, no rules for me I'm free![21]

The larger story is summed up in that one little phrase by the animated snowman who says, "An act of true love will thaw a frozen heart." Elsa, the elder sister, who sings the song, thought she was pursuing freedom. "I don't want anyone to tell me what to do. I'm going to live my life anyway. I'm going to slam the door. I will be free." Yet she was enslaved, and at the end of the story, which had an ironic and upside-down conclusion, her younger sister Anna, who is the savior figure, is willing to sacrifice her life, an act of true love in order to save her older sister. The coldness of our hearts can only get thawed and softened when there is an act of true sacrificial love rather than the achievement of self-discovery.

It is only through the power of a gift-giving, self-donating Savior that sinners can have their hardened hearts softened and their cold hearts thawed. The amazing power of God's grace for us is that we get the gift reception Jesus deserved because he got the gift rejection we deserved.

23

The Gift of Interdependence

1 CORINTHIANS 12:12–31a

MODERN PEOPLE DO NOT LIKE the idea of dependence. They major on independence. They do not want to *need* others, nor do they want to be defined by others. Dependence sounds like weakness or deficiency. For the most part, people enjoy and take pride in autonomy. So when readers approach a passage in the Bible that speaks about interdependence in the church, while many contemporary people might find themselves attracted to the picture of a harmonious community, they do not ultimately want it if it is at the expense of their independence. They might want community, but the only thing they are unwilling to pay for it is their autonomy. Paul enters into this tension as he continues his discussion about internal matters within the church community. He is concerned about the propriety of Christian worship and wants to ensure that the Corinthians' life together reflects the upside-down nature of the gospel that they have received. The fact of the matter was that it was not being reflected in the church community. They looked a whole lot like they did before they received the gospel. They had essentially imported the entirety of their culture into the life of the church (hierarchy, classism, sexual deviance, etc.). Paul's goal is to get them to take a hard look at themselves and help them make a mid-course adjustment so that their community becomes a witness to the beauty of the gospel.

The main point that Paul is trying to get across is this: God has designed his church to be a community of *complementary interdependence*. The church is to be complementary; that is, each member brings something to the table that the others need and is enhanced by interdependence. It is also a place where each member can be harmoniously dependent upon others for his or her identity. We will consider Paul's discussion of interdependence under three headings:

- The Beauty of Interdependence
- The Lack of Interdependence
- The Recovery of Interdependence

The Beauty of Interdependence

Paul uses the body metaphor[1] to build his case for the beauty of the church (introduced in vv. 12–20; reiterated in v. 27). Verse 27 says: "Now you are the body of Christ and individually members of it." The church does not function as a collection of separate individuals. The church does not even function like a democracy. There is never a 51 percent to 49 percent victory in the church. It does not split up along party lines. It is far more vitally connected than that. The church functions as a body.[2]

Consider our own bodies. When we stub our toe, our whole body reacts. Our legs react; we bend our knees and raise our feet. Our arms react; we reach down and grab our toe. Our mouths cringe, and we yell. Our eyes dart to see what we stubbed our toe on. The body works seamlessly and organically together. There are no individual decisions to be made. The body reacts as a whole unit. It is not as though certain members of the body decide to opt out when they don't feel like assisting. And yet the body exhibits great diversity.[3] Toes are unlike ears; eyes are unlike elbows. Their diversity is not a hindrance to their unity, but absolutely necessary for it. The body could not function as it does if it were made up of 100 ears or 100 elbows. Paul wants church members to see themselves as integrally tied to one another like the various members of the human body.

The beauty of interdependence is grounded in each member's *indispensability*.[4] Verses 21–24a tell us: "The eye cannot say to the hand, 'I have no need of you,' nor again the head to the feet, 'I have no need of you.' On the contrary, the parts of the body that seem to be weaker are *indispensable*, and on those parts of the body that we think less honorable we bestow the greater honor, and our unpresentable parts are treated with greater modesty, which our more presentable parts do not require." It is almost ridiculous to consider members of the body deciding they don't need one another. Paul wants us to see that we are this preposterous when we fail to see the indispensability of others. Even the weakest members of the body, likely referring to sensitive internal organs, are indispensable.[5]

This is something that many Christians need to hear: We are all deathly afraid of being dispensable—we do not want to be used and tossed aside. We are consistently concerned about whether we fit in—whether we're accepted. Many people hop around to different communities looking for the right fit. If we are members of a local church, we are indispensable. And all of the other members are indispensable parts of our lives. They, too, are part of the body that God has put together to display the beauty of the gospel.

As an illustration, there are many important and indispensable parts of a hospital. The medical director, the head of a department, the many attending physicians, the chief resident, the senior resident, the junior resident, the many interns and medical students are all indispensable members of this medical community. This doesn't even include nurses, administrative staff, building maintenance personnel, and cleaning crew. Take any one of these groups out and things will eventually collapse. The church is not a hospital. There is less actual hierarchy; we are completely interdependent upon one another, and this is seen in the indispensability of each member.

If an individual who has back problems reaches for something and injures his back, the other parts of the body would have to compensate for the role his back plays in his body. As he is trying to brush his teeth he has to lean over a certain way. If he has to bend his knees, he needs to put one of his arms down on the counter to help support his weight. What if his arm doesn't want to help and says to his back, "You should have gone to the gym to work out." But this is not the way different parts of the body react. It instinctively reacts and responds. If one part gives way, if it has difficulties, if there are deficiencies, other parts will naturally compensate. If there is an injury, of course other parts are going to be inconvenienced, but this is the nature of what it means to exhibit the beauty of interdependence.

The Beauty of Interdependence, a Result of God's Composition

Verse 24b says: "But God has so composed the body, giving greater honor to the part that lacked it . . . ." Rather than being a sign of weakness, interdependency is God's design for the church. The church is to be a microcosmic picture of a restored humanity and is to reflect God's original intention for humanity (i.e., interdependence). Rather than embracing the hierarchy and celebrity culture in the world surrounding the church, it is called to be a countercultural community. The weaker are indispensable. The "less honorable" and "unpresentable"[6] are actually seen as deserving more honor and greater care. God has so composed the body that the "members" that don't fit elsewhere in the world—those that are weak, ugly, or unpresentable—have a primary place.

The Beauty of Interdependence Expressed through Mutual Care[7]

Verses 25, 26 tell us: ". . . that there may be no division in the body, but that the members may have the same care for one another. If one member suffers, all suffer together; if one member is honored, all rejoice together." If church members are organically interdependent upon one another, they experience the joys and pains of the body as a unit. If our hand is crushed in a tragic accident, our entire body experiences the pain. Furthermore, if our hand is permanently damaged, the entire body will continue to struggle as it works to make up for the loss of the hand. And if our hand were to be cut off, our body would experience permanent loss (not to mention the fact that our hand itself would die in isolation from the body). In the same way, when the hand is functioning normally, the entire body enjoys the benefits of a healthy hand. Similarly, if a hand were to go rogue and decide that it no longer wanted to serve the body for one reason or another, it would bring great harm to the entire body. It would be a denial of interdependence.

Mutual Care Expressed through the Exercising of Grace Gifts

Verses 27, 28 state: "Now you are the body of Christ and individually members of it. And God has appointed in the church first apostles, second prophets, third teachers, then miracles, then gifts of healing, helping, administrating, and various kinds of tongues." Paul says, "God has appointed." In the same way that God has composed the body for interdependence, he has also "appointed" grace gifts that are intended to be used for mutual care. In the same way that each member of our own body contributes its unique gift to the rest of the body as it carries out its role, every Christian is intended to participate in a culture of mutual care for the body of Christ. In these ways we see the beauty of interdependence. However, we rarely see churches functioning in this way. If we did, our churches would be packed; our communities would be so compelling, so refreshingly countercultural that we would not be able to keep people away. Unfortunately, this is not what we typically see.

The Lack of Interdependence

If the Bible lays out the paradigm for an alternate community of God's grace, why is there so much counterevidence in the church? Why is the church so often the place where there is hierarchy, celebrity culture, backbiting, etc.?

There is a *lack of interdependence because we view others as dispensable.* One of our worst fears is to be considered dispensable, disposable, or replaceable. Ironically, the way people attempt to guard against this is to inflate their view of self (i.e., "I am indispensable") and deflate their view of others (i.e., "you are dispensable"). In other words, they inflate themselves, and they deflate other people. We think some are indispensable, and others can be replaced. There is an application of business, transactional principles in the way others are evaluated, rather than an application of covenantal principles of mutual self-service.

Consumers relate to other consumers in ways that only consumers know when it comes to relating to others. People do this in an attempt to insulate themselves, but they end up isolating themselves. It creates a culture where others are usable commodities. Community itself becomes a commodity to be consumed. They view others as dispensable because they fail to recognize the necessity of diversity. Verses 29, 30 say: "Are all apostles? Are all prophets? Are all teachers? Do all work miracles? Do all possess gifts of healing? Do all speak with tongues? Do all interpret?" The grammar indicates that the answer to all of these questions is no. The church is incomplete unless its members operate by being interdependent.

God has given various gift sets to individuals in the church. Some have prophetic gifts (apostles, prophets, teachers, tongues); others have priestly gifts (miracles, healing) or kingly gifts (helping, administrating [literally "piloting"]).[8] God has given every member grace gifts, but he has not given any individual all the grace gifts. Even if one's grace gifts are those that are more readily visible (preaching, teaching, etc.), we are incomplete without the gifts of others. We are incomplete in and of ourselves. In other words, if we look at all of the gift mixes, we need prophetic types, we need priestly types, and we need kingly types.

In addition, there can be a dark side to all of our grace gifts because humanity is fallen. So, for example, some who have strong prophetic gifts can tend to be impatient, and that takes them away from being more pastoral and relational. Others are very priestly and pastoral, and they shepherd people well, but they might be inefficient in the ways they organize things. Certain members are kingly; they can get things done by being very efficient with their time and all of the resources they have, but they might abandon the people in the process because they just want to get the job done in the most productive way. There are potential dark sides to the different gift mixes that people possess. God brings together all of the different parts, and he puts them into a constellation where there is mutual service and benefit for the entire body. To the extent that there is failure to see the necessity of the diversity of gifts in the body, to that extent others will be viewed as dispensable, and God's compositional design for humanity will be missed.

When God's compositional design is missed, there is nothing left but self-composition. There is a lack of interdependence because members of a body are more interested in self-composition. Rather than seeing that God is the composer of the body and the appointer of gifts, the Corinthians viewed themselves as composers and believed that they could attain skills and competencies through hard work. Similarly, if believers today believe their identity can be built on their own, they will need to protect it and keep others at arm's length by insulating themselves from the interdependency of the community. They will end up isolating themselves from the context for which they were created and will fail to be recipients of God's grace. Christians can end up placing themselves in a position where they are unable to recognize the beauty of God's communal composition. The weak should not be viewed as indispensable and unworthy of honor.

A Lack of Interdependence Because of Self-Care

Because church members are oftentimes interested in self-protection and self-care, they are unable to fulfill their role in the body (mutual care). They are called to suffer when others suffer, to rejoice when others rejoice. But sharing in the suffering of others seems too costly. So they become rebellious body parts. In the process they lose their identity as body parts. Hands cease to function as hands are supposed to function, and they ultimately cannot share in the rejoicing of others. Their grace gifts become an occasion for competition and stratification. If an individual is all about self-care rather than mutual care, his gifts become a means of distinguishing and advancing himself rather than advancing the interest of others.

In these ways the church often becomes a mirror image of the surrounding culture. We have to honestly ask ourselves if our local churches reflect the culture in this way. In valuing the intellect, has there been an undervaluing of the heart? In valuing excellence, has there been an undervaluing of simplicity? Have the grace gifts of some members been overlooked because we overvalue the grace gifts of others? Have we viewed people in our community groups as dispensable? Have we become more interested in self-composition and lost sight of God's composition? Are we more concerned with self-care than mutual care? The answer to many of these questions is likely yes. Is there any hope of our community being transformed to reflect the beautiful interdependence that God intends?

The Recovery of Interdependence

Complementary interdependence can be recovered, first, because Christ could have viewed sinners as dispensable, but in his grace he saw them as indispensable. In fact, he became dispensable in their place. The imagery of the body is not generic; it is specific. It is the body of Christ. The health, well-being, and future of the body are in the hands of the head—Christ. Individual sinners have been incorporated into his body by grace. No one has earned his way in. Even if we have falsely determined that we are dispensable, the head of the body has declared that we are not! The most presentable part—the head—was willingly dishonored so that the least presentable parts—you and I—might receive honor. The strongest member was made weak and dispensable in order that the weaker members—you and I—might be considered indispensable. This love transforms the sinner's reality. Christians need to recognize that they are utterly dependent upon Christ and the community in which he has placed them. When they realize that they are dispensable, they are able to receive the grace that tells them they are indispensable.

Secondly, interdependence can be recovered because Christ saves sinners from the myth of self-composition. We are God's composition, and he has made us a part of his body.

Being in a dating relationship can create an exhausting experience of self-promotion, similar to marketing one's goods. The person may feel the need to be able to always be on, to impress continually because he doesn't want to scare the other person away. He's never at rest because he's not quite sure exactly how that person views or evaluates him. So he wants to be fully aware and wants to make the right decisions. He wants to make sure he is bringing his best to the table. When we think about it deeply, that's not so much a covenantal dynamic; it's really the marketplace transactional relationship between a consumer and a vendor. In other words, people are involved in consumer relationships and thus are always insecure and a little nervous.

Because Christians have been united to Christ's body by grace, we are free to abandon all attempts at self-creation and self-composition. Members do not need to distinguish themselves or compete for a higher position; their position in the body has been secured. They can rest in the fact that their identity is given to them by Christ and is affirmed in community.

Interdependence can be restored because Christ cares for sinners by making them interdependent members of his body. We mutually care for one another because we have experienced his care. Christ completely eschewed self-protection and self-care in order to care for us. The ultimate work of Another makes every Christian ultimately concerned about others. Anyone who has experienced the self-giving love of Another—the ultimate grace gift—can use his grace gifts as a conduit to express that same self-giving love.

24

What Is Love?

1 CORINTHIANS 12:31b—13:13

CHAPTER 13 OF 1 CORINTHIANS is a beautiful passage. There are times in 1 Corinthians when the reader could sense a sort of collective head-scratching after reading a passage in this letter. Head coverings, meat sacrificed to idols, people getting drunk at church—to name a few of the issues. Because Christians believe that all Scripture is given to them by God, the reader is not supposed to play down the importance and relevance of those slightly hairy passages. But there are some passages of the Bible that simply go down a bit easier than others. And this one goes down nice and easy.

This passage is often read at weddings, even nonreligious weddings. Why? Because the idea that "love never ends," that there's something that never fails, that there's something that can endure anything—that's one of the most beautiful ideas that a human heart can hear. And at that moment, when husband and wife "may now kiss" one another during the wedding ceremony, it's this kind of love that is coursing through their newly married minds. Love is resonant. It sounds true, even if it's often elusive.

But unfortunately for many who have been going to church for a while, this might be the 26th time they've heard 1 Corinthians 13 referenced, and they're thinking, "Yep. Love never ends. Got that one. Yawn." If that's you, come back, please! The Apostle Paul, who wrote this letter to the church in the city of Corinth, is concerned to get this message through to the very people who have heard it a million times.

The Corinthian Christians had the religious thing down. They did what Christians do every week (they went to church, they prayed, sang, listened to a sermon, and even shared a meal together). But in all the coming and going, in all their churchly activity, in spite of all the sermons they had ever heard on 1 Corinthians 13, they struggled to keep love at the center of their lives.

In this particular instance, the Corinthians had gotten themselves caught up in arguments about who was most eloquent, who was the smartest, who had the most spiritual sensitivity, who made the most money, who did the most community service, etc. They were interested in excellence, in what set them apart.

Paul steps into this setting—and into our setting today—and says, "I know you love your excellence, but let me show you an even more excellent way" (12:31)—the way of love. "The way of love?" they ask. "What's love got to do with it?" Most people are curious to know "What is love?" The answers emerge from this passage as it describes what love does in four points:

- Love Fills Life with Necessary Meaning
- Love Fills Life with Beautiful Impossibility
- Love Fills Life with Lasting Significance
- Love Redefines Life

Love Fills Life with Necessary Meaning (vv. 1–3)

While there may be a few jaded detractors, for the most part humanity seems to think that love is a good thing. When John Lennon and Paul McCartney sing, "All you need is love," people may find themselves feeling slightly suspicious, and rightly so. But people always sing along because there's at least a part of every human heart that thinks there's some truth in it. We want it to be true. In a way we need it to be true. Maybe it's as the ever-charming Francis Spufford put it: "Given the cruel world, it's the love song we need, to help us bear what we must; and, if we can, go on loving."[1]

In any case, most people hold in common the belief that love, whatever it may be, strikes at the heart of what it means to be human, that it provides human lives with necessary meaning. There are plenty of things we can live without, but love is not one of them To quote a popular 1997 hit, "I don't care who you are, where you're from, what you did, as long as you love me."[2] Love trumps identity, pedigree, and history. Another singer agrees: "As long as you love me, we could be starving, we could be homeless, we could be broke, as long you love me."[3] Love is that essential element in life that simultaneously makes everything important and everything else unimportant. If it is taken away, life inevitably lacks necessary meaning. But if it can be added in, then whatever may come down the line can be faced with courage and hope.

In the words of relational psychotherapist James Olthius, "Loving is not merely one thing among others that we are called to do. Love is not an additive. Loving is of the essence of being human, the connective tissue of reality, the oxygen of life."[4] Love is like oxygen. Take it away, and it is difficult to breathe; without oxygen, and without love, a part of every human being dies.

In an attempt to underscore the necessity of love, and to highlight the absurdity of the Corinthians' communal stratification over issues of excellence, Paul invites them to sing a song that is the inverse of "As Long as You Love Me." He asks them to consider a world without love. Take a look at verses 1–3:

> If I speak in the tongues of men and of angels, but have not love, I am a noisy gong or a clanging cymbal. And if I have prophetic powers, and understand all mysteries and all knowledge, and if I have all faith, so as to remove mountains, but have not love, I am nothing. If I give away all I have, and if I deliver up my body to be burned, but have not love, I gain nothing.

In these three verses Paul lays out three elements that will be important to keep in mind. He's interested primarily in what the Christian *says*, what he *knows*, and what he *does*. And in each instance he asks the believer to imagine a world minus love.

In verse 1 he focuses on what we say: "If I speak in the tongues of men and of angels, but have not love, I am a noisy gong or a clanging cymbal." The Corinthians were obsessed with impressive speech, and they were also intrigued by the idea that they might be able to speak supernatural languages. Now what you may or may not think about the idea of speaking in tongues is beside the point. In any case Paul is unimpressed. An individual can speak any language he wants, and he can be as eloquent as he'd like to be. But if it's not undergirded and infused with love, it's just white noise.

He is saying a believer can sing all the love songs he'd like, but if he doesn't mean it, if it is just a means to some other end, then Paul doesn't want to hear it. It's just noise. Turn down those clanging cymbals![5] What is said is impressive, it's eloquent, but it's empty of necessary meaning. Love fills what is said with necessary meaning.

Love also matters in relation to the issue of what we know (v. 2): "And if I have prophetic powers, and understand all mysteries and all knowledge, and if I have all faith, so as to remove mountains, but have not love, I am nothing." The Corinthians were obsessed with excellence, and this carried over into their understanding of knowledge. They placed a high premium on intelligence, insight, and secret knowledge. They were intrigued with the idea that they could access some higher plane of spiritual knowledge. Again Paul is unimpressed and asks them to consider what knowledge looks like when stripped of love.

Contemporary people know what this looks like. If we run into an incredibly intelligent, knowledgeable person, and yet he lacks kindness, humility, and gentleness, we are not impressed with him. Knowledge devoid of love is nothing. Intelligence minus love equals ignorance. Even if we are in the right, others would rather likely not want to hear what we have to say. Paul says that whenever a person "foregrounds" knowledge and "backgrounds" love, he is nothing.

If love infuses what we say and know with necessary meaning, it also gives meaning to what we do: "If I give away all I have, and if I deliver up my body to be burned, but have not love, I gain nothing" (v. 3). Charity is all the rage, but what about loveless charity? Let's say a person is in great need of financial assistance, and our family has limitless amounts of money, and we agree to help him out under one condition: he must understand that we do not love him, we do not care about him. Rather, we are only interested in giving to him because it will make us look really good and because we need to unload some money for tax purposes. So long as he understands that he is inconsequential, that he is nothing to us, we're good. "Do you want our money?" Now the pragmatist in all of us says, "Sure. Hand it over." But the love-desiring human in all of us says, "You know what, keep it. If you don't love me, I'd rather be starving, I'd rather be homeless, I'd rather be broke. If you don't love me, this transaction means nothing. Your charity and nobility are worthless."

Thankfully we don't live in a world devoid of love. Instead love fills life with necessary meaning. Our longing for it trumps eloquence, intelligence, and even charity. What is more meaningful than hearing someone say, "I love you" is knowing that they mean it all the way down to their core.

Everyone longs to be more than noise. We all long to know and be known—to really get someone, and to feel totally gotten—to know that we are not nothing. Why do we desire these things? Because love has filled our lives.

Love Fills Life with Beautiful Impossibility (vv. 4–7)

The most resonant verses in this passage are contained here in verses 4–7. Paul provides a perspective on love that is strikingly beautiful, yet seemingly beyond human experience. "Love is patient and kind; love does not envy or boast; it is not arrogant or rude. It does not insist on its own way; it is not irritable or resentful; it does not rejoice at wrongdoing, but rejoices with the truth. Love bears all things, believes all things, hopes all things, endures all things."

On our best days we long to give this love,[6] and on our worst days we long to receive this love. What people wouldn't give to be more patient and kind with their loved ones. And it is ever so beautiful when others are unusually patient or uncommonly kind with us. We catch glimpses of it all the time, and our hearts are drawn out by the beauty. These instances of love reinstate hope in the face of hopelessness. They breathe life into lifeless situations. They draw us out of ourselves. They make us more human, more alive.

However, isn't there reason to be suspicious of this kind of idealistic love? After all, there appears to be a significant amount of counterevidence to suggest that it is probably unattainable.

One might ask, where is this counterevidence? Well, there is plenty of it in our own lives. Take a quick look at any relationship, and there is quite a bit of unlovely stuff taking place. Though there are times when love mysteriously and beautifully breaks through, there's a whole lot of ugly stuff happening too.

Look at verses 4–7 again. Patience? Imagine an individual who got bent out of shape in line at a coffee shop because the guy in front of him couldn't make up his mind. Kindness? No one would characterize his brief interaction with the man as very kind. But here are some things he is familiar with (and so are we). "Envy." The same individual definitely envied one of his coworkers this week—she has things together in a way that he doesn't. "Rude." Oh, yes. "Insisting on [his] own way"? "You should have heard the conversation I had with my father on Thursday. I really told him what's what." "Irritable." Yep. "Resentful." Check. Must we continue?

The beautiful thing that everyone longs for, perhaps more than anything in the world, looks to be out of reach—impossible really. But here's the strange thing: the very impossibility draws us back into it. It's almost what makes love so tantalizing, so enticing. It's like a game really. There's simply no way to get it right every time, but the fun of playing, the beauty of experiencing love, somehow manages to outweigh the real pain that everyone experiences in the absence of love.

In baseball the best players in the game typically only successfully hit the ball three out of every ten times. The best hitter who ever lived—Ted Williams, a legendary obsessive who measured the weight of his bats down to a tenth of an ounce—only hit the ball thirty-four times for every 100 times he went to the plate.[7] And still he was obsessed. He couldn't sleep at night because he was thinking about the pitcher he would face the next day. The joy of playing the game—of seeing the ball fly off the bat 34 percent of the time—kept him coming back.[8]

Maybe love is the primary game of our lives. Most of the time we strike out. The curveballs of life are just too much to handle. Or the fastball pace of the city gets the best of us. But every now and again the impossible seems possible, and we catch a glimpse of love, and so we keep at it. Love shapes what we say, it shapes how we think, it shapes what we do. Like Ted Williams we stay up at night thinking about the people we'll encounter the next day. We hang on their words. We search their eyes. We measure their actions—all for signs of love. Because more than anything in the world, this is what we're looking for.

I want you to say that you love me—and once you come to know me in all of my unacceptability, I still want you to love me—and then I want you to say that you love me again—and I then want you to prove it, to prove that you're not going anywhere, to prove that this isn't a game, but that what we share is in the life-or-death category, in the until-death-do-us-part category. And then I want you to promise that it will never stop. This leads us to our third observation about love.

Love Fills Life with Lasting Significance (vv. 8–13)

In 1960 The Shirelles became the first all-girl group to reach #1 on the Billboard charts with their hit song, "Will You Still Love Me Tomorrow?"[9] We may have heard it. The song ends with these lines: "I'd like to know that your love is love I can be sure of, so tell me now and I won't ask again, will you still love me tomorrow?" And even though the singer has just promised that she won't ask again, the song fades out as she asks again three more times, "Will you still love me tomorrow?" The hearer gets the feeling that even though the record has faded out, she's still asking. Isn't that what everyone is asking?

Even though love fills one's life with necessary meaning, and the game of love gives glimpses of beautiful impossibility, there is a nagging sense that love is just like everything else—perishable, temporary, limited, fleeting, momentary.

The Apostle Paul is not naive. He recognizes the limits in our humanity. "As for prophecies, they will pass away; as for tongues, they will cease; as for knowledge, it will pass away. For we know in part and we prophesy in part, but when the perfect comes, the partial will pass away" (vv. 8b–10). Here he pulls back in the categories from verses 1–3. What we say and know and do will pass away. All these things are partial. Our gifts, our skills, our actions, even our spiritual insights are perishable, spoilable, biodegradable. Death is hot on our trails, and nothing we say, know, or do will help us escape it. None of the skills we've acquired in this game of love ultimately gain us anything.

However, there is one thing that is nonperishable, unspoilable, death-proof—love itself. Verse 8a says: "Love never ends."[10] Love is categorically different. It fills life with permanent significance. It injects eternal importance into the present. And again this is exactly what people long for. There is a longing for love that doesn't end, that isn't bounded by the same limits that we find in ourselves.

Some of the most beautiful stories of love are those in which there is a preview of the permanence of love. Consider, for example, cases in which a wife or husband makes the excruciating decision to care for a spouse who has ceased to be the engaging partner and friend they once were. I think of my grandmother who was diagnosed with Alzheimer's and spent the last few years of her life stuck somewhere between the present and the past. She no longer recognized her husband and even called him by the name of an old boyfriend. She was well cared for and surrounded by family, but this much was clear: she had nothing to offer.

Our desire for the permanent significance of love causes us to ask, "Will you invest in me with permanent significance when I have nothing to invest in this relationship?" "Will you love me when it's not a game anymore? When I can't play catch?" "Are there limits and conditions?" "Was this love really about a transaction, about what I brought to the table?"

Those are heavy questions, but everyone asks them, because they reveal one's deepest fears. Even though there is a longing for limitless, permanent love, there are also limits and impermanence in ourselves. Can a person ever bear all things, endure all things? That's a recipe for a nervous breakdown. People do not have an endless reservoir of belief and hope. We can't even endure a ten-minute conversation in many cases, let alone "all things." Love is impossible. So what is a person to do?

Barbara Fredrickson, professor of psychology at the University of North Carolina, in her new book *Love 2.0* suggests that love needs an upgrade. The old love—the kind we've been talking about—is outmoded, and we need a new model. What does Fredrickson's new model look like? Here are her words: "Love is not exclusive." "Love's timescale is far shorter than we typically think. Love, as you'll see, is not lasting." "And perhaps most challenging of all, love is not unconditional."[11]

What then is love for Fredrickson? "Love is that micro-moment of warmth and connection that you share with another living being."[12] "Love is an emotion, a momentary state."[13] And what is the result of this upgrade to Love 2.0? "Right now—at this very moment in which I am crafting this sentence—I do not love my husband. Our positivity resonance, after all, only lasts as long as we two are engaged with one another. The same goes for you and your loved ones. Unless you're cuddled up with someone reading these words aloud to him or her, right now, you don't love anyone."[14] Does Love 2.0 sound like an upgrade to anyone? It sounds like going from an iPhone 6 to a rotary phone.

But this move is actually very logical. Fredrickson simply recognizes the limitations of human love and seeks to redefine it so that its definition is in line with the way that it often functions. It seems to me that in light of the meaningful, beautiful impossibility of permanent love, we really only have two options: 1) we can keep playing the game—try to be awesome at love—in an attempt to do what we are unable to do—the impossible. Or 2) we can redefine love—rewrite the rules of the game so that love is easily accomplishable. But my guess is that, having been exposed to the old, genuine article, Love 2.0 is untenable, unpalatable. We are simply unwilling to give up our smartphones. We shouldn't want to let go of this vision that we've had of a *necessarily meaningful, beautifully impossible, permanently significant love*, and we should urge others not to let go of it either. But how can we hold on?

We can hold on by recognizing that we've made a fatal error. What is that error? We have located love within ourselves. We have viewed it as something we do, a muscle we exercise, an emotion we feel, an experience we have. The cost of locating love within ourselves is that we have given it an expiration date.

If love is to be love, if it is to be what we come to know it to be in all of its mystery and magic, if love is to be the love that we desire, crave, and long for, then it will necessarily have to come from outside of us. And this is why Paul suggests that love is categorically different and permanently significant. Love happens outside of us. Love happens to us. Love is not words we say. It is not feelings we feel. It is not even deeds we do. It is something far bigger than all of that, and only this kind of love can redefine our lives.

Love Redefines Life

If love must be outside of us to remain the love that we want it to be, then God himself is the only one fit for the role to love.

What does love say? Love says you are not noise — "I hear you, I understand you." Love says, "I know you all the way through, and despite your deepest fears, you are absolutely *not* nothing. You are highly valuable." Love says, "You are worth giving away everything I have." Love says, "I would die for you." Do we have anything less than this in the good news that has been reported to us about Jesus Christ? Jesus looks at all of our issues, at all of our lovelessness, our terrible batting average, whatever mess we've made most recently, and says not simply, "I would die for you" but "I did die for you. It's already done. I became nothing so you would know that you're not nothing." In this way God, who after all is love (1 John 4:8, 16), fills life with all the necessary meaning that we crave.

But what are believers supposed to do with all the impatience, cruelty, envy, boasting, arrogance, rudeness, self-insistence, irritability, resentfulness, and wrongdoing they find within themselves? What about all these limits? What about how hard it is to love our spouse, our kids? It's hard to love my church! If we are completely honest about our sin, it's even hard to love God at times! We're running on empty.

Instead of hearing what we need to do for God, or even for others, we need to hear what love has done for us. This is God's posture toward us in all our brokenness. In love God is patient with the sinner. In love God is kind to us. In love God bears the believer upon his shoulders. In love God endures us in all of our unendureableness. We can't wear him out, and he's not backing down. His love never ends. The beautiful impossibility of love is a beautiful possibility in the hands of God.

If love is the primary game that humans play — the one people expend all of their time, energy, words, thoughts, and actions on — the gospel is a declaration that the game is over. The game has already been won. In Christ, the creator of the game of love stepped onto the playing field, and through what looked like the most tragic loss in history — a loss that included his own death — he accomplished the ultimate victory — a victory signified/sealed by his defeat of death in his resurrection. This is how humanity knows that love never ends. It has already beaten death. Love killed death.

What does this mean? It means that we can put all of the games we play in perspective. When I was a kid, I used to play games in my front yard and pretend that I was my favorite athlete, Larry Bird. I imagined myself having all of his skill and finesse. Of course I didn't, but I was able to enjoy pretending to be Larry Bird because the game had already been won. He was already the all-star. He was already a champion. But what if I was deluded and thought that I actually was Larry Bird, that it was my responsibility to lead the Celtics to a championship? There would be no fun in that at all.

We tend to be like that! The game has already been won, and we are called to enjoy and share the benefits in a backyard game, but we act like the world is riding on our shoulders, like we have to bear and endure it all. It has already been borne; it has already been endured. Love faced death, and love won. All this time we've been playing the game of love as if our lives depended on it, while Jesus—love incarnate—has been trying to break in and say, "Love is dependent on my death. You get to live and love because I died in love, for love, for you, my love!"

Alain de Botton, a thought-provoking philosopher of the atheist stripe, has a remarkable reflection on love:

> Passing an unfortunate woman in the street one day, [my girlfriend] asked me, "Would you have loved me if I'd had an enormous birthmark on my face like she does?" The yearning is that the answer be yes—an answer that would place love above the mundane surfaces of the body, or more particularly, its cruel unchangeable ones (i.e. "I will love you not just for your wit and talent and beauty, but simply because you are you, with no strings attached. I love you for who you are deep in your soul, not for the colour of your eyes or the length of your legs or size of your chequebook"). The longing is that the lover admire us stripped of our external assets, appreciating the essence of our being without accomplishment. . . . Even if we are beautiful and rich, then we do not wish to be loved on account of these things, for they may fail us, and with them, love. . . . The desire is that I be loved even if I lose everything: leaving nothing but me, this mysterious me taken to be the self at its weakest, most vulnerable point. Do you love me enough that I may be weak with you? Everyone loves strength, but do you love me for my weakness?[15]

And the answer of love—the answer of the God who is love—is yes.
Allow this God who is love to fill your life with necessary meaning.
Allow this God who is love to erupt in your life with beautiful possibility.
Allow this God who is love to invest your life with permanent significance.
"Love never ends."

25

An Upbuilding Project

1 CORINTHIANS 14:1–25

TO UNDERSTAND THIS PASSAGE, one must situate it in its proper literary and cultural context. Paul is addressing an internal church controversy at Corinth about the use of prophecy and tongues. Christians were obsessed with these seemingly more miraculous speech gifts—particularly with the gift of tongues. Meanwhile, non-Christians were confused by their unintelligible speech. Paul calls the Corinthians to place an emphasis on intelligible speech that builds up the church. Grace gifts, which are given for the building up of the church, should never become an occasion for division within the church. Paul makes this very clear. So when considering charismatic speech gifts such as tongues or prophecy, one must understand that Paul wants to situate this within the context of the building up of the church.

Though many do not have problems with this particular issue in their churches or denominations, there is certainly modern-day controversy about the same gifts that Paul addresses here. The result is the same: non-Christians are often confused. Talk of "tongues" and "prophecy" is foreign enough. When Christians themselves seem unable to understand what they're talking about, that can create a significant barrier to faith. In an attempt to place the emphasis where Paul places it (i.e., on the building up of the church) we are not going to explore the modern-day practices of tongues and prophecy in much depth. That said, as we engage the text some distinctives emerge from Paul's teaching. Paul's main focus here is on building up the church, and the primary means of doing that (in the context of speech gifts) is communicating in a way that can be understood by everyone present. This will be looked at through three different discussion points:

- The Call to Build Up the Church with Our Gifts
- The Danger of Tearing Down the Church with Our Gifts
- The Beauty of a Church Rebuilt

The Call to Build Up the Church with Our Gifts

In 12:11 Paul argues that the Spirit apportions to each member a particular gift. Everyone has a gift matrix — probably a combination of gifts from the various gift clusters (i.e., prophetic, kingly, and priestly gifts). The kingly cluster[1] consists of administrative, organization, help, and guidance/leading. The priestly[2] consists of hospitality, healing, and counseling. The prophetic[3] consists of preaching, teaching, prophecy, and tongues. No gift is inherently better than the others ("to each," 12:7). Gifts are not something that we earn ("is given," 12:7), and each member and the exercising of his or her gift is indispensable (even the "weaker" parts, 12:22).

The church of Corinth had failed to recognize the beauty of the interdependence and indispensability of all of these gifts and had begun to overemphasize prophetic speech[4] grace gifts. This has happened in some parts of the modern church as well. To put things in perspective, when was the last time you heard about a controversy in the local church about the gift of hospitality? There aren't two camps or positions on the gift of hospitality. There should be no division over gifts from the prophetic cluster either. Although certain gifts are minimized and speech gifts are often elevated, they shouldn't be. They are all different and useful. Each person has been apportioned at least one gift (and not all believers have the same gifts), and he has a gift matrix that is a combination of all of the different gifts in the gift clusters.

Spiritual gifts are "for the common good" (12:7) — for building up the church. In our current passage Paul focuses on two particular gifts that fall into the prophetic category, namely, prophecy[5] and tongues.[6] The way Paul handles these two particular gifts will show that no matter which gifts God has given an individual, the purpose of these gifts is for the building up of the church. Prophecy and tongues did not drop out of thin air in the Corinthian church. Prophecy had a long history within the Old and New Testament. Moses was the first prophet (Deuteronomy 18), and there is a rich history of Old Testament prophets who consistently called Israel back to the covenant that God had made with them. Furthermore, these prophets called Israel to seek God; to abandon their high places, altars, and idols; and to repent and obey his commandments.[7] But now for the church, the person of Jesus is the fulfillment of the office of prophet ("but in these last days he has spoken to us by his Son," Hebrews 1:2). So prophecy is intelligible speech by which God calls his people to fidelity and faithfulness (i.e., it is not primarily predictive). God puts his words in the mouth of the prophet, and the community is responsible to obey. Deuteronomy 18:18, 19 says, "I will raise up for them a prophet like you from among their brothers. And I will put my words in his mouth, and he shall speak to them all that I command him. And whoever will not listen to my words that he shall speak in my name, I myself will require it of him."

Tongues too has a history within the Old and New Testaments. A multiplicity of languages or tongues was initially seen as judgment in Genesis 11 (the Tower of Babel). Similarly, when God's people would not listen to him through intelligible prophecy, he sent people speaking in other languages as a sign of judgment. Paul makes reference to Isaiah 28 in verse 21: "By people of strange tongues and by the lips of foreigners will I speak to this people, and even then they will not listen to me, says the Lord." In the New Testament, tongues no longer represent judgment but redemption. In Acts 2, during Pentecost, when the Holy Spirit was poured out on the church, the judgment of the Tower of Babel was essentially reversed. God's word was spoken and heard intelligibly in multiple languages. So in the New Testament, "tongues" are actual languages miraculously spoken by people who are not familiar with those languages. The language would then either be understood by a native speaker (a sign of God's power) or interpreted by a member of the community who miraculously had been given the gift of interpreting a language with which they also were unfamiliar (also a sign of God's power).

Prophecy and interpreted tongues essentially did the same thing: they were intelligible words from God to his people meant to build up the church and convince non-Christians of the reality of faith. The problem in the Corinthian church was that they had gotten it backwards. They were more interested in the unintelligible, uninterpreted tongues. As a result the community could not be built up, and non-Christians would remain unconvinced. They were prioritizing the impressive over the intelligible. The problem was that the "impressive" was not making a good impression; it was actually doing the very opposite. Paul is looking to correct their misuse of their grace gifts so the church can be built up. Verses 1–4 say:

> Pursue love, and earnestly desire the spiritual gifts, especially that you may prophesy. For one who speaks in a tongue speaks not to men but to God; for no one understands him, but he utters mysteries in the Spirit. On the other hand, the one who prophesies speaks to people for their upbuilding and

encouragement and consolation. The one who speaks in a tongue builds up himself, but the one who prophesies builds up the church.

Note that love again is at the forefront: "Pursue love." And here are the things that prophecy does—things that all grace gifts ought to aim for: (1) "upbuilding": if a grace gift is ever used to tear someone else down, or even if it is being exercised without reference to the upbuilding of others, the point is being missed. (2) "Encouragement": the Greek here is *paraklesis*— "the same root as the word used in John 14 to describe the Holy Spirit as Paraclete, Advocate, Counselor. It literally means 'to be called in alongside' to assist and support."[8] (3) "Consolation": "This has the sense of whispering in the church's ear, probably in the sense of allaying fear and enabling God's people to be calm under pressure."[9] All in all, Paul wants us to "strive to excel in building up the church" (14:12). And part of this striving will include a willingness to recognize the potential misuse of grace gifts in the church.

The Danger of Tearing Down the Church with Our Gifts

Paul wanted the Corinthians to see that even though they may have been getting a kind of spiritual high from speaking in tongues, the effect is detrimental. Verse 9 says: ". . . if with your tongue you utter speech that is not intelligible, how will anyone know what is said? For you will be speaking into the air." When our grace gifts are used for our own individual ends without reference to others, one of the results is that non-Christians are left in the dark and are unable to hear the gospel: ". . . if you give thanks with your spirit, how can anyone in the position of an outsider say 'Amen' to your thanksgiving when he does not know what you are saying?" (v. 16). The church is unable to be built up: "For you may be giving thanks well enough, but the other person is not being built up" (v. 17).

This is true of any grace gift. It is possible to use grace gifts for a selfish end. Take the example of teaching. It is possible to take the spiritual gift of teaching and abuse it in order to appear smart, to gain a following, or to impress listeners. When pastors load up their teaching with Christianese and theological lingo that is unintelligible to Christians or non-Christians, they effectively do the same thing that the Corinthians were doing. They put a basic understanding of the faith out of reach. Or consider the gift of hospitality: it is possible to abuse the gift of hospitality by only being hospitable to the people whom one is comfortable having around or to feed an ego. This will not negate the given gift, but it will essentially make it useless.

It is possible to use gifts in a way that is unintelligible. If our hospitality is entirely shaped by strange traditions—if we only welcome people on our own terms and refuse to meet them where they are, creating a comfortable environment where they can experience community and grace—our "hospitality" is unintelligible. In essence if we are more concerned about feeling like we are welcoming (according to our own standards) than whether or not our guests feel welcomed (in ways that they can comprehend), we are missing the point. The problem is not with the gift itself, but with our use of it. Verses 18, 19 continue: "I thank God that I speak in tongues more than all of you. Nevertheless, in church I would rather speak five words with my mind in order to instruct others, than ten thousand words in a tongue." Paul is not disparaging tongues—after all, they are a gift from God! He is disparaging the misuse of the gift.

We have to make sure that if we've been given a tool or a gift, we use and apply it properly. A hammer and a saw are two different tools meant for two different purposes. Someone can try to saw a nail all he wants, but it won't budge, and he may actually do damage to the nail. Similarly, he could try to hammer a piece of wood all he wants, but in the end he won't be able to replicate the clean cut of a saw. If anything, he'll have a broken, battered piece of wood. We are called to recognize the nature of the tools we've been given and to use them appropriately. No matter what tool an individual has been given, it is to be used for the upbuilding of the church through intelligible use.

When we misuse our gifts, we do not lose our gifts, but they lose their potency and purpose. Using our gifts selfishly and unintelligibly turns them on their head. Verses 21–23 tell us: "In the Law it is written, 'By people of strange tongues and by the lips of foreigners will I speak to this people, and even then they will not listen to me, says the Lord.' Thus tongues are a sign not for believers but for unbelievers, while prophecy is a sign not for unbelievers but for believers. If, therefore, the whole church comes together and all speak in tongues, and outsiders or unbelievers enter, will they not say that you are out of your minds?"

Acts 2 and the practice of interpreted tongues were a sign of God's global restorative work—the message of the gospel was spreading to all nations. When tongues were interpreted (thus becoming intelligible), it was a sign that the hearers were no longer left in the dark about God's purposes and plans of redemption. However, when the Corinthians ceased to use the gift of tongues as it was intended to be used (i.e., intelligibly for edification), it ceased to function as a sign of redemption and actually reverted to a sign of judgment. Knowing that this is a possibility with all of our gifts, we must come to terms with our tendency to twist the good gifts that God has given us for selfish ends. How can our gifts be redirected to their original use? How can we redirect our course in order to ensure that our gifts are being intelligibly and contextually used for edification?

The Beauty of a Church Rebuilt

Christians commonly think of non-Christians as being in need of grace, but Christians' own fractured communities demonstrate that they are just as much in need of grace! As individuals, Christians need a God who has given them grace gifts in order to give even more grace! Grace is needed in order to know how to properly use grace gifts. At the end of his discourse on these gifts, Paul envisions the gifts being restored to their proper use. "But if all prophesy, and an unbeliever or outsider enters, he is convicted by all, he is called to account by all, the secrets of his heart are disclosed, and so, falling on his face, he will worship God and declare that God is really among you" (vv. 24, 25).

When gifts are used intelligibly for the purpose of edification, the result is that the message of the gospel rings clear and true. For unbelievers and believers alike, as God's word is declared, we experience *conviction*.[10] We recognize the ways in which we are out of step with God's will. We are *called to account*.[11] We are not allowed to remain unmoved or unaffected. "The secrets of [our] heart are disclosed." We are not straining to be understood, but we realize that we have been understood at the deepest level. We "fall on [our] face[s]." We assume a posture of humility and repentance as we recognize that God is present in his word. We "worship God." We turn away from self-interest, placing God at the center of our lives.

How can we be sure this will happen? "God is really among you" (v. 25). This has never been in doubt in the passage. The question has simply been whether or not this reality was clear. We can be certain that the church will be rebuilt from the rubble we create because God is really among us. Our edifying and upbuilding of the church is based upon God's building work. We are parts of a building of which Christ is "the cornerstone" (Ephesians 2:20). It is Christ who builds the church, and "the gates of hell shall not prevail against it" (Matthew 16:18). If the gates of Hell will not prevail against the church, what makes us think that our failures will cause it to crumble? Jesus is not under any illusions about his church; he built it upon a broken rock (Peter).

Our intelligibility and contextualization is grounded in the accommodating, intelligible work of God in Christ. Though he could have been self-interested, he chose to be other-interested. Though he could have spoken another language—one that was beyond us, a heavenly coded language—he literally took on the *lingua franca*. He adapted himself to our language in order that he might be understood. And in order to make clear his commitment to us, and to overcome our self-interest and sin, he gave himself up in the most intelligible act of all time — the cross of Christ. This act made it forever clear and undeniable that "God so loved the world." How could he have made it any clearer? And now all of our gifts are intended to be used to make this redemptive act of God clear and compelling.

When the Apostle Paul uses the word for "building up" (v. 26; some translations say "edify"),[12] he is using an architectural term. Often the word is used metaphorically, as when someone says, "Oh, I want to build that person up." But it's an architectural term that is being applied organically to the different members of the body of the church. But the Apostle Paul mixes metaphors when he uses the architectural terms of being built up organically to describe the vitality of growth and the edification of church members.

This architectural imagery calls to mind Ephesians 2:19–22: "So then you are no longer strangers and aliens, but you are fellow citizens with the saints and members of the household of God, built on the foundation of the apostles and prophets, Christ Jesus himself being the cornerstone, in whom the whole structure, being joined together, grows into a holy temple in the Lord. In him you also are being built together into a dwelling place for God by the Spirit." He's saying that if we want to know what it means to be tightly knit and joined together as a body, we must know that we are all building blocks of this big structure, this big temple, the church, and Jesus Christ is the cornerstone. As we understand this relationship to one another, we will continue to grow and be built up.

There's nothing more beautiful than when somebody comes and is able to exercise speech grace gifts and people's hearts are moved. Someone with this gift speaks winsomely, and there is an insightful "ah-ha" moment when there is deep conviction about serving a particular idol. It is a beautiful use of that speech grace gift when someone is speaking the truth in love and the listener is gripped by its loving truth, so those words should not be refused or rejected. The individual who has this particular gift should use it and wield it carefully and humbly, not for his or her own benefit, not to be impressive, but in order to build up another believer.

The whole point here is not, do I have the gift of prophecy or the gift of tongues or the gift of healing? It's not about appearing to be impressive because a certain gift is possessed. It's a matter of those speech gifts being used and exercised in a skillful way to speak the gospel into a person's life so the human heart will be enlarged by the reality of what Christ has done.

26

Order out of Chaos

1 CORINTHIANS 14:26-40

SINCE CHAPTER 11 Paul has been talking about life within the body of Christ, the church. He has been particularly interested in the proper order of Christian worship. Each member's place and contribution to the body of Christ through the use of his or her grace gifts was emphasized. In this final sub-section his attention turns toward the subject of *order in public worship.*

It is important for the reader to understand that some elements in this passage have been controversial. Admittedly, on first reading some things strike us as being odd, perhaps even unsettling. There is controversy among scholars and within churches. Christians may find themselves troubled by this, but Paul's strong language about the role of women in the public assembly of the church has a particular setting and context. Paul is not leading with the subject of gender roles; he is responding to an occasion or development in the Corinthian church. Disruption in the church is the *occasion* for his teaching. The *content* of his teaching is order for the sake of freedom. This is similar to his teaching on spiritual gifts when the occasion was the misuse of prophecy and tongues. The content of the teaching was unity and upbuilding.

Christians need to seek to submit themselves to the full counsel of God's Word because there will be times when the cultural setting and personal presuppositions will cause an individual to be challenged by the Bible. The question is, will we allow the Bible to challenge our built-in assumptions? Will we allow it to say what it says? Will we wrestle with what it actually says, or have we predetermined what it is and is not allowed to say? When readers engage the text honestly, they find there is actually a significant amount of contextual nuance to what Paul is saying.[1] When we approach the

Biblical text we come with certain preunderstandings or presuppositions or an established set of beliefs that have been culturally conditioned. So when it comes to certain topics or issues that are a little more challenging—such as this one—we need to know that we come with a preconceived, presuppositional set of beliefs by which we have been culturally conditioned. There needs to be not only interpretive humility but also interpretive conviction because this passage can rub right up against the way modern people view reality.

When a Christian speaks the truth in that way—from where the Bible stands—he should assume that every ideology is going to be suspicious of Christianity. To those who are on the right it's going to seem like it's on the left, and to those who are on the left it's going to seem like it's on the right. A Christian needs to communicate with winsomeness and with a great amount of grace. "What is Paul saying here? Why this strong language?" will be a typical response. The Bible has to be able to contradict the reader, and God has to be able to contradict our views. If he can't do that, we're not in a real relationship with him.

When Christians seek to hear what the Bible is actually saying, at times they realize that their cultural blinders have hindered them from understanding what it was saying in the first place. One must strive for interpretive humility. Submission to the text should be the pursuit, rather than causing the text to be submitted to the modern reader. In due time these more controversial matters will be addressed, but we will major on what Paul majors on—the way the God of the Bible seeks to bring order out of chaos, particularly as it pertains to the proper order of public worship. Three points will guide the discussion:

- The Desire for Order
- The Occasions for Order
- The Beauty of Order

The Desire for Order

Individuals all have a desire for order. A thought-provoking modern philosopher by the name of Alain de Botton states it this way:

> Order contributes to the appeal of almost all substantial works of architecture. So fundamental is this quality, in fact, that it is written into even the most modest of projects at their very inception, in careful diagrams of electricity circuits and pipework, in elevations and plans—documents of beauty in which every cable and door frame has been measured and in

which, though one may fail to grasp the exact meaning of certain symbols and numbers, he or she may nonetheless sense, and delight in the overwhelming presence of precision and intent. Order is the means by which one makes sense of life.[2]

People live their lives each day because there are discernible patterns and routines. There is order of the workplace, order of schedules, order of public transit, etc. At a restaurant food is "ordered" because the person ordering the food is simply placing herself under the order of the institution that will ultimately deliver her the food for which she is paying.

Despite the fact that individuals desire order, they all approach it differently.

Pursuing freedom for the sake of freedom is chaotic (anarchy). Some reject all forms of order as enslaving. Many creative persons may lean this way, although everyone is dependent on order whether he knows it or not.

Ordering simply for the sake of order is despotic (tyranny). Some reject all forms of freedom as a sign of weakness. Certain type-A personalities might lean this way. It's actually unlivable because the ultimate order one seeks is out of reach and uncontrollable.

However, *order for the sake of freedom is liberating (liberty).* This third way sees order as a means of achieving freedom because it recognizes the necessity of having both systematic order and organic energy.

Think about the streets that people walk down each day in a city. The pedestrian needs to know multiple things—whether a street is one-directional or two-way, whether there are checkpoints (e.g., stop signs, traffic lights, etc.), guideposts (e.g., speed limit or caution signs), crosswalks or walk signals. If the anarchy paradigm (chaotic freedom/disorder) is embraced, the streets will be dangerous and unusable. Imagine what a mess it would be if individuals removed every single traffic light, stop sign, crosswalk, speed limit sign, and walk signal. They would experience gridlock, not to mention multiple accidents and injuries. If others embraced the tyranny paradigm (stifled freedom/forced order), the streets would be unpleasant, like a military state. They might be orderly, but individuals would likely seek to avoid them because they wouldn't look forward to strolling around. If the order freedom paradigm were accepted, there would be cars and pedestrians living in relative harmony. People could get where they need to go in a decent amount of time, but if they wanted to stroll and window-shop they would be able to enjoy themselves. The freedom one experiences is dependent upon and enabled by the order set in place by wise city planners. This text presents the reader with a view of Biblical worship that embraces this harmonious dance between freedom and order.

Biblical Worship Characterized by Freedom

Verse 26 says: "What then, brothers? When you come together, each one has a hymn, a lesson, a revelation, a tongue, or an interpretation. Let all things be done for building up." "Each one" is invited to fully participate, and this is not limited only to men. This is a beautiful picture of each member of the body making a meaningful contribution.[3] There is a variety of gifts[4] mentioned for the purpose of building up—namely, singing, teaching, prophecy, tongues, and interpretation. Paul reiterates what he argued for in the previous passage.[5] When Christians exercise their spiritual gifts, the main goal is the building up of the community.

Biblical Worship Also Characterized by Order (v. 40)

Whatever Paul is saying, he is not discouraging freedom and participation in worship. For all of the trouble that the gifts of tongues and prophecy have caused, he still encourages the Corinthians to desire and practice them. In verse 39 he says: "So, my brothers, earnestly desire to prophesy, and do not forbid speaking in tongues." However, he is seeking to provide needed guidelines to ensure that worship doesn't devolve into chaos. A well-functioning street needs design, signage, and good flow. Likewise, a well-functioning church service needs the same elements. Verse 40 continues: "But all things should be done decently and in order." This verse needs to be read with caution because it is not supposed to be read restrictively. Paul is encouraging the Corinthians to pursue order for freedom's sake.

The Occasions for Order

Paul is addressing two occasions for the sake of maintaining order: 1) tongues and interpretation, and 2) prophecy and discernment. Verses 27, 28 say: "If any speak in a tongue, let there be only two or at most three, and each in turn, and let someone interpret. But if there is no one to interpret, let each of them keep silent in church and speak to himself and to God." A freedom is granted to use one's gift in corporate worship, but there must be order: There can't be too many people speaking in tongues; otherwise one gift will dominate, and the flow will be disrupted. In other words, the participants can't be speaking over one another. Respect and concern for others is necessary, and personal silence (across genders) is preferable over creating disorder or confusion.[6]

The larger controversy is encased within a discussion about the practice of prophecy: "Let two or three prophets speak, and let the others weigh what is said. If a revelation is made to another sitting there, let the first be silent. For you can all prophesy one by one, so that all may learn and all be encouraged, and the spirits of prophets are subject to prophets. For God is not a God of confusion but of peace" (vv. 29–33). Again Paul emphasizes freedom, but it is to be characterized and accentuated by order. There was widespread participation in prophecy (including women): "You can all prophesy one by one," but not too many people in a given service ("two or three"). Personal silence is also preferable to talking over and disrespecting a brother or sister ("let the first be silent"). Therefore, the prophets are intended to remain in control (v. 32) (i.e., prophecy is not an ecstatic, uncontrollable experience[7]). The order of freedom is based in God's character,[8] and confusion must be avoided in order to reflect God's character as a God of peace.

Just as tongues need to be interpreted, prophecies need to be "weighed" and discerned: "Let the others weigh what is said" (v. 29). It is in this context that Paul's statements about the role of women in corporate worship need to be read. Whatever Paul may be saying, he is not saying that women ought to remain silent at all times—he has already encouraged them to pray and prophesy! But what are these verses saying? Verses 33b–35 continue: "As in all the churches of the saints, the women should keep silent in the churches. For they are not permitted to speak, but should be in submission, as the Law also says. If there is anything they desire to learn, let them ask their husbands at home. For it is shameful for a woman to speak in church." Paul is talking about the authoritative weighing of prophecies. Apparently there was a situation in Corinth where, when the prophecies were being weighed (presumably by male leaders) certain women were interjecting, asking questions, perhaps even challenging the rulings.[9] In a broader cultural context where women were generally submissive (e.g., a married woman would not talk to men who were not her husband), this would have brought shame upon the husbands of such women. It would be dishonorable. She would be dishonoring her husband by challenging the authority of the church leadership in this way.

Nevertheless, Paul does not want such women to be left in the dark, so he encourages them to ask their questions in a more appropriate context.[10] Paul's appeal to the Law is simply an appeal to the general principles of how the genders are to relate to one another in Genesis 2, 3.[11] This was not a question of nature but of function.

Need for Ordered Freedom Arising out of the Slavery of Chaos

Verses 36–38 tell us: "Or was it from you that the word of God came? Or are you the only ones it has reached? If anyone thinks that he is a prophet, or spiritual, he should acknowledge that the things I am writing to you are a command of the Lord. If anyone does not recognize this, he is not recognized." The Corinthians thought they had received a unique word from God and knew better than the apostle.[12] They believed that in their own wisdom they had arrived at a better way to worship than the one they had received. Christians risk the same error whenever they dismiss the teaching of the Bible—whether it be on spiritual gifts, gender roles, or other issues. But despite the fact that they viewed themselves as having great spiritual insight and importance, Paul says that if they are unable to receive his words as a command of the Lord, then they are not actually who they thought they were.[13]

Chances are that most individuals are caught somewhere between order and chaos. Corporate worship is incredibly ordered, while personal worship is chaotic. Others long for corporate worship to be more chaotic or free because they find personal worship to be incredibly dry and boring. What Christians are craving is the unique intervention of God to bring about an order that serves freedom. Christians do not want anarchy-driven traffic jams or a police state. They want a place to live—a street to stroll down, an order in which they can come alive. But where can they get it?

The Beauty of Order

The order of freedom is the result of the creative and redemptive activity of the triune God. "For God is not a God of confusion but of peace" (v. 33). We see the creative activity of God in Genesis 1:1–5: "In the beginning, God created the heavens and the earth. The earth was without form and void, and darkness was over the face of the deep. And the Spirit of God was hovering over the face of the waters. And God said, 'Let there be light,' and there was light. And God saw that the light was good. And God separated the light from the darkness. God called the light Day, and the darkness he called Night. And there was evening and there was morning, the first day." God takes chaos (void) and orders it. He fills the void and gives form, and his creative work brings about ordered freedom. God's design is neither anarchy (the universe is ordered and predictable), nor tyranny (people are free to cultivate and create), but an ordered freedom (the order and design of the universe compel his people to exercise their freedom in an orderly way).

The order of freedom is also the result of God's redemptive activity. There is perfect harmony within the three persons of the Godhead. Each person has a particular focus. The Father sends the Son, and the Son submits to the Father's sending, and the Spirit is sent by the Father and the Son in order to highlight the Son's work. The Trinity is an ultimate picture of an ordered, free community in which the persons give themselves freely for the good and joy of the others. When individuals get a picture of this beautiful harmony, there is no way they can misconceive their own place in the ordered freedom of corporate worship as restrictive. The Son is not less than the Father because he willingly submits to him. If anything, the Son's greatness is highlighted by his willing submission. Christians can trust God's design for ordered freedom because they see it at work in his own mutual interiority. And we see that he was willing to experience the chaos of our anarchy and the evil of our tyranny in order to free us from our slavery, to place us in a community of a beautified, ordered freedom where we find ourselves coming alive to who we were intended to be.

Jesus' self-donating sacrifice is a picture of his greatness, not his weakness. And when his disciples are willing to submit to the authority that God has established within his church for the sake of ordered freedom within the propriety of corporate worship, then there is harmony within the church. It is a master who becomes a servant who rules not with abusive leadership but servant leadership. When this reality is applied to members of the church, it is absolutely glorious.

27

The Power of the Gospel

1 CORINTHIANS 15:1–11

"If Jesus rose from the dead, then you have to accept all that he said; if he didn't rise from the dead, then why worry about any of what he said?"[1] If Jesus really defeated death, that gives credence to every claim he made. If Jesus did not defeat death, every claim he ever made is proven false. In the words of Jaroslav Pelikan: "If Christ is risen—then nothing else matters. And if Christ is not risen—then nothing else matters."

Christians and non-Christians have taken various positions on the topic of Christ's resurrection. Those who hold to an ahistorical position assert that Christians overspiritualize the resurrection and so remove it from its cultural setting. Many non-Christians flat out deny it. Those on the periphery state that Christians overemphasize various aspects of Christ's life and ministry at the expense of a proper treatment of the resurrection. Christian humanists tend to overemphasize the incarnation. Christian legalists overemphasize the life and teaching of Jesus, while Christian fundamentalists overemphasize the death of Christ to the exclusion of all other aspects. Some non-Christians, on the other hand, treat the resurrection as the novel belief of a minority rather than a claim with which we must reckon. The impersonal perspective argues that Christians over-doctrinalize and over-theologize so that the reality of Christ's resurrection has little to no impact on life. Non-Christian skeptics keep Christ and his claims at arm's length to avoid any need for a real encounter.

I like what Tim Keller has said about the doctrine of the resurrection: "I like the doctrine of the resurrection because it is just as hard or harsh as life itself." In other words, the resurrection has a sharp, intolerable, hard edge. When it evaluates life, there is something very hard and sharp about what it is trying to say. If Jesus Christ was bodily raised from the dead—a real historical event—that should change everything. We have both hope and joy. It changes the way we view ourselves, the world, our neighbors, creation, God, and history. It changes everything. But if Jesus Christ were not bodily raised from the grave, then Christianity has nothing to say. No hope. No joy. No exhortation. No inspiration. But Christianity is not just an optimistic pile of stories; real power emerges. If it is true, then we have real hope. And if it is not true, then we as Christians are most to be pitied of all people. The current text tells us that the gospel, rather than being ahistorical, is unmistakably historical; rather than being peripheral, it is necessarily central; and rather than being impersonal, it is radically personal. We'll look at three points:

- The Gospel Is Historical
- The Gospel Is Central
- The Gospel Is Personal

The Gospel Is Historical (Apologetic)

All religions and worldviews attempt to provide an answer to the age-old question of death. What is death? Why is there death? How do we relate to death?

There have been various approaches: One position simply desires to ignore or deny death by transcending or dissociating from it. Others fight or delay death by searching for the fountain of youth or either embrace or cave into death and giving up hope. However, each of these approaches falls short. Denying death is not an option because death is unavoidable. Delaying death is only temporary because death is universal. Embracing death is unsatisfying because death is unnatural.

If a religion is to have something meaningful to say about death, it must happen on the plane where life and death happen—it must take place in the realm of human history. It needs to give resolve in the face of death's unavoidability. It must give humanity an antidote for death's universality. It must give hope in the face of death's unnaturalness. The Christian gospel is not removed from this world, nor does it seek to remove us from the world. It does not seek to deny, delay, or embrace death; rather, it confronts death head-on in the middle of history. The gospel is not simply an idea, principle, or perspective—it is news—news that happened in history, news that revolves around a person.

The Gospel Centers on the Person and Work of Jesus Christ

Gospel piece #1: Incarnation. The text does not explicitly address the incarnation, but it implicitly assumes it. The gospel declares that God became man in the person of Jesus Christ in order to carry out his plan of redemption.

Gospel piece #2: Life. This text does not mention the life of Christ, but it is confirmed by all but the most radical revisionist historians that Jesus Christ was a historical figure. Even Christianity's radical opponents defend the historicity of the person of Jesus. But the gospel claims that Christ did more than simply exist. He lived a life of perfect obedience to God's Law, meeting the demands that individuals never could.

Gospel piece #3: Death. Here is where this text picks up the narrative. Verse 3 says: "For I delivered to you as of first importance what I also received: that Christ died for our sins in accordance with the Scriptures." This is a historical reality accepted by everyone who believes that Christ existed.[2] "Christ died"[3] for a purpose (i.e., "for our sins"). He had no sins of his own to die for, but the wages of our sin was Jesus' death. He died in order that individual sinners might be reconciled to God. And this happened "in accordance with the Scriptures."[4] Christ's death was according to God's redemptive plan and in line with what had been foretold in the Old Testament Scriptures.

Gospel piece #4: Burial. Verse 4 tells "he was buried."[5] Christ's death was no mere illusion because his body was treated like any other corpse by the Roman officials and by his friends who grieved the loss of his life.

Gospel piece #5: Resurrection. Verse 4 tells us "he was raised[6] on the third day[7] in accordance with the Scriptures." A human being in history on a particular day was raised from the dead. The phrase "in accordance with the Scriptures" argues that the historical nature of the gospel hinges on the resurrection. The resurrection would have been just as unbelievable to a first-century person as it would be for a modern individual living in a more developed scientific age.

Many simply dismiss the idea of resurrection as ahistorical, but in order to do so four clear historical realities must be erased. William Lane Craig argues for these historical realities:[8]

Historical reality #1: The burial of Jesus. Jesus Christ was buried by Joseph of Arimathea in his personal tomb, and the tomb was guarded by Roman guards. It was a known location that could be checked. Joseph of Arimathea was a member of the Jewish court that condemned Jesus, so this was not likely fabricated by Christians.

Historical reality #2: The empty tomb. "The tomb of Jesus was found empty by a group of his female followers." "The fact that the women's testimony was considered worthless in a first-century Palestinian court gives credence to the historicity of the account"[9] (i.e., they didn't choose strong witnesses). Everyone agrees that the tomb was empty—either by resurrection or some other explanation.

Historical reality #3: Post-resurrection appearances. Verses 4–8 say: ". . . he was raised on the third day in accordance with the Scriptures, and . . . he appeared to Cephas, then to the twelve. Then he appeared to more than five hundred brothers at one time, most of whom are still alive, though some have fallen asleep. Then he appeared to James, then to all the apostles. Last of all, as to one untimely born, he appeared also to me." Jesus appeared to all of the leaders of the early church[10]—Peter, Paul, and all of the apostles. If he only appeared to them, it would make sense that some people doubted the veracity of the sightings. But Paul appeals to a crowd of "more than 500 brothers," most of whom were still alive and could have confirmed or denied Paul's claim. Five hundred rational people who did not have a category for seeing a dead person raised claimed to have seen the risen Jesus. This claim itself is a historical reality.

Historical reality #4: The reaction of the early disciples. Early disciples had every reason not to believe in the resurrection of Jesus unless he had actually been raised. Their leader was dead. Their leader was a condemned heretic—a man under the curse of God because of his death on a tree. Nevertheless, they were prepared to die over their belief in the resurrection of Christ. In spite of the fact that there was no benefit to their believing in the resurrection, they chose to defend this claim at all costs.

These four realities must be explained—the burial, the empty tomb, the appearances, and the reaction of the disciples. An actual historical resurrection makes the most sense of the historical realities that we have before us. One must come up with a more compelling alternative explanation if one wishes to deny the historical records of Scripture.

The skeptic must come up with a historically feasible, plausible account—an alternative explanation—for why there is an empty tomb, why there was an established burial, why there were eyewitness accounts, why there was the emergence of the early church. The reality is that the general population did not have a worldview that could receive the truth of the resurrection. In other words, if there were simply the empty tomb and not the eyewitness testimony, or if the converse were true, then the resurrection could be explained. If we had the empty tomb, but we didn't have eyewitness testimony, someone could come up with a conspiracy theory and simply say, "They stole the body." Even if the Roman guards were deeply asleep, what needs to be understood is that for a Roman guard to allow somebody to break into a tomb like that would ultimately mean he was forfeiting his own life. Also the report of Jesus' resurrection would have been unthinkable for a Greek individual, and it would have been inconceivable in the mind of a Jewish individual. In a dualistic Greek world, they did not have categories for a bodily resurrection. Judaism had no category for understanding that somebody in the middle of history could actually rise from the dead. The historical data and the evidence that was presented challenged these world-views. Even if people can't believe in the resurrection, they should *want* it to be true. The gospel is historical, and it takes place in real time and space and thus has implications for every human life.

The Gospel Is Central (Theological)

Verses 1–4 state: "Now I would remind you, brothers, of the gospel I preached to you, which you received, in which you stand, and by which you are being saved, if you hold fast to the word I preached to you—unless you believed in vain. For I delivered to you as of first importance what I also received: that Christ died for our sins in accordance with the Scriptures, that he was buried, that he was raised on the third day in accordance with the Scriptures." Here is the flow of Paul's logic. The gospel is news that must be communicated[11] because it is something that Paul himself "received" (v. 3) (he heard it).[12] It is news that Paul "preached" (v. 1) and "delivered" (v. 3) because the gospel is news that breaks into a hearer's world (it is "received," v. 1). The reception of the gospel is part of a Christian's past, but it is also a reality that has an ongoing present importance ("and so you believed" [v. 11]). The gospel is doing a present saving work in their lives ("and by which you are being saved," v. 2), and it is a power that continues to have future significance in the life of a believer. Therefore, the Corinthians must "hold fast" to the gospel (v. 2).

Three common mistakes about gospel centrality include:

1. "The gospel is something that happened merely in my *past*." It was the beginning of my Christian life, but I accepted the gospel, and now I'm moving on to deeper things.
   - Problem 1: This misses the present, holistic significance of the gospel.
   - Problem 2: It also misses the future promises and security of the gospel.

2. "The gospel is something I need only occasionally in *the present*." Sometimes Christians slip and fall and need grace, but when God picks them up, they think they can move on by trying harder to earn God's favor. When times get difficult Christians can turn to God for grace, but Christians are by and large self-sufficient (this may be implicit).
   - Problem 1: This common mistake misses the past done-ness of the gospel that ensures the security of one's future.
   - Problem 2: It also ignores the constant, ongoing need for grace in every dimension of one's life.
3. "The gospel is primarily about what is going to happen in *the future*." Personal relationship with God is primarily understood as it relates to one's eternal destiny—"I'm all set and on my way to Heaven."
   - Problem 1: This makes the relationship with God primarily transactional—"I believe the gospel out of fear (escape) or desire for pleasure."
   - Problem 2: It misses the present significance and fullness of the gospel.

The gospel is intended to be part of the past, present, and future reality of a Christian's salvific experience. One's *past* is settled. Christ entered into history to die for one's sins and raise him or her again to new life. One no longer needs to fear death as the punishment for his or her past sins—resurrection is a reward because of the work of Christ. An individual's *present* is secure. One can stand firm and hold fast because God is ultimately holding fast to him or her. The resources of the gospel are sufficient to meet every challenge and temptation that one may face. The ultimate end of all our fears is death, but Christ has defeated death in his resurrection; so all of these derivative fears are stripped of their power. Our *future* is certain. Individuals do not have to strive to create and maintain a future for themselves because Christ has already done the work for them. The resurrection is clear evidence of Christ's death-conquering work on our behalf. Look at Christ, and you will see your future.

The gospel is intended to be the central power around which one's life revolves. If a Christian's life revolves around another person, that other person will inevitably crush that individual. If a Christian's life revolves around himself, he will implode. But if his life is centered around the gospel, then he orbits around the one person who will not crush him (he was already crushed for you), and the believer will not implode because his center of gravity is properly aligned.

If the truth of the centrality of the gospel brings harmonious balance into a sinner's life, why make the mistake of pushing the gospel to the periphery?

Individuals doubt the present reliability of the foundation of the gospel, and they seek other foundations upon which to stand (cf. v. 1). Most of them are self-constructed (vocation, family, etc.). In the midst of the uncertainties and imbalances of life, people look for other things to take hold of for stability ("If you hold fast," v. 2). They take hold of whatever is nearby. When taking a subway, if a passenger is trying to ride without holding on to the sturdy pole right beside her, she will inevitably keep slipping and will lose her balance. Christians have been given something to which they can hold fast and that will see them through life's uncertainties, yet they try to balance themselves and take hold of alternate stabilizers that actually offer no stability at all.

The resurrection was not purely a naked display of power. One commentator put it this way, referring to verse 17: "'If Christ were not raised then you would still be dead in your sins.' So the resurrection proves that something is over, and the question is, what is over?"[13] Attending the funeral of a deceased family member is often a very difficult experience. Our culture attempts to appease the pain by saying that death is natural. That is why the dead body is presented in a way that seems very natural—the way he or she looked before death. However, death is *not* natural. Death is actually outright ugly because it has been inflicted. Death is a judgment. And when Jesus died, if he didn't rise, everyone would still be in their sins because death would still be owed to them. Death would still have authority over human lives. This is the reason why Jesus' resurrection from the dead is essentially telling the believer that a payment for sin has been made The debt has been paid, and Christians have overcome sin, and sin will no longer have power and authority over them. Our sins have been paid for in full; the resurrection of new life has already begun in us.

So the gospel is unmistakably historical, it is necessarily central, and lastly it is personal.

The Gospel Is Personal (Existential)

Verses 8–10 say: "Last of all, as to one untimely born, he appeared also to me. For I am the least of the apostles, unworthy to be called an apostle, because I persecuted the church of God. But by the grace of God I am what I am, and his grace toward me was not in vain. On the contrary, I worked harder than any of them, though it was not I, but the grace of God that is with me." Paul speaks about the gospel as something that he has experienced—something that ought to be having an effect on the Corinthian believers. It is not merely an idea or an institutional religion. It is not even a way of looking at the world. It is historical news with ultimate personal impact. Paul recounts his own story by saying that he was a persecutor of the church, making him utterly unworthy to be a recipient of God's favor and grace, but ironically this is precisely what he is given in Jesus. Jesus made a personal appearance to him.[14] Paul recognizes his "unworthiness" and even calls himself "the least of all the apostles."[15] It is ultimately the free grace of God that makes Paul what he is.

The gospel de-centers unbelievers from the center of their own life. They recognize their unworthiness. They recognize they are what they are by grace. The gospel is now a functional identity. Without effort or work Christians are put in perfect relationship with God and experience all the benefits of union with Christ. His *incarnation* means that he always meets everyone where he or she is. His perfect life means that Christians are perfectly accepted by God regardless of their ability to be righteous. His *substitutionary death* means that Christians need no longer fear punishment for their sins—he has borne the full penalty. His *burial* means that his death on one's behalf was no mirage and that someone has gone to face the consequences to replace death. His *resurrection* means that death has been defeated—it has been stripped of its power and sting. Christians will ultimately be raised again to new life because of their union with the resurrected Christ.

The result of this free, full grace is that Christians live their lives to the full.[16] Verse 10 says: "But by the grace of God I am what I am, and his grace toward me was not in vain. On the contrary, I worked harder than any of them, though it was not I, but the grace of God that is with me." The grace of God does not create laziness, but actually works in individuals to lead them toward deeper engagement. His incarnation leads individuals to put others before themselves. One accommodates others because he or she has experienced accommodating grace. Jesus' life and teaching lead individuals to live lives of compelling, sacrificial love. His death enables individuals to live free from the guilt of sin and to be certain of God's acceptance and approval. Rather than trying to wash oneself from guilt or earn the approval of others, one is free to live in light of God's full acceptance and a cleansed conscience. His resurrection enables individuals to take risks and to be fearless in the face of death. The ultimate enemy has been defeated, so all of our other minor enemies are stripped of their power. Individuals are enabled to "work harder," but not for gain or building an identity or security—Christians already have all of those things. We don't even work from our own power; rather it is "the grace of God that it is with [us]."

At Easter the resurrection is at the center of a story that God has placed at the center of history and that, we are here reminded, is the only thing that can really carry the weight of being at the center of our lives. The gospel is historical: it makes the most sense of the facts. The gospel is central: it's the very heart of Christianity. The gospel is personal: it is news that must be reckoned with at the heart level.

In other words, Christianity refuses to be left- or right-brained. It doesn't just emphasize the objective historical reality, but also talks about the personal nature of its truth. It's not just for cognitives, and it's not just for mystics. God takes the truth—the historical truth of the resurrection—and burns it deep into human hearts so that the gospel will be received and the personal implications will be recognized.

28

Resurrection

1 CORINTHIANS 15:12–34

IF THE RESURRECTION IS TRUE, then everything would change for those who do not embrace the faith. If the resurrection is true, then unbelief is implausible. If Jesus has been raised from the dead, that validates Paul's preaching of the gospel. And if the resurrection is *not* true, then everything would change for those who do embrace the faith. If the resurrection is false, belief is implausible. If Jesus has not been raised from the dead, then the gospel is invalidated.

Timothy Keller describes the resurrection as "the hinge upon which the story of the world pivots."[1] The doctrine of the resurrection has profound implications for how anyone lives. The resurrection of Christ in the past and the resurrection of human beings in the future have deep practical significance for the present. It changes the way both death and life are understood and experienced. Paul addresses the topic of the resurrection this way:

- The Realities of the Resurrection
- The Implications of the Resurrection
- The Application of the Resurrection

The Realities of the Resurrection (What Is the Resurrection?)
Apologetic Credibility

Modern individuals have a difficult time accepting the idea that someone could rise from the dead. To claim that a human being actually expired, was buried, and three days later rose again from the ground without any human intervention seems too fantastic and nearly unbelievable. Typically people assume that the gullibility of ancient people allowed them to believe in something this incredulous. However, ancient people had just as much difficulty with the resurrection as moderns do.[2] Death is death—it is not as though the ancients had a permeable understanding of death in which individuals might return at will. Resurrection was just as preposterous to an ancient individual as it is to a modern person. People aren't supposed to rise from the dead—this is true regardless of anyone's cultural or historical context. Suspicion is natural and warranted, but it's not unique. It was unthinkable even for the Greeks at that time because they had a gnostic, dualistic way of looking at the material world and the spiritual world. In other words, they considered the soul to be wonderful and beautiful, but they considered the physical body, the flesh, to be evil. The Greeks, even Greek Christians, did not have a worldview to accommodate a belief in the bodily, physical resurrection of Jesus.

What about the Jews? Although there is an assumption that they had a robust understanding of the resurrection, there are only two explicit references to the resurrection in the Old Testament—Isaiah 26:19 and Daniel 12:1, 2. There may be more references, but these are the only two on which there is consensus among scholars. The Jews did believe that at the very end of the world everything would be renovated. They anticipated the new heavens and the new earth at the end of time when there would be bodily, physical resurrection. However, they did not have a worldview to accommodate a belief in a bodily, physical resurrection in the middle of history.

What's surprising is that the amount of evidence for the resurrection is actually substantial. Even some renowned atheists have acknowledged this. Anthony Flew, one of the most respected atheistic philosophers within the last fifty or sixty years, claims: "The evidence for the resurrection is better than for claimed miracles in any other religion. It's outstandingly different in quality and quantity from the evidence offered for the occurrence of most other supposedly miraculous events."[3] Flew eventually became a theist, but he did not become a Christian. Though he thought the evidence was strong for the resurrection, he never actually embraced it.

Even if one does not believe in the resurrection, one would want it to be true. If there is a concern for justice, good stewardship of the environment, and other great causes in this physical world, then believing in the resurrection provides the proper context and understanding for desiring a greater or better world. If this life is all there is, what incentive or motivation would one have to try to work for a greater or better world? N. T Wright writes, "The message of the resurrection is that this world matters."[4] Believing in the resurrection supports an individual who wants to stand up for that which is right and to be the best possible steward he can be.

Doctrinal Centrality

Resurrection is more important than people might think. If Christians fail to believe in the resurrection, everything falls apart.[5] 1) Paul's work as an apostle is then in vain, and 2) the Christian faith itself is in vain.[6] "And if Christ has not been raised, then our preaching is in vain and your faith is in vain"[7] (v. 14). So 3) Paul is a liar who misrepresents God. "We are even found to be misrepresenting God, because we testified about God that he raised Christ"[8] (v. 15).

If there is no resurrection, 4) Christian faith is futile—it accomplishes nothing, and thus the sin problem is still a live problem that needs a solution. "And if Christ has not been raised, your faith is futile and you are still in your sins"[9] (v. 17). 5) The promises of a new heavens and new earth are empty—there is no afterlife for those who have died. "Then those also who have fallen asleep in Christ have perished" (v. 18). 6) The present life experience of Christians is pointless and to be pitied. "If in Christ we have hope in this life only, we are of all people most to be pitied"[10] (v. 19).

The resurrection is the truth on which everything else hinges. Without it Christian ministry is pointless, personal faith is ineffective, God's character is called into question, Christians are still in need of salvation, any sense of future hope is removed, and our present experience is meaningless. On the other hand, if Christ did indeed rise from the dead, then the opposite is true! The Corinthians had not taken into account the importance of the resurrection. They didn't realize all the things that would fall apart without the validity of the resurrection. Interestingly enough, they had pulled out another piece of the puzzle that had caused the doctrine of the resurrection of Christ to come tumbling down. In order to understand this, one needs to make a quick categorical expansion in relation to his or her understanding of the resurrection.

Categorical Expansion

Resurrection is a bigger topic than people might think. People tend to think that the Christian doctrine of resurrection has simply to do with the resurrection of Christ in the past. It is that, but it is more. The Christian doctrine of the resurrection includes the belief that not only was Christ raised in the past, but also that all believers will be raised in the future. According to this passage, Christ is "the firstfruits" of God's resurrecting work (v. 23) that will be completed when he returns. This is basic Christian teaching, and it is found in the Apostles' Creed: "I believe in . . . the resurrection of the body."

Sadly, many Christians are unaware of this doctrine. Many Christians have embraced a view of the future that is un-Biblical.[11] God's intention is not that Christians would be disembodied souls floating around in the clouds, but that they would live with him forever as whole persons, both body and soul. Therefore, the Christian understanding of the resurrection ought to make individuals more this-worldly and not merely other-worldly. This has profound implications for the way life should be approached precisely because it has shaped the way death is to be understood in light of the resurrection.

The Implications of Resurrection (Is Resurrection Existentially Plausible?)

The Problem of Death

Everyone must come to terms with the reality of death one way or another. People can 1) passively deny death by ignoring the reality and avoiding talking about it, 2) actively battle death by warding off its fast approaching signs via diet, or 3) tragically embrace it by psychologically twisting death into something that it is not. Even the Corinthians were attempting to cope with death. According to verse 29 they were undergoing vicarious baptisms on behalf of the dead.[12] Paul doesn't outright condemn them for this practice, but neither does he condone it. He uses it against them.

Everyone must come to terms with what happens after death, and there are three major explanations for understanding this. 1) Body and soul cease to exist after death (hedonism/survival).[13] In this view there is nothing beyond this life, so this position often leads to hedonism. "Let us eat and drink, for tomorrow we die" (v. 32). If a person simply ceases to exist, then this life becomes about survival and indulgence. Though plenty of people who hold this view happen to be upstanding, moral people, they lack a robust grounding for their morality or humanitarianism. 2) The body ceases to exist, but the soul lives on (dualism/mysticism). Many ancients held that the body was intrinsically evil, while the soul was intrinsically good. This viewpoint is still quite common today, even among Christians. This perspective can lead to a form of escapism that ignores the physical world. 3) Body and soul continue to exist by way of resurrection (holism). This is the view that the Scriptures present, but it is nearly impossible to comprehend because of the pervasiveness and certainty of death. There is no reason to believe that holistic humans, being body and soul, will continue to exist at some point in the future, unless there is reason to believe that death has been defeated. That is precisely what the Bible states—death has been swallowed up by the resurrecting power of Jesus Christ.

The Defeat of Death

"But in fact Christ has been raised from the dead, the firstfruits of those who have fallen asleep. For as by a man came death, by a man has come also the resurrection of the dead. For as in Adam all die, so also in Christ shall all be made alive. But each in his own order: Christ the firstfruits, then at his coming those who belong to Christ" (vv. 20–23). The resurrection of Christ was not a one-time event that was never meant to be repeated again; it was the "firstfruits" of a greater plan.[14] In agricultural terms, the "firstfruits" is the very first showing of a given harvest. If the firstfruits are good, that is a good sign that the rest of the harvest will be good. Christ's resurrection is only the beginning of God's greater plan of the resurrection. Adam functioned as the federal representative of his people (i.e., humanity), and everyone inherited death because of his fall into sin.[15] Jesus functioned as the federal head of his people, and everyone who is in him inherits resurrection life because of his defeat of death.[16]

The Victory of Life

Then comes the end, when he delivers the kingdom to God the Father after destroying every rule and every authority and power. For he must reign until he has put all his enemies under his feet. The last enemy to be destroyed is death. For "God has put all things in subjection under his feet." But when it says, "all things are put in subjection," it is plain that he is excepted who put all things in subjection under him. When all things are subjected to him, then the Son himself will also be subjected to him who put all things in subjection under him, that God may be all in all (vv. 24–28).

Individuals live in the time between Christ's past historical resurrection and his future historical return, but it's important for Christians to grab hold of a vision of God's future, the end-time plan for this world.[17] Jesus will ultimately destroy every ruler, authority, and power associated with death, sin, and decay and thereby establish a world free from death, sin, and decay.[18] In the beautiful self-giving order of the Trinity, the Father sends the Son to accomplish this work, and the Son willingly accomplishes it and then presents it to the Father.[19] The victory of life is ultimately seen in the fact that God is "all in all." There will come a day when death is no more, and only the eternal life that God freely gives will remain. Admittedly, as soon as one begins to talk about eschatology, the future, the defeat of death, he begins to scratch at the limits of his understanding. However, the doctrine of the resurrection is profoundly applicable to all human life. God has a way of entering into people's lives, breaking through with the shattering, disrupting, powerful event of the resurrection. He has a way of throwing things off balance, but it is in these moments that he builds the believer up with the powerful implications of the resurrection.

The Application of Resurrection
(How Does It Change the Way Life Is Lived?)

The only way to overcome death, pain, wounds, sins, and struggles is to understand the deep internal application of the doctrine of the resurrection.

If the Resurrection Is False . . .

Individuals may or may not believe that the resurrection is true, but if these individuals do not believe that it is true and they take their perspective to its logical conclusion, they will have a profound lack of future hope. Then this life is all that anyone has, and it could be destroyed at any moment. A person would have to strive to get everything that can be gained out of this life. This approach to life may be understood as radical hedonism (willing to take a risk over trivial matters). "If the dead are not raised, 'Let us eat and drink, for tomorrow we die'" (v. 32). If an individual does not believe the resurrection is true, on what basis does his life have meaning beyond this moment? One has to engage in the never-ending game of self-preservation. This may cause an individual to be self-protectionistic (unwilling to give himself for crucial matters). If this is all that anyone has and death is inevitable, then that person will have to preserve everything at the cost of relationships and a full-throttle embracing of life. Ironically, individuals get stuck moving alone back and forth between exploration and self-preservation. They want everything in the world, but everything in the world is a potential threat to survival. If this is all there is, then they have to have it all and avoid it all at all costs.

If the Resurrection Is True . . .

Christians have a profound hope. "Resurrection means endless hope, but no resurrection means hopeless end."[20] No matter what one may face in the here and now, he or she will know that it is not ultimately determinative—this is not all there is. Similarly, when loved ones pass away, one is not filled with final grief but with expectant joy. Individuals will embrace risky living (willing to give oneself for crucial matters). "Why are we in danger every hour? I protest, brothers, by my pride in you, which I have in Christ Jesus our Lord, I die every day! What do I gain if, humanly speaking, I fought with beasts at Ephesus?" (vv. 30–32a). Christians do not need to engage in self-preservation and self-protection because they cannot ultimately lose. Even the loss of life is not an ultimate loss.[21] Christians can look death in the eye without ultimate fear.[22] Ironically, it is the resurrection that gives Christians what hedonism and self-exploration falsely promise: the ability to live and enjoy life to the full without fear. Christians will be able to conduct themselves with moral composure (an unwillingness to overvalue trivial matters). "If the dead are not raised, 'Let us eat and drink, for tomorrow we die.' Do not be deceived: 'Bad company ruins good morals'" (vv. 32b, 33). Because this is not the end, individuals are able to take the light things of life lightly. Additionally, Christians are able to have proper perspective on what really lasts. Rather than creating a pie-in-the-sky piety, the resurrection provides a framework for understanding the importance of righteous living in the present, something that a naturalistic understanding of life cannot entirely provide.

But the problem is that there is a remaining disconnect: "Wake up from your drunken stupor, as is right, and do not go on sinning. For some have no knowledge of God. I say this to your shame" (v. 34). Many who have an intellectual knowledge of the resurrection lack a transformative knowledge.[23] Paul compares this to a drunken stupor—functionally living without resurrection hope. But note that Paul doesn't offer them anything more than what they already have in Christ. It is not as though there is something more profound than the death and resurrection of Christ. Paul's approach is to call their attention to the foolishness of ignoring the incredible significance of the resurrection life that they have. In other words, there is no need for something more—we need to drill down deeper into what we already have. We have a profound hope that gives us the ability to live riskily with moral composure because death has been defeated!

The resurrection narrative tells a story with a beautiful, happy ending. The end of redemptive history is: God wins, and those who are in union with Christ will win along with him. He will renew the entire world to make it the way it is supposed to be and will undo all of the disintegration. The resurrection is a picture of what that future will look like. Why do we have difficulty dealing with suffering? Why do we have difficulty with death? Why do we worry about potentially losing money or career? It is difficult because we think that this broken world is the only world that we're ever going to have. We want greater certainty than that. And Paul is trying to say that the greater certainty has already been validated and solidified through the life, death, and resurrection of Jesus Christ. We have inherited this resurrection life as a gift—a power that is already inherited by faith in Jesus, that helps us look suffering and death in the eye and see hope. Death will not ultimately have the victory because of what Jesus Christ has done. It's not possible that we could ever fail or consider ourselves as losers. Because Jesus Christ lost everything for us, we can't ultimately lose anything.

29

The Resurrection Body

1 CORINTHIANS 15:35–49

CAN THE CHRISTIAN DOCTRINE of the resurrection make sense? Where is there overlap and continuity with the present world? Where is there discontinuity? Does the Christian doctrine of the resurrection of the dead have any practical significance? Paul continues with his focus on the resurrection of the body. He is talking to the Corinthians about the claim that all Christians will be raised from the dead when Christ returns. In essence, if Jesus was raised, it follows that all those who are in him will also be raised. If he has defeated death, then death will not ultimately reign in the lives of those who belong to him. He is "the firstfruits" (15:20, 23), the first of many to be raised from the dead. If Jesus was not raised, it follows that there is no means of escaping death or hoping for something beyond the present life. But because Christ was raised from the dead, Christians must attempt to comprehend the claim that he is going to raise from the dead those who belong to him.

The most significant implication of the passage is the importance of the body. How the human body is viewed will radically shape the way one thinks and lives. If the body is unimportant, one will either be an escapist mystic or an unfettered hedonist. The material world will not matter. However, many today are beginning to recognize the importance of the body. This is seen through healthy eating, exercising, and caring for the environment. Historic Christianity provides the most robust framework for pursuing material, bodily health and wholeness. Admittedly, this is contrary to popular belief and goes against much of modern-day Christian practice. But if individuals follow the teaching of Scripture and allow it to speak for itself, they may be pleasantly surprised by what they find. Flannery O'Connor once said: "For me it is the virgin birth, the Incarnation, the resurrection which are the true laws of the flesh and the physical. Death, decay, destruction are the suspension of these laws. I am always astonished at the emphasis the Church puts on the body. It is not the soul she says that will rise but the body, glorified."[1] This passage will be examined in the following three movements:

- The Resurrection Is Intelligible
- The Resurrection Is Incomprehensible
- The Resurrection Is Indescribably Beautiful

The Resurrection Is Intelligible (vv. 35–41)

The first notable observation is that the resurrection is intelligible. In other words, the resurrection is natural. There is continuity between resurrection and what is typically seen in the world on a daily basis. The resurrection in this sense is intelligible even though it is incomprehensible.

"But someone will ask, 'How are the dead raised? With what kind of body do they come?'" (v. 35). The Corinthians were having a hard time believing the implication that all Christians will be raised in a body because Christ was raised in a body. They had categories for the soul living on indefinitely, but there was no category for the body living on indefinitely.[2] They had a dualistic understanding of the human person. The soul—the immaterial part of the person—was seen as the good, immortal part, but the body—the material part of the person—was seen as the bad, mortal part.[3] The goal was to slough off the limited, filthy body so the soul could experience purity and limitlessness. This is still a commonly held belief. Many believe that the body is just a container for the soul. Death is seen as a release from the mortal body. The soul ascends to some netherworld where individuals can finally be free. This view is improperly held by many Christians who view Heaven as a bodiless, amorphous existence in an otherworldly, heavenly location. This idea is also held by most spiritualists (and those in other religions). Paul wants to confront this misunderstanding about the body and its eventual resurrection, and he does so by making two arguments in verses 35–41: 1) The resurrection of the body lines up with the understanding of *change/transformation of quality* (vv. 36–38); 2) the resurrection of the body lines up with the understanding of *variety/difference of kind* (vv. 39–41).

(1) The resurrection of the body lines up with the understanding of the *transformation of quality*. Verses 36–38 say: "You foolish person! What you sow does not come to life unless it dies. And what you sow is not the body that is to be, but a bare kernel, perhaps of wheat or of some other grain. But God gives it a body as he has chosen, and to each kind of seed its own body."

It is natural to assume that bodies will not rise from the dead. Most people do not have firsthand experience of a resurrection; neither did the Corinthians. But there are corollaries in this world that might cause one to consider it. Paul looks at the subject of transformation and change. *Transformation is counterintuitive.* Paul uses the example of a seed that sprouts into something that looks completely different than it originally did. The seed undergoes a burial and is later transformed. The DNA is the same, but there is transformation. Transformation is counterintuitive in our own lives. Life transformation and meaningful change usually happen at moments of crisis. Life often emerges from what feels like death. The idea of life forming out of death then proves itself to be a perfectly intelligible concept.

Transformation is out of one's control. The seed is buried and left to forces outside of its control; it needs good soil and moisture. It is God who enacts this transformational work. "God gives it a body as he has chosen, and to each kind of seed its own body" (v. 38). It is God who gives the seed its body, and it is God who gives the tree its body. It is God who gave us our bodies; it is also God who gives resurrection bodies. God provides the transformation of quality, which is intelligible but is also foreign because it happens out of one's control.

(2) The resurrection of the body lines up with the understanding of *variety/difference of kind.* Verses 39–41 say: "For not all flesh is the same, but there is one kind for humans, another for animals, another for birds, and another for fish. There are heavenly bodies and earthly bodies, but the glory of the heavenly is of one kind, and the glory of the earthly is of another. There is one glory of the sun, and another glory of the moon, and another glory of the stars; for star differs from star in glory." Paul is saying that just because individuals cannot imagine a body that is different than the body that one has now does not mean it isn't possible. God has created all kinds of bodies. Each one is fit for its environment—the animal for the land, the bird for the air, the fish for the sea. God is the ultimate Creator of bodies. God has created different and specific kinds of bodies that can thrive within a particular environment or natural habitat. The very variety that is visible and noticeable should lead us to believe that he is capable of creating a human body that is different in quality and kind than our present earthly bodies. Paul is strategically using metaphors and illustrations of the natural world in order to explain the intelligibility of the resurrection.

But despite the ways the resurrection lines up with this world, it is also beyond us. In other words, there is continuity, but there are equal measures of discontinuity. We cannot predict what a resurrection body will look like because it is outside of the realm of our experience.

Resurrection Is Incomprehensible (vv. 42–46)

The resurrection is intelligible, but it is also incomprehensible. The resurrection is natural, but it is also supernatural. The resurrection is like something in the world, but it is also unlike anything in this world.

There is an incomprehensible change in quality, *from perishable to imperishable.* "So is it with the resurrection of the dead. What is sown is perishable;[4] what is raised is imperishable. It is sown in dishonor; it is raised in glory. It is sown in weakness; it is raised in power" (vv. 42, 43). Though the reader can understand that transformation does happen in some cases, it is impossible for one to understand how something could go from perishable to imperishable, from dishonorable to glorious, and from weak to strong. Everyone longs for the imperishable. We see from the health and cosmetic industries that many people attempt to fight death with all kinds of tools because they know their bodies are extremely fragile. If there were a way to make perishable life imperishable, it's likely that it would have been found! But individuals will try anything to lengthen their lives. The resurrection of the body claims that Christians will be raised and the quality of their bodies will be utterly transformed—from the perishable to the imperishable, from dishonor to glory, from weakness to power. Christianity affirms the longing to overcome death, disease, sickness, and decay, but it doesn't do so by escaping from the body but by transforming the body itself!

There will be an incomprehensible change in kind—*from natural to supernatural.*[5] Verses 44–46 say: "It is sown a natural body; it is raised a spiritual body. If there is a natural body, there is also a spiritual body. Thus it is written, "The first man Adam became a living being"; the last Adam became a life-giving spirit. But it is not the spiritual that is first but the natural, and then the spiritual." The transformation of the body consists in its being infused and re-created by the life-giving Spirit of Jesus. It is a move from a natural body to a supernatural body. It is a move from mortal to immortal. But the body is still present. Consider Jesus' resurrection body,[6] which is the closest thing Christians have to an encounter with a resurrected body. He was human; he was recognizable; he had scars; he ate fish. But there was a supernatural quality to his body since he walked through walls! This is beyond normal comprehension. It is something that many people would like to believe is true. It is something they likely find difficult to believe because it seems so speculative. What Christians believe about the body truly matters. If individuals believe that the body is done with at death, they are most likely mystic escapists. Christians can fall on both sides of this. Why care for the body anyway? Death can't be beaten! At best it can only be delayed a few years. Similarly, why care for the earth? It's decaying and headed toward destruction! If people believe the body has eternal significance, they can fight death because it has already been defeated. Stewardship for the created world can also be achieved because it also has lasting significance. The body, like the physical things of this world, is not something to escape from but to embrace and beautify.

How can this be believed? How can Christians be assured they will experience this incomprehensible transformation of quality and kind? In short, it is in the beauty of the Resurrected One, Jesus, that this truth can become a believable reality and a future promise for those who believe.

The Resurrection Is Indescribably Beautiful (vv. 47–49)

How can one come to a realization that the resurrection is indescribably beautiful and compelling? How can one see that there is a convergence of the natural and the supernatural or that the resurrection has entered the world in the person of Jesus Christ?

> Thus it is written, "The first man Adam became a living being"; the last Adam became a life-giving spirit. But it is not the spiritual that is first but the natural, and then the spiritual. The first man was from the earth, a man of dust; the second man is from heaven. As was the man of dust, so also are those who are of the dust, and as is the man of heaven, so also are those who are of heaven. Just as we have borne the image of the man of dust, we shall also bear the image of the man of heaven. (vv. 45–49)

First Adam and Last Adam[7]

Our bodies are inherited from Adam. Adam was the first federal head of humanity. He represented humanity and fell into sin, which led to death. Everybody is perishable because of Adam. For the bodies to be something other than perishable, there is a need for a second Adam. Jesus was the federal head who came to represent his people. He perfectly did what Adam could never do and paid the penalty of death for Adam's sin. Our natural bodies are inherited because we belong to Adam. We will inherit our supernatural bodies because we belong to Jesus.

The Grace of Resurrection

God has made the incomprehensible comprehensible in Jesus. Jesus reversed the cosmic order for his people! In order to save his people, Jesus, the only naturally imperishable one, became perishable on their behalf. The man of Heaven took on a body of dust in order that people who are made of dust might take on a heavenly body. He became like a grain of wheat—buried in the ground—but counterintuitively transformed to bear much fruit. In John 12:24 Jesus states: "Truly, truly, I say to you, unless a grain of wheat falls into the earth and dies, it remains alone; but if it dies, it bears much fruit." The imperishable became perishable that the perishable might become imperishable. Jesus, the glorious one, experienced dishonor so that the dishonorable might experience glory. Jesus, the powerful one, became weak so that the weak might become powerful. Jesus who deserved life experienced death so that those who deserved death might experience new life. Jesus, "the man of heaven" (v. 49), made himself a Son of Man—a man of the earth—so that the sons of Adam, men of the earth, might become men of Heaven. In this Jesus the natural and the supernatural come together. The present and future converge. This is how individuals can be certain that "just as we have borne the image of the man of dust, we shall also bear the image of the man of heaven" (v. 49). If one belongs to Jesus, his or her future supernatural resurrection body is just as certain as his or her present natural body. Christ is in us—we already have the DNA! We are like a seed that will be planted and will sprout to counterintuitive, unexpected new life.

So what would the grace of resurrection mean for those who belong to Jesus? How does the indescribable beauty of resurrection manifest itself in a person's life?

Hebrews 11 talks about the roll call of the faithful. The passage lists wonderful examples of people who were faithful to God. To better understand Hebrews 11, it is important to be aware of the literary structure of the book of Hebrews. The overall structure of the book is clearly introduced in chapter 1, which declares Jesus as the one who is superior over all individuals and institutions. So when looking at Hebrews 11, the core implication of the passage is not that the reader must emulate the faithfulness of the people mentioned in the text; rather, one must recognize that even their faithfulness is not superior to the faithfulness of the one whom the writer of Hebrews is emphasizing, namely Jesus Christ. With this in mind, a proper examination of Hebrews 11:33, 34 can be considered: "who through faith conquered kingdoms, enforced justice, obtained promises, stopped the mouths of lions, quenched the power of fire, escaped the edge of the sword, were made strong out of weakness, became mighty in war, put foreign armies to flight." This text clearly alludes back to the story of Daniel, his three friends, and King

Nebuchadnezzar. If the overall structure of the book of Hebrews is not taken into consideration, the implication of these two verses may be seen as moralistic. The reader may think, "These people had faith, and therefore whenever I'm in the lion's den of life, then if I simply show faith like these men, God will certainly deliver me!"

But the point is not to determine whether or not God can deliver his people because he certainly can and often does. When God's people are being saved from the lion's den of life, it is easy to give credit to our own faith. But what happens if there is no immediate deliverance? The answer lies in the power of the resurrection. If we hang on to the resurrection, we can face anything in life. There can be peace in the midst of difficult circumstances in life when the reality and hope of the resurrection is indeed the foundation of one's life. How do we know this? The writer of Hebrews goes on to say, "Women received back their dead by resurrection. Some were tortured, refusing to accept release, so that they might rise again to a better life. Others suffered mocking and flogging, and even chains and imprisonment. They were stoned, they were sawn in two, they were killed with the sword. They went about in skins of sheep and goats, destitute, afflicted, mistreated" (11:35–37). If there is no concept of this "better life," referring to resurrection life, then the Christian has no way of facing difficult circumstances that come his way. We would be able to handle them only to the extent that we are spared.

Hebrews 11:35–37 provides a summary of what happened in history, during the Maccabean period in early Judaism before Christ. The story can be found in the book of 2 Maccabees. That book is not part of the canonical Scriptures, but it is good extra-canonical Jewish history. Second Maccabees 7 relates a story based on seven sons, their mother, and the emperor at the time. The emperor, Antiochus Epiphanes, urged the seven sons to denounce their faith in Yahweh. Death was their only other option. The mother encouraged the sons to stand firm in their faith. The vicious dictator then prepared a big frying pan and a cauldron of boiling water and was ready to kill whoever wouldn't denounce their faith in God. One by one every son was getting killed off. Even until the last son, the mother refused to give in. She continued to encourage her sons to stand firm in their faith. How was she able to endure this pain and suffering? How did she face death? What sustained this woman? Resurrection life. Hebrews 11:35 says, "Women received back their dead by resurrection. Some were tortured, refusing to accept release, so that they might rise again to a better life." The literal translation of "a better life" is "a better resurrection." What is "a better resurrection"? It is the death and resurrection of all genuine believers because of the death and resurrection of Jesus Christ. Knowing there is a better resurrection sustained this mother to live courageously. She knew that one day God's people would be transformed with glorified supernatural bodies.[8]

30

Victory over Death

1 CORINTHIANS 15:50–58

IF JESUS ROSE FROM THE DEAD, what does this mean for humanity? What does the reality of the resurrection say about the present circumstances and future prospects for God's people? Paul answers these questions by framing his final section with the language of victory.

Conversations about victory are typically reserved for official contests or battles, such as the victory of an Olympic athlete. Victory is sought in the context of war. Sir Winston Churchill declares: "You ask, what is our policy? I can say: It is to wage war, by sea, land and air, with all our might and with all the strength that God can give us: to wage war against a monstrous tyranny, never surpassed in the dark lamentable catalogue of human crime. That is our policy. You ask, What is our aim? I can answer with one word: Victory—victory at all costs, victory in spite of all terror, victory however long and hard the road may be; for without victory there is no survival."[1]

But victory is often understood as an unofficial reality in personal contexts. When someone beats an addiction or overcomes an unreasonable fear, the phrase *personal victory* is used. Typically victory language gets scaled back to the language of winning. We win competitions, drawings, office pools, races, etc. One famous actor has said, "If I'm doing good in life—if I'm achieving, earning, climbing, purchasing . . . I'm winning."

Victory presumes two things: 1) There is an adversary. It may be other people (coworkers, friends, etc.), a power structure ("the man," capitalism, etc.), or yourself (personal limits, bad habits, etc.). 2) It is better to win than to lose. Given the clear choice, who would ever choose to lose? Though some are more competitive than others in some areas of life, there is no one who is simply not competitive. We are all playing a game, and whether we set the rules or someone else does, we are seeking to win. Paul's discussion about victory is in reference to the ultimate adversary—death. This passage answers the following three questions:

- Why Do We Need Victory?
- How Do We Get Victory?
- What Does Victory Look Like?

Why Do We Need Victory?

Because We Feel Perishable or Like We're Losing

Paul draws a number of contrasts throughout our passage. "I tell you this, brothers: flesh and blood cannot inherit the kingdom of God, nor does the perishable inherit the imperishable" (v. 50). When Paul uses the words "flesh and blood" and "the kingdom of God," it's his concrete way of saying "this world" as opposed to "that world." The present decaying world is opposed to the future undecaying world, The way things are is opposed to the way things will be; the perishable is opposed to the imperishable. It is his way of talking about the frailty of human nature—mortality against immortality (v. 54: "the mortal puts on immortality").[2]

Since all things are subject to death, one of humanity's greatest desires is to have victory over that which is perishable.[3] Individuals need to be faster, stronger, smarter, richer, more beautiful than others in order to assure themselves of their relative importance and permanence. Individuals may not be firing on all cylinders, but if they can make themselves the best or the most important one, they can be assured of their indispensability. Overly competitive individuals desire victory so much that they invent things to conquer. The entire history of sports is an attempt to make victory less dangerous.

Contemporary people pursue imperishability by transforming and modifying themselves. This is seen in any area of life where perfectionism is present. Anne Lamott states: "[P]erfectionism is based on the obsessive belief that if you run carefully enough, hitting each stepping-stone just right, you won't have to die. The truth is that you will die anyway and that a lot of people who aren't even looking at their feet are going to do a whole lot better than you, and have a lot more fun while they're doing it."[4] This strategy of life is largely seen in the health industry culture with its insane workout regimens. Physical fitness, which can indeed enhance and even prolong human life, becomes a religion that dominates modern life. One can feel "religious" in the gym—guilt about not working out, shame about the way one looks, a sense of being judged by others, justification for one's lack of exercise. There is also a stringent dietary regimen. A healthy diet, which can indeed benefit one's life, becomes a religion that dominates people's lives. Healthy food has become a religion—people are now concerned about the *purity* of their food because they want to know the food's origin and its relationship to the environment. Furthermore, they also want to know whether or not their meat was raised and slaughtered *ethically*.

There is nothing wrong with this—you'll likely be healthier if you avoid preservatives and trans fats, but the trouble comes when Christians view fitness and diet as a means of self-salvation. A workout regimen or healthy diet cannot save anyone. One can follow all of the rules—listen to the *gurus* and make all the dietary sacrifices he wants—and he can even feel self-righteous about his obedience to the approach he has chosen, but it will not make him any less perishable. What is ultimately desired is victory over death.

Because We Will Ultimately Die—We Will Lose

C. S. Lewis has said that "100 percent of us die, and the percentage cannot be increased."[5] The thrill of victory at all costs is pursued because the agony of defeat is an appetizer of death, namely an echo from the future reminding all people that they are perishable. Death has the power to scale backwards into life. Decay, disintegration, deterioration, and loss are fought against because they are all signposts on the road that leads to death. Limitations are rebelled against to ensure ourselves that we are not moving in the direction in which we know we're moving. The reason there is a yearning within humanity to burst these limits is that death is not natural! Individuals fight against death because it is the ultimate enemy.

You will never find any old myth, a legend, or a story of a single culture with all of its accumulated wisdom and ancient teaching that says anything like death is just a great circle of life. Whatever the myth or story is, it will always talk about death being unnatural. Death is always traumatic. Death is obscene. It is counter to everything that is living. Death is ugly, painful, sad, brutal, and terrible. It is an aberration. It is terrifying. Death is absolutely not natural. It is monstrous. It doesn't give you any options. Death is immutable in that sense.[6]

Everyone has to decide as an individual whether he believes death will ultimately win or not. If individuals believe that death wins in the end, why fight? If people believe that death does not win in the end, what is the basis for that belief? If victory is possible, how can it be obtained?

How Do We Get Victory?

Human lives are perishable, and people can do nothing to change that—the greatest athletes and the healthiest individuals in the world meet the same end as the laziest and unhealthy people in the world. To understand how to get victory over death, we need to go to the source of its power. Verse 56 says, "The sting of death is sin, and the power of sin is the law." "The sting of death is sin." Human death entered the world through sin; without sin, death has no power—it would have been a moot point. The original word for "sting" (*kentron*) was often used to refer to the sting of a bee or a scorpion.[7] Without sin, death has no means of stinging the human race. But everyone has been stung; everyone is a sinner. Sin is the instrument of death, and death is the needle with sin as its poison. The Law is the environment in which the poison spreads. There are two approaches to the Law that ignore the problem of death ("The power of sin is the law"):

(1) People ignore the Law because sinners are lawbreakers. In many instances breaking laws cannot be resisted, particularly if they are judged to be unnecessary or superfluous. The Law—though it is righteous and God-given by nature—has the effect of increasing transgressions because it points out more areas in which individuals can be the rulers of their own lives. Christians sin against God when they ignore his law, which perpetuates the cycle of death.

(2) Some who try to trust the Law by following all the rules wrongly believe they will be able to defeat death on their own. Even if they are not trusting in God's Law, they are often trusting in whatever law they have adopted for their own lives. What laws do Christians believe can bring them fulfillment, satisfaction, and legacy? People sin against God when they view the Law as a means of overcoming death. It is simply a means of managing and temporarily delaying the inevitability of it.

How do individuals get victory over this ultimate enemy? "Behold! I tell you a mystery. We shall not all sleep, but we shall all be changed, in a moment, in the twinkling of an eye, at the last trumpet. For the trumpet will sound, and the dead will be raised imperishable, and we shall be changed. For this perishable body must put on the imperishable, and this mortal body must put on immortality" (vv. 51–53). Paul claims to have divine revelation about the way to beat death. "Behold! I tell you a mystery." He's saying, "Look! I have new information about the future that up until this time has been hidden. Listen up." Something must happen outside of us! A "change" (v. 51) must occur.[8] The dead must be raised by someone else—they cannot raise themselves (v. 52). The perishable must put on the imperishable (v. 53), and this comes from outside of us. Lives are spent trying to put on the imperishable, to no avail. The mortal must put on immortality (v. 53). This transformation happens in an instant and at the end of time. It will happen "in a moment" (the smallest fraction of time), "in the twinkling of an eye" (the batting of an eyelash).[9] This transformation is an external work that happens in a moment, but people have been trying for their entire lives and failing to add a minute to their lives. With the phrase "at the last trumpet" Paul is drawing on Old Testament imagery used to describe the last day.[10]

"When the perishable puts on the imperishable, and the mortal puts on immortality, then shall come to pass the saying that is written: 'Death is swallowed up in victory.' 'O death, where is your victory? O death, where is your sting?'" (vv. 54, 55). Paul declares that death will ultimately be defeated, and there will come a day when all of this actually takes place. The perishable and mortal will put on imperishability and immortality. Christians will be raised from the dead as bodies—they will "put on" imperishability and immortality. This will signal the death of death. Paul draws on the Old Testament (Isaiah 25:8; Hosea 13:14) to sing a song in mockery of death.[11] No one sings the song "We Are the Champions" unless victory is beyond doubt and secured. Death is not simply erased of its power; it is literally swallowed up, never to be seen again.

What is the basis for Paul's confidence? It is found in verse 57: "But thanks be to God, who gives us the victory through our Lord Jesus Christ." The victory is already secure in Christ because the King of the kingdom took on flesh and blood. The imperishable one became perishable on our behalf. The immortal one became mortal on behalf of the sinner he wanted to save by absorbing the sting of death. "Its venom has been absorbed by Christ and drained of its potency so that the victory over death now belongs to God and to God's people who benefit from it."[12] He took away the power of sin by fulfilling the Law on our behalf. There is nothing a sinner can do to defeat death because Jesus has already defeated it for him. There is no law that he must fulfill in order to be given imperishability—Jesus fulfilled the Law in his place. The Christian inherits the kingdom of God, imperishability, and immortality because of the work of Christ.

What Does Victory Look Like?

This victory has present-day implications. The victory is something that God gives to the believer—not simply something that he *will* give. The ultimate victory is already possessed by the believer, so he no longer needs to live an anxiety-ridden life in an attempt to win life—it has already been won. He can rest in the finished work of Jesus Christ. What are the areas of our lives that we're trying to win? What keeps us up at night? Money, relationships, health? We don't have to win—we are free to lose. This probably scares most people. "What will my motivation be?" The world runs on laws that promise but can't deliver on the defeat of death, so once we leave the realm of law we get nervous. But paradoxically it is this very freedom that allows the believer to work diligently, to work well, and to work with hope.

Verse 58 says: "Therefore, my beloved brothers, be steadfast, immovable, always abounding in the work of the Lord, knowing that in the Lord your labor is not in vain." "Therefore" in light of Christ's victory, which is the ground for one's faith, the redeemed sinner can live a victorious life. The apostle says, "my beloved brothers," live in the context of community and "be steadfast."[13] The Christian's motivation for steadfastness is not his own winning, but the winning of Christ. We don't have to be moved by the things that normally throw us off course when we're focused on winning. It's like watching a soccer match of which we already know the outcome. We can enjoy it. We can pay attention to even more detail. But we can watch it without anxiety or fear.

Furthermore, Jesus Christ was so moved in love toward you that he set up an unshakable foundation of redemption through his work. Therefore, the church will be "immovable." We can enjoy the spoils of victory as it overcomes the agonies of defeat. This truth motivates the believer to know that in the Lord "[his] labor is not in vain." Paul says in 15:10, "But by the grace of God I am what I am, and his grace toward me was not in vain. On the contrary, I worked harder than any of them, though it was not I, but the grace of God that is with me." We can quit playing the game of winning. We can start living life as if we have already won (because we have).

There is an amazing line in Psalm 112. The psalmist says that "the righteous will never be moved." He will be immovable. He will "not [be] afraid of bad news." There are so many days when we wake up in the morning and we are afraid we are going to receive some bad news. Something's not going to go right. Someone is going to say something to ruin our day. So the hope is that the day will go well. This righteous person, whose righteousness is rooted in the enduring, full "righteousness" of the Lord (Psalm 112:3), is immovable and will not be afraid of bad news. In other words, this person's heart is "steady" and "firm" (Psalm 112:7, 8). He will be triumphant as he looks at all of his adversaries. The way that God's righteous people are going to have a victorious life is to know that they are going to win and conquer over all of their adversaries, ultimately even death itself, because of the blood-bought work of Jesus.

C. S. Lewis says it this way: "It is a serious thing to live in a society of possible gods and goddesses, to remember that the dullest and the most uninteresting person you talk to may one day be a creature, which that if you saw it now, you would be strongly tempted to worship."[14] He's talking about the fallen but redeemed sinner who has been created in the image of God. He is talking about human immortality and imperishability. The person next to us, who might seem dull and uninteresting, we will one day in the new heavens and new earth be tempted to worship. Even though we are weak, we will be strong. Even though we are foolish, we will be wise. Even though we are useless, we will be missional. Even though we are slaves, we are of royal blood.

This victory and imperishable life is not something that we will possess only in the future—we already have it now as an inheritance in Christ. If we already know that life has already been won, if death has been defeated, if life has been secured, if it has been given to us, then we can walk forward with great confidence, joy, and victory.

31

A Community of Reconciliation

1 CORINTHIANS 16:1-11

THE FINAL CHAPTER of this letter seems a bit anticlimactic. Chapter 15 was a lengthy and beautiful treatment of *the* most pivotal event in human history—the resurrection of Jesus Christ. So anything that comes after that seems like a postscript. In fact, at the end of Paul's letters he appears to be cramming in a bunch of disjointed thoughts before the curtain closes. But through these final instructions, what the reader sees emerging is a portrait of a community that lives in light of that event that changed the world—the kind of community that the church is supposed to be. And very simply put, it's one that mends what's torn, that rights what's wrong—that reconciles. How?

- By Sharing Its Goods
- By Sharing Its Life
- Across Every Dividing Line

By Sharing Its Goods (Through Economic Justice)

Paul was writing to the Corinthians to tell them about the church in Jerusalem that had fallen on hard times because of a famine. Basically this famine created a climate of economic inequality. The church in Jerusalem had nothing, while the churches around them had everything. So Paul arranges for a special fund to be collected in response to this growing problem. And that's where our passage picks up. Verses 1–4 say, "Now concerning the collection for the saints: as I directed the churches of Galatia, so you also are to do. On the first day of every week, each of you is to put something aside and store it up, as he may prosper, so that there will be no collecting when I come.

And when I arrive, I will send those whom you accredit by letter to carry your gift to Jerusalem. If it seems advisable that I should go also, they will accompany me."

Paul's instruction here is actually quite simple. He is saying, share your goods, share your money, share your things—especially in a climate of economic inequality. Why? Time and again the Bible frames inequality in a way that might come as a surprise to many. It defines it not in terms of misfortune, as most people would, but rather in terms of *injustice*.[1] But why does it do this? It's because when there's inequality, there are only two possible scenarios—either there's not enough to go around, or it's not going around. And there is plenty to go around—now more than ever before. We live in a society in which wealth is no longer a zero-sum game. In ancient times one's wealth was basically tied to one's land, so in order for an individual to get more, it meant someone would have to get less. That is not the way it happens today. Today wealth can be generated, not just transferred.[2] There's more to go around now than ever before. It's just not going around.

And in light of this, the modern church is oftentimes not the countercultural community it is supposed to be. Reconciliation is not happening—and it can't in conditions like this! A fascinating article in *The Atlantic* exposed hundreds of school districts in our country concerning a new segregation that is emerging, this time along economic lines.[3] The most staggering thing about this is that everyone said this would never happen. We're progressive people! Segregation isn't an issue anymore! In fact, this was the very argument that the districts made to get the court orders for mandatory integration lifted. Then this happened. But along with segregation, and this was the real problem, came a debilitating *inequality*. Imagine going to a school where no teacher worth his salt would be caught dead in the classroom. Imagine having to use resources deemed inadequate for kids on the other side of town but as perfectly fine for us. Imagine colleges and employers refusing to give us the time of day because we went to "that school." And imagine people of privilege all the while shaking their heads at us because we couldn't do better. If that were our lot, could we even begin to think about reconciliation? We probably couldn't.

Social psychologist Christena Cleveland put it well when she said:

> (We just want it to magically happen because, like, *grace covers a multitude of sins*, right?). . . . We want oppressed people to come to *our* privileged spaces, assimilate to *our* culture, *never* speak out against our oppressive ways, and all the while be *super* grateful that we're nice enough to even let them hang around. . . . In short, many Christians want reconciliation

without justice, much like we want the resurrection without the crucifixion. . . . [When we do this] on the surface . . . everything looks cheery and bright. . . . But the structural inequalities that caused the division in the first place remain unnoticed and untouched. As a result, people of color report . . . feelings of disempowerment, loneliness, marginalization, exclusion and misunderstanding. They feel out of place, on the edge of the circle, silenced, and disconnected. . . . Reconciliation without justice is simply oppression disguised.[4]

But there is good news for us—God's people have failed, but he has not. And through a pivotal event that changed the world as we know it, he is now forging together for himself a new community that will take things that aren't right and make them right. A community that will look at the plight of the poor and say not *your* problem but *our* problem. A community that will look at the distress of the oppressed and say *what's yours is mine* and *what's mine is yours*. A community of reconciliation animated by the Spirit of a resurrected God who's making all things right.[5]

How can we be a community that looks more like this? Learning how to share is the place to start. In verse 2 Paul gives specific instructions[6] on how to do this, not because he's trying to be pejorative, but because he knows that sharing isn't natural and that sinners need help getting out of themselves because they turn inward, especially with their money and their things. Verse 2 gives us three practical principles of sharing. First, we need to share *consistently*. Paul says that we are to do this "on the first day of every week." Sharing, remember, isn't natural. But regularity is the first step in making it more so. Second, we have to share *proportionally*. "Each of you is to put something aside and store it up, *as he may prosper*."[7] What Paul is getting at here is that the more you gain, the more you can give. For example, someone who has $50,000 can share $5,000 and it's no small thing. But for someone who has $5 million, what's $5,000? Or $50,000 or $500,000 or even $1 million? The more you gain, the more you can give— and a higher percentage, not just a higher amount. And finally, we have to share *deliberately* ". . . so that there will be no collecting when I come."[8] Sharing cannot be an afterthought. Christians can't just rummage through what's left over and scrape something together after they've obtained everything else they want. If they do this, I guarantee they won't have anything left to share because money and things, remember, turn us inward when we're not deliberate.

So the church is to be a community that reconciles, and its members do this first by sharing their goods. But the church does this, secondly, by sharing its life.

By Sharing Its Life (Through Friendship)

Verses 5–9 say, "I will visit you after passing through Macedonia, for I intend to pass through Macedonia, and perhaps I will stay with you or even spend the winter, so that you may help me on my journey, wherever I go. For I do not want to see you now just in passing. I hope to spend some time with you, if the Lord permits. But I will stay in Ephesus until Pentecost, for a wide door for effective work has opened to me, and there are many adversaries." Paul's beating heart is not only for economic justice, but also for friendship. Paul wants more than just the Corinthians' money, he wants *them*. He says in verse 6 that he wants to stay and spend a season with them, even if it is winter. He doesn't want to simply see them in passing[9] (v. 7), but he wants to be with them and share life together. This is also why he doesn't just send the gift to Jerusalem but sends people from the Corinthian community along with it (v. 3) and why he's even willing to go in person himself (v. 4). This community that the church is called to be reconciles not only by sharing its goods but also *by sharing its life*.

Given our cultural moment, a community like this would be incredibly compelling. It's no secret that we live in a climate where inequality is a growing problem. But the thing is, every proposed solution misses this crucial point. Conservatives typically say that charity or philanthropy is the answer, that individuals should share.[10] Liberals, on the other hand, more or less go the welfare route—the state, with our tax dollars in hand, should share.[11] Now both of these are true—individuals and the state *should* share! But both also miss something absolutely crucial (which is why both charity and welfare come off clunky and arrogant, even offensive when you think about it). Both say, "Let me give you what I think you need without taking the time to get to know you, let alone share life with you, so I can just pat myself on the back and return to business as usual with my conscience clear." If reconciliation without justice is just oppression, as Christena Cleveland put it, then justice without friendship is just arrogance! But we can avoid both dangers by sharing our *goods* and our *lives*.

Or maybe more precisely, by sharing our goods *as* we share our lives—doing justice *through* friendship. This is so crucial. Sharing, as we've said, is hard. But when the poor aren't just a concept but are our friends, when we know their dreams and their stories because we do life together, it makes it much harder to keep our stuff to ourselves. So we share. At the same time it's this same friendship, this same shared life, that guards the Christian from arrogance. Paul says something absolutely fascinating in verse 6[12] "perhaps I will stay with you or even spend the winter, *so that you may help me on my journey, wherever I go.*" For Paul, friendship was a two-way street. It wasn't Paul bringing the goods and the people bringing the needs. He *got* as much from his friends as he *gave*, sometimes even more. And that always happens when people build deep meaningful friendships, when they share life together. When they find this happening in friendships with *the poor*, the arrogance melts away.

Christopher Heuertz answered this call to reconciliation, but was disillusioned by how so many were missing the mark. So he set out to build a community that reconciled by doing justice, and he accomplished this through friendship and a shared life together. After reflecting upon his experience, he coauthored a book with his friend Christine Pohl, and they called it *Friendship at the Margins*. He writes:

> Ministry with people who are poor often assumes that "our" task is to meet "their" needs. A focus on friendship rearranges our assumptions. From the start, our emphasis included rejecting certain assumptions—that gifts flow in one direction and that a substantial social distance between donors and recipients is necessary. We were particularly troubled by the unintended consequences that followed from these assumptions—efforts to love "the stranger" while remaining separate from her life, reducing the "poor" to objects of charity.[13] [As a result], we've tried instead to cultivate a shared life [with] friendship at the heart. [And as these] friendships grew, the needs of our friends became an invitation to practice generosity. Our own excess indicted us without anyone saying anything explicitly. Friendships put pressure on our lifestyle choices because our possessions and consumption patterns were hard to hide from our friends. That's why it is often easier to keep people who are poor at a distance, or to arrange to enter their world only through brief visits.[14] [At the same time] when we started fiddling with the notion that resources don't flow in one direction, we found grace and wisdom and gifts in our friends who were poor. Many have suffered unspeakable trauma, abuse, violence and exploitation. And yet they continued to find the courage to pray. Their faith was resilient. They lived with gratitude and hope. From their poverty they practiced abundant generosity, giving freely with joy.[15] [After this], we could no longer see these people as projects, because we came to understand that we were not ministering "to" our friends, but in ministry among them.[16]

So the church is to be a community that reconciles by sharing its goods as it shares its life. But lastly, it is called to do all of this to everyone.

Across Every Dividing Line

Up to this point reconciliation has been addressed exclusively across economic lines. And it's fitting, because that's the central focus of the passage. However, there is a much richer portrait of reconciliation. *It reaches across every possible dividing line.*

Verse 3 tells us that this fund was going to the church in Jerusalem, the capital city of the Jews. So by sheer virtue of its location, it would have been made up of a lot of Jewish Christians. But now look where the fund was *coming* from, namely Galatia and Corinth. Galatia was located in modern-day Turkey, and Corinth was one of the most influential *Greek* cities in the ancient world. By sheer virtue of their locations, these two churches would have been made up of a whole lot of Gentiles. And as anyone who knows anything about the ancient world will tell you, Jews and Gentiles weren't exactly the best of friends. There was no love lost between them, and yet they are coming together here. This community is reconciling across not only economic lines but also across even the most hostile *racial* lines.[17]

Likewise, look at what Paul says in verses 10, 11: "When Timothy comes, see that you put him at ease among you, for he is doing the work of the Lord, as I am. So let no one despise him. Help him on his way in peace, that he may return to me, for I am expecting him with the brothers." Paul uses a very strong word in verse 11—"despise." It's a word that captured an intense hatred, the word that was probably used to describe relations between Jews and Gentiles at the time. But the question is, why would the Corinthians feel this strongly about Timothy? Corinth was a city where only the best and the brightest came to play. Credentials and status were everything. Where an individual attended school mattered. Degrees mattered; one's occupation mattered. People would ask questions like "How much do you make?" or "Where do you live?" This was the kind of sizing up that happened time and again. They had started off with Paul, who basically had the equivalency of a couple of modern PhDs, along with the entrepreneurial success of founding more than fourteen new churches, which in turn spawned countless daughter churches of their own—and they still gave him a hard time![18] Now Timothy wasn't half the man Paul was. He was not as accomplished or flashy, and neither credentials nor commanding charisma were his thing. He wasn't really the Corinthians' type. But Paul pleads with them to receive Timothy, to do what this community is supposed to do—reach across every dividing line, including those of competency, credentialing, and status.[19]

And this is what the church is supposed to be like. A community that reaches across not only *a* dividing line but across *all* dividing lines, with its members sharing everything—their things and their lives. It is very easy to get more and more discouraged when looking at what Paul is asking the church to be. Oftentimes our communities don't look anything like this. And that has a lot to do with us! We should be glad that this passage comes on the coattails of a long passage focusing on the resurrection. The road ahead looks pretty grim if the Christian needs to look to himself and try to walk it alone. But the good news is that we don't have to do that because there's Someone else to whom we can look. Someone who's walked the road before us, swallowing up sin and death and injustice along the way. Someone who's gone first to disarm the sting of division and inequality by rising in triumph over it all.[20] Someone who keeps walking that road with us, sharing his things and his life, even giving it away for us on a cross.[21] If we just look to ourselves and the road ahead, there's no reason to hold out hope, no reason to press on. But when we look to him, we find hope at what seems like hope's end. We find the courage to keep pressing on.

As crucial as that is, we actually need one more thing because even with proper courage and hope, a task this big can be paralyzing. It's hard to even know where to begin. In a scene from a popular sitcom a groom is about to have a nervous breakdown the morning of his wedding. His close friend is helping him overcome his fears by saying, "Forget getting married for a second. Just forget about it. Can you just come home and take a shower?" "Yeah, but then . . ." "Ahh, ahh, ahh we're just going to go home and take a shower." These are, oddly enough, really wise words. A lot of times we think that we need to be what we're supposed to be overnight, that we need to change in an instant, when what we really simply need is to go home and take a shower.

So this passage gives us four really practical things by way of application. First, Christians need to share—consistently, proportionally and deliberately. We need to sit down and set aside a portion of our income every week and share it. And each week we need to share a little more and keep doing this until it becomes second nature to us. It might feel clunky at first, but we have to start somewhere. Second, we need to get to know, *really* get to know, people who are different from us. We must begin to share life with others and get deeply into their lives and allow them to enter deeply into ours, so we can actually start to call them friends. There are plenty of people in our church communities who are different from us. That is not a bad place to start. Third, if some of us live in a place of privilege—and that would include most modern people—we need to intentionally put ourselves in places of dis-privilege. We're most likely to worry about the people we see first thing in the morning. And given where we are, this means that we need to deliberately put one foot in another world.[22] Finally, we must do all of this in light of the victory that has already been won. "Thanks be to God, who gives us the victory through our Lord Jesus Christ. Therefore, my beloved brothers, be steadfast, immovable, always abounding in the work of the Lord, knowing that in the Lord your labor is not in vain" (15:57, 58).

32

A Common Bond

1 CORINTHIANS 16:12–24

FIRST CORINTHIANS FOCUSES ON what it means to be part of a gospel-shaped community of God's grace. Throughout these chapters we have had occasion to consider many challenging and controversial questions, themes, and issues. We have seen that the gospel has the power to shape our communities in personal, practical, and powerful ways. With the end of this preaching commentary, we've also come to the end of a lengthy letter. Paul is now in conclusion mode. He is getting very practical and talking about future plans and is sending his own greetings along with greetings from other believers. In what ways can this portion of the letter be helpful? God chose to communicate his word through inspired but ordinary human beings. He chose to communicate his word through ordinary literary genres. First Corinthians 16 is just as inspired and profitable as 1 Corinthians 15 with its treatment of the resurrection. What does 1 Corinthians 16 mean for Christian lives?

Paul makes the argument that all humans long for a common bond and for a community characterized by several factors. The first is *love*. Everyone wants to be accepted as each one is and have the resources to love others as himself. A common bond is also characterized by *mutual care*. Everyone wants to be cared for in his or her time of need and wants to know a version of themselves that cares for others. Third, a common bond is characterized by *a balance of community and individuality*—everyone wants to be part of something bigger than himself, but each wants to remain distinctly himself. No one wants his or her identity to be steamrolled by a community, but at the same time no one wants to build his or her identity alone in isolation from community. And lastly, a common bond is characterized by *connection*. Everyone wants to be locally plugged in but globally connected. Most err toward one side or the other. First Corinthians gives a picture of a community that was characterized by all these things that people desire. In this chapter we will examine the common bond of the early Christians to see if there is any potential for us to experience something similar. We will consider these matters under three points:

- The Existence of a Common Bond
- The Characteristics of a Common Bond
- The Recovery of a Common Bond

The Existence of a Common Bond

Local and Global Network

The first is the existence of a common bond. Paul is writing from Ephesus in Asia (western edge of modern Turkey) to the Christians of Corinth in Achaia (modern-day Greece). What does this tell us? Local communities of believers were spreading broadly and rapidly just twenty years after the death and resurrection of Christ. These local communities had strong ties to other local communities in other parts of the world, so much so that they would send representatives to one another (for example, Stephanas, Fortunatus, and Achaicus were believers from the Corinthian church who had traveled to see Paul in Ephesus, v. 17). One's membership in a local church connects him or her to a global movement, a global family. The language of "brothers" shows up three times here (vv. 12, 15, 20). The global family members greet each other with a holy kiss (v. 20). The early church was made up of vibrant local communities that were richly intertwined in a global family network.

Individual and Communal Network

Not only is there a local and global network, but also an individual and communal network. Note how many personal names are mentioned throughout this passage: Apollos (v. 12), Stephanas (vv. 15, 17), Fortunatus and Achaicus (v. 17), Aquila, Prisca, and their house church (v. 19b), Paul himself (v. 21), and Christ Jesus (v. 24). Not only do Christians around the globe know that each other exist (the way Christians in Boston know that the church in Seattle exists), they have a personal knowledge of individuals in the other communities. This underscores the familial nature of the church. Though they are tied to one another by virtue of their membership in the community, individuality is still maintained. Apollos' own desires and interests are respected (v. 12). Stephanas and his household are named and honored for their devotion (v. 15). Stephanas, Fortunatus, and Achaicus are refreshing gifts to Paul and are deserving of recognition (vv. 17, 18). Aquila and Prisca are known to the Corinthian believers as well (v. 19). Though it is hard for people today to grasp the remarkable nature of this community in the age of cell phones and social media, it is extraordinary that this type of meaningful network was created without regard for business, politics, race, class, etc. That would have been absolutely unheard of in that day. It is sadly unheard of today. What were the characteristics of this community? What was the nature of their common bond?

The Characteristics of a Common Bond

The first characteristic of this common bond is that it is reinforced by gospel truth. "Be watchful, stand firm in the faith, act like men, be strong" (v. 13). Paul says "Be[1] watchful'"[2] in order to provide a word of caution for the Corinthians to remain alert and to have their hope engaged for the return of the Lord who will make all things right. The verse further reads, "Stand firm in the faith."[3] This is shorthand for believing the core doctrines of Christianity. "Faith" is a call to mind the historical realities of what God has done for them in Christ. He is saying, "Make the gospel one of your core values." In the following commands, "Act like men, be strong"[4] Paul is not contrasting masculinity and femininity, but fullgrownness and childlikeness. In 13:11 we read, "When I was a child, I spoke like a child, I thought like a child, I reasoned like a child. When I became a man, I gave up childish ways." The gospel is to be central to all that the Corinthians say and do. Their present situation (which includes uncertainty, the lack of a trustworthy leader, and the doctrinal mess they are in) should not distract them from growing into maturity. Nothing can hold them together apart from the gospel. Personal interests, tastes, preferences, and desires are not grounds for any kind of true, lasting unity. The gospel, which is for everyone regardless of background, overcomes every boundary present in other human communities.

The characteristic of a common bond is secondly realized in the context of one-anothering love (vv. 14–18). Verse 14 states: "Let all that you do be done in love."[5] Love is a comprehensive mode of operation. No function or action of the community is allowed to be untouched and unshaped by love. A community that has experienced the love of God in Christ will necessarily share the love of God with one another. How does this love play out? Consider verses 15–18:

> Now I urge you, brothers—you know that the household[6] of Stephanas were the first converts in Achaia, and that they have devoted themselves to the service of the saints—*be subject to such as these, and to every fellow worker and laborer.* I rejoice at the coming of Stephanas and Fortunatus and Achaicus, because they have made up for your absence, for *they refreshed my spirit* as well as yours. *Give recognition to such people.*

There is the dynamic interplay of a one-anothering community at work here. A common bond is realized through loving relationships of mutual subjection. Subjection takes place regardless of position, pedigree, or any other identity marker. Some do not like subjection because it takes them out of a position of control and power. Others do not like subjection because it will call their comfort and approval into question. But the gospel allows power-hungry control freaks to subject themselves to others. The gospel also allows approval hungry comfort seekers to boldly take positions of influence they might otherwise avoid.

A common bond is realized through loving and self-giving service for the refreshment of others. Leaders are refreshed by members even as members are refreshed by leaders. Refreshment in the gospel is never unidirectional. Each member is equipped to refresh others in the gospel. Gospel refreshment is multidirectional. It's in this context that one must understand the interesting pronouncement in verse 22: "If anyone has no love for the Lord, let him be accursed." If we do not love someone, that person's rejection of us is meaningless. Paul is simply saying, if someone chooses not to respond to the love of God in Christ, then let him remain outside of the blessings of this community on the basis of his own decision. We will not be bothered by this unless we actually desire to be a part of the community. The common bond is realized through honoring and recognizing the contributions of each member of the community. We ought to be liberal and generous with recognition. While the surrounding culture reserves recognition for those who stand a head above the rest, the church seeks for ways to recognize and honor members of the community for ordinary gospel work.

Paul is saying, "Make community one of your core values." A common bond was cause for rejoicing across distance (vv. 17–20). Verses 19, 20 say: "The churches of Asia send you greetings. Aquila and Prisca, together with the church in their house, send you hearty greetings in the Lord. All the brothers send you greetings. Greet one another with a holy kiss." Paul is calling the Corinthians to recognize their core level connection to Christians in other parts of the world. Moreover, he is calling the ordinary Christians hearing this letter read on a Sunday morning to "make this movement one of your core values." He is essentially saying, "Take an interest in what's happening in the churches around you. Pray for their success and for the advancement of the gospel. Take an interest in the global movement of the gospel; support it through prayer, relationships, and finances. Ultimately these are your family members. Think of the connection you have to your extended family—your connection to other Christians ought to be at least that strong. The church is filled with your brothers and sisters!"

Sadly, the majority of our interactions are not characterized by love. Some steamroll the individual for the sake of the community. Others devalue the community for the sake of the individual. Mutual devotion and submission are rare. We approach the community with hierarchical lenses. We value flashiness over faithfulness. Rather than reaching across great distances, we isolate ourselves. Is it possible to recover this ideal common bond among Christians?

The Recovery of a Common Bond

Verses 23, 24 say: "The grace of the Lord Jesus be with you. My love be with you all in Christ Jesus. Amen." The only basis for this kind of common communal bond is Jesus Christ. He is the only one who did everything out of love! He subjected himself to our desire to destroy him in order to restore and rescue us. He is the one and only Son who welcomes brothers and sisters into the family of God by means of his redemptive work. Look at the words of Paul again: "My love be with you all in Christ Jesus." Start at the end: "in Christ Jesus." Union with Christ—being in Christ Jesus—is the basis of our common bond. "My love be with you all." The same preposition is used in "be with you." Paul introduces his letter by saying "grace to you and peace," but when he concludes his letter he says "grace . . . be with you." Communion with one another only happens through our union with Christ. And union with Christ necessarily brings us into communion with one another. When we're in Christ together as a community we naturally move together.

In a works-based community, people calculate for fairness. One does not love someone unless he shows himself worthy. One does not subject himself or herself to someone unless he or she knows the other person is qualified. One does not recognize someone unless he does something outstanding.

But in a grace-fueled community one doesn't calculate, one doesn't expect anything in return; he or she is not in it for reciprocation. Grace is not equity. Grace is treating others in a loving way though they deserve the opposite. So when they deserve judgment or disdain, rather than responding to them in the same way and taking vengeance into our own hands, we respond with generosity, love, and grace. This means treating somebody in the opposite way of what they deserve. Therefore it is not equity. Equity is just being fair if somebody has wronged another. It's reciprocating the payment or responding proportionally to the extent of that person's crime. We might be very fair people. But that doesn't necessarily mean we are gracious people. Through Christ we can love someone who is unworthy. We can be loved when we are unworthy. We can subject ourselves to someone less qualified than ourselves. We can be empowered to do things that we haven't previously done. We can share honor and recognition in counterintuitive situations and in counterintuitive ways. Within the common bond of our communion with Christ, all of life is shared! No one is supposed to live in isolation, but rather we all are to live as one.

There are two main usages for the concept of "one" in Scripture. First, "one" can signify uniqueness or singularity. The other way to understand "one" is to signify unity and being united in contrast to singularity, "one" as opposed to many. The contrast to unity is division. These two dimensions of meaning for "one" are what we find in Scripture. When one looks at the Old Testament and early Jewish background, one sees clearly an emphasis on the singularity and uniqueness of God. We get this from the *shema*, the basic Jewish monotheistic creed from Deuteronomy 6:4 that every Jew recited. Every day they would say, "Hear O Israel: the Oʀᴜɢ our God, the Oʀᴜɢ is one." The Lord is "one," and whenever this word is used it is echoing the *shema* as well as referring to the singularity and uniqueness of the one true God.

Another dimension of the meaning of the word "one" in early Jewish background emphasizes unity as opposed to division among God's people. So one dimension highlights the meaning of singularity, and another usage emphasizes unity or oneness in terms of being united as God's people.[7]

What is the point here? The Old Testament background makes an amazing connection between the two dimensions of "one" as both singularity and unity.

What is the novel contribution that the New Testament authors make when using this term "one" and the theme of oneness? The obvious parallel is that the New Testament writers and Jesus himself say that he is singularly unique as the one true God (see note 11 in chapter 15 of this book, on 8:6; John 10:30). If one believes in the deity of Christ, one would expect that to be the natural progression. But the amazing connection that the New Testament writers make is to apply the unity dimension of the word "one" not only to God's people, the church, but also to the interior community of the Godhead.

Jesus prays, in his farewell discourse, for his disciples to "be one even as we are one" (John 17:22). That is, just as the Father and the Son are "one," may his disciples be "one." God's people cannot be singular, for God is unique, but they can be united and unified just as the persons of the Godhead are unified even in their diversity. In other words, the love foundation of the relationship that the Son has with the Father is what now fuels the church's love for one another (v. 20, "Greet one another with a holy kiss"). The common bond in Christ enables Christians to create and enjoy a culture of one-anothering. "Let all that you do be done in love. . . . My love be with you all in Christ Jesus" (vv. 14, 24).

Soli Deo gloria!

Notes

Chapter One: Surprised by Encouragement

1. There is very little doubt about the Pauline authorship of this epistle. Aside from the fact that it is stated to have been written by Paul, the theological concerns, vocabulary, and historical connections with other Pauline epistles affirm his authorship. There is much to note about Paul's relations with the Corinthian church, but mainly his identity as a Jew, Roman citizen, follower of Jesus, eschatological herald, and apostle to the Gentiles (see Roy E. Ciampa and Brian S. Rosner, *The First Letter to the Corinthians*, The Pillar New Testament Commentary [Grand Rapids: Eerdmans, 2010], pp. 6–16). The phrase in verse 1, "called by the will of God to be an apostle of Christ Jesus," establishes Paul's divine call and authority to speak to the Corinthian church.

2. "Strabo (*Geographica* 8.6.20) attributes the city's wealth to the fortune of being 'the master of two harbors.' The narrow land bridge of Cenchrea . . . connected the two ports, enabling cargo and even small ships to be hauled across the isthmus to the other gulf. . . . Corinth was a natural crossroad for land and sea travel" (David E. Garland, *1 Corinthians*, Baker Exegetical Commentary on the New Testament [Grand Rapids: Baker Academic, 2003], p. 1). After Rome sacked and destroyed the chief city of the Achaean league, the destruction and fall of the city of Corinth in 146 BC became inevitable. When Julius Caesar reestablished the city in 44 BC, that "created a new Roman heritage . . . with an imposed city plan, architecture, political organization, and ethos different from the Greek predecessor" (ibid., p. 2).

3. "No matter the choice of discipline, you will find in cities the structures that produce the best, brightest, and most successful contributors to their respective industries. . . . This is why cities are packed with students, singles, young marrieds, entrepreneurs, high achievers, immigrants, and what has been termed the 'creative class.' Cities are talent magnets. If you want to make a name for yourself, there is no other place to do it than in the big city" (Stephen T. Um and Justin Buzzard, *Why Cities Matter* [Wheaton: Crossway, 2013], pp. 39, 40).

4. "The denizens of Corinth in Paul's day were known for their wealth and ostentation. The new city allowed many aggressive freedmen and their heirs, who would have been freeborn, the chance to acquire wealth through commercial ventures. Without an entrenched aristocracy, the citizens of Corinth were not fated 'to remain in their allotted position on the social scale' but had a real opportunity for upward social mobility, primarily by attaining wealth and buying friendships and clients (T. L. Carter, "Big Men' in Corinth," *Journal for the Study of the New Testament 66* (1997, p. 53). . . . However, this society was not egalitarian. It was an oligarchy that was 'hierarchic and elitist'" (Garland, *1 Corinthians*, p. 2). In other words, an absence of an aristocracy gave rise for a meritocracy through various scales of social upward mobility, and this in turn created an environment that became elitist and sectarian, hence becoming a new kind of an "aristocracy."

5. Many of the city dwellers were so affluent that "wealth and ostentatious display became the hallmark of Corinth" (H. D. Betz, *2 Corinthians 8 and 9: A*

Commentary on Two Administrative Letters of the Apostle Paul, Hermeneia (Philadelphia: Fortress, 1985), p. 53.

6. Corinth "seems to have been a city designed for those who were preoccupied with the marks of social status" (B. K. Peterson, *Eloquence and the Proclamation of the Gospel in Corinth*, Society of Biblical Literature Dissertation Series 163 [Atlanta: Scholars Press, 1998], p. 61), and they idolized the idea of "the value which others place on one's goods and achievements" (J. M. G. Barclay, "Thessalonica and Corinth: Social Contrasts in Pauline Christianity," *Journal for the Study of the New Testament*, pp. 47, 56). Wayne Meeks (*The First Urban Christians: The Social World of the Apostle Paul* [New Haven, CT: Yale University Press, 1983], p. 54) states that the social climate of Corinth gave rise to an individual's propensity to develop his identity formation built on values such as "occupational prestige, income or wealth, education and knowledge, religious purity, family and ethnic group position, and local-community status" or as one other scholar suggests, "a combination of patronage, marriage, wealth, and patient cultivation of connections" (H. A. Stansbury, "Corinthian Honor, Corinthian Conflict: A Social History of Early Roman Corinth and Its Pauline Community," PhD diss. [Irvine: University of California, 1990], p. 87).

7. Anthony C. Thiselton, *The First Epistle to the Corinthians: A Commentary on the Greek Text*, New International Greek Testament Commentary (Grand Rapids: Eerdmans, 2000), p. 4.

8. T. B. Savage, *Power through Weakness: Paul's Understanding of the Christian Ministry in 2 Corinthians*, Society for New Testament Studies Monograph Series 86 (Cambridge: Cambridge University Press, 1996), p. 35.

9. Garland, *1 Corinthians*, p. 5.

10. John Pollock, *The Apostle: A Life of Paul* (Colorado Springs: David C. Cook, 2012), p. 157.

11. Garland, *1 Corinthians*, p. 9.

12. Von Dobschütz, quoted in Leon Morris, *The First Epistle of Paul to the Corinthians*, The Tyndale New Testament Commentaries (Grand Rapids: Eerdmans, 1989), p. 19.

13. Ciampa and Rosner, *The First Letter to the Corinthians*, p. 55 state that the sanctified "are set apart for God's special purpose and use, just as the utensils in the Temple, the priests, and so on." The term is a perfect passive participle (cf. Constantine Campbell, *Verbal Aspect and Non-Indicative Verbs* [New York: Peter Lang, 2009], pp. 28, 29), which could suggest that Paul wanted to provide greater emphasis or to stress "the present state of affairs." In other words, "thanks to Christ's work on the cross, believers find themselves in a state of sanctification (are now sanctified), made acceptable to God (Rom. 15:16). . . . The phrase in Christ refers to 'faith-union with Christ, through which they share his risen life' (cf. Acts 26:18)" (F. F. Bruce, *Paul, Apostle of the Heart Set Free* [Grand Rapids: Eerdmans, 1977], p. 30).

14. In reference to the term "holy" or "called to be saints," Ciampa and Rosner (*The First Letter to the Corinthians*, p. 56) observe that "because God has sanctified them, they should worship him in holiness." They have been designated and called as "saints" or "holy" (cf. 2 Corinthians 1:1; Romans 1:7; 8:27; Ephesians 1:1; Philippians 1:1; Colossians 1:2), and since they belong "to the holy people of God [which] qualifies them as saints set apart to serve God's purposes, not their own," they should live a "lifestyle . . . bound by moral strictures and standards of behavior

because God is holy" (Leviticus 19:1–2; Exodus 19:5–6; 22:31; 1 Corinthians 3:17 (Garland, *1 Corinthians*, p. 28).

15. Cf. 1:12, 31; 7:22, 23; 8:1–6; 9:19–23. Many issues of the Corinthian church dealt with their various allegiances to different patrons.

16. Paul gives thanks not merely for the Corinthians' enrichment of various gifts but "because of the grace of God that was given you in Christ Jesus." "He selects the gifts of which the Corinthians were especially proud" (Morris, *The First Epistle of Paul to the Corinthians*, p. 37), and he "concentrates on these two clusters of gifts, because the Corinthians majored on them" (David Prior, *The Message of 1 Corinthians*, The Bible Speaks Today [Downers Grove: InterVarsity Press, 1985], p. 24). And ironically, their "greatest liabilities and greatest strengths lie in their gifts" (Garland, *1 Corinthians*, p. 34). Gordon D. Fee (*The First Epistle to the Corinthians*, The New International Commentary of the New Testament [Grand Rapids: Eerdmans, 1989], p. 38) elaborates on this observation by saying that "Paul selects these almost certainly because they were noticeably evident in the community. But they also happen to be items that function in some very negative ways in the church. What Paul appears to be doing, then, is redirecting their focus from their 'graces' (good things in themselves because they edify the church) to God, who has given them, and to Christ, 'in whom' they have been made available ('in him' refers back to 'in Christ Jesus' in v. 2)."

17. These words "speech" and "knowledge," or literally "word" and "knowledge," are gifts of the Spirit (cf. chapters 12—14) and occur more times in 1 Corinthians than in Paul's other letters. The phrase generally refers to the "spiritual graces which make up the Christian character . . . alluding to certain spiritual gifts but not confined to them" (Ciampa and Rosner, *The First Letter to the Corinthians*, p. 64).

18. B. K. Peterson (*Eloquence and the Proclamation of the Gospel in Corinth*, Society of Biblical Literature Dissertation Series 163 [Atlanta: Scholars Press, 1998], p. 59) describes the ancient world's fascination with the art of rhetoric by saying that "in Hellenistic society the practice and expectations of rhetorical eloquence were pervasive. Not only were political leaders expected to speak persuasively and eloquently, but also those who claimed authority in philosophy and religion. Among such people there was great competition, and success depended upon one's ability to express the power of the divine in his or her performance—not only through miracles, but also through rhetorical performances."

19. Fee, *The First Epistle to the Corinthians*, p. 43 points out that this verb "sustain" is the same as the verb in verse 6, "confirmed," which carries on the legal metaphor emphasizing the confirmation of "being pronounced not guilty, blameless" or "guiltless" as it pertains to the Law (see also Ciampa and Rosner, *The First Letter to the Corinthians*, p. 66).

20. Cf. Garland, *1 Corinthians*, p. 35: "Christian experience depends entirely on God's faithfulness (cf. Phil 1:6), not on individual giftedness."

21. "Instead of standing on their dignity as those enriched with speech and knowledge, they should be standing on tiptoe in anticipation of what is to come when God will establish or confirm them as blameless on the day of the Lord." Ibid.

22. Garland (ibid.) translates this word as "common-union" that signifies sharing "the status of being-in-Christ and of being shareholders in a sonship derived from the sonship of Christ." See also Thiselton, *The First Epistle to the Corinthians*, p. 104.

Chapter Two: The Appeal of Unity

1. Cornelius Plantinga, *Not the Way It's Supposed to Be* (Grand Rapids: Eerdmans, 1995), p. 10.

2. In addition to his tone, it's interesting to note Paul's position. Blomberg writes that "Paul does not side with one particular faction; this would exacerbate the problem. Instead, he is after whatever it takes to dispel factiousness and create harmony. But he cannot be requesting unanimity of perspective on every issue nor requiring uniformity of action, inasmuch as his emphasis on the diversity of spiritual gifts in chapters 12—14 precludes demands for Christian 'cloning.' Cooperation, mutual concern, peaceful coexistence, edification in love—all these are the positive antidotes for divisiveness" (*NIV Application Commentary for 1 Corinthians* [Grand Rapids: Zondervan, 1995], p. 45).

3. Paul invokes a classical Greek expression here that connotes "to make up differences" or "be at peace" with individuals or groups. His use of "speak the same" would have brought to mind the writings of Aristotle and Thucydides (Joseph B. Lightfoot, *Notes on Epistles of St. Paul from Unpublished Commentaries* [London: Macmillan, 1895], p. 151) to his readers and listeners. Paul not only demonstrates his knowledge of classical culture, but is appealing in the vernacular of the Greco-Roman rhetoric.

4. This can be better rendered as "cliques," "cracks," or "dissensions" in this context (Leon Morris, *The First Epistle of Paul to the Corinthians*, The Tyndale New Testament Commentaries [Grand Rapids: Eerdmans, 1989], p. 94).

5. Ben Witherington, *Conflict and Community in Corinth* (Grand Rapids: Eerdmans, 1995), p. 95.

6. Possibly even one of Paul's first converts, as Witherington suggests (in ibid., p. 99).

7. What bothered Paul the most was that the Corinthians had "absorbed the spirit of partisanship. . . . He does not attack the teaching of any of the parties, but the fact that there were parties. He does not exempt those who clung to his own name" (Morris, *The First Epistle of Paul to the Corinthians*, p. 41).

8. David E. Garland, *1 Corinthians*, Baker Exegetical Commentary on the New Testament (Grand Rapids: Baker Academic, 2003), p. 42.

9. Those converted by Paul directly would have felt a very strong attachment to him and considered themselves "forever in his debt" (David Prior, *The Message of 1 Corinthians*, The Bible Speaks Today [Nottingham, UK: Inter-Varsity Press, 1985], p. 30). They felt such a strong indebtedness to him that they would have accepted his teachings word for word.

10. Because of Apollos' academic background, those keen to follow him would have consisted of the intellectually elite of the Corinthian church. From what little is known about Apollos, it is widely accepted that he was from Alexandria, "one of the most respected and creative university cities of the Mediterranean" (ibid., pp. 31, 32). Because of his intellect, rhetoric, expository knowledge of the Old Testament Scriptures, accurate teaching about Jesus, and bold preaching, Apollos would have been a very attractive public figure.

11. Given the backdrop of Peter's ministry outlined in the book of Acts, it would be reasonable to assume that many of Peter's followers were from Jewish Christianity. Prior notes, "there is ample evidence of legalistic tendencies in the church at Corinth,

particularly in the debate about the rights and wrongs of eating food offered to idols in chapters 8—10. . . . [and] Paul's clash with Peter about food laws . . . the 'kosher' issue may well have continued to be a smouldering fire between the apostle to the Gentiles and the one 'entrusted with the gospel to the circumcised'" (ibid., p. 33).

12. Those who deemed themselves a part of the "Christ-party" would have considered themselves among the spiritual elite (ibid., p. 34). In their anti-authoritarian eyes, following a particular leader/hero would have been foolish. As Prior speculates, a very plausible motto for those in the Christ-party may have been: "Who needs leaders anyway? Christ is our leader. He is the head of the body. We depend on him alone and we go straight to him. He tells us what to do and, when we wait on him, he lets us know his will" (ibid.).

13. Much of the Corinthians' struggles, as outlined in verses 1–9, were rooted from "setting too high a value on human wisdom and human eloquence in line with the typical Greek admiration for rhetoric and philosophical studies" (Morris, *The First Epistle of Paul to the Corinthians*, p. 42). And most of the Corinthians "were caught up in the pattern of behavior that characterized those who were zealous for oratory and eloquence and became the students of the various famous Sophists and other rhetors" (Ben Witherington, *Conflict and Community in Corinth* [Grand Rapids: Eerdmans, 1995], p. 100).

14. There many reasons for and examples of factionalism in the modern church. Blomberg writes that the "disunity of the church of Jesus Christ remains one of the greatest scandals which compromises its witness today. . . . Church should be a place where people who have no other natural reason for associating with each other come together in love . . . a fully mature congregation should integrate people of disparate races, nationalities, socioeconomic strata, and societal status. . . . Views on baptism, the Lord's Supper, the millennium or the rapture, women in ministry, spiritual gifts, and numerous other items should not stand in the way of intensive networking and cooperation among a wide variety of churches in a given community or region for the larger purposes of the kingdom" (Craig L. Blomberg, *1 Corinthians*, NIV Application Commentary [Grand Rapids: Zondervan, 1995], p. 49).

15. The reference to baptism further reinforces the Corinthian attachment to the particular leader who baptized them. The patronage associated with their physical baptism continues to be the root of the factionalism. Paul is reminding them here of their true "spiritual baptism" (Roy E. Ciampa and Brian S. Rosner, *The First Letter to the Corinthians*, The Pillar New Testament Commentary [Grand Rapids: Eerdmans, 2010], p. 81).

16. As Paul does in Romans 10:15, he invokes the eschatological nature of Isaiah to reinforce his perspective of "preaching the gospel." Paul viewed his "heralding of the gospel as an eschatological, divinely, commissioned activity" (ibid., p. 86).

17. To be unpacked in the concluding section of chapter 1, Paul rejects earthly wisdom and eloquence, for the reliance upon it empties the cross of its power. Ciampa notes that the "cross of Christ" mentioned here is more than just the mere historical event of Jesus' crucifixion, but stands for all that his death accomplishes (ibid.).

Chapter Three: Rewriting the Storyline

1. There is a grammatical emphasis here on the "word" or the act of preaching, as also repeated in verses 21 and 23.

2. "'Perish' stands for a definitive destruction, not merely in the sense of the extinction of physical existence, but rather of an eternal plunge into Hades, and a hopeless destiny of death, in the depiction of which such terms are used as 'wrath and fury, tribulation and distress'" (A. Oepke, in Kittel, TWNT, vol. I, p. 396, quoted by David Prior, *The Message of 1 Corinthians*, The Bible Speaks Today [Nottingham, UK: Inter-Varsity Press, 1985], p. 44).

3. Quoted from Isaiah 29:14, "from a context in which the prophet is proclaiming God's intentions to judge Israel for her superficial and hypocritical religion" (Craig L. Blomberg, *1 Corinthians*, NIV Application Commentary [Grand Rapids: Zondervan, 1995], p. 52).

4. See "wisdom" in Willem Van Gemeren, *New International Dictionary of Old Testament Theology and Exegesis*, vol. 4 (Grand Rapids: Zondervan, 2012), p. 1277.

5. Cf. Isaiah 19:12. These questions are posed in a sarcastically rhetorical tone.

6. The phrase "of this age" conveys eschatological language, reflecting phrases from rabbinic and apocalyptic Judaism (Gordon D. Fee, *The First Epistle to the Corinthians*, The New International Commentary of the New Testament [Grand Rapids: Eerdmans, 1989], 71).

7. See Chapter 1 of this book.

8. For more information, see chapter 5 of Stephen T. Um and Justin Buzzard, *Why Cities Matter* (Wheaton: Crossway, 2013).

9. Ben Witherington, *Conflict and Community in Corinth* (Grand Rapids: Eerdmans, 1995), p. 23.

10. Ibid.

11. From Harriet Rubin, "Success and Excess"; www.fastcompany.com/node/35583/; accessed March 28, 2009.

12. See Robert Fuller, *Somebodies and Nobodies* (Gabriola Island, BC, Canada: New Society Publishers, 2004).

13. Left to themselves, human beings or mere creatures cannot fully know the living God (Romans 1:18–31). True knowledge of God probably refers here to a correct understanding of what God is doing in the world rather than a proper apprehension of God's being and character (Fee, *The First Epistle to the Corinthians*, p. 72).

14. The adversative conjunction "but" and emphatic pronoun "we" in the Greek presents a stark contrast between the wisdom of men and the preaching of "Christ crucified" (Leon Morris, *The First Epistle of Paul to the Corinthians*, The Tyndale New Testament Commentaries [Grand Rapids: Eerdmans, 1989], p. 45).

15. Translated as "a stumbling block," or quite literally "a scandal."

16. Gordon Fee, *The First Epistle to the Corinthians*, The New International Commentary of the New Testament (Grand Rapids: Eerdmans, 1989), p. 74.

17. Greeks prided themselves in speculative philosophy, where honor was attributed to the outstanding thinkers.

18. Jews were looking for physical evidence and were interested in the practical. Much like they did with Jesus, they demanded a sign (cf. Matthew 12:28; 16:1, 4; Mark 8:11, 12; John 6:30). A messiah, in the minds of the Jews, was manifested in majesty and power, so a crucified one would have been contradictory on their terms (see Morris, *The First Epistle of Paul to the Corinthians*).

19. Cf. Galatians 3:13, 14.

20. Richard Bauckham, *Jesus: A Very Short Introduction* (New York: Oxford University Press), 2011.

21. Much of these insights are derived from Malcolm Gladwell, *Outliers* (New York: Little, Brown & Company, 2008).

22. See ibid., pp. 123–28. Calculating for inflation, $250 billion in 1980 would compute to nearly $760 billion in 2014 (more than three times the amount).

23. See chart in ibid., p. 134.

Chapter Four: A New Understanding of Community

1. As Prior notes, "for the Corinthians, knowledge mattered more than love; for Paul, the key to knowing all that God has prepared for us is in loving him" (David Prior, *The Message of 1 Corinthians*, The Bible Speaks Today [Nottingham, UK: Inter-Varsity Press, 1985], p. 52).

2. When referring to "the mature" here, Paul is not referencing the philosophically elite, politically influential, or religiously pious. Seeing its antonym in "infants" (3:1), he connects "the mature" to those who are spiritual adults as opposed to the spiritual infants (14:20; cf. 13:11; Philippians 3:15; Ephesians 4:13, 14; Hebrews 5:13, 14). Garland notes ". . . the distinction between juvenile Christians who fail to incarnate the cross by nursing jealousies and stoking rivalries, and the 'mature' who accept God's foolishness as wisdom and the world's wisdom as foolishness. Being spiritually adult means recognizing and embracing God's wisdom in the cross and knowing that it invalidates the wisdom of this age" (David E. Garland, *1 Corinthians*, Baker Exegetical Commentary on the New Testament [Grand Rapids: Baker Academic, 2003], pp. 92, 93).

3. "Wisdom" is used fifteen times in 1:17 – 2:13. Numerous commentators have deduced that the Corinthians were obsessed with wisdom, and Paul certainly intends to address the situation here (see Roy E. Ciampa and Brian S. Rosner, *The First Letter to the Corinthians*, The Pillar New Testament Commentary [Grand Rapids: Eerdmans, 2010]). Thiselton points out that not only "wisdom" but "maturity" and "spirituality" were contextual catchwords that "had become embedded in the life of the church at Corinth, and [Paul's] most urgent task at this point is . . . to reclaim the terms for the gospel by redefining them in the light of the nature of God and of the gospel" (Anthony C. Thiselton, *The First Epistle to the Corinthians: A Commentary on the Greek Text*, New International Greek Testament Commentary [Grand Rapids: Eerdmans, 2000], p. 224).

4. *Hoi archontes'* is mainly used to signify earthly rulers (vs. spiritual/supernatural rulers) (see Cullmann 1960: 91; Caird 1956: 17, as quoted in Thiselton, *The First Epistle to the Corinthians*). Paul uses this phrase in Romans 13:3 to clearly refer to earthly rulers (cf. Matthew 20:25), and sixteen other occurrences in the New Testament support this view.

5. "Just as earlier human wisdom is under God's judgment, here the rulers who advocate it likewise 'come to nothing . . .' They have no part in the age to come. The Corinthian Christians are part of and destined for the new age. To embrace human wisdom, then, is bad eschatology, for it is an alignment with a party that God opposes and whose fate is set" (Ciampa, *The First Letter to the Corinthians*, p. 125).

6. Tony Reinke, *Lit! A Christian Guide to Reading Books* (Wheaton: Crossway, 2011), pp. 93, 94.

7. The nearest source of Paul's citation is from Isaiah 64:4; other passages that read similarly in part are Psalm 31:20; Isaiah 52:15; 65:17. Others have argued it

may have come from a unrecorded saying of Christ in the Gospels. Leon Morris best describes this quotation to be a "free citation of Isaiah 64:4, with reminisces of other scriptural passages" (*The First Epistle of Paul to the Corinthians*, The Tyndale New Testament Commentaries [Grand Rapids: Eerdmans, 1989], p. 55).

8. C. S. Lewis, *Mere Christianity* (New York: Harper Collins, 1952), p. 159.

9. "Nobody can really know what is going on in a man's mind, nobody but the man's own spirit. From outside we can guess. But the spirit of the man does not guess. He knows. In the same way, reasons Paul, no one outside God can know what takes place within God, nobody but the Spirit of God. The Spirit knows God from the inside. This ascribes full deity to the Spirit. And it shows that the revelation of which Paul has been speaking is authentic. Because the Spirit who reveals is truly God, what he reveals is the truth of God" (Morris, *The First Epistle of Paul to the Corinthians*, p. 57).

10. It is interesting to note that Paul refers to the gospel as a "mystery" or "secret" (v. 7). "The mystery that Paul speaks here is not something additional to the saving message of Christ crucified: it is in Christ crucified that the wisdom of God is embodied. It consists rather in the more detailed unfolding of the divine purpose summed up in Christ crucified" (F. F. Bruce, *Paul, Apostle of the Heart Set Free* [Grand Rapids: Eerdmans, 1977], p. 38). The three great sources of human knowledge—seeing, hearing, and thought—alike fail here (Prior, *The Message of 1 Corinthians*, p. 51).

11. "Instead of sharing the fate of the 'rulers of this age,' that is, 'come to nothing' (2:6b), believers anticipate an altogether better destiny (2 Cor. 3:18; Rom. 8:30; Phil. 3:21). . . . The use of 'Lord of glory' as a title for Christ in v. 9 gives a hint as to the way in which such exaltation is possible . . . believers expect glory because of their union with the risen and exalted Christ" (Ciampa, *The First Letter to the Corinthians*, p. 126).

12. This could refer to Satan, the spirit who leads people away from God (2 Corinthians 4:4; Ephesians 6:11; John 12:31). But because of the rejection of supernatural influences proposed for verses 6, 7, the spirit here most likely refers to the spirit of human wisdom that opposes God (ibid., p. 131).

13. "Thus, as we will see in later verses, to be 'spiritual' is not to have some extra light from within or even somehow to be extraordinarily sensitive to the divine, as in much popular use of the term but to appropriate and live in accordance with God's saving work through Christ by God's Spirit" (cf. E. Schweizer, TDNT 6:436, 437; quoted from Ciampa, *The Message of 1 Corinthians*, p. 129).

14. Gordon Fee highlights the verb "discerned" in verse 14 as a crucial one. It only appears in this Pauline letter, occurring ten times. "Here there seems to be a play on the word; many think it is also ironical, anticipating the usage in 4:3–4. Probably it means something very close to 'discern' in the sense of being able to make appropriate 'judgments' about what God is doing in the world; and the person 'without the Spirit' obviously cannot do that. As such it is immediately picked up in v. 15 as the one proper activity of the truly 'spiritual' person" (*The First Epistle to the Corinthians*, The New International Commentary of the New Testament [Grand Rapids: Eerdmans, 1989], p. 117).

15. "A Divine and Supernatural Light," *The Works of Jonathan Edwards*, vol. 2 (Peabody, MA: Hendrickson, 2005), p. 14.

16. Luc Ferry, *A Brief History of Ideas* (New York: Harper Collins, 2003).

17. Derived from Timothy Keller's *Walking with God through Pain and Suffering* (New York: Penguin Books, 2013), p. 38.

18. While only mentioned once up to this point, Paul begins to emphasize the activity of the Spirit by mentioning him six times in verses 10–14.

19. The quoted question in verse 16 is from Isaiah 40:13. Paul does not mean that every Christian can understand all of Christ's thoughts. He means that the indwelling Spirit reveals Christ. The spiritual person accordingly does not see things from the viewpoint of the world. He sees them from the viewpoint of Christ.

Chapter Five: God-Given Growth

1. See Chapters 1 and 2 of this book.

2. This is an affectionate address. *Adelphoi* softens the rebuke Paul is about to make and affirms that it is being made out of both necessity and love. See Leon Morris, *The First Epistle of Paul to the Corinthians*, The Tyndale New Testament Commentaries (Grand Rapids: Eerdmans, 1989), p. 61.

3. John LaRosa, "Self-Improvement Market Has Unfilled Niches For Entrepreneurs," March 26, 2012; http://www.prweb.com/releases/2012/3/prweb9323729.htm.

4. "They were not ready for it, even some years on from their conversion to Christ. 'Mere lapse of time does not bring Christian maturity'" (David Prior, *The Message of 1 Corinthians*, The Bible Speaks Today [Nottingham, UK: Inter-Varsity Press, 1985], p. 56).

5. "Paul's basic accusation against the Corinthians is that in acting divisively they behave as if they belong to 'this age' and as if they do not have the Spirit. In other words, they live as if they were no different from anyone else in Corinth. . . . Proof of their worldliness, Paul says, can be seen in the fact that 'there is jealousy and strife among you.'" Continuing on to cite Galatians 5, Ciampa notes that of the list of fifteen items that characterize worldly behavior, six of them have to do with division (Roy E. Ciampa and Brian S. Rosner, *The First Letter to the Corinthians*, The Pillar New Testament Commentary [Grand Rapids: Eerdmans, 2010], p. 135).

6. Hence Paul's use of "children" language toward the Corinthians. Their pursuit of growth in the worldly sense has brought little progress in the areas of spiritual growth since Paul's planting of the church.

7. To distinguish between the difference of *sarkikos* in verse 3 and *sarkinos* in verse 1, this question here is better translated, "Are you not fleshly?"

8. Morris notes that "there was nothing blameworthy in their being 'not yet ready for it.' But it is otherwise when he says 'you are *still* not ready . . .' Paul gets to the root of the matter with his accusation that they are *still worldly*. The difference between *sarkinos* and *sarkikos* is like that between 'fleshy' and 'fleshly.' The more thoroughgoing word is *sarkinos*, but there is no blame attaching to it as applied to those who are young in the faith. But *sarkikos . . .* when used of those who have been Christians for years, is blameworthy. To be characterized instead by flesh, as the Corinthians were, is the very opposite of what Christians should be" (Morris, *The First Epistle of Paul to the Corinthians*, pp. 61, 62).

9. From 2004 Presidential Debate, found in "Transcript Part 3: How Can the U.S. Remain Competitive?" http://www.cnn.com/2004/ALLPOLITICS/10/08/debate.transcript3/.

10. Cf. Isaiah 5:1–7.

11. "'To each' . . . probably means that these servants act as they were gifted by God. Paul claims to be the planter of the congregation; Apollos only watered. This means that Paul came first, laid the foundation, and converted the Corinthians, that Apollos nurtured them, and that a certain distinction of labor exists between Paul and Apollos. Though both are servants . . . he argues that it is God who causes conversions and church growth regardless of what human instruments God uses" (Ben Witherington, *Conflict and Community in Corinth* [Grand Rapids: Eerdmans, 1995], p. 132).

12. Or defuses the personality-cult controversy. See Prior, *The Message of 1 Corinthians*, p. 57.

13. This is further affirmed in the emphasis found in verse 9, where God is mentioned first in all three descriptions: "God's fellow workers," "God's field," and "God's building" (both in English and Greek).

14. "This emphasis on serving is crucial for recovering a biblical perspective on leadership. Jesus taught precisely the same: 'Let the greatest among you become as the youngest, and the leader as one who serves. For which is greater, one who sits at table, or one who serves? Is it not the one who sits at the table? But I am among you as one who serves' (Lk. 22:24–27). Division, rivalry, jealousy arise in the church because certain leaders lord it over the flock and God's people often love to have it so; it is less demanding, less disturbing. Authority in the church, truly Christian authority, comes from those who lay down their lives for the brethren in service and availability. Any other authority is worldly authority and is to be rejected" (Prior, *The Message of 1 Corinthians*, p. 57).

Chapter Six: The Architecture of Community

1. David E. Garland, *1 Corinthians*, Baker Exegetical Commentary on the New Testament (Grand Rapids: Baker Academic, 2003), p. 114.

2. Greek *sophos*, literally translated "wise" (cf. 3:18, "wise in this age").

3. That is, Christ crucified.

4. As Ciampa and Rosner note, "The major Old Testament background to Paul's comparison of the Corinthians to a temple in 3:10–17 is Solomon's garden-like Temple and the end-time temple of Malachi 3—4. In terms of specific connections, Paul echoes Isaiah 3:3 in 3:10; 1 Chronicles 29:2 in 3:10; and Malachi 3:2–3 in 3:12–15. As 'God's temple' (3:16), the Corinthians are the antitype of the imposing temple of Solomon and the fulfillment of Malachi's version of the end-time temple" (Roy E. Ciampa and Brian S. Rosner, *The First Letter to the Corinthians*, The Pillar New Testament Commentary [Grand Rapids: Eerdmans, 2010], p. 150).

5. This points out the individual responsibility of all.

6. "'To build upon' refers to preaching and instruction (2 Cor. 10:8; 12:19; 13:10; cf. Ep. 2:19–22), but that task need not be limited to 'apostles, prophets, evangelists, pastors, and teachers,' since they are given 'to equip the saints for the work of ministry, for building up the body of Christ' (Eph. 4:11–12; cf. 4:16, 29)" (Garland, *1 Corinthians*, p. 115).

7. Paul uses the Greek word *naos* here to describe the Corinthian church, which would have differed from the usual use of *hieron* (describing the temple). The noun comes from the root *naein*, which literally means "to dwell." Witherington points

out that the *naos* was usually a part of the ancient temple where the god was thought to dwell—the sanctuary proper. "Remarkably, Paul believes that even these badly mixed-up Christians are still God's temple where God still dwells" (Ben Witherington, *Conflict and Community in Corinth* [Grand Rapids: Eerdmans, 1995], p. 134).

8. As Ciampa and Rosner suggest, the judgment here is "not of all humankind, of the justified over against (other) sinners, but of wise and unwise builders of the church" (*The First Letter to the Corinthians*, p. 150). The fire is more meant for purification and refinement than judgment and punishment.

9. "A subordinate error equates the people trying to destroy God's temple with the poor builders of the previous paragraph. Even shoddy construction is at least *erecting* a building of some kind, but those Paul warns . . . are trying to *demolish* it" (Craig L. Blomberg, *1 Corinthians*, NIV Application Commentary [Grand Rapids: Zondervan, 1995], p. 81).

10. The repetition of "destroy" here shows that the "punishment is not arbitrary; it 'fits the crime.' To engage in making divisions is to destroy the divine society and thus to invite God to destroy the sinner" (Leon Morris, *The First Epistle of Paul to the Corinthians*, The Tyndale New Testament Commentaries [Grand Rapids: Eerdmans, 1989], p. 67).

11. See the previous chapters in this book for discussions of earthly wisdom and foolishness versus divine wisdom and foolishness.

Chapter Seven: A Proper Evaluation

1. The word for "servants" (Greek *hyperetas*) literally means "under-rower" or "someone who is simply responding to higher authority and doing his job." The word for "stewards" (Greek *oikonomos*) literally meant "housekeeper, overseer, or slave" in New Testament contexts. "They were charged with providing the establishment of a large estate with food and all things needful. He was responsible, not to his fellows, but to his lord. He was not expected to exercise his own initiative, still less his own personal authority. He simply did his master's bidding and looked after his affairs" (David Prior, *The Message of 1 Corinthians*, The Bible Speaks Today [Nottingham, UK: Inter-Varsity Press, 1985], p. 62). All these ideas were ways in which Paul thought Christians should be regarded—as servants and stewards of Christ.

2. The Greek begins the verse grammatically with an emphasis on "but with me," contrasting Paul's stance with the Corinthians and their method of evaluation (Leon Morris, *The First Epistle of Paul to the Corinthians*, The Tyndale New Testament Commentaries [Grand Rapids: Eerdmans, 1989], p. 72).

3. See Matt Smethurst, "You Can't Exhaust It," October 8, 2013; http://www.thegospelcoalition.org/article/you-cant-exhaust-it.

4. *Hyperetas* is a "happy change of metaphors for Paul" (compared to the use of *diakonoi* up until this point for "servants"), because "not only is it pregnant with the notion of accountability that is in the forefront of this paragraph, but it inherently conveys the motif of delegated authority as well. . . . Thus apostles are supposed to be regarded as 'servants of Christ,' reemphasizing their humble position and their belonging to Christ alone; at the same time they are 'stewards of the mysteries of God' (RSV), emphasizing both their trusted position and their accountability to God" (Gordon D. Fee, *The First Epistle to the Corinthians*, The New International Commentary of the New Testament [Grand Rapids: Eerdmans, 1989], p. 159).

5. Paul's understanding and awareness of himself, or his conscience, is seen in his letter to the Romans (2:14, 15). "'When Gentiles who have not the law do by nature what the law requires . . . they should show that what the law requires is written on their hearts, while their conscience also bears witness and their conflicting thoughts accuse or perhaps excuse them on that day when, according to my gospel, God judges the secrets of men by Christ Jesus.' Paul himself told the Roman governor of Judea, Felix, 'I always take pains to have a clear conscience toward God and toward men' (Acts 24:16). Even if this conscience did accuse him, there were two cleansing and strengthening secrets, summed up in these two passages: 'How much more shall the blood of Christ . . . purify your conscience from dead works to serve the living God' (Heb. 9:14) and 'God is greater than our hearts, and he knows everything' (1 Jn. 3:20)" (Prior, *The Message of 1 Corinthians*, p. 63).

6. Paul uses a different word for "wise" (*phronimos*) here than he does until this point in the letter (*sophos*). While there is little that distinguishes the meaning of the two words in the Greek, Morris notes that just by using a different word, Paul "puts some difference between his readers and the worldly-wise he has castigated earlier" (*The First Epistle*, 78).

7. "Cf. 1 Thes. 2:9; 3:8; 4:11; Paul refers to the fact that he physically labored to earn a living; which would have been despised by the Greeks, thinking of it as only fit work for slaves" (ibid.).

8. *David and Goliath* (New York: Little, Brown and Company, 2013), pp. 61, 62.

9. "Paul's weaknesses reflect the 'weakness of God,' which is displayed in the cross as his saving power; and in 2:4–5 they are seen as the proper channels through which God's power might be manifested . . . 'you are strong!' . . . is the ultimate irony. They are not in fact among the powerful and influential in Corinth, but by their judging Paul they are assuming the seat of such. Yet again, in Christ they should be among the truly 'strong'" (Fee, *The First Epistle to the Corinthians*, p. 176).

10. Greek plural *perikatharmata*, literally "things removed as the result of cleaning all around" (Morris, *The First Epistle of Paul to the Corinthians*, p. 79).

11. Greek *peripsema*, "that which is wiped off by rubbing all around" (ibid., p. 78).

12. "Because the removal of filth has the effect of cleansing, both words came to have the derived meaning of 'propitiatory offering,' that offering that cleanses from sin. It was not used of sacrifices in general, but of human sacrifices which were offered in some places. We might think this would give the words a noble tinge, but not so. The people who were sacrificed were those who could most easily be spared, the meanest and most worthless in the community. . . . Paul's point then is that the apostles were regarded as the most contemptible of people (cf. La. 3:45). . . . He was describing the present position of the apostles" (ibid., p. 79).

13. J. K. Rowling speech available at https://www.youtube.com/watch?v= wHGqp8lz36c.

14. Sarah Pulliam, "Interview: Malcolm Gladwell on His Return to Faith While Writing 'David and Goliath,'" October 9, 2013; http://www.religionnews.com/2013 /10/09/interview-malcolm-gladwell-return-faith-writing-david-goliath/.

Chapter Eight: The Indispensability of Authority

1. From excerpt in Victor Lee Austin's *Up With Authority* (New York: T&T Clark, 2010), p. 79.

2. From *Oxford Dictionary*.

3. Austin, *Up with Authority*, p. 27.

4. Paul appeals to his spiritual fatherhood toward the Corinthian church by means of reminding them that he "became (Gk. *egennesa*, a regular verb for begetting children and referring either to the father or mother's role) [their] father through the gospel" (Gordon D. Fee, *The First Epistle to the Corinthians*, The New International Commentary of the New Testament [Grand Rapids: Eerdmans, 1989], p. 185).

5. While trying to reestablish his authority, Paul is also trying to gain back their loyalty. He makes it a point to say his relationship with them is unique; he is not only their "father" but their "*only* father." "This is not intended to be a putdown of their other teachers, of whom Paul has thus far spoken favorably. Rather, the metaphor intends to simply distinguish his own relationship to them from that of all others, including of course Apollos and Peter, but also those within their community who are currently exercising influence, not to mention all others who ever would. His unique relationship to them was that of 'father,' and that gave him a special authority over and responsibility toward them. With this language, therefore, he is both reasserting his authority and appealing to their loyalty, which had obviously eroded in this church" (ibid., p. 185).

6. The Greek, *mimetai mou ginesthe*, emphasizes the verb of "being" rather than "imitating," further reinforcing the character exhortation, and not just behavior modification.

7. C. S. Lewis, *Surprised by Joy* (New York: Harcourt, 1955), p. 172.

8. The Greek word *noutheto* is used by Paul throughout the New Testament (cf. Romans 15:14; Colossians 1:28; 3:16; 1 Thessalonians 5:12, 14; 2 Thessalonians 3:15). "'Admonish' seems to be capture a better nuance. It has the primary connotation of trying to have a corrective influence on someone, an 'admonition that is designed to correct while not provoking or embittering'" (J. Behm, TDNT IV, 1021; quoted by Fee, *The First Epistle to the Corinthians*, p. 184).

9. Richard Bauckham, *God and the Crisis of Freedom* (Louisville: Westminster, John Knox Press, 2002), p. 66.

10. Walter Isaacson, *Steve Jobs* (New York: Simon & Shuster, 2011).

11. Ibid., p. 454.

12. Roy E. Ciampa and Brian S. Rosner, *The First Letter to the Corinthians*, The Pillar New Testament Commentary (Grand Rapids: Eerdmans, 2010), p. 188, quoting Garland.

13. Further affirmation and evidence of the father-children motif.

14. Andy Crouch, *Playing God* (Downers Grove: InterVarsity Press, 2013), p. 25.

15. See ibid.

16. Bauckham, quoting Water Bruedermann, *God and the Crisis of Freedom*, p. 68.

17. Richard Sibbes, *Care for the Soul: Exploring the Intersection of Psychology & Theology* (Downers Grove: InterVarsity Press, 2001), p. 209.

18. Richard Lints, "Rewoven Into the Fabric of Redemption: Section V," May 13, 2010; http://www.centerforgospelculture.org/2010/05/rewoven-into-the-fabric-of-redemption-section-v/.

19. Tim Keller, John 12 sermon; www.redeemer.com/sermons.

Chapter Nine: The Grace of Discipline

1. Jonathan Leeman, *The Church and the Surprising Offense of God's Love: Reintroducing the Doctrines of Church Membership and Discipline* (Wheaton: Crossway, 2010), p. 44.

2. "... a case of incest that is either being tolerated or condoned within the church . . . a believer is living in an incestuous relationship that even pagans disallowed is bad enough; but far worse is the church's relaxed attitude toward it—they are arrogant" (Gordon D. Fee, *The First Epistle to the Corinthians*, The New International Commentary of the New Testament [Grand Rapids: Eerdmans, 1989], p. 196).

3. Blomberg (*1 Corinthians*, NIV Application Commentary [Grand Rapids: Zondervan, 1995]), Ciampa and Rosner (*The First Letter to the Corinthians*, The Pillar New Testament Commentary [Grand Rapids: Eerdmans, 2010]), and Morris all support the observation that the woman was the guilty's stepmother, and not biological mother. Otherwise Paul would have specified her as such. Morris further explicates that it could have also been involving "the woman [who] was divorced from his father, or that the father had died, leaving her a widow . . ." (Leon Morris, *The First Epistle of Paul to the Corinthians*, The Tyndale New Testament Commentaries [Grand Rapids: Eerdmans, 1989], p. 83).

4. Many commentators recall the account of Cicero (*Pro Cluentio*, 15) and his outrage toward a woman wedded to her son-in-law. For more relevant Greco-Roman perspectives, see Charles H. Talbert, *Reading Corinthians* (New York: Crossroads, 1989), pp. 13, 14.

5. "It is easy to overlook the peccadilloes of those who contribute generously to the church funds, or open their homes for church meetings" (Goulder, 1999, p. 348; quoted in David E. Garland, *1 Corinthians*, Baker Exegetical Commentary on the New Testament [Grand Rapids: Baker Academic, 2003], p. 158).

6. Lewis Smedes, *Sex for Christians* (Grand Rapids: Eerdmans, 1994), p. 67.

7. Greek *pleonektais*; cf. 5:11; 6:10; Ephesians 5:5.

8. Garland, *1 Corinthians*, p. 186.

9. See exposition on the Lord's Supper in Chapter 20 of this book.

10. "Where anyone claims to be a Christian but leads a life that belies his profession, there is to be no such close fellowship as will countenance his sin" (Morris, *The First Epistle of Paul to the Corinthians*, p. 89).

11. "The mention of 'leaven' in v. 6 naturally suggests imagery from Paul's own history as a law-abiding Jew, namely the two religious rituals of Passover. He begins with a direct allusion to the ceremonial removal of all leaven from their homes (Exod. 12:15), which in turn prompts an allusion to the most important event of all, the sacrifice of the Paschal Lamb (Exod. 12:6)" (Fee, *The First Epistle to the Corinthians*, p. 216).

12. Fee notes that Paul's mentioning of yeast is similar to our modern folk wisdom of "a bad apple spoils the whole barrel." "Leaven . . . consisted of keeping back a 'little' portion of last week's dough, which in turn was thoroughly fermented to give it lightness (= sourdough bread). Although the OT does not expressly so specify, the Feast of Unleavened Bread, as well as being a religious celebration, was probably a health provision. Because of the fermentation process, which week after week increased dangers of infection, the Israelites were commanded once a year to purge their homes of all leaven (Exod. 12:14–20). During the Feast, they would bake

only unleavened bread, from which dough they would then start up the process again after the Feast. Thus in the NT leaven became a symbol of the process by which an evil spreads insidiously in a community until the whole has been infected by it (cf. Mark 8:15). So it was in Corinth. Their problem was that they were not taking this matter seriously, either the evil itself or their danger of being thoroughly contaminated by it" (ibid.).

13. Greek *elikrineias*, "the quality or state of being free of dissimulation" (*The Greek-English Lexicon of the New Testament*, Walter Bauer, Frederick W. Danker, eds. [Chicago: University of Chicago Press, 2001]).

14. Cf. Exodus 12.

Chapter Ten: Grace and Grievances

1. Paul draws on the eschatological literature (cf. Daniel 7:22; Matthew 19:28; Revelation 20:4). Witherington suggests that "on judgment day believers will judge the outside world and even angels. . . . Paul's point in v. 2 is that if they are going to go on and judge the world, then surely they can handle an ordinary mundane matter now on their own" (Ben Witherington, *Conflict and Community in Corinth* [Grand Rapids: Eerdmans, 1995], p. 165). The way Paul appeals to the saints sharing in judgment infers that it was well known to his audience (Leon Morris, *The First Epistle of Paul to the Corinthians*, The Tyndale New Testament Commentaries [Grand Rapids: Eerdmans, 1989], p. 91).

2. See the discussion on *shalom* in Chapter 2 of this book.

3. Greek *adikeite* (cf. Matthew 20:13; Luke 10:19; Acts 7:24, 26, 27; 25:10, 11; 2 Corinthians 7:2,12; Galatians 4:12; Colossians 3:25).

4. Greek *apostereite* (cf. 7:5; Mark 10:19; 1 Timothy 6:5; James 5:4).

5. "In deciding to sue, one first had to calculate the cost and the chances of winning, not on the basis of the merits of the case but on the defendant's social status and powerful connections . . . people in the ancient world contended for honor in the law courts, and one gained on her by beating a rival down. The pursuit of litigation often has little to do with the pursuit of justice" (Garland, *1 Corinthians*, pp. 200, 201).

6. Warren Burger, "Christian Conciliation: An Alternative to Ordinary ADR— Part 1"; http://www.peacemaker.net/site/c.nuIWL7MOJtE/b.5369217/k.9B7D /Christian_Conciliation_An_Alternative_to_Ordinary_ADR__Part_1.htm.

7. Ibid.

8. Quoted from http://www.peacemaker.net/site/c.nuIWL7MOJtE/b.5392247/k .8144/Frequently_Asked_Questions.htm.

9. Ken Sande, *The Peacemaker* (Grand Rapids: Baker Books, 2004).

10. See Miroslav Volf, *Exclusion and Embrace* (Nashville: Abingdon, 1996).

Chapter Eleven: Sex

1. "Going to a prostitute is culturally so natural to the Greek that such an undertaking did not first have to be introduced or maintained by a new libertine program." Becker, quoted in Anthony C. Thiselton, *The First Epistle to the Corinthians: A Commentary on the Greek Text*, New International Greek Testament Commentary (Grand Rapids: Eerdmans, 2000), p. 227. Cf. David E. Garland, *1 Corinthians*, Baker Exegetical Commentary on the New Testament (Grand Rapids: Baker Academic, 2003), pp. 240, 241.

2. "If there is anyone who thinks that youth should be forbidden affairs even with the courtesans, he is doubtless austere (I cannot deny it), but his view is contrary not only to the licence of this age, but also to the custom and concessions of our ancestors. For when was this not a common practice? When was it blamed? When was it forbidden?" Cicero, *Pro Caelio*, quoted in Garland, *1 Corinthians*, p. 227.

3. "There can be no question that the initial clause of v. 12 represents a quotation used as a maxim by some or by many at Corinth . . . probably a slogan bandied about among some of the Christians in Corinth and used . . . to justify an indiscriminate exercise of their rights (Collins)." Thiselton, *The First Epistle to the Corinthians*, pp. 460, 461.

4. "In many cultural situations, slogans often appeal to freedom or liberty for their emotive power." Ibid., p. 461.

5. Cf. Song of Solomon 4:5; 7:1–3, 6–8.

6. Consider this story from Lauren Winner: "I want to tell you a story about my friends Charlie and Suzanne. They should have had a picture-perfect wedding night. . . . But [instead it] was, in Suzanne's words, 'a disaster.' Though Charlie was eager to make the beast with two backs (that's Shakespeare's felicitous phrase, not my own), she simply did not want to have sex. . . . Nor did she want to have sex much during their first three years of marriage, until they started meeting with a counselor. . . . 'I knew there would be a learning curve with sex, but I thought that meant learning about mechanics. What I really had to learn was that sex is OK—that it is OK to desire my husband.' Rather than spending our unmarried years stewarding and disciplining our desires, we have become ashamed of them. We persuade ourselves that the desires themselves are horrible. . . . We spend years guarding our virginity, but find, upon getting married, that we cannot just flip a switch. Now that sex is licit, sanctioned—even blessed by our community—we are stuck with years of work (and sometimes therapy) to unlearn . . . anxiety about sex; to learn, instead, that sex is good" (Lauren Winner, *Real Sex: The Naked Truth About Chastity* [Grand Rapids: Brazos Press, 2005], p. 95).

7. Cf. Genesis 2:24.

8. "People inevitably become enslaved. . . . Paul reminds them that embodied humans easily can become hostage to their bodily appetites" (Garland, *1 Corinthians*, p. 229). "If freedom or liberty is absolutized without qualification, it brings bondage" (Thiselton, *The First Epistle to the Corinthians*, p. 462).

9. "The sex drive is so intense that it becomes a temptation to manipulate and even exploit the other person. To the extent that the functional is predominant in our sex lives, we treat the other person as a means and thus dehumanize him. When this happens, sexual intercourse is immoral . . . because it distorts and destroys a personal relationship" (Lewis Smedes, *Sex for Christians* (Grand Rapids: Eerdmans, 1994), p. 104). "When one has sex with a prostitute [or outside of marriage], what God intended to be a means of sharing one's life with another is dehumanized into a momentary coupling for the sole purpose of sexual release" (Garland, *1 Corinthians*, p. 237).

10. Wendy Shalit, *A Return to Modesty* (New York: Touchstone, 1999), p. 88.

11. Ibid., p. 237.

12. Ibid., p. 220.

13. Ibid., p. 131.

14. Ibid., p. 46.

15. Ibid., p. 54.

16. Jean-Jacques Rousseau, *Emile*, quoted in ibid., p. 120.

17. Ibid., p. 192.

18. "As numerous modern writers agree . . . Paul now quotes another Corinthian slogan. The purpose of the slogan was to articulate the sense of distance between deeds done in the physical body, especially matters relating to food, sex, or property, and the supposedly 'spiritual' level of life, which some would like to think operates on a 'higher' plane which can be isolated from the 'lower.' This supposed dualism of 'levels' is foreign to Pauline thought, but commonplace in those circles influenced by a popular form of quasi-Platonic thought" (Thiselton, *The First Epistle to the Corinthians*, p. 462).

19. "The Christian story . . . has very positive things to say about bodies, but throughout its history the church has sometimes equivocated. We Christians get embarrassed about our bodies. . . . We are not sure whether [they] are good or bad; it follows that we are not sure whether sex is good or bad" (Winner, *Real Sex: The Naked Truth About Chastity*, p. 95).

20. "Paul assumes that the body is not an outer shell that the soul will slough off at death—something he develops fully in chapter 15. The Christian's body is destined for resurrection . . . since the body will be raised, it is important now" (Garland, *1 Corinthians*, pp. 231, 232).

21. Smedes, *Sex for Christians*, p. 110.

22. Ibid., p. 101.

23. Ibid., pp. 112, 113.

24. "The context and rhetorical tone suggest that Paul wants to draw out the distinctive character of sexual sin compared to every other sin a person could possibly commit. That these other sins are 'outside the body' implies that they are not sins 'against the body,' not that the body is not involved in committing them. Sexual sin, by contrast, is labeled a direct assault on the body . . . [and is] destructive *against one's self*. . . . Commentators, however, have long asked how drunkenness, gluttony, suicide, and self-mutilation do not qualify also as sins against the body. But Paul is not referring to what might physically injure the body. . . . To take one example, drunkenness does not have the capacity to make a person one flesh with alcohol. This one-flesh union is true only of the sex act. Because intercourse with a prostitute [or outside of marriage] is 'uniquely body joining, it is uniquely body defiling' (Fisk)" (Garland, *1 Corinthians*, pp. 237, 238).

25. "It is assumed that the Corinthians argued that . . . one has a stomach to digest food and hunger pangs to announce when it is time to eat; the same goes for sex organs. The argument may have run thus: sex organs exist to be used, and sexual appetites should be fulfilled, not frustrated" (ibid., p. 230).

26. Cf. Hosea 3, 4.

Chapter Twelve: The Beauty of Marriage

1. From Chris Rock's *Never Scared* album (Dreamworks, 2005).

2. Adam Sternbergh, "A Brutally Candid Oral History of Breaking Up," *New York Times Magazine*, March 11, 2011; http://www.nytimes.com/2011/03/13/magazine/mag–13Monogmy-t.html?_r=0.

3. In this case many struggled with overzealous asceticism as well. Hays observes that "sexual abstinence was widely viewed as a means to personal wholeness

and religious power" (1997: 114, quoted in David E. Garland, *1 Corinthians*, Baker Exegetical Commentary on the New Testament [Grand Rapids: Baker Academic, 2003, p. 263]). "Some Corinthians apparently regarded sexual asceticism to be a good and had the example of Paul, who had renounced marriage to be free for the service of the gospel. Their motivation, however, was quite different from Paul's as he seeks to elucidate. What caused them to vaunt sexual asceticism as a good is unclear. Several options have been proposed to explain its emergency in the community: repudiation . . . Gnostic dualism . . . the inheritance from Judaism . . . devotion to Sophia . . . the debate between Cynics and Stoics . . . over-realized eschatology . . . divine men . . . eschatological women . . . Corinthian pneumatism . . . the Corinthians' cultural heritage . . . debates among physicians . . . and cataclysmic external circumstances" (for further exposition and explication, see ibid., pp. 263–65).

4. See 1 Corinthians 5 and Chapter 9 of this book.

5. See Garland's notes on 6:16–20 and prostitution (*1 Corinthians*, pp. 219–41).

6. "Marriage Rate Declines to Historic Low, Study Finds," *Huffington Post*, July 22, 2013; http://www.huffingtonpost.com/2013/07/22/marriage-rate_n_3625222.html.

7. 1 Corinthians 7:39; 11:11.

8. "Though life was better for women during the empire than during the earlier period of the Roman Republic, marriage was still basically an asymmetrical relationship with the husband wielding greater power and authority. The *patria potesta* had by no means disappeared. The phrase 'buying a wife' was still common during the empire (Gaius Inst. 113). The relationship between husband and wife was often much like that between father and daughter or uncle and niece, because a man was often considerably older than his wife. When Quintilian writes that a notable trait of a good husband is restraint in his relationship with his wife and that this is a sign of his affection, he is voicing common assumptions about the dominant position of the husband" (Ben Witherington, *Conflict and Community in Corinth* [Grand Rapids: Eerdmans, 1995], p. 170).

9. C. S. Lewis, *The Four Loves* (Orlando: Harcourt Books, 1960).

10. Morris rightfully makes the distinction between unequally yoked marriages in which the nonbelieving spouse is willing to live with the believer and marriages in which the nonbeliever is not willing to live with the believer. In the case of willingness, the believer is not to divorce him/her (vv. 12, 13). When the unbeliever willingly leaves the marital relationship, Paul deems it to "be so," and the believer is free to remarry (v. 15) (Leon Morris, *The First Epistle of Paul to the Corinthians*, The Tyndale New Testament Commentaries [Grand Rapids: Eerdmans, 1989]).

11. See Chapter 14 of this book.

12. 1 Corinthians 5:1–5.

13. 1 Corinthians 6:12–20.

14. See Timothy and Kathy Keller, *The Meaning of Marriage* (New York: Riverhead, 2011), pp. 50, 57, 60, 107, 110, 177, 178.

15. Tara Parker-Pope, "The Happy Marriage Is the 'Me' Marriage," December 31, 2010; http://www.nytimes.com/2011/01/02/weekinreview/02parkerpope.html.

16. "Why Men Won't Commit: Men's Atitudes About Sex, Dating and Marriage," October 22, 2002; http://www.freerepublic.com/focus/news/773847/posts.

17. Derived from Keller, *The Meaning of Marriage*, p. 23.

18. Tim Keller, quoted in Collin Hansen, "The Mirage and Marriage," January 27, 2013; http://www.thegospelcoalition.org/article/the-mirage-and-marriage.

19. Timothy Keller, quoting Stanley Hauerwas, in "You Never Marry the Right Person," *Relevant Magazine*, January 5, 2012; http://www.relevantmagazine.com/life/relationship/features/27749-you-never-marry-the-right-person.

20. Ernest Becker, *The Denial of Death* (New York: Free Press, 1973), p. 160.

21. Cf. the book of Hosea.

Chapter Thirteen: On Calling

1. Jeanne Meister, "Job Hopping Is the 'New Normal' for Millennials: Three Ways to Prevent a Human Resource Nightmare," *Forbes Magazine*, August 14, 2013; http://www.forbes.com/sites/jeannemeister/2012/08/14/job-hopping-is-the-new-normal-for-millennials-three-ways-to-prevent-a-human-resource-nightmare/.

2. Quoted from Timothy Keller, *Counterfeit Gods* (New York: Penguin, 2009), p. 79.

3. Greek *kalein*; cf. 1:9; 7:15; 15:9.

4. "Paul's usage suggests that he has in mind God's call to salvation. It transcends and transforms all external circumstances, and the perfect tense hints at the continuing effects of that call. As a consequence, he insists that they are not to make unnecessary changes in their life circumstances that their conversion and response to God's call do not require" (David E. Garland, *1 Corinthians*, Baker Exegetical Commentary on the New Testament [Grand Rapids: Baker Academic, 2003], p. 303).

5. ". . . since the divine call came to each individual without regard to his or her social context, God does not esteem one particular state to be more valuable or more advantageous than another. The implication is that the only criterion of how they should live as Christians is determined by God, who called them, not by humans with their faulty judgments. Paul commands them to conduct their lives [literally "walk"] accordingly. That is, they are to walk as those called by God and in accord with God's commands and not be driven by human aims and aspirations" (ibid., p. 304).

6. John Pless, as quoted by Gene Edward Veith, "Our Calling and God's Glory," *Modern Reformation Magazine*, November/December 2007, vol. 16, no. 6, pp. 22–28.

7. See note 2 from Chapter 12.

8. Paul recognizes that a shift in illustration to encompass social status is a strategic move in verse 21, as a third of Corinth's population were slaves, and another third former slaves who had been freed (Garland, *1 Corinthians*, p. 307),

9. Greek *doulos* (cf. 12:13).

10. "Many (some argue most) first century household slaves at some time in their life had the opportunity for manumission. They could save money on the side to buy their freedom. . . . Freedpersons remained members of their former holder's extended household, and their former holders as patrons were obligated to help them advance" (Craig S. Keener, *First-Second Corinthians* [New York: Cambridge University Press, 2005], p. 67).

11. Adapted from Keller, *Counterfeit Gods*.

12. See Dave Harvey, *Rescuing Ambition* (Wheaton: Crossway, 2010), pp. 12, 68, 123.

Chapter Fourteen: Singleness

1. Today 50.2 percent of those who are sixteen years or older are single, according to the Bureau of Labor Statistics.

2. The word translated "betrothed" is often taken to mean "virgins." "That word today belongs usually to medical discourse or to sexual discourse with prior value-judgments . . . Either 'those who have not married' or 'those who have not yet married' seems best for modern English and public reading. The former matches the Greek more closely, but the latter reflects the Greek-in-context more clearly" (Anthony C. Thiselton, *The First Epistle to the Corinthians: A Commentary on the Greek Text:* New International Greek Testament Commentary [Grand Rapids: Eerdmans, 2000], 571).

3. ". . . that he wants them to be free from anxieties (7:32), that he offers counsel for their own benefit, and that he has no intention of lassoing them (7:35). [He refuses] to castigate as 'sin' any decision to reject his advice on this particular matter (7:28, 36). He allows room for a variety of stances on how to live in obedience to God's call" (David E. Garland, *1 Corinthians*, Baker Exegetical Commentary on the New Testament [Grand Rapids: Baker Academic, 2003], p. 322).

4. Lori Gottlieb, "Marry Him! The Case for Settling for Mr. Good Enough," *The Atlantic*, March 1, 2008.

5. "Some understand the phrase 'because of the present necessity' to be a reference to the end-time woes that will engulf the world and are already portended in the sufferings of Christians (Barrett 1968: 175; Conzelmann 1975: 132). . . . Paul urges them to stay single in light of the imminent coming of Christ, which is preceded by a time of woe. But his use of the participle always refers to what is already present, which makes the rendering 'impending' problematic. . . . This usage of the participle suggests that he refers to something they are already experiencing. Consequently, some opt to translate the phrase as 'the present difficulty,' referring to the pinch of present circumstances instead of impending end-time disasters" (Garland, *1 Corinthians*, p. 323). Cf. Thiselton, *The First Epistle to the Corinthians*, pp. 573–75.

6. The Greek word used here ". . . refers to a specific quality of a particular period of time as against . . . time as chronological duration and further . . . [it] constitutes a critical moment in which much is at stake. This is often but not always a time of opportunity which will not last indefinitely. . . . It is limited; it is a critical time" (Thiselton, *The First Epistle to the Corinthians*, p. 579). "[Paul] is talking not about how little time is left but about how Christ's death and resurrection have changed how Christians should look at the time that is left" (Garland, *1 Corinthians*, p. 328).

7. "Paul does not advocate indifference to the world or flight from it . . . since the 'as thoughs' presuppose involvement in the world. What these 'as thoughs' do is pose a question: What is it that molds one's life? . . . Christians must be mindful that marriage is . . . not ultimate . . . that laughter and tears are not the last word . . . that inordinate love of things make them possess us rather than we them . . . that being engaged with the world is one thing; becoming enmeshed in it is another" (Garland, *1 Corinthians*, pp. 327–31).

8. "We encounter a permanent theological principle of the relativizing of all civic, family, and commercial commitments on the basis of eschatological realities" (Thiselton, *The First Epistle to the Corinthians*, p. 579). "Paul does not argue, 'the end might come tomorrow with its terrible afflictions; therefore do not get married.'

He argues instead, 'The end has broken into the present, and it requires a reevaluation of all that we do in a world already on its last legs'" (Garland, *1 Corinthians*, p. 327).

9. "'The form of this world is passing away' . . . [this] refers to the world's outward array, its arrangement, its fashion. The metaphor perhaps is drawn from the shifting scenes in a theater (Trench 188: 266, Edwards 1885: 197), or perhaps is related to the costume and mask of an actor" (Garland, *1 Corinthians*, p. 331).

10. "Christians must be mindful that marriage is . . . not ultimate" (ibid., p. 329).

11. Again, remember that "some opt to translate the phrase as 'the present difficulty,' referring to the pinch of present circumstances instead of impending end-time disasters" (ibid., p. 323).

12. The word translated "anxieties" (v. 32) carries a sense of "being anxious, being unduly concerned [or] being properly concerned for [and] devoting concern to" (Thiselton, *The First Epistle to the Corinthians*, p. 586). Paul probably had the former in mind here.

13. This is probably an example of the second way of translating "anxieties"—a proper concern for others. "Paul [also] uses the word 'anxiety' elsewhere . . . in the sense of encouraging concern for other people (Philippians 2:20)" (ibid., p. 586).

14. "Being holy in body does not mean that she is pure because she avoids the sexual relations that marriage imposes. All Christians are to be holy in body, whether married or not (1 Thessalonians 5:23; cf. Romans 6:12, 19; 12:1; 1 Corinthians 6:13, 19–20; 2 Corinthians 7:1; Philippians 1:30; 1 Thessalonians 4:4). The combination of body and spirit describes the whole person and means that she strives to be holy in every way and is totally devoted to the Lord (Schrage 1995: 180)" (Garland, *1 Corinthians*, p. 335).

15. We must "translate the terms in a way which brings together the public world of the whole person . . . with the transcendent realm of the whole person's intimacy with God . . . [so it should translate] in order to be holy both publicly and in the Spirit" (Thiselton, *The First Epistle to the Corinthians*, p. 591).

16. Eric Klinenberg, *Going Solo: The Extraordinary Rise and Surprising Appeal of Living Alone* (London: Penguin 2012), p. 230.

17. Ibid., p. 232.

18. Ibid., pp. 8, 9.

19. Ibid., pp. 8, 18, 230, 231.

20. Ibid., p. 87.

21. Ibid., p. 72.

Chapter Fifteen: The Right Use of Rights

1. Witherington shows the practicality of this seemingly irrelevant issue by stating, "this discussion is primarily about interpersonal behavior in certain contexts, not about cuisine." Behind this summary, Witherington basically frames his argument with "knowledge" (*gnosis*) language, in which the Christians Paul had issue with were "defending their right to go to a temple for a meal . . ." based on the knowledge that "only God is God and food is morally neutral" (Ben Witherington, *Conflict and Community in Corinth* [Grand Rapids: Eerdmans, 1995, pp. 187, 186).

2. John Stuart Mill said famously, "The only freedom which deserves the name, is that of pursuing our own good in our own way, so long as we do not attempt to

deprive others of theirs, or impede their efforts to attain it." Quoted in Richard Bauckham, *Crisis of Freedom* (Louisville: Westminster John Knox Press, 2002), p. 20.

3. Gordon Fee is helpful to show that the main problem Paul is addressing in this passage is "attitudinal." He explains that the Corinthian believers "think Christian conduct is predicated on *gnosis* (knowledge) and that knowledge gives them *exousia* (rights/freedom) to act as they will in this manner. Paul has another view: The content of their knowledge is only partially correct; but more importantly, *gnosis* is not the ground of Christian behavior, love is. Thus Paul begins by refuting the opening words of their argument, 'we all possess knowledge'" (Gordon D. Fee, *The First Epistle to the Corinthians*, The New International Commentary of the New Testament [Grand Rapids: Eerdmans, 1989], p. 363).

4. Thiselton's heavy treatment of the various interpretations of verse 8a reveal that he follows the interpretation of Jeremias and Murphy-O'Connor by putting his translation in quotations, seeing it as a slogan or catchphrase of "the strong": "Food will not bring us to God's judgment. . . ." In other words, "their principle [was]: if we do not eat, we fall prey to a lack; if we do eat, we abound." He notes that many commentators differ on whether it was a slogan or not and welcomes Fee's synthesis: "Both sentences [8a and 8b] reflect what the Corinthians were arguing in their letter, whether they are direct quotations or not" (Anthony C. Thiselton, *The First Epistle to the Corinthians: A Commentary on the Greek Text*, New International Greek Testament Commentary (Grand Rapids: Eerdmans, 2000), pp. 647, 648).

5. Craig Blomberg uses the language of the "gray areas of life" and "morally neutral areas." For example, he groups chapter 8 with 9:1–18 as "a second application of the principle of freedom tempered by love in morally neutral areas by the issue of accepting money for ministry" (Craig L. Blomberg, *1 Corinthians*, NIV Application Commentary [Grand Rapids: Zondervan, 1995], p. 168).

6. Thiselton comments on the verb "puffed up" (*physioo*), suggesting ". . . something pretentiously enlarged by virtue of being pumped full of air or wind. Love, by contrast, builds solidly, and does not pretend to be what it is not. If it gives stature to a person or to a community, that enlargement remains solid and genuine" (Thiselton, *The First Epistle to the Corinthians*, p. 622).

7. Blomberg sums this up by saying, ". . . there is this sense in which Paul can agree but not without immediate qualification (vv. 1b–3). Love, not knowledge, must form the foundation of Christian behavior" (*1 Corinthians*, p. 161).

8. Fee's summary statement on the difference between knowledge and love in this verse is excellent: "Not only is love 'not puffed up' (13:4, the final occurrence of this word in the letter), but quite the opposite, it 'builds up.' The aim of Christian ethics is not Stoic self-sufficiency, which requires proper knowledge; rather its aim is the benefit and advantage of a brother or sister. Thus it is the opposite of their behavior in vv. 7–12, which sets a stumbling block before others" (Fee, *1 Corinthians*, pp. 366, 367).

9. Paul is not condemning knowledge here or elsewhere. But, as Prior elaborates, "[Paul] is concerned that true *agape*-love should control and characterize their gnosis. The spirit in which we say what is right is as much a part of the truth as the knowledge we articulate. As Godet puts it, 'knowledge devoid of love and of the power to edify, when we look at it more nearly, it is not even true knowledge'" (David Prior, *The Message of 1 Corinthians* [Downers Grove: InterVarsity Press, 1985], p. 142).

10. David Brooks, *Bobos in Paradise* (New York; Simon & Schuster, 2000), p. 261.

11. Richard Bauckham, *Jesus and the God of Israel* (Grand Rapids: Eerdmans, 2008), p. 29.

12. The Apostle Paul probably said this best in the Christ hymn in Philippians 2:5–11: "Have this mind among yourselves, which is yours in Christ Jesus, who, though he was in the form of God, did not count equality with God a thing to be grasped, but emptied himself, by taking the form of a servant, being born in the likeness of men. And being found in human form, he humbled himself by becoming obedient to the point of death, even death on a cross. Therefore God has highly exalted him and bestowed on him the name that is above every name, so that at the name of Jesus every knee should bow, in heaven and on earth and under the earth, and every tongue confess that Jesus Christ is Lord, to the glory of God the Father."

13. The emphasis on the word "brother" is picked up by Morris: ". . . it occurs four times in the last three verses (NIV makes the last one *him*)" (Leon Morris, *The First Epistle of Paul to the Corinthians*, The Tyndale New Testament Commentaries [Grand Rapids: Eerdmans, 1989], p.128). This emphasis is important when considering Paul's push to apply the sociological implications of the cross.

14. Morris helpfully explains Paul's connecting the sociological implications of the cross with the believers' union with Christ: "[The Corinthian believers] are 'in Christ', and anything done against them is therefore done against him (cf. Mt. 25:42–45). There is a high dignity in being Christian. It is easy to look down on some church members as unimportant. But they are not so. No temple of the Holy Spirit (6:19) is unimportant. God lives in the weak. We must honour them as members of Christ, and beware of sinning against the Lord." Ibid.

15. Morris summarizes Paul's point in verse 13 this way: "Paul himself will do his utmost to see that he does not hinder the weak. In the context he might have confined himself to 'meat offered to idols', but he speaks of 'food' (NIV, *what I eat*). If need be he will become a vegetarian and *never eat meat again*. The important thing is not his own rights, nor his own comfort, but the well-being of the brotherhood." Ibid.

Chapter Sixteen: The End(s) of Entitlement

1. Many of these thoughts were derived from Jean M. Twenge and W. Keith Campbell, *The Narcissism Epidemic: Living in the Age of Entitlement* (New York: Free Press, 2009), p. 77.

2. Ibid.

3. Tim Urban, "Why Generation Y Yuppies are Unhappy," *Huffington Post*, September 15, 2013; http://www.huffingtonpost.com/wait-but-why/generation-y -unhappy_b_3930620.html.

4. Paul asks four rhetorical questions that each beg the positive affirmation in response.

5. Paul mentions the "seal" of his apostleship in verse 2 (Greek *sphragis*). The Geek words *apologeia* and *anakrinousin* in verse 3 translate as "defense" and "examine" respectively. The Greek word *exousia*, "right" (see the notes in Chapter 15 of this book) is found in verse 4.

6. When he refused and continued to rely on tentmaking instead, they charged that his unwillingness to go along with their patronage demonstrated that he did not

have the same authority as other itinerant apostles or preachers (Craig L. Blomberg, *1 Corinthians*, NIV Application Commentary [Grand Rapids: Zondervan, 1995], p. 173).

7. Cf. 2 Corinthians 11:7.

8. Itinerant Greco-Roman philosophers and religious teachers supported themselves in one of four ways: charging fees, staying in well-to-do households, begging, or working in a trade. The last of these was least common but generally acknowledged to give the philosophers the greatest freedom to teach however he liked. Powerful patrons in the Corinthian church doubtless would have preferred to have Paul accept their money but give them deference and political support in return (Blomberg, *1 Corinthians*, p. 173).

9. See David Prior, *The Message of 1 Corinthians*, The Bible Speaks Today (Nottingham, UK: Inter-Varsity Press, 1985), pp. 153–56.

10. Cf. 2 Corinthians 11.

11. "Paul's 'I' is emphatic. Whatever the practice of others, 'he' has not exercised his rights. Nor is his purpose in writing in this strain to establish a basis for a change of practice. So fiercely does he hold his conviction that he says I would rather die than change it. The text here it is very difficult. Paul appears to break off a sentence and never complete it: 'it would be better for me to die than no one will make this boast of mine an empty one!' The break in construction marks Paul's deep emotion, and his emotion shows the importance he ascribed to his practice" (Leon Morris, *The First Epistle of Paul to the Corinthians*, The Tyndale New Testament Commentaries [Grand Rapids: Eerdmans, 1989], p. 134).

12. Garland likens Paul's woes more to that of Amos than Jeremiah. "The lion has roared; who will not fear? The ORUG God has spoken; who can but prophesy?" (Amos 3:8). Paul's woe is more linked toward the potential inability of *not* preaching the gospel, whereas for Jeremiah, "the consequences for preaching [were] adversity and suffering" (David E. Garland, *1 Corinthians*, Baker Exegetical Commentary on the New Testament [Grand Rapids: Baker Academic, 2003], p. 424).

Chapter Seventeen: An Effective Witness

1. In the past, many in the West could assume an essentially Christian public. The worldview that shaped the structures and goals of society were running on the borrowed capital of the Christendom experiment. But as the world continues to globalize, people of very different cultures are being brought together and are now facing the need to give shape to their shared life together. In this context it can no longer be assumed that the social world is formed along a generally Christian (or at least Christendom) worldview. Christians can no longer lean on the borrowed capital of Christendom and assume that the goals and reasons set for any societal task (whether it be in career, family, education, wealth-generation) will be consistent with their Christian faith. What could be assumed a generation ago now requires constructive thought.

2. See Lesslie Newbigin, *The Gospel in a Pluralist Society* (Grand Rapids: Eerdmans, 1989) for more on this issue.

3. "Those outside the law . . . in other contexts could mean the unjust, unrighteous, or godless (cf. Acts 2:23; 3 Macc. 6:9; Ezek. 18:24 LXX; Luke 22:37) or to the lawless or outlaw (2 Thess 2:8), but clearly in this context denotes Gentiles who

are outside the revealed law of the OT and Judaism" (Anthony C. Thiselton, *The First Epistle to the Corinthians: A Commentary on the Greek Text*, New International Greek Testament Commentary [Grand Rapids: Eerdmans, 2000], p. 703).

4. "The clearest example of what Paul means by becoming 'as a Jew' and as 'one under the law' is his description of the thirty-nine lashes he suffered at the hands of the Jews (2 Cor. 11:24). . . . He bowed to synagogue discipline to maintain his Jewish connections (Harvey 1985: 93). . . . Paul accepted these penalties to keep open the option of preaching the gospel message in the synagogue. For Paul to submit to this punishment five times testifies not only to his mettle but also to his extraordinary sense of obligation to his people" (David E. Garland, *1 Corinthians*, Baker Exegetical Commentary on the New Testament [Grand Rapids: Baker Academic, 2003], p. 430).

5. "How did Paul become without the law? He is not simply talking about forsaking distinctively Jewish practices such as Jewish food laws or Sabbath celebrations . . . nor is he talking about his presentation of the gospel, using arguments that would be more persuasive to the Gentile world. . . . He did not become a pagan sinner, but . . . like a Gentile, as one without heritage, without the merit of the fathers, without works of law to set him apart from others or to justify his salvation. Paul lived among the Galatians simply as a Christian, not as a Jew or a Pharisee of Pharisees (see Betz 1979: 223)" (ibid., pp. 431, 432).

6. Andrew Walls, *The Cross-Cultural Process in Christian History* (New York: Orbis Books, 2002), p. 245.

7. See Newbigin, *The Gospel in a Pluralist Society* and Lesslie Newbigin, *Foolishness to the Greeks: The Gospel and Western Culture* (Grand Rapids: Eerdmans, 1986) for more on this issue.

8. "Paul refers to 'the law of Christ' . . . it is neither the Mosaic law code revamped and promulgated by the Messiah (contra W. Davies 1963: 109–90) nor the specific precepts given by Christ to his disciples (e.g., 1 Cor. 7:10; 9:14; contra C. Dodd 1968: 137). . . . Carson (1986: 12) asserts that Paul is not simply bound by 'certain teachings of Jesus but by all that Christ accomplished and represents' . . . the pattern of the one who gave his life as a ransom for the many (Mark 10:43–45)" (Garland, *1 Corinthians*, p. 432).

9. "Being free from the Law does not mean that Paul runs wild with self-indulgence—a word pointedly spoken to the Corinthians who are proclaiming 'I am free to do anything.' Instead, he lives with a powerful sense of obligation to God, defined now by his relationship to Christ" (Hays, quoted in Thiselton, *The First Epistle to the Corinthians*, pp. 704, 705).

10. Walls, *The Cross-Cultural Process in Christian History*, pp. 269, 270.

11. See Timothy Keller, *The Reason for God: Belief in an Age of Skepticism* (New York: Penguin, 2008) for more on these issues.

12. See Michael Gerson and Peter Wehner, *City of Man: Religion and Politics in a New Era* (Moody: Chicago, 2010) and Vaclav Havel, *Politics, Morality and Civility* (Washington, D.C.: The Trinity Forum, 2006) for more on the issue of politics.

13. See Joshua J. Yates and James Davison Hunter, eds., *Thrift and Thriving in America: Capitalism and Moral Order from the Puritans to the Present* (New York: Oxford University Press, 2011) and Daniel Bell, *The Economy of Desire: Christianity and Capitalism in a Postmodern World* (Grand Rapids: Baker, 2012) for more on the issue of economics.

14. See Mark R. Gornik, *To Live in Peace: Biblical Faith and the Changing Inner City* (Grand Rapids: Eerdmans, 2002) for more on the issue of peacemaking.

15. See Christopher Heuertz and Christine D. Pohl, *Friendship at the Margins: Discovering Mutuality in Service and Mission* (Downers Grove: InterVarsity Press, 2010) and Nicholas Wolterstorff, *Hearing the Call: Liturgy, Justice, Church and World* (Grand Rapids: Eerdmans, 2011) for more on the issue of neighboring.

16. See Jonathan Sacks, *The Dignity of Difference: How to Avoid the Clash of Civilizations* (New York: Bloomsbury, 2003), Miroslav Volf, *A Public Faith: How Followers of Christ Should Serve the Common Good* (Grand Rapids: Brazos Press, 2011), and Richard Mouw, *Uncommon Decency: Christian Civility in an Uncivil World* (Downers Grove: InterVarsity Press, 2010) for more on the issue of civil society and the public sphere.

17. "Paul appeals to a general rule: 'Every competitor in the games abstains in every way.' The image of 'running' suggests a continuing exertion (cf. Phil. 3:12–14, with its image of the runner straining to cross the finish line), but the key is 'self-control.' Every reader knew that winning a race or a boxing match required of the athlete hard training (expressed in the modern motto 'no pain, no gain') and self-denial, particularly when it came to diet. . . . Athletes who want to win cannot conform to the world and eat the same things as those who are not preparing for the rigors of competition (Epictetus, *Diatr.* 3.15.10, Philo, *Dreams* 2.2.9, Horace, *Ars poetica* 412–14; Xenophon, *Symposium* 8.37)" (Garland, *1 Corinthians*, pp. 440, 441).

18. "Even the intensity of effort demanded of the athlete to make the prize yours belongs to the stage setting of the picture: an athlete goes through anything, both effort and abstinence, to win, because he or she has an eye on the ultimate goal" (Thiselton, *The First Epistle to the Corinthians*, p. 711).

19. "The word [translated as 'disqualified'] is much stronger than [that]. It means 'proven false,' as with coinage, 'to be shown as counterfeit.' Hebrews 6:8 contains a vivid picture of what 'failing the proof' entails: 'But land that produces thorns and thistles is worthless and is in danger of being cursed. In the end it will be burned'" (Garland, *1 Corinthians*, p. 445).

20. "For once the restraint and literalism of the AV/KJV may serve us better: *that I might be a partaker thereof with you.* In our view (with Collins) the issue is neither that of bringing benefit to others (NJB), nor that of sharing in these benefits as a missionary pastor (NRSV, NIV, REB, Fee). To stand alongside the Jew, the Gentile, the socially dependent and vulnerable, or to live and act in solidarity with every kind of person in every kind of situation is to have a share in the nature of the gospel, i.e. *to instantiate what the gospel is and how it operates*" (Thiselton, *The First Epistle to the Corinthians*, p. 707).

21. See Hebrews 12:2.

Chapter Eighteen: Escaping Idolatry

1. "Idols exist . . . as a pretext for setting ourselves at the centre of reality and worshiping the work of our own hands. Once man has lost the fundamental orientation which unifies his existence, he breaks down into the multiplicity of his desires; in refusing to await the time of promise, his life-story disintegrates into a myriad of unconnected instants. Idolatry, then, is always polytheism, an aimless passing from one lord to another. Idolatry does not offer a journey but rather a plethora of paths

leading nowhere and forming a vast labyrinth. . . . Herein lies the paradox: by constantly turning towards the Lord, we discover a sure path which liberates us from the dissolution imposed upon us by idols." Pope Francis, *Lumen Fidei*, June 29, 2013; http://w2.vatican.va/content/francesco/en/encyclicals/documents/papa-francesco_20130629_enciclica-lumen-fidei.html.

2. "When human beings give their heartfelt allegiance to and worship that which is not God, they progressively cease to reflect the image of God. One of the primary laws of human life is that you become like what you worship; what's more, you reflect what you worship not only to the object itself but also outward to the world around. Those who worship money increasingly define themselves in terms of it and increasingly treat other people as creditors, debtors, partners, or customers rather than as human beings. Those who worship sex define themselves in terms of it (their preferences, their practices, their past histories) and increasingly treat other people as actual or potential sex objects. Those who worship power define themselves in terms of it and treat other people as either collaborators, competitors, or pawns. These and many other forms of idolatry combine in a thousand ways, all of them damaging to the image-bearing quality of the people concerned and of those whose lives they touch" (N. T. Wright, *Surprised by Hope* [New York: Harper Collins, 1989], p. 182).

3. Greek *epithymias*; cf. Mark 4:19; Luke 22:15; John 8:44; Romans 1:24; 6:12; 7:7; 13:14; Galatians 5:16; Ephesians 2:3; 4:22; Philippians 1:23; Colossians 3:5; 1 Thessalonians 2:17.

4. "[Humans are] intentional beings who first and foremost (and ultimately) intend the world in the mode of love. We are primordially and essentially agents of love, which takes the structure of desire or longing. We are essentially and ultimately desiring animals, which is simply to say that we are essentially and ultimately lovers. To be human is to love, and it is what we love that defines who we are. Our (ultimate) love is constitutive of our identity. So we're not talking about trivial loves, like when we say we 'love' pizza or the Boston Red Sox; we're not even quite talking about significant loves, like when we say we 'love' our parents or we 'love' a spouse (though these will be wrapped up in the sort of love we're concerned with). Rather, we are talking about ultimate loves—that to which we are fundamentally oriented, what ultimately governs our vision of the good life, what shapes and molds our being-in-the-world—in other words, what we desire above all else, the ultimate desire that shapes and positions and makes sense of all our penultimate desires and actions. This sort of ultimate love could also be described as that to which we ultimately pledge allegiance; or, to evoke language that is both religious and ancient, our ultimate love is what we worship" (James K. A. Smith, *Desiring the Kingdom* [Grand Rapids: Baker Academic, 2009], pp. 50, 51).

5. The comparison between the Israelites and Corinthians is discussed throughout all major commentaries. "The Israelites of old experienced redemption, baptism and God's continuing help. But they flirted with idolatry and nearly all of them perished in the wilderness. It may be that some of the Corinthians felt that their baptism and their use of Holy Communion guaranteed their final salvation, no matter what they did. Paul warns them that this is not so. Idolatry brings ruin" (Leon Morris, *The First Epistle of Paul to the Corinthians*, The Tyndale New Testament Commentaries [Grand Rapids: Eerdmans, 1989], p. 138).

6. Smith, *Desiring the Kingdom*, p. 25.

7. Dick Keyes, "The Idol Factory," in Os Guinness and John Seel, eds., *No God but God: Breaking with the Idols of Our Age* (Chicago: Moody, 1992), p. 31.

8. ". . . The OT event that is referred to (Num. 25:1–9) specifically joins the particular event of sexual immorality with eating in the presence of Baal Peor. Second, the preceding text also alludes to idolatrous eating joined with sexual play. Third, in the prohibition against prostitution in 6:12–20, Paul deliberately reapplies the 'temple' imagery of 3:16–17 to the Christian's body that was being 'joined' to a prostitute. . . . Fourth, every other mention of 'idol food' in the NT is accompanied by a reference to sexual immorality (Acts 15:29; Rev. 2:14, 20). Moreover, Rev. 2:14 has the same allusion to Num. 25:1–2. It is highly probable, therefore, that in each case these two sins really belong *together*, as they did in the OT and pagan precedents; and they go together at the meals in the pagan temples" (Gordon D. Fee, *The First Epistle to the Corinthians*, The New International Commentary of the New Testament [Grand Rapids: Eerdmans, 1989], p. 455).

9. See Chapters 2 and 7 of Timothy Keller's *Counterfeit Gods* (New York: Dutton, 2009), pp. 22–47, 154–64.

10. There are similar undertones with "exodus" in the Israelite account of the escape and exodus from Egypt.

11. "Paul describes Israel's experience of the miraculous bread (Exod. 16:4–30) and miraculous drinking of water from the rock (Exod. 17:1–7; Num. 20:2–13) as a form of 'spiritual eating,' unquestionably viewing it as a type/analogy of the Lord's Supper: 'They all ate the same spiritual food and drank the same spiritual drink'" (Gordon D. Fee, *The First Epistle to the Corinthians*, The New International Commentary of the New Testament [Grand Rapids: Eerdmans, 1989], p. 446).

Chapter Nineteen: The Glory of God and the Good of Neighbor

1. "The principle is clear. The Christian is not concerned with his rights, but with the glory of God (cf. Col. 3:17). Eating, drinking, everything must be subordinated to this" (Leon Morris, *The First Epistle of Paul to the Corinthians*, The Tyndale New Testament Commentaries [Grand Rapids: Eerdmans, 1989], p. 148).

2. Greek *exousia*; cf. Hebrew *kabod*, literally meaning "weighty."

3. Regardless of the stance of the two parties, the origin of the food ultimately did not matter. "On these matters one is truly free, especially in the matters of food, since in the prayer of benediction alluded to in v. 30 one acknowledges that the ultimate origin of all food, no matter who butchered it or where it appeared in process, is God himself" (Gordon D. Fee, *The First Epistle to the Corinthians*, The New International Commentary of the New Testament [Grand Rapids: Eerdmans, 1989], p. 480). Paul addresses "the Christian community, which is neither Jewish nor Greek but a 'third race': the church of God (32). Paul is not concerned at this stage with barriers or stumbling blocks, with rights or with responsibilities" (David Prior, *The Message of 1 Corinthians*, The Bible Speaks Today [Nottingham, UK: Inter-Varsity Press, 1985], p. 176). Cf. Psalm 24:1; 1 Timothy 4:1–5; 6:17.

4. "The reason for addressing this issue is that what was sold in the market (*macellum*) often contained meat butchered by the priests, much of it having been part of the pagan sacrifices. Since such meat was expressly forbidden to Jews, and since in their earliest days followers of 'the Way' were considered to be a sect of the

Jews, the whole issue of the Christians' relationship to the meat market was a thorny one" (Fee, *The First Epistle to the Corinthians*, p. 481).

5. "Avoiding all foods that had any associations with an idol was a tall order because any food purchased in the market or served at a friend's home potentially was tainted by some idolatrous rite. That possibility does not mean that they must avoid all food on the chance it had some past contact with an idol" (David E. Garland, *1 Corinthians*, Baker Exegetical Commentary on the New Testament [Grand Rapids: Baker Academic, 2003], p. 489).

6. Cf. 1 John 4:19.

7. C. S. Lewis, "The Weight of Glory," *Theology*, November 1941.

8. Tullian Tchividjian, "Does Grace Make You Lazy?" *Christian Post*, March 2, 2013.

9. Prior's helpful "five ground-rules for life together in Christ" are helpful:

    i. 'Do all to the glory of God' (31)—not to establish my freedom.

    ii. 'Try to please all men in everything' (33)—not claiming my rights.

    iii. 'Seek the advantages of many' (33)—not my benefit or fulfillment.

    iv. 'Seek that many may be saved' (33)—not being preoccupied with my personal salvation.

    v. 'Be an imitator of Christ' (11:1)—not boosting my reputation.

That is Christian freedom: "being free from ourselves to glorify God by being like Christ" (Prior, *The Message of 1 Corinthians*, p. 177).

Chapter Twenty: Issues in the Worshiping Community

1. Tom Schreiner agrees that 11:2 is a hinge verse: "It is probably the case . . . that 11:2 is the introductory statement for all of chapters eleven through fourteen. Even though the Corinthians are not following the traditions regarding women (11:3–16), the Lord's Supper (11:17–34), and spiritual gifts (12:1 — 14:40), the situation of the church is not bleak in every respect" (Thomas R. Schreiner, "Head Coverings, Prophecies, and the Trinity: 1 Corinthians 11:2–16," in *Biblical Manhood and Womanhood*, eds. Wayne Grudem and John Piper [Wheaton; Crossway, 1991], p. 125).

2. The language of "liberated traditionalism" comes from Craig L. Blomberg, *1 Corinthians*, NIV Application Commentary (Grand Rapids: Zondervan, 1995), p. 218. He furthers his discussion "for a balanced application of this 'liberated traditionalism' to contemporary marriages" on pp. 223–26.

3. Ibid., p. 211.

4. Leon Morris makes this background crystal clear: "In Judaism, women had a very minor place; they were not even counted in the number required for a synagogue (ten males). Christianity gave them a new and significant place, and their head-covering is a mark of their new authority. The differences arising from creation remain; Paul is not trying to obliterate them. But he is clear that Christian women have *authority*" (Leon Morris, *The First Epistle of Paul to the Corinthians*, The Tyndale New Testament Commentaries [Grand Rapids: Eerdmans, 1989], p. 152).

5. We must see, Schreiner argues, "that Paul argues from creation, not the fall. The distinctions between make and female are part of the created order, and Paul

apparently did not think redemption in Christ negated creation" (Schreiner, "Head Coverings, Prophecies, and the Trinity," *Biblical Manhood and Womanhood*, p. 133).

6. David Prior, *The Message of 1 Corinthians*, The Bible Speaks Today (Nottingham, UK: Inter-Varsity Press, 1985), p. 180.

7. Language of "liberated traditionalism" comes from Craig Blomberg, *1 Corinthians*, p. 218. He furthers his discussion "for a balanced application of this 'liberated traditionalism' to contemporary marriages" on pp. 223–26.

8. Kathy Keller, *Jesus, Justice, and Gender Roles: A Case for Gender Roles in Ministry* (Grand Rapids: Zondervan, 2014), p. 492.

Chapter Twenty-One: Discerning the Body

1. Carolyn Steel, *Hungry City: How Food Shapes Our Lives* (London: Vintage Books, 2013), p. 212.

2. Tim Chester, "Meals Matter to the Mission"; http://theresurgence.com/2012/12/27/meals-matter-to-the-mission.

3. Ben Witherington, *Conflict and Community in Corinth* (Grand Rapids: Eerdmans, 1995), p. 244.

4. Gerd Theissen, *The Social Setting of Pauline Christianity: Essays on Corinth* (Philadelphia: Fortress, 1982), pp. 145–74.

5. See Leonard J. Vander Zee, *Christ, Baptism, & The Lord's Supper: Recovering the Sacraments for Evangelical Worship* (Downers Grove: InterVarsity Press, 2004), pp. 161–86 for a discussion of the historical development of the doctrine of the Lord's Supper in the church. Also see Gary Macy, *The Banquet's Wisdom: A Short History of the Theologies of the Lord's Supper* (New York: Paulist, 1992).

6. These views can also be found in further detail in John Armstrong, ed., *Understanding Four Views on the Lord's Supper* (Grand Rapids: Zondervan, 2007). They are described as the Baptist view (memorialism), the Roman Catholic view (transubstantiation), the Lutheran view (consubstantiation), and the Reformed view (spiritual presence).

7. Witherington, *Conflict and Community in Corinth*, p. 242.

8. Craig L. Blomberg, *1 Corinthians*, NIV Application Commentary (Grand Rapids: Zondervan, 1995), p. 228.

9. Theissen, *The Social Setting of Pauline Christianity*, pp. 145–74.

10. Blomberg, *1 Corinthians*, p. 236.

11. Blomberg notes, "The reason Paul, like the gospel writers, calls it the 'cup' rather than using the word wine is because the expression would evoke Old Testament associations of suffering the 'cup' of God's wrath (e.g. Ps. 75:8; Isa. 51:17). Christ's shed blood demonstrated that he accepted the wrath we deserved to experience and so made possible for us peace with God" (ibid., p. 230).

12. Cf. Vander Zee, *Christ, Baptism, & the Lord's Supper*, pp. 143–53.

13. The temporal emphasis of the Lord's Supper not only looks back in history at Christ's finished work on the cross, but also looks forward to the future hope of a heavenly banquet. As Witherington correctly notes, the focus is on "the past, the present, and the future" (*Conflict and Community in Corinth*, p. 251).

14. One does not partake in the Lord's Supper because he or she is considered worthy. The invitation is solely a gift of God's grace. Marshall adds that his "warning was not to those who were leading unworthy lives and longed for forgiveness but to

those who were making a mockery of that which should have been most sacred and solemn by their behavior at the meal" (I. Howard Marshall, *Last Supper and Lord's Supper* [Grand Rapids: Eerdmans, 1980], p. 116).

15. D. A. Carson, *Love in Hard Places* (Wheaton: Crossway, 2002), p. 61.

Chapter Twenty-Two: A Gift-Giving God

1. Leon Morris, *The First Epistle of Paul to the Corinthians*, The Tyndale New Testament Commentaries (Grand Rapids: Eerdmans, 1989), p. 163.

2. D. A. Carson, *Showing the Spirit: A Theological Exposition of 1 Corinthians 12–14* (Grand Rapids: Baker, 1987), p. 19. The Greek *charisma* is found sixteen times in Pauline writings alone (and once more in the New Testament in 1 Peter 4:10). Carson notes that Paul uses this word in a variety of contexts:

- To the Romans as: a mutual encouragement of faith (cf. Rom. 1:11), that which generates life over against Adam's sin (5:5–16), the gift of God in Jesus Christ (6:23), to the election of Israel (11:29); and the list of gifts presents in Romans (12:6–7). . . .
- In 1 Timothy, Timothy is told not to neglect the "gift" given him through prophetic message when the elders laid hands on him; and,
- In 2 Timothy, a similar account when Timothy is called to "fan into flame the gift of God" from the laying of hands. (p. 20)

3. See notes above. Paired with "the same Spirit."

4. Greek *diaknoion*; paired with "the same Lord." Garland points out that "'services' match nicely with the Lord's ministry and with his self-sacrifice proclaimed in the Lord's Supper" (David E. Garland, *1 Corinthians*, Baker Exegetical Commentary on the New Testament [Grand Rapids: Baker Academic, 2003], p. 576).

5. Greek *energematon*; paired with "the same God." Fee comments that "activities" is appropriately paired with "the same God" (Galatians 2:8; Ephesians 1:11; 3:20; Philippians 2:13) and implies that all things accomplished in the church are effected by God's power (Gordon D. Fee, *The First Epistle to the Corinthians*, The New International Commentary of the New Testament [Grand Rapids: Eerdmans, 1989], p. 588).

6. Fee draws on the context of this passage situated before chapters 13, 14 of Paul's letter in which he will push for the gifts being for the benefit of the community as a whole. Spiritual gifts are for "the common good" and building up the community, not primarily for the benefit of the individual (ibid., p. 589).

7. Greek *sophia*; see Chapter 2. Wisdom here harks back to Paul's message in 2:6–16, where we see wisdom is not about deeper things revolving around the mysteries of God. Instead Paul connotes a wisdom that recognizes the message of Christ crucified, which can only be received through the Spirit (Fee, *The First Epistle to the Corinthians*, p. 592).

8. Greek *gnosis*. Many commentators attribute this gift to be akin to inspired teaching, namely insight into the meaning of Scripture (ibid., p. 593).

9. Greek *pistis*. It's interesting to note that even faith is a gift. While Paul is clearly referring to faith that leads to the salvific work of the Spirit enlightening the

believer to believe in the life, death, and resurrection of Jesus Christ, Paul has in mind here a "supernatural faith that can 'move mountains' (13:2)" (ibid.).

10. Greek *lamaton*, referring to physical acts of healing.

11. Greek *dynameon*. While Paul might subsume healing under the gifts of miracles, this gift most likely refers to all other kinds of supernatural activities outside of healing the sick (ibid., p. 594).

12. Greek *propheteia*; see Chapter 25 of this book.

13. Or literally, "discernments of spirits." Most likely this refers to the phenomenon of "'discerning, differentiating, or properly judging' prophecies" (Fee, *The First Epistle to the Corinthians*, p. 594).

14. Greek *glosson*; see Chapter 25 of this book.

15. See Chapter 25 of this book.

16. I am indebted to Tim Keller for these insights.

17. Tim Keller, *Theology and Practice of Church Ministry* (New York: Redeemer Presbyterian Church, 2004), p. 23.

18. Ibid., p. 24.

19. In Romans 12:8 the Greek *prosistamenos ev spouda* is literally, "leading in zeal," or uniting toward a vision.

20. Greek *kuberneseis*, the ability to organize a task and get it done.

21. Idina Menzel, "Let it Go," *Frozen*, original motion picture soundtrack, Sunset Sound/Capital Studios, 2013.

Chapter Twenty-Three: The Gift of Interdependence

1. Greek *soma*. The body proves to be the perfect picture that marries both unity and diversity.

2. Morris's observation of the significance of baptism for the church body helps us note the unity theme throughout the body metaphor. "Baptism into one body symbolizes this truth (from other standpoints baptism is 'into Christ', Gal. 3:27, or 'into his death', Rom. 6:3). Early in this letter Paul appealed to baptism into Christ as pointing the Corinthians away from their factions and rivalries to their essential unity (1:13ff). The same thought is put in a different form here. Jews or Greeks, slave or free, all alike are baptized into one body, and thus into a unity that transcends all human distinctions" (Leon Morris, *The First Epistle of Paul to the Corinthians*, The Tyndale New Testament Commentaries [Grand Rapids: Eerdmans, 1989], p. 171).

3. Diversity is no accidental attribute of the body. It is of its very essence. No one member is to be equated with the body. It takes many members to make up one body.

4. Witherington notes that in 21ff. Paul's emphasis is that no one particular body member can "devalue another or declare it to be of no worth" (Ben Witherington, *Conflict and Community in Corinth* [Grand Rapids: Eerdmans, 1995], p. 259).

5. Witherington's sidebar on the Roman colony pecking order is helpful to consult (ibid., pp. 259, 260).

6. Greek *aschemona*, literally less "honorable" and "shameful." For usage of this word as meaning sexual shame, see Deuteronomy 24:1, LXX. "Paul is undoubtedly referring to the sexual organs, on which we bestow greater honor, and which therefore have greater decorum, because we cover them while the more decorous parts (e.g. the face) do not have such need. Although the analogy with the preceding sentence is not precise, Paul's point seems to be similar. Bodily appearances are deceiving;

all the parts are necessary, which is reflected in this case by the very way we treat some parts of our bodies that seem 'lesser' to us" (Gordon D. Fee, *The First Epistle to the Corinthians*, The New International Commentary of the New Testament [Grand Rapids: Eerdmans, 1989, pp. 613, 614).

7. Many commentators take extended looks into Paul's apparent ranking of the offices of spiritual gifts (see Fee, *The First Epistle to the Corinthians* and David Prior, *The Message of 1 Corinthians*, The Bible Speaks Today [Nottingham, UK: Inter-Varsity Press, 1985]). Paul's crux here of mutual care within the church builds the tension as he leads into "a still more excellent way" mentioned in 12:28 and portrayed in 1 Corinthians 13.

8. See the previous chapter of this book for exposition of the three different offices of Christ that laid the foundation for spiritual gifts.

Chapter Twenty-Four: What Is Love?

1. Francis Spufford, *Unapologetic: Why, Despite Everything, Christianity Can Still Make Surprising Emotional Sense* (San Francisco: HarperOne, 2014), p. 104.

2. Backstreet Boys, "As Long as You Love Me," Max Martin and Kristian Lundin, *Backstreet's Back*, 1997.

3. Justin Bieber, "As Long as You Love Me," Andrew Lindal and Darkchild, *Believe*, 2012.

4. James H. Olthius, *The Beautiful Risk: A New Psychology of Loving and Being Loved* (Grand Rapids: Zondervan, 2001), p. 44.

5. Carson notes: "This value judgment is meant to be shocking. Part of its power is that Paul does not merely say that under this condition—that is, under the condition of speaking in tongues but without love—it is not the gift of tongues that is only a resounding gong or a clanging cymbal, but I, myself . . . as if my action of speaking in tongues without love has left a permanent effect on me that has diminished my value and transformed me into something I should not be" (D. A. Carson, *Showing the Spirit: A Theological Exposition of 1 Corinthians 12 – 14* [Grand Rapids: Baker, 1987], p. 59).

6. Carson teases out the use of the Greek *agapao* in his commentary, but his main discussion revolves around what distinguishes this kind of love and makes it "Christian love." He writes, ". . . the first three verses insistently speak of the love you and I are supposed to exercise . . . perhaps the real distinction in 1 Cor. 13 is between egocentric and altruistic love. The line is not drawn between love of God and love of man, but between both of these and self-love . . . what is distinctive about God's love for us, it is that it is self-originating. . . . God loves what is unlovely" (*Showing the Spirit: A Theological Exposition of 1 Corinthians 12 – 14*, pp. 64, 65).

7. Ted Williams's lifetime batting average was .344; http://www.baseball -reference.com/players/w/willite01.shtml.

8. For more on Ted Williams, see Leigh Monteville, *Ted Williams* (New York: Broadway Books, 2005).

9. The Shirelles, "Will You Love Me Tomorrow?" Gerry Goffin and Carole King, *Tonight's the Night*, 1960.

10. The Greek word *pipitei* literally means "falls" or "collapses." Love will never collapse.

11. Barbara Fredrickson, *Love 2.0* (New York: Penguin Group, 2013), p. 6.

12. Ibid., p. 10.

13. Ibid., p. 15.

14. Ibid., p. 36.

15. Alain de Botton, *On Love* (New York: Alain de Botton, 1993), p. 168.

Chapter Twenty-Five: An Upbuilding Project

1. "Doing" gifts.

2. "Being" gifts.

3. "Saying" gifts.

4. Witherington wisely summarizes the major concern of this passage—and the use of speech gifts in the Corinthian church—as how worship should manifest intelligibility for the purpose of building up the church. This building up happens twofold: when individual believers are edified by one another; when nonbelievers present in an assembly are challenged by the gospel, convicted, and converted (Ben Witherington, *Conflict and Community in Corinth* [Grand Rapids: Eerdmans, 1995], p. 276).

5. "... prophecy . . . is something like our preaching, but it is not identical with it. It is not the delivery of a carefully prepared sermon, but the uttering of words directly inspired by God" (Leon Morris, *The First Epistle of Paul to the Corinthians*, The Tyndale New Testament Commentaries [Grand Rapids: Eerdmans, 1989], p. 187). Its function is to build up, exhort, and console (v. 3). It is not reserved for a particular group of Christians, but should be, in fact, a gift sought after by all Christians (Witherington, *Conflict and Community in Corinth*, p. 280).

6. Most simply put, the gift of tongues (Greek *glossolalia*) was seen as "a prayer language or as a way to talk to God, not as a human language . . . the Spirit speaking mysteries" (Witherington, *Conflict and Community in Corinth*, p. 281). Paul deems that prophecy is an inherently superior gift to tongues because it does not need interpretation. But the "'greater-lesser' language is based on the criterion of intelligibility and edification, not on the inherent worth of some gifts as functions" (ibid., p. 282).

7. Cf. 1 Kings 13:32; 2 Kings 12:3; 14:4; 15:4; 15:35; 18:4; 2 Chronicles 14:3, 5; Isaiah 36:7; Jeremiah 19:5; 32:35; Hosea 10:8; Amos 7:9; Micah 1:3.

8. David Prior, *The Message of 1 Corinthians*, The Bible Speaks Today (Nottingham, UK: Inter-Varsity Press, 1985), p. 243.

9. Ibid.

10. The Greek word translated "disclosed" is *elenchetai*, "exposed," "reproved," or "rebuked" (cf. Matthew 18:15; Luke 3:19; John 3:20; 8:46; 16:8; Ephesians 5:11, 13; 1 Timothy 5:20; 2 Timothy 4:2; Titus 1:9, 13; 2:15; Hebrews 12:5; James 2:9).

11. The Greek word translated "called to account" is *anakrinetai*, "examined" or "judged" (cf. 2 Corinthians 2:14, 15; 4:3, 4; 9:3; 10:25, 27; also Luke 23:14; Acts 4:9; 12:19; 17:11; 24:8; 28:18).

12. Greek *oikodomen*, from the root *oikos* or "house."

Chapter Twenty-Six: Order out of Chaos

1. See Timothy Keller, *The Reason for God* (New York: Dutton, 2008), pp. 83, 84, 111.

2. Alain de Botton, *The Architecture of Happiness* (New York: Random House, 2006), p. 78.

3. This speaks to the progressive nature of Christian worship. Jewish worship was characterized by people in specialized roles, including worship leaders and those reading the Torah. The picture of worship that Paul outlines is one where there is not as much of a distinction between the clergy and laity. Each one is able to contribute to corporate worship. Worship, then, is not guided by cultural norms (Ben Witherington, *Conflict and Community in Corinth* [Grand Rapids: Eerdmans, 1995], p. 285).

4. "Of the nature of each gift here mentioned we cannot be certain. Does the person who brings a 'hymn,' for example, simply introduce a known composition for all to sing? Does it mean a fresh contribution each time, as many have suggested? The brief answer is that we possess too little information to warrant firm conclusions. It is clear that the Corinthian service was not boring!" (D. A. Carson, *Showing the Spirit: A Theological Exposition of 1 Corinthians 12–14* [Grand Rapids: Baker, 1987], p. 118).

5. "'Building up' others becomes the litmus test for determining the relative value of gifts, and Paul underscores its importance throughout this chapter (1 Cor. 14:3, 4, 5, 12, 17; see also 8:1; 10:23)" (David E. Garland, *1 Corinthians*, Baker Exegetical Commentary on the New Testament [Grand Rapids: Baker Academic, 2003], p. 658).

6. The act of being silent is a demonstration of self-control. Those who have the gift of speaking in tongues have the ability to speak or refrain from speaking. The expression of this gift is not spontaneous nor sporadic, but controlled and measured (cf. David Prior, *The Message of 1 Corinthians*, The Bible Speaks Today [Nottingham, UK: Inter-Varsity Press, 1985], p. 250; Carson, *Showing the Spirit*, p. 119; Leon Morris, *The First Epistle of Paul to the Corinthians*, The Tyndale New Testament Commentaries [Grand Rapids: Eerdmans, 1989], p. 195).

7. "This truth does not of course sanction mere traditionalism in worship, or sanctify stuffiness; but it does warn us sharply about the dangers of the opposite end of the spectrum. That is not wise and biblically informed Christian worship that pursues freedom at the expense of order, or unrestrained spontaneity at the expense of reverence" (Carson, *Showing the Spirit*, p. 121).

8. Garland, *1 Corinthians*, p. 664.

9. Witherington, *Conflict and Community in Corinth*, p. 287.

10. In ancient Greek culture, it was more common for husbands not to look highly upon their wives with respect to their intellect. So it's surprising and somewhat progressive that Paul would have the husbands take time to teach and instruct their wives in the home. Paul is giving dignity and worth to the wives here because the greater culture would see them as being invisible and not worth their time (Craig S. Keener, *First-Second Corinthians* [New York : Cambridge University Press, 2005), p. 171).

11. D. A. Carson, "Silent in the Churches"; https://bible.org/seriespage/silent-churches-role-women-1-corinthians-1433b-36.

12. Prior, *The Message of 1 Corinthians*, p. 253.

13. Garland, *1 Corinthians*, p. 674.

Chapter Twenty-Seven: The Power of the Gospel

1. Timothy Keller, *The Reason for God* (New York: Dutton, 2008), p. 203.

2. "'That Christ died' refutes those docetists who believed that Christ only seems to be human (because they also believed that matter was inherently evil)." (Craig L.

Blomberg, *1 Corinthians*, NIV Application Commentary [Grand Rapids: Zondervan, 1995], p. 296).

3. Garland affirms that the concept of dying for someone else was not unique among the secular writers of that time. "As Origen notes (*Cels.* 1.30.31), Celsus affirmed that a life laid down for others could and did remove evils that have fallen upon cities and countries, but he denied any value to Christ's death because his manner of dying was so inglorious and shameful in comparison with that of the Greco-Roman heroes" (David E. Garland, *1 Corinthians*, Baker Exegetical Commentary on the New Testament [Grand Rapids: Baker Academic, 2003], p. 685).

4. Most scholars agree that Paul is here referring to Isaiah 52, 53, which talks about God's Suffering Servant.

5. "In the present context it emphasizes the fact that a dead corpse was laid in the grave, so that the resurrection that follows will be recognized as an objective reality, not merely a 'spiritual' phenomenon, a phantasm of some kind. Therefore, even though the point is incidental to Paul's own concern this very early expression of Christian faith also verifies the reality of the empty tomb stories" (Gordon D. Fee, *The First Epistle to the Corinthians*, The New International Commentary of the New Testament [Grand Rapids: Eerdmans, 1989], p. 805).

6. "Paul shifts from using the aorist tense to describe Christ's death and burial to the perfect tense (*egegertai*) to describe Christ's resurrection. It is not something that belongs to the past, but something that has an effect on present reality (Schrage 2001:38)" (Garland, *1 Corinthians*, p. 686).

7. "'On the third day' uses inclusive reckoning: Good Friday is day one, Saturday is day two, Easter morning is day three. It is less clear which Scriptures point to the *resurrection* on the third day. Perhaps Paul meant only that the Scriptures testified to Christ's resurrection, with passages like Psalms 16:8–11 and 110:1–4 in view (cf. Acts 2:24–36). In that case, 'according to the Scriptures' would modify only the verb 'raised' and not the phrase 'on the third day.' But he may also have found some typological significance in the third-day references to God's vindication of his people in such texts as Genesis 42:18, Exodus 19:16, Joshua 2:22, Ezra 8:2, Esther 5:1, Jonah 1:17 (cf. Matt. 12:40), and especially Hosea 6:2" (Blomberg, *1 Corinthians*, p. 296).

8. Paul Copan, ed., *Jesus' Resurrection* (Downers Grove: InterVarsity Press), p. 32ff.

9. Ibid.

10. Blomberg suggests that the appearances of Jesus to all the apostles could have happened on several occasions such as the Sunday night following Easter (John 20:24–29), the Great Commission (Matthew 28:16–20), or on the day of Christ's ascension (Acts 1:1–11) (Blomberg, *1 Corinthians*, p. 296).

11. "Paul did not originate the message he gave them. He simply *passed on* what he had *received*. This is the accepted language for the handing on of tradition. What follows is a very early summary of the church's traditional teaching. Paul is not working on some views he has worked out for himself; he is passing on what had been told him. This is the *kerygma*, the proclamation, the gospel preached by the early church" (Leon Morris, *The First Epistle of Paul to the Corinthians*, The Tyndale New Testament Commentaries [Grand Rapids: Eerdmans, 1989], p. 201). Fee says it is clear that the two basic doctrines of the Christian faith — the atoning death of

Christ and his resurrection—were well taught before Paul came onto the scene (Fee, *The First Epistle to the Corinthians*, p. 801).

12. "The statement that he received the gospel from others is only an apparent contradiction of his declaration in Gal. 1:11–12 that he did not receive the gospel that he preached 'from a man,' nor was he taught it, but he received it through a revelation of Jesus Christ. The same verb (*paralambanein*), a technical term for receiving tradition, appears in both passages. In Cor. 15:3–5, however, Paul is speaking only about the fact surrounding Jesus' death and resurrection. Many agree that he was not an eyewitness to Jesus' ministry, and these facts were passed on to him by the tradition. In Gal. 1:11–12, he does not have in view the historical details on which the gospel is based but the interpretation of what those facts mean. The gospel is not simply a litany of facts, but something much more. It is the message that by grace God has acted decisively to save all humans, Jews and Gentiles, through Jesus Christ alone, apart from the law and human performance" (Garland, *1 Corinthians*, pp. 683, 684.)

13. Keller, *The Reason for God*, p. 210.

14. Morris argues that Paul is placing his encounter with the Lord on the road of Damascus on the same order as the other resurrection appearances (Morris, *The First Epistle of Paul to the Corinthians*, p. 203).

15. "With this sentence and the next Paul offers an explanation of the preceding self-deprecating words (v. 8) which serve at the same time as an apologetic of his apostleship and especially of his ministry among them" (Fee, *The First Epistle to the Corinthians*, p. 814).

16. "We come to the heart of Paul's point. Undeserved, unmerited grace which springs from the free, sovereign love of God alone and becomes operative in human life not only determines Paul's life and apostolic vocation but also characterizes all Christian existence, not least the promise of resurrection and the reality of the activity of Christ as Lord" (Anthony C. Thiselton, *The First Epistle to the Corinthians: A Commentary on the Greek Text*, New International Greek Testament Commentary [Grand Rapids: Eerdmans, 2000], p. 1211).

Chapter Twenty-Eight: Resurrection

1. Timothy Keller, *King's Cross* (London: Hodder & Stoughton, 2012), p. 221.

2. It is exactly for that reason Paul is responding to some in the Corinthian congregation who denied the resurrection from the dead (v. 12). Blomberg argues that everyone in the ancient world believed in life after death, as the Corinthians certainly did. Instead the doubters were "disputing the Jewish and Christian doctrine of *bodily* resurrection and endorsing one of the more Greek forms of belief that limited the after-life to disembodied immortality of the soul" (Craig L. Blomberg, *1 Corinthians*, NIV Application Commentary [Grand Rapids: Zondervan, 1995], p. 295). Morris adds that "death for such meant the liberation of the soul from its prison in the body, for the body (*soma*), they held, was a tomb (*sema*). They may have thought of the state of the departed as the life of the 'shades' in Hades" (Leon Morris, *The First Epistle of Paul to the Corinthians*, The Tyndale New Testament Commentaries [Grand Rapids: Eerdmans, 1989], pp. 205, 206).

3. Gary R. Habermas and Anthony Flew, *Did the Resurrection Happen?* (Downers Grove: InterVarsity Press, 2009), p. 85.

4. Timothy Keller, *The Reason for God* (New York: Dutton, 2008).

5. "Christ's death and resurrection in space and time, as bone fide historical events, actually sets Christianity apart from all its major rivals. Later Western religions that developed in part in reaction to Christianity do not claim deity or resurrections for their originators, merely prophetic status. . . . Older Eastern religions do not even require the actual historical existence of their founders for their beliefs and practices to make sense. In some ways they are more akin to philosophies than to historical truth-claims. But Christianity lives or dies with the claim of Christ's resurrection. To be sure, it is possible to believe in Jesus' resurrection and not become a Christian. But without the bodily resurrection Christianity crumbles. Finding the bones of Jesus would assuredly disprove our religion" (Blomberg, *1 Corinthians*, p. 308).

6. "Without the resurrection, the life of Paul would have been a complete waste of time. All the persecutions, sufferings, and hardships he endured were pointless. His ministry would have been founded on a fraud and a hoax" (David Prior, *The Message of 1 Corinthians*, The Bible Speaks Today [Nottingham, UK: Inter-Varsity Press, 1985], p. 263).

7. The faith of the Corinthians being based entirely on the preaching of Paul, "the collapse of the ground of his preaching necessarily meant the collapse of their faith." The Greek word *kenos*, translated "in vain" literally means "empty" implying that taking out the resurrection of Jesus, nothing was left of their faith (ibid.).

8. Morris (*The First Epistle of Paul to the Corinthians*, p. 207) states that the further consequence of such denial reveals the apostles to be liars: "It cannot be said that they were honest men, who in sincerity have given advice they thought to be good, though it is now shown to be not as good as they had imagined."

9. "To 'be in one's sins' is uncommon through the Scriptures even though Jesus talked about 'dying in sin (Jn. 8:21, 24) and Paul of being 'dead in sins.' Two meanings can be taken into consideration. The death of Christ without the resurrection would not have given a justified Christ, but a condemned one, implying he would not be able to justify others (Godet). Or 'believers would still be living in their sins like any pagan'" (ibid., pp. 207, 208).

10. According to Garland, Christians are pathetic dupes if Christ was not raised. Indeed, he says, "They are the most pitiable of all human beings because they have embraced Christ's death and suffering in this life for nothing. Christianity would be an ineffective religion that is detrimental to one's health since it bestows only suffering on its followers. Suffering the loss of all things because of Christ and sharing his sufferings by becoming like him in his death with the hope of attaining the resurrection (Phil. 3:7–11) turns out to be foolish" (David E. Garland, *1 Corinthians*, Baker Exegetical Commentary on the New Testament [Grand Rapids: Baker Academic, 2003], p. 703).

11. "Even referring to the life to come simply as 'heaven' points out a serious misconception. The biblical hope is for believers to experience all of the wonders and glories of a fully re-created heavens and earth (Rev. 21−22)" (Blomberg, *1 Corinthians*, p. 311).

12. Blomberg calls this "some sort of proxy baptism" that the early church fathers (Tertullian, Chrysostom, Epiphanius, Philaster) alluded to in reference to a practice among the Gnostic groups during the second-century. "Given the Corinthians' tendencies toward early Gnostic belief and practice, it is not difficult to imagine something similar having begun among at least a few in Corinth already in

the first century. Paul neither condemns nor condones such a practice but argues for its relevance if Christ is not raised. In other words, those who are baptizing people on behalf of the dead contradict their own theology that denies the resurrection. The Corinthians might well have replied that they performed such baptisms for the sake of disembodied souls, but Paul is convinced that without a body there is no further life at all" (ibid., p. 299). Garland gives a few options concerning the motivations that pushed the Corinthians to baptize on behalf of the dead: "to claim a place for the deceased in the world of the dead (DeMaris 1995a:679), to ward off the threat from hostile cosmic principalities and powers to their nonbaptized dead (Downey 1985), to assure an early resurrection for the deceased to participate in the messianic kingdom (Schweitzer 1931: 279, 285), or generally to impart the benefits of their spirituality or their salvation to the dead (cf 2 Macc. 12:43–45)" (*1 Corinthians*, p. 716).

13. Garland claims that Epicurean thought was prevalent during that time, believing the soul existed no longer after the dissolution of the body. He appeals to Greek literature (Plato, Aseschylus) to support his argument. Based on that, Garland asserts that "such fatalism led people to want to live life now to the fullest," some of the Corinthians were primarily concerned about the blessings and pleasures of their earthly life and not the life to come, and "salvation had to do with matters of this life and present benefits: health, wealth, protection, sustenance" (*1 Corinthians*, p. 698).

14. Morris notes "the *firstfruits* point us to the first sheaf of the harvest, which was brought to the temple and offered to God (Lev. 23:10f.); it consecrated the whole harvest. Moreover, *firstfruits* imply later fruits" (*The First Epistle of Paul to the Corinthians*, p. 209). But Witherington goes further: "With 'firstfruits' Paul might be alluding to OT practices in regard to the wheat sheaf after Passover, but he more likely uses the idea to stress the connection between Jesus' resurrection and the believer's future resurrection. Christ's resurrection is the first part of the harvest of those who have 'fallen asleep' and also that which assures the Corinthians that the rest of the harvest will eventually come in" (Ben Witherington, *Conflict and Community in Corinth* [Grand Rapids: Eerdmans, 1995], p. 304).

15. "Paul is not interested in making the point that Adam's sin brought death, but in showing how Adam's sin had a universal effect on all who came after. The same applies to Christ's resurrection. As physical death came inevitably from Adam's sin, so physical resurrection comes inevitably from Christ's resurrection. He underscores the incarnation with the phrase 'through man.' This detail prevents anyone from arguing that Christ was some divine figure whom death could not really touch. It also foiled the argument that his resurrection was of a different order because he was divine" (Garland, *1 Corinthians*, p. 706).

16. The point made by the Apostle Paul concerning this parallelism between Adam and Christ (as in Romans 5) was to highlight the fact that Christ, like Adam, is the progenitor of a new humanity (Prior, *The Message of 1 Corinthians*, p. 267).

17. Witherington makes an interesting point here: "Paul is probably countering Roman imperial eschatology in this section, which may also explain his stress on the fatherhood of God, because in the imperial propaganda the emperor was portrayed as not only divine but also as 'father of the fatherland' (*pater patriae*).'The *Pater-Patriae* image had more appeal to Roman citizens and subjects with a Roman background, wherefore it was primarily in the city of Rome and in Italy and probably in Roman *coloniae* that this aspect of the Roman propaganda was the strongest' (E. M. Lassen

"The Use of the Father Image in Imperial Propaganda and 1 Corinthians 4.12–21" TynB 42–1991, pp. 127–36). . . . Paul is trying to supplant the imperial eschatology, which was clearly extant in Corinth and which looked to the emperor as the father and benefactor providing the current blessings, with an eschatology that involves Christ and a truly divine Father. . . . The evidence just cited shows that Roman Corinth was not dominated by the old Greek democratic ideals but by the more hierarchical ideals propagated by the emperor and his officials in the colonies" (*Conflict and Community in Corinth*, p. 295).

18. "There is a dynamic meaning to the Greek *basileia* (*kingdom*); it is 'rule' rather than 'realm.' Paul's thought is that Christ will at the last exercise full and complete authority over all things and all people; he will reign in majesty (cf. 2 Thes. 1:7ff). Then he will 'deliver up' this authority, this rule, to his Father. All that opposes God will be subdued. So Paul speaks of Christ as destroying *all dominion, authority and power*. These three words are probably not meant to define with precision different kinds of authority. Rather they together emphasize that in that day there will be no governing power of any kind that will not be completely subservient to Christ" (Morris, *The First Epistle of Paul to the Corinthians*, p. 211).

19. Blomberg sums up the dynamic of the relationship between the Father and the Son: "Although God the Son is *essentially* equal to the Father, he remains *functionally* subordinate, just as his glorified humanity keeps him distinct from what he was prior to the incarnation" (*1 Corinthians*, p. 298).

20. Garland, *1 Corinthians*, p. 721.

21. "Far more apposite and intelligible is Paul's indignation about the value of his own sufferings. *I die every day* (31) is his experience. . . . He pressed on with such a dangerous life, because he was convinced that something infinitely better awaited him in the resurrection-life of heaven. He was prepared to persevere with such ministry, because, in this carrying about in his body the death of Jesus, life was released in the Corinthians—and that made him very proud of them (31)" (Prior, *The Message of 1 Corinthians*, p. 270).

22. For Garland, Paul's fighting against the beast of Ephesus refers to a metaphor concerning dangers that threatened his life: "If he is writing this from Ephesus, he speaks of an open door of opportunity but many adversaries (1 Cor. 16:8–9). The 'wild beasts' plausibly are bloodthirsty human antagonists who would eagerly tear him to pieces. His Roman citizenship did not provide him protection from mob violence, but only the right to certain formal procedures (*1 Corinthians*, p. 721). According to Prior, this refers to a direct encounter with occult forces and his mob lynching under the influence of fanatics of the local goddess Artemis recorded in Acts 19: "The theatre at Ephesus is specifically mentioned, the scene of literal battles-to-the-death with wild beasts: Paul's memory of the events was probably jogged, as in Ephesus he dictated this letter to his amanuensis. What is the point, asks the apostle, of subjecting one self to such a lifestyle, if there is no resurrection?" (*The Message of 1 Corinthians*, p. 270).

23. "Appropriately, then, Paul tells them to come out of their drunken stupor and stop sinning (the present continual tense indicating the cessation of ongoing action). They should know God better. There will be eschatological consequences to their actions, a judgment of deeds, as ch. 3 makes clear. They will be held accountable when they rise from the dead. Paul publicly shames them, asking, in effect, 'How could you

be so ignorant of God that you do not know about the future resurrection and future judgment?' The mention of 'knowledge' of eschatological mysteries (v. 51) suggests that Paul is criticizing the same group whose claims of 'knowledge' of the faith's mysteries and of Christian freedom to dine in temples he mentions in chs. 8–10" (Witherington, *Conflict and Community in Corinth*, p. 306).

Chapter Twenty-Nine: The Resurrection Body

1. Flannery O'Connor, *The Habit of Being* (Toronto: HarperCollins, 1979), p. 100.

2. Gordon D. Fee, *The First Epistle to the Corinthians*, The New International Commentary of the New Testament (Grand Rapids: Eerdmans, 1989), p. 779.

3. "Apparently a major stumbling block—if not *the* major stumbling block—for the Corinthians in accepting the notion of resurrection was that having a body seemed synonymous with mortality and corruptibility so that the combination of body and immortality did not make sense. This, along with the Greek idea that immortality involved the soul and was inherent to having a soul, as opposed to the Christian idea that eternal life or salvation is a gift that will affect both body and spirit, makes the confusion understandable" (Ben Witherington, *Conflict and Community in Corinth* [Grand Rapids: Eerdmans, 1995], p. 307).

4. Greek *phtora*, literally "destruction, decay, corruption" (cf. 9:25; 1 Peter 1:18, 23).

5. Paul uses an agricultural metaphor here to speak of the supernatural mystery that is the resurrection. "The same mystery shrouds the germination of seeds. Moderns, influenced by a scientific understanding of germination as a natural process of development, may misunderstand what Paul says. He is not talking about a natural development but thinks in terms of God's transforming a bare grain and making it into something different. He understands God to give the growth in physical and spiritual harvests (3:6–7). The farmer does not know how the seed grows in the earth (Mk. 4:27) but only trusts that God is active and will bring it to pass. What is true in the case of seeds planted in the earth provides a lesson that can help the objector appreciate the possibility that a human corpse buried in the earth can also be transformed into something new" (David E. Garland, *1 Corinthians*, Baker Exegetical Commentary on the New Testament [Grand Rapids: Baker Academic, 2003], p. 728).

6. Cf. Matthew 28; Mark 16; Luke 24; John 20, 21. ". . . the Scripture as a whole witnesses to Christ as a life-giving spirit. . . . Paul sees Christ as having become a life-giving spirit in his work of saving sinners" (Leon Morris, *The First Epistle of Paul to the Corinthians*, The Tyndale New Testament Commentaries [Grand Rapids: Eerdmans, 1989], p. 224).

7. "Paul refers to Genesis 2:7 . . . his point appears to be that the characteristic of man from the very beginning is *psyche*, 'soul.' That was true of Adam and it is true of all his descendants. The first Adam passed on his nature to those who came after. . . . Adam was the progenitor of the race, and his characteristics are stamped on the race. In the same way, 'Christ is the last Adam,' the progenitor of the race of spiritual people. . . . There is finality about 'the last Adam': 'There will be no other Head of the human race.' By virtue of his office as the last Adam he stamps his characteristics on those who are his" (ibid.).

8. Derived from Timothy Keller, *Counterfeit Gods* (New York: Penguin, 2009), Chapter 5, "The Power and Glory," pp. 97–125.

Chapter Thirty: Victory over Death

1. Winston Churchill, taken from his speech given on May 13, 1940, entitled "Blood, Toil, Tears and Sweat"; http://www.winstonchurchill.org/learn/speeches /speeches-of-winston-churchill/92-blood-toil-tears-and-sweat.

2. Throughout the epistle, Paul dismisses any Corinthian believer's cosmology not under the authority of Christ. The late Swiss New Testament scholar Eduard Schweizer shows that by stating the double nominative "flesh and blood" (*sarx kai haima*), Paul denounces any latent or visible Hellenistic dualism among the believers: "Unlike Greek thought, he is not distinguishing an incorruptible part of man from a corruptible. On the contrary, Paul's concern is to present the new state as an absolutely different and unimaginable gift of God, as a miracle." The miracle lies not only in their identification with the saving gospel (1:2, 30; 6:11; 7:23; 15:2) but also in their sharing in his victory over death (15:57). Taken from E. Schweizer, "σὰρξ," *TDNT* 7:129, quoted from David E. Garland, 1 Corinthians, Baker Exegetical Commentary on the New Testament (Grand Rapids: Baker Academic, 2003).

3. Paul also used "perishable" and "imperishable" (*phthora* and *aphthora*) to describe the difference between the "perishable" wreath sought by athletes and the "imperishable" wreath desired by Christians (9:25). This supports the spiritual thrust of the passage as Paul is reflecting on his needing self-control in his calling to preach to win more people for Christ (9:26, 27).

4. Anne Lamott, *Bird by Bird: Some Instructions on Writing and Life* (Toronto: Pantheon, 1994), p. 28.

5. C. S. Lewis, *The Weight of Glory* (San Francisco: HarperCollins, 2001), p. 61.

6. Ibid., pp. 45, 46.

7. Garland explains that the noun "sting" (*kentron*) "can refer to a goad that drives on or wounds (Acts 26:14; Prov. 26:3; Sir. 38:25; Ps. Sol. 16:4), or to a stinger (Rev. 9:10 [of scorpions]; 4 Macc. 14:19 [of insects])." Garland's insights are helpful: "Here [*kentron*] must refer to something that harms far more seriously than either a goad or a stinger, and it must be synonymous with 'power' in 1 Cor. 15:56. . . . It enables death to exercise dominion over the entire world, but its venom has been absorbed by Christ and drained of its potency so that the victory over death now belongs to God and to God's people, who benefit from it" (David E. Garland, *1 Corinthians*, Baker Exegetical Commentary on the New Testament [Grand Rapids: Baker Academic, 2003], pp. 745, 746).

8. The interjection translated by the HVV, "Behold!" is like saying, "Listen up!" or "Pay attention!" It is unique to this letter and is rarely used by Paul (cf. 2 Corinthians 5:17; 6:2, 9; 7:11; 12:14; Galatians 1:20). These references are found in Simon J. Kistemaker, *1 Corinthians*, New Testament Commentary (Grand Rapids: Baker, 1993), p. 581.

9. The word the HVV translates as "twinkling" (*rhipe*) only occurs here in the New Testament, but in extra-Biblical literature "it can denote the *rapid wing movement* which causes the *buzz of a gnat* or the twinkling . . . of a star." Thiselton is helpful in translating the phrase "in the blinking of an eye" because it does away with the dependence on an idiom that may not translate into every contemporary culture

(Anthony C. Thiselton, *The First Epistle to the Corinthians: A Commentary on the Greek Text*, New International Greek Testament Commentary [Grand Rapids: Eerdmans, 2000], pp. 1295, 1296). John MacArthur points to the rapid movement of the eye: "The eye can move faster than any other visible part of our bodies, and Paul's point was that the change will be extremely fast, instantaneous" (John MacArthur Jr., *First Corinthians: The MacArthur New Testament Commentary* [Chicago: Moody Press, 1984], p. 443).

10. Thiselton points to other Biblical episodes throughout the canon where the trumpet is used "to announce manifestations of God" such as Exodus 19:16, Zechariah 9:14; 1 Thessalonians 4:16. Thiselton, *The First Epistle to the Corinthians*, p. 1296.

11. Thiselton unpacks the rhetorical purpose behind Paul substituting the LXX rendering of "Hades" in Hosea 13:14 for "death": "With regard to the substitution of Death for *Hades*, the two function as rhetorical synonyms; death without the resurrection of the body is a reductive demotion to the realm of the shades, or *She'ol* presented in its Greek form" (ibid., p. 1300).

12. Garland, *1 Corinthians*, p. 746.

13. The participle *perisseuo* generally means "abounding" but has the specific notion of "excelling" in God's work (*BDAG*, p. 805). Kistemaker's comments are helpful: "Paul is not talking about retaining the status quo in the church. He wants the people to grow in their love for the Lord and to communicate this in their deeds" (Kistemaker, *1 Corinthians*, p. 587).

14. Lewis, *The Weight of Glory*, p. 45.

Chapter Thirty-One: A Community of Reconciliation

1. "The poor have a right unto part of thine estate . . . in which respect the Spirit of God calleth . . . part of the rich man's stock . . . the poor man's 'due,' unto whom of right it doth belong; for saith he [Proverbs 3:27], 'withhold not good from them to whom it is due, when it is in the power of thine hand to do it.' . . . So that thy relieving the poor is not only an act of mercy . . . but of justice" (Thomas Gouge, *Riches Increased, or the Surest and Safest Way of Thriving* [London: Partridge and Company, 1856], p. 147).

2. See John R. Schneider, *The Good of Affluence: Seeking God in a Culture of Wealth* (Grand Rapids: Eerdmans, 2002), pp. 26, 31, 32.

3. Nikole Hannah-Jones, "Segregation Now," *The Atlantic*, May 2014.

4. Christena Cleveland, "Why Reconciliation Needs Justice," June 10, 2013; http://www.christenacleveland.com/2013/06/why-reconciliation-needs-justice/.

5. "As Dieter Georgi argues, here a link with the resurrection chapter emerges in two ways: (a) 'bodily' existence entails taking responsibility for the corporeity of believers in the everyday public domain; and (b) a debt to the communities founded by the first witnesses of the resurrection may be implied by the moral debt to their 'founding' role" (Anthony C. Thiselton, *The First Epistle to the Corinthians: A Commentary on the Greek Text*, New International Greek Testament Commentary [Grand Rapids: Eerdmans, 2000], p. 1320).

6. "Soards (1999: 357) and Talbert (1987: 105) identify principles that undergird Paul's instructions for the collection. It is to be done regularly ('on the first day of the week'), universally ('let each one of you'), systematically ('set aside,' 'save up'), proportionately ('as one has been prospered') and freely ('so that no collections

might take place when I come')" (David E. Garland, *1 Corinthians*, Baker Exegetical Commentary on the New Testament [Grand Rapids: Baker Academic, 2003], p. 753).

7. "Fee suggests that the NIV, in keeping with his income, is 'a bit too modern,' but it has the advantage of avoiding the notion of giving only when one is making a profit (Barrett, Collins, BAGD), or deciding what a donor can spare (NJB) or afford (REB). In spirit, the tradition of the widow's mite lies behind Paul's phraseology: 'Whoever sows sparingly will also reap sparingly, and whoever sows generously with reap generously . . . God loves a cheerful giver . . .' (2 Cor 9:6, 7; cf. 2 Cor 8:1—9:15)" (Thiselton, *The First Epistle to the Corinthians*, p. 1323).

8. "There is to be no last-minute, superficial scraping around for funds as an unplanned off-the-cuff gesture. . . . Each is to play his or her part in a planned strategy of regular giving in weekly response to God's blessing and his financial provision, for the benefit of those who suffer deeper poverty and in mutuality and solidarity with a local church community" (ibid., p. 1324).

9. "Our modern, compressed sense of time . . . should not limit the span of 'passing through' to an overnight stay (cf. the use of the same verb in Acts 8:4, 40; 11:19; 13:6, 14; 14:24; 15:3, 41; 16:6; 18:23, 27; 19:1, 21; 2 Cor. 1:16)" (Garland, *1 Corinthians*, p. 757).

10. See Daniel Bell, *The Economy of Desire* (Grand Rapids:, Baker, 2012), pp. 199–203.

11. See ibid., pp. 203–205.

12. "[The verb translated 'help me on my journey'] is used in the NT for sending departing travelers on their way and can entail providing them with all the resources—such as money, supplies, and companions—necessary for the journey (see 2 Cor. 1:16; see also Acts 15:3; Rom. 15:24; Titus 3:13; 3 John 6; 1 Macc. 12:4). Although Paul did not receive support from a congregation while he was working among them, he did allow them to equip him for his travel to his next mission point" (Garland, *1 Corinthians*, p. 757).

13. Christopher L. Heuertz and Christine D. Pohl, *Friendship at the Margins: Discovering Mutuality in Service and Mission* (Downers Grove: InterVarsity Press, 2010), p. 26.

14. Ibid., pp. 85, 86.

15. Ibid., pp. 76–78.

16. Ibid., p. 33.

17. "We know from 2 Corinthians and Romans that [Paul] hoped that the gift would cement the bond between the Gentile and the Jewish Christian communities and that it would demonstrate that Christian unity transcended ethnic barriers and did not require Gentile Christians to become Jewish proselytes" (Garland, *1 Corinthians*, p. 752).

18. "Fee identifies a key point: Timothy is to 'remind them of Paul's ways' (4:17), and he is portrayed here as continuing the work which Paul himself began. Hence any hostility toward Paul would be likely to rub off onto Timothy as Paul's 'delegate,' 'representative' or 'co-worker'" (Thiselton, *The First Epistle to the Corinthians*, p. 1330).

19. "Paul is deeply concerned about how Timothy will be received at Corinth. . . . They may perhaps have preferred to welcome Apollos rather than Timothy. . . . Paul's concern is that at Corinth Timothy may be regarded as of little or no account. In 1:28

Paul referred to the nobodies or nothings (neuter) whom God chose, while in 6:4 the nobodies in the church might better judge civil cases than civil magistrates who had been linked or influenced by favors from the wealthy. Corinth must not regard Timothy so" (ibid., p. 1331).

20. See Ephesians 2:11–22; Colossians 2:15.

21. "Much more than (just giving) is involved. In 2 Cor 4:5–7 the gospel itself is a 'treasure,' and the issue of the collection is interwoven inseparably with a basic reformulation of the gospel: 'For you know the grace of our Lord Jesus Christ, that for you he became poor, though he was rich, so that you might become rich through his poverty' (2 Cor 8:9). David Ford argues that Paul 'plays' with and upon this theme to let 'the economy of God' speak to the practical financial dealings of Christians. 'Resources, work, production, distribution, value and exchange, together with the processes and relationships that these involve,' provide in one direction powerful metaphors for the nature and operation of the gospel, but then in turn come to speak back to the Christian's own attitude toward his or her own resources, work, production, value, exchange, reciprocity, mutuality, giving'" (Thiselton, *The First Epistle to the Corinthians*, p. 1319).

22. See Heuertz and Pohl, *Friendship at the Margins*, p. 130.

Chapter Thirty-Two: A Common Bond

1. As indicated by his grammar, Paul is not speaking of momentary attitudes, but rather uses the present imperative to bring out continuative states (Leon Morris, *The First Epistle of Paul to the Corinthians*, The Tyndale New Testament Commentaries [Grand Rapids: Eerdmans, 1989], p. 238).

2. Conveying more than a mere lack of sleep, the phrase carries significant eschatological overtones (cf. Matthew 24:42, 43).

3. As seen in the immaturity of the Corinthian people addressed throughout the letter, the strength and steadfastness of people cannot be derived from self, but only from God.

4. "Be courageous and strong" (David E. Garland, *1 Corinthians*, Baker Exegetical Commentary on the New Testament [Grand Rapids: Baker Academic, 2003, p. 743; also see Anthony C. Thiselton, *The First Epistle to the Corinthians: A Commentary on the Greek Text*, New International Greek Testament Commentary [Grand Rapids: Eerdmans, 2000], p. 1336).

5. Cf. 1 Corinthians 13 (discussed in Chapter 24 of this book).

6. The fact that Stephanus' entire household was mentioned suggests that he was a man of considerable means (Ben Witherington, *Conflict and Community in Corinth* [Grand Rapids: Eerdmans, 1995], p. 319).

7. Israelites were separated in the *diaspora*, but God brings all the tribes together to become one. We find in Ezekiel 37:16, 17, 19, 22, 24: "For Judah and the people associated with him . . . then take another stick and write on it, 'For Joseph . . . and all the house of Israel associated with him.' And join them one to another into one stick, that they may become one in your hand . . . and make them one stick, that they be one hand in my hand. . . . And I will make them one nation in the land, on the mountains of Israel. And one king shall be king over them all, and they shall be no longer two nations, and no longer divided into two kingdoms. . . . My servant David shall be king over them, and they shall have one shepherd."

Scripture Index

4:4	312n12, 338n11	4:22	331n3
4:5–7	349n21	4:29	314n6
5:17	346n8	5:5	318n7
6:2	346n8	5:11	338n10
6:9	346n8	5:13	338n10
7:1	325n14	5:22–30	200–201
7:2	319n3	5:25–32	130
7:11	346n8	6:11	312n12
7:12	319n3		
8:1—9:15	348n7	**Philippians**	
8:9	349n21	1:1	306n14
9:3	338n11	1:6	307n20
9:6	348n7	1:23	331n3
9:7	348n7	1:30	325n14
10:8	314n6	2	123, 191
10:25	338n11	2:5–11	327n12
10:27	338n11	2:13	335n5
11	328n10	2:20	325n13
11:7	328n7	3:7–11	342n10
11:24	329n4	3:12–14	330n17
12:14	346n8	3:15	311n2
12:29	314n6	3:21	312n11
13:10	314n6		
		Colossians	
Galatians		1:2	306n14
1:11–12	341n12	1:28	317n8
1:20	346n8	2:15	349n20
2:8	335n5	3:5	331n3
3:13	310n19	3:16	317n8
3:14	310n19	3:17	332n1
3:27	336n2	3:25	319n3
4:12	319n3		
5	153, 313n5	**1 Thessalonians**	
5:16	331n3	2:9	316n7
5:19	54	2:17	331n3
5:20	54	3:8	316n7
		4:4	325n14
Ephesians		4:11	316n7
1:1	306n14	4:16	347n10
1:11	335n5	5:12	317n8
2:3	331n3	5:14	317n8
2:8	56	5:23	325n14
2:11–22	349n20		
2:19–22	245, 314n6	**2 Thessalonians**	
2:20	244	1:7ff.	344n18
3:20	335n5	2:8	328n3
4:11	215, 216	3:15	317n8
4:11–12	314n6		
4:13	311n2	**1 Timothy**	
4:14	311n2	Book of	335n2
4:15	86	1:10	137
4:16	314n6	4:1–5	323n3

General Index

Abel, 27
accountability, 65
Adam, 277, 343n15
adultery, 108, 184–85
ambition, 138–39
Apollos, 308n10, 317n5
asceticism, 121–22, 128, 189, 322n3
assimilation, 31
authoritarianism, 79–80, 83, 87
authority, 71, 73, 79–89

Baal, 181, 332n8
baptism, 27, 268, 309n15, 336n2,
  342n12
Bauckham, Richard, 155–56
Becker, Ernest, 128, 136
Bell, Mary, 35
Blomberg, Craig, 206
Brooks, David, 155
Buerger, Warren, 107

Cain, 27
Carson, Don, 209, 212
Chloe, 25
Christian community
  bonds of, 298–303
  building and restoration of, 59–67
  as gospel-shaped, 105–6, 109–11
  growth of, 51–58
  issues of entitlement, 159–70
  liberties and privileges of, 151–57
  and power of the gospel, 255–63
  principles of sharing in, 291–96
  and speaking truth in love, 88–89
  victory in, 281–87
church
  building of with spiritual gifts, 239–45
  as Christian witness, 171–77
  complementary interdependence in,
    221–28
  discipline in, 99–101

divisions in, 19–20, 62–63, 103–4,
  309n14
healthy foundation of, 63
identity of, 104–5
reconciliation in, 289–96
separatists vs. accommodationists to
  the world, 94–95
stratification in, 209
unity in, 23–30, 61, 157
women's role in, 196–98, 251–52
and worldly validation, 26
circumcision, 137
Cleveland, Christena, 290–91
conviction, 244
Corinth, 16–17, 34–35, 203, 294, 305nn2-
  5, 306n6
Corinthian church
  and charismatic speech gifts, 239–45,
    250–53
  dispute and grievances in, 103–12,
    206–7
  and eating meat sacrificed to idols,
    152–55, 181–82, 189–90, 332n4,
    332n5
  economic justice of, 289–96
  emphasis on intellect and influence,
    33–34, 231–32, 307n18, 309n13
  evaluation of Paul, 69–77, 308n9
  jealousy and strife within, 54–55,
    313n5
  local and global network of, 298–99
  role of women in, 196–97, 251–52,
    333n4
  sense of entitlement, 159–70
  socioeconomic stratification in, 203–9
  spirit of competition and achievement
    in, 34–35, 211
Craig, William Lane, 257
creation, 57, 123, 200, 252
Crouch, Andy, 87
culture

Index of Sermon Illustrations

Authority

There is a cosmic evaluating authority, and unless an evaluation of others and of oneself is done in light of this cosmic authority, it is going to be out of alignment with reality, 71

Authority is necessary for human flourishing. The more free we become, and the more gifted we become as individuals, the more we will need thoughtful and careful authority to help us flourish, 80

Steve Jobs story as example of ultimate values and authority leading to human diminishing, 84–85

Christian Community

As an agricultural metaphor, 51

As an architectural metaphor, 59

No function or action of the community is allowed to be untouched and unshaped by love. A community that has experienced the love of God in Christ will necessarily share the love of God with one another, 299

David Prior: five ground rules for life together in Christ, 333n9

Antonin Scalia: "I think we are too ready today to see vindication or vengeance through adversary proceedings, rather than peace through mediation. . . . Good Christians, just as they are slow to anger, should be slow to sue," 107

Anthony Thiselton: "There is to be no last-minute, superficial scraping around for funds as an unplanned off-the-cuff gesture. . . . Each is to play his or her part in a planned strategy

of regular giving in weekly response to God's blessing and his financial provision, for the benefit of those who suffer deeper poverty and in mutuality and solidarity with a local church community," 348n8

Discernment

Gordon Fee: Highlights the verb discerned as a crucial one. It only appears in this Pauline letter, occurring ten times. "Probably it means something very close to 'discern' in the sense of being able to make appropriate 'judgments' about what God is doing in the world; and the person 'without the Spirit' obviously cannot do that," 312

Evil

Gordon Fee: "Paul's mentioning of yeast is similar to our modern folk wisdom of 'a bad apple spoils the whole barrel.' Thus in the NT leaven became a symbol of the process by which an evil spreads insidiously in a community until the whole has been infected by it. So it was in Corinth. Their problem was that they were not taking this matter seriously, either the evil itself or their danger of being thoroughly contaminated by it," 318–19

Forgiveness

This free-of-charge gospel allows us to stop putting the world on trial. We can forgive and find room for the people whom we once attempted to write off and write out, 169

Grace

Grace and justice are perfectly balanced in the heavenly law court. We don't simply demand justice, and we don't simply hand out grace. Because of the work of Christ, justice and grace meet perfectly, 110

Jonathan Edwards: "There is a difference between having an opinion that God is holy and gracious, and having a sense of the loveliness and beauty of that holiness and grace," 47

Tullian Tchividjian: "The news of God's inexhaustible grace has never been more urgent because the world has never been so exhausted. In our culture where success equals life and failure equals death, people spend their lives trying to secure their own meaning, worth, and significance," 72

Anthony C. Thiselton: "We come to the heart of Paul's point. Undeserved, unmerited grace which springs from the free, sovereign love of God alone and becomes operative in human life not only determines Paul's life and apostolic vocation but also characterizes all Christian existence, not least the promise of resurrection and the reality of the activity of Christ as Lord," 341n16

Idolatry

When you find your identity in any idol— whether it is your money, your work, your relationships, the things you consume, or even your own sexuality or your sexual ethic—it will lead to personal and communal breakdown, 109

Leon Morris: "The Israelites of old experienced redemption, baptism and God's continuing help. But they flirted with idolatry and nearly all of them perished in the wilderness. It may be that some of the Corinthians felt that their baptism and their use of Holy Communion

guaranteed their final salvation, no matter what they did. Paul warns them that this is not so. Idolatry brings ruin," 331

N. T. Wright: "When human beings give their heartfelt allegiance to and worship that which is not God, they progressively cease to reflect the image of God. One of the primary laws of human life is that you become like what you worship; what's more, you reflect what you worship not only to the object itself but also outward to the world around. . . . These and many other forms of idolatry combine in a thousand ways, all of them damaging to the image-bearing quality of the people concerned and of those whose lives they touch," 331

Leadership

Gospel life is about deferring, about elevating others, about pursuing someone else's interests, about being humble and not being arrogant, about giving and not always receiving, about wealth distribution and not wealth accumulation, about leveraging one's power and influence for those who are powerless, 77

David Prior: "Authority in the church, truly Christian authority, comes from those who lay down their lives for the brethren in service and availability. Any other authority is worldly authority and is to be rejected," 314

Lord's Supper

The purpose of the Supper is to wake up the spiritually sleepy person from his numbness to his wrong, give him grace to overcome it, and then restore him and the community at large, 96

The Lord's Supper was designed to demonstrate something radically different. It was intended to create, sustain, and display an alternate community—an upside-down social order. The Lord's Supper is the meal, the dinner table,

until he wants to play with it again . . .
you can't go to bed with someone and
leave your soul parked outside," 95

Lauren Winner: "Rather than spending our unmarried years stewarding and disciplining our desires, we
have become ashamed of them. We
persuade ourselves that the desires
themselves are horrible. . . . We spend
years guarding our virginity, but find,
upon getting married, that we cannot
just flip a switch. Now that sex is
licit, sanctioned—even blessed by our
community—we are stuck with years
of work (and sometimes therapy) to
unlearn . . . anxiety about sex; to learn,
instead, that sex is good," 320

Sin

Metaphor of leaven or yeast to capture
the social consequences of wrongdoing. "Yeast doesn't stay in one corner
of the loaf; it permeates the whole. In
fact, even a very small amount of it
will gradually expand and work its way
through the entire loaf. The same is
true with sin or social wrong because
the community is all one loaf," 97

Christians have the essential fuel for honest reconciliation. We were sanctified.

The grip of sin has been released. We
are freed, 110

Trinity

Criag Blomberg: "Although God the Son
is *essentially* equal to the Father, he
remains *functionally* subordinate, just
as his glorified humanity keeps him
distinct from what he was prior to the
incarnation," 344n19

Union with Christ

Communion with one another only happens through our union with Christ.
And union with Christ necessarily
brings us into communion with one
another. When we're in Christ together
as a community we naturally move
together, 301

Leon Morris: "[The Corinthian believ-
ers] are 'in Christ', and anything done
against them is therefore done against
him. There is a high dignity in being
Christian. It is easy to look down on
some church members as unimportant.
But they are not so. No temple of the
Holy Spirit is unimportant. God lives
in the weak. We must honour them as
members of Christ, and beware of sinning against the Lord," 327

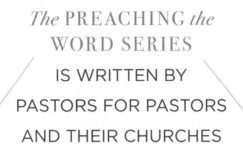